McGraw-Hill Series in Speech

CLARENCE T. SIMON, *Consulting Editor*

*Fundamentals of Speech*

## McGraw-Hill Series in Speech

Clarence T. Simon, *Consulting Editor*

Baird·Argumentation, Discussion, and Debate

Baird·Discussion: Principles and Types

Baird and Knower·General Speech

Brigance (Ed.)·A History and Criticism of American Public Address

Callahan·Radio Workshop for Children

Powers·Fundamentals of Speech

Van Dusen·Training the Voice for Speech

# *Fundamentals of*
# SPEECH

**David Guy Powers, Ph.D., Ed.D.**

*Queens College*

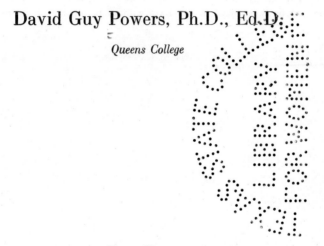

FIRST EDITION

1951

McGRAW-HILL BOOK COMPANY, INC.

New York     Toronto     London

FUNDAMENTALS OF SPEECH

*To*

ALONZO F. MYERS

*An inspiring leader and true friend
whose many gifts have enriched
higher education in our country*

# PREFACE

This is a fundamental course in speech. It combines training in the four basic speech skills with public speaking, discussion, and the speech arts. Through developing skill in word usage, voice, articulation, and social sensitivity, it seeks to weld an expressive personality. Hence, the scope of the course is broad, the arrangement of material is cumulative, activity is the method, and effectiveness is the aim. Time is not spent in lecturing or in the analysis of the scientific aspects of speech. The student *prepares* his speech, *outlines* it, *delivers* it in class, *reviews* the results, *indicates* a plan for improvement, and *prepares to repeat* the process in the following projects. Activity reigns supreme.

Directed practice is the method used to achieve effectiveness. Questions for critical discussion of performance set the standard of achievement by isolating the significant factors in each objective. These questions force the student to perceive, evaluate, and express throughout the entire class time. Moreover, they establish the habit of observation. This method is effective because each factor recurs constantly in a variety of situations of different complexity. Such repetition is not monotonous because it assumes its place in the total situation; *e.g.*, communication is specifically studied in the first chapter but recurs in every performance during the course. The student studies the nature of communication in isolation, but the application is always in the total situation. Hence, the art of speaking is learned in the speaking situation.

Good speech training integrates the work of other courses. It fosters interest in community speech activities and instills a love of the excellent. To accomplish this the projects encourage students to use the materials of other courses as the "basis of fact" necessary in their speeches; to engage in the speaking situations afforded by clubs, extracurricular activities, and social groups; to criticize current speakers and attend professional plays. The more thoroughly speechwork permeates the life of the student, the more profitable and permanent will be the results. The variety of experiences provided forms an interest in scholarly and graceful living. Extensive references have been included to enable thorough study of any particular activity.

The attention given to vocabulary and pronunciation is designed to fulfill known needs of all college students. In a survey conducted over a number of years at Fordham University, the most universally expressed needs of the students were "enrichment of vocabulary" and "improvement of pronunciation." Such skills are the result of continued activity. A single project cannot form the habit of vocabulary building or correct pronunciation. Hence, "Developing Semantic Skill" has been extended throughout the book.

The first half of the course deals specifically with the student's skill. He is equipping himself with skills that he will use later in group life. The second half deals with the application of skills in real situations. The first half concentrates on words, voice, and articulation, while the later projects accentuate skill in informing, gaining group decisions, securing action, entertaining, and sharing aesthetic experiences. Thus the two aims of the fundamental course, knowledge and skill, are attained through guided practice. The student first acquires skills and then is taught the judicious use of the skills acquired. Fourteen projects provide drills for the four fundamental skills. Each skill is critically studied, tested in actual situations, and evaluated individually. This is necessary because understanding is a matter of apprehension, which may come quickly, but skill is acquired only after long practice. It is relatively easy to understand the structure of the piano or the scientific elements of a chord in Bach, but to learn to play Bach is a much longer process. So it is with the art of speech. To understand takes time, but to be skilled in speaking takes a lifetime.

Skill in speaking, however, is not an end in itself. And so it is that the second half of the course deals with the student's total effectiveness in the forms of public address, conference, debating, oral interpretation, conversation, and radio and television speaking. Such activities will serve to set the skills acquired and introduce the student to the total forms in which the speaker must function. The variety of forms included will enable the instructor to fashion the course to the student's greatest needs. A special section on visual materials will be helpful in inciting interest.

The course has been planned to reveal to the student the importance of genuine study and practice. Clear, forceful, and effective expression is the result of directed practice in a variety of situations. No chart, diagram, or series of suggestions can ever replace self-activity of the student. Every attempt has been made to have the student realize that he must take the responsibility for his development as an effective speaker. The "critical approach" used in this book is an important element in self-activity. It develops a critical acumen that will remain with the student after the course is finished. This should serve as a continuing stimulus for acquiring not only better speech habits but a fuller life.

DAVID GUY POWERS

FOREST HILLS, N.Y.
*April,* 1951

# CONTENTS

# CONTENTS

## PART VI. CONFERENCE SPEAKING

## PART VII. SPEECH ARTS

# FOREWORD TO STUDENTS

You are in college to become a cultured person and each course should contribute toward that goal. This course has been organized to help you acquire a more effective speaking personality.

Personal effectiveness in speaking requires the possession of definite skills and knowledge. Without knowledge, skill is wasted, and without skill, knowledge loses its power. Knowledge tells you the "who," the "how," the "where," and the "why" of the situation, but skill gives you facility in directing these factors. To have skill and no knowledge leads to loquaciousness and bombast; to have knowledge and no skill leads to rancor and discontent. Hence, the aim of the course is to produce the skilled speaker, sensitive to the psychological forces in human situations, and trained in directing the minds of others.

Each chapter is arranged to achieve the two aims of the course. After sufficient treatment of the factors in the situation, you proceed directly to actual practice in speaking. Study the assignment, the treatment of factors involved, the purpose, the audience, and the specific skill to be employed. Remember, it is the smooth combination of all these that produces the skilled speaker.

Chapters are arranged in the following way: first, you are given a general discussion of the topic; second, you are given an assignment based upon this reading and an outline form to be followed; third, you present your talk to the class; fourth, your performance is discussed by the class; and fifth, you study these criticisms and compare your results with your preparation. This process helps you see yourself objectively in three stages of activity: the preliminary planning, the actual presentation, and the final check on the results. An intelligent student will strive to eliminate his difficulties systematically.

## USE OF OUTLINES

Your outline streamlines your thoughts. It presents to your mind the reasonable connections between the parts of your speech; the clearer your thoughts, the easier the task of communicating them to others. Remember that order is as essential to an outline as the steel structure is to a building. It determines the form of the building to be erected. A false connection in an outline is as serious as a skyscraper with a base floor made of poor material, and a gap in your thought pattern is like a building without a third floor. The building can't be erected, but in thought organization the calamity of vagueness and misunderstanding ensues. So try to make each outline represent the framework you wish to imprint on the minds of your listeners.

Throughout this course you will engage in the process of outlining. Various forms are given so that you may experiment and find which type is most suitable for you. A combination of many features may suit you best. Moreover, by careful outlining you develop the mental habit of organizing. You discover the most effective method of arranging your thoughts for communication. At first this process will seem difficult, but you will soon develop skill, and it will become part of you. The first outline will start with the simplest division: beginning, middle, and end. As your speeches require a more detailed arrangement of thoughts, you will find need for variations in your outlines. Follow the instructions given with each outline and see wherein it provides efficient organization for your thoughts and feelings.

### Developing Semantic Skill

Hundreds of former students have requested a simple but effective method of building their vocabularies. They were conscious that the most infallible index of thinking capacity is a full and rich vocabulary. After much experiment, this easy and productive device was worked out. Its value has been established thousands of times. This is it. Three sources of words are used: first, words encountered in the treatment of the chapter; second, frequently used words difficult to define and pronounce; third, words personally encountered in other activities. Look up these words in a dictionary for meaning and pronunciation. The latter is indicated by diacritical markings or phonetic symbols. It is left to the student's discretion whether he wants to include the etymology and special meanings of the words. All are required, however, to use the words in one or more sentences.

It has been found convenient to do the vocabulary work on 3 by 5 index cards. These cards can be kept permanently in a small wooden box readily accessible. If you can arrange to carry a few cards around with you daily and refer to them in your spare time, you will find your passive vocabulary soon becoming active. An example of one of these cards is given below (definition from *Webster's New International Dictionary*):

### FRONT

semantics—sĕ-măn′tĭks

The science of meanings, as contrasted with *phonetics*, the science of sounds; the historical and psychological study and the classification of changes in the signification of words or forms, viewed as normal and vital factors in linguistic development, including such phenomena as specialization and expansion of meaning, meliorative and pejorative tendencies, metaphor, adaptation, and the like. *Semantics* is usually construed as a singular noun.

(After F. *sémantique*, from Gr. *sēmantikos* significant meaning, from *sēmainein* to signify, from *sēma* a sign; akin to Sanskrit *dhyāti* he thinks.)

### BACK

Proficiency in speaking involves four types of skill: phonetic skill, semantic skill, social skill, and vocal skill.

Semantic skill refers to the ability to use words in meaningful patterns.

Mr. Breal wrote a book called *Semantics* in 1896; it attempted to initiate a science of symbols.

# PART I. SOCIAL SKILL

Social skill is the ability to participate effectively in human relationships. It requires that you express your ideas appropriately, that you understand the forces molding situations, and that your speech and actions are socially acceptable. It further requires that you groom the personal factors which are an intimate part of you as a person. You can acquire this skill by developing your sense of communication and becoming sensitive to the factors which influence human behavior. As you develop your social skill you will become aware of the motivations that guide human actions, and you will become a more mature personality.

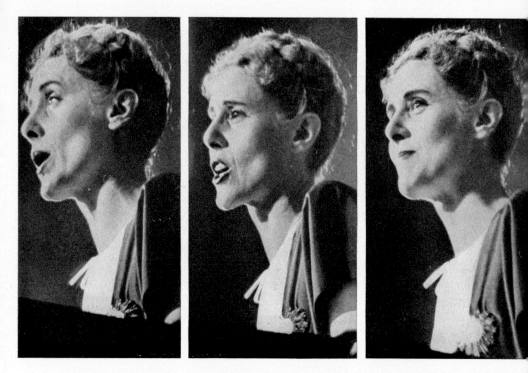

*Press Association, Inc*

Clare Booth Luce is one of America's foremost speakers. As a playwright, publisher, and congresswoman she has influenced the political and social life of our nation. Her personal charm, wit, social and semantic skill are legendary. Many of her expressions have become the slogans of her party, and the incisive comments in her plays have made audiences rollick with laughter. Her clear thinking and forceful expression won high respect when she represented the state of Connecticut in the United States Congress. In addition to her superb semantic skill notice the direct contact she achieves with her audience. She literally relishes in the thought she has given them. This is the essence of communication.

## Chapter 1

# COMMUNICATION

All life comes back to the question of our speech—the medium
through which we communicated.
                                        —HENRY JAMES

Man has always wondered at his ability to speak. To primitive man
it was the characteristic which set him apart from all other forms
of animal life. He could speak. And no other living thing uttered a
word. The ancient Vedic hymns characterized *Vāk* (speech) as a
creation of the gods, and the eternality of speech was advocated
by the *Mimāmsakās.* Panini, early Hindu scholar, denoted man by
the expression *"vyaktavak," i.e.,* "one possessing distinct speech."
So wondrous did the Greeks consider this gift that they called the
animal *a'logon,* meaning "without word," and Plato in *Cratylus* says,
"Man alone, of all animals, is rightly denoted *anthropos,* meaning
capable of thought and speech." In like manner the Anglo-Saxons
called man the "word-carrier," and when he spoke he unlocked his
"word-hoard." Early man wove a myth about the nature of speech
and modern man scientifically examines its minutest elements. The
mystery of this uniquely human ability continues to intrigue scholar
and layman alike.

Whence came this power to speak? Was it a direct gift of God, or
did man play a part in establishing himself as a speaking animal?
Several theories have been offered to explain the origin of speech.
These theories have varied degrees of ingenuity, and it is not un-
reasonable to suppose each has some degree of truth. Still, all come
to the basic truth that man was endowed with a mechanism capable
of performing the speech act and he alone continues to use that
power.

*Speech as a Mode of Acting*

Man shares his sound-making ability with other animals. The cry of the child for food and the wail of the wolf have common phonetic aspects. Both are instinctive, and both are total body responses to needs. Danger, fear, and want occasion both outbursts, and the sounds bear striking phonetic resemblances. Charles Callet, in his fascinating book, *Le mystère du langage,* suggests that all sounds of man and animal are simply the result of hissing, bellowing, growling, and rasping. An even more fundamental similarity is that all these sounds are strident sounds. All are the result of tensing the entire mechanism. Normal wants or abnormal conditions call them forth. The fact that body constrictions accompany these sounds may explain their common phonetic ring. In like manner, the purring and cooing sounds of animals and birds have a counterpart in the gurgling, babbling, and prattling of children. They denote the contented state of the mechanism. Still, these activities cannot be designated as speech. They are the responses of living mechanisms in need, or the overtones of beings functioning harmoniously within their environment.

During this stage, sounds are dependent upon the action at hand. They emerge as the roar of the sea or the thud of the breaking wave, and are inextricably dependent on the mechanism of production. Yet within this very mode of acting lies the essential difference in the nature of child and animal. The animal makes traditional calls and continues to make them in response to natural needs. The character of the call does not differ, and only its intensity has been known to change. The same call that primitive man heard from the beast attracts the hunter today. This is significant. The animal possesses no power to modify the call. It is as natural as the sniff of the dog, and it is as unvarying. It not only gives rise to no phonetic adaptation but denotes that there is no underlying power capable of such modifications.

In human beings, however, certain factors are present which change the whole nature of the act. The child's call gradually changes to a more effective call. It is adapted to the known calls of the child's environment. These phonetic changes give evidence of a power of modification, and this advantage makes man the inevitable superior of the animal. It typifies him as the master of phonetic habits rather than the subject of phonetic limitations of cries and whelps. This phonetic ability confers rational life upon the child and forever sets the boundary of brute life for the animal.

It is obvious, therefore, that the calls of animals are alinguistic, while the cries of the child are prelinguistic. The child possesses a linguistic power and will learn to use it, while the animal will continue despite age and experience to emit the same calls. In the early stages of linguistic growth, certain sounds are shared in common with animal noises denoting basic drives, but these are not speech. They are emotive manifestations. The act of speech is a more involved process of action and interaction. It is not merely a total body response or a mode of action. *It is a purposeful activity establishing relationship through the use of phonetic sounds.* Only man codifies his utterances and thus indicates the possession of higher faculties. In other words, man alone uses speech as a mode of communication.

## Speech as a Mode of Communication

Man is a social animal, and his first and most significant act is a social act—an act in which an experience is exchanged, a thought transferred, a feeling mutually enjoyed, or a conviction expressed and agreed upon. For this act to take place there must be many common elements. The Latin root *communis* is the basis for "common," "community," and "communication." It suggests that there is something shared and understood by a number of people. And, indeed, men live in groups called "communities" because of common beliefs and understanding. For it is not mere proximity that makes a community but a oneness of outlook and a common purpose.

Communication welds individuals into groups by crystallizing common concepts, by preserving common bonds of interest, by creating a unity of symbols distinct from other groups, and by establishing a common heritage. Underlying each of these acts is the basic fact that without language communities could not exist. Some social philosophers go so far as to say that society exists in linguistic communication. Certainly it is true that modern society would be impossible without its highly intricate systems of communication. If, for example, the means for transmitting the spoken word alone were eliminated for a week, what would our cities be like? Picture New York without telephones, telegraph, radio, or television. Our great cities would lose their efficiency quite rapidly under such conditions.

Speech as a mode of communication affects our individual lives most intimately. It is the system through which we exchange ideas, feelings, and wishes by means of symbols called "words." It deals with the effectiveness of the individual in establishing mental and emotional contact with his fellow men. It goes beyond the notion that speech is merely the expression of one's own ideas, and emphasizes the give-and-take in human relationships. It acknowledges the role of habits and skills, but insists that such habits be used in communicative activities. So conceived speech is a composite activity that permeates the whole process of living. It is the means by which you communicate with those around you. And, by virtue of that fact, it either releases you for full living or, like the speechless animals, condemns you to an isolated life.

Speech is not an end in itself. It is a means by which necessary human relationships are established. It is the nervous system of the body social. A visit to the United Nations would make this truth quite evident. The United Nations could not exist without its well-regulated system of almost instantaneous translations into the three principal languages and, on occasion, into several other tongues. So it is with you as an individual. Unless you are able to participate effectively in social situations you cannot achieve your full development. You are incapable of participating effectively in significant experiences, and you are lessening the opportunities of your own growth. You cannot become a mature personality because the necessary skills are not yours. But as you acquire these skills you achieve maturity. You become a more vital personality leading a more abundant life.

## The Essential Skills

Four essential skills are characteristic of a mature personality: the social, the semantic, the phonetic, and the vocal. Through the development of these skills you acquire proficiency in communicating your ideas, in gaining cooperation, in persuading others, and in achieving leadership. Such skills cannot be acquired all at once. Each skill must be analyzed separately and concentrated upon individually. To try to do everything at once results in chaos. You must make each skill a goal and direct all your energies toward that particular goal. In this way, each skill will become part of you, and you may then proceed to develop another skill.

You have developed a share of these skills already, so the task is not as arduous as it first appears. In many instances you will be perfecting skills which you now possess. You will be isolating a particular operation for closer scrutiny. Just as the dancer attacks a specific step, drills until he has perfected it, and only then incorporates it into his routine, so it is with your speech. You isolate to perfect. In this way, what seems unbelievably intricate in the finished performance becomes in reality simple. And, *mirabile dictu,* as you develop each skill, you improve your entire personality.

### The social skill

*Social skill is your ability to participate effectively in human relationships.* It demands that you know what to say, how to say it, when to say it, and when not to say it. It demands that you understand the psychological forces molding the situation and that the forms, customs, and rubrics of the group are apparent to you. Social skill demands that the unspoken cues of human intercourse are readily perceived and correctly interpreted. It demands that you are aware of the forces motivating the other participants, and that you possess the foresight to direct their energies toward mutually acceptable solutions. It demands that you know how to clarify ideas, to give examples, and to assist all members of the group to deeper understandings. It demands that you know how to use patience, tact, and compassion. And, finally, it demands that you can mediate conflicts by discovering common areas of agreement, especially when such areas seem not to exist. Such social skill is a priceless commodity. As you acquire it you will become an indispensable force in human affairs.

### The semantic skill

*Semantic skill is your ability to use words meaningfully.* To acquire semantic skill you must have a wide knowledge of the meanings behind words and sufficient practice in using words. Only in this way do words come readily and easily to mind. You must combine knowledge with use in order to acquire semantic skill. For merely to know words does not confer skill in using them. Nor do words become part of your thinking pattern unless you think in terms of them frequently. Be patient, for this skill is not acquired easily. It takes effort and time. That is why it has been integrated throughout your course.

### The phonetic skill

*Phonetic skill is the ability to form the phonemic elements of your language properly.* Such skill is necessary because it carries social approval or disapproval. It is an element in personal relationships which either identifies you as a member of a group or castigates you as an outsider. Realize that every human society has a preferred form of speech, a more desirable way of emitting sounds. Your ability to use the preferred forms will facilitate your social acceptance and will graphically reflect the cultural advantages you have enjoyed.

### The vocal skill

*Vocal skill is the ability to create the desired emotional effect with your voice.* A rich, resonant voice indicates a well-developed and assured person, while a strident, whispering, or breathy voice suggests an unimpressive personality. You can make your voice pleasant and vibrant. And such a voice will assure you of an enthusiastic response from your listeners. It will help you express your thoughts in clear, forceful, and artistic sound patterns.

### How to Develop Skills

The most efficient way ever discovered to develop a skill is by practice. You must constantly do an action in order to do that action freely. As Aristotle observed, "You learn to play the flute by playing the flute." At a later date, John Dewey expressed the same thought in his famous dictum, "You learn to do by doing." This axiom is true in a double sense in acquiring speech skills, for speaking is not only an expressive skill but a receptive skill as well. You must not only be able to speak but to engage in listening and speaking situations. As St. Augustine pointed out, "Without the rules of rhetoric many have become better speakers than those who learned the rules, but we have never known one who became a speaker without reading or hearing the discussions and speeches of others."

The four fundamental skills will be acquired in actual speaking situations. You will develop your communicative sense by speaking with an audience, discussing the effect of your efforts, and criticizing positively the performances of your classmates. This is the most effective method. It exercises your creative and critical powers during every class hour.

## PROJECTS

Every moment of speaking time is a battle to hold the attention of your listeners. You must contact them with your eyes, with your voice, and with bodily gestures. Even the fact that they are looking at you is no guarantee that they are listening. People quickly learn that it is easier to look as though they are listening than to listen. You must command their attention, for it is your responsibility to direct their minds to your ideas. There is no such thing as a bad listener. There are disinterested listeners waiting to become good listeners if you interest them. This is true of all audiences.

In your first talk to the class the purpose will be to develop your sense of communication. You now have some notion of what communication is, and the following four specific suggestions will help you to achieve contact with your audience. Make these suggestions part of every speech you give.

1. *Be direct.* Directness comes from talking with your audience, not at them. Observe the grotesque picture created by two cronies who meet on the corner and talk without looking at each other. Or note the suspicious impression created by people who talk to you and favor you only with surreptitious glances. Quintilian points out that the first requisite of a good orator is that he give the impression to the audience of straightforward dealing and honesty. To give the impression you are concealing something robs you of the power to influence. Believe what you have to say and say what you believe. This requires that you look the audience in the eye and make your voice and manner carry conviction. Looking out the window or at the floor distracts the audience. If you look at your audience, they will help you make your talk. They will encourage you with signs of approval and inspire you with their interest. Skilled speakers can interpret the thoughts of their audiences by watching the expressions on their faces. You will acquire the same skill if you make a habit of noting audience reactions as you speak. Remember, the floor and the window will never respond but the audience always will.

2. *Be interested in your subject.* The speaker who thinks his message is valueless communicates his attitude long before his message. Avoid telling the audience the uninteresting details of an uninteresting event. What appeals to you poignantly, or has left a lasting impression on you, will appeal to an audience. Have the confidence that your experience will

appeal to them as it did to you. This will give you an animation that is both pleasant to behold and infectious.

In your first assignment, you are going to present a fellow classmate to the group. You can make your talk interesting if you become interested in your partner. Every person has something interesting to confide if you have the patience to find it out. For example, Paul Henri Spaak, first president of the General Assembly of the United Nations and premier of Belgium at the age of thirty-nine, when I asked him the secret of his success, said, "I have only one rule by which my actions are guided. Each human being has something in him that deserves attention, and when once discovered it becomes an enrichment of your own person. Seek the good in others continually. If you make this a permanent trait, you have the key to understanding others." In your interview, capture the spirit of Paul Henri Spaak. Search for the quality in your classmate that makes him unique.

3. *Have a definite purpose.* Poor speakers aim at nothing—and hit it. A speaker without a purpose is as harrowing a sight as a general without an objective who insists upon attacking furiously in all directions. Both are soon reduced to nothing. A purpose in speaking furnishes a desire to communicate. A worth-while thought is generally too big for one person; it carries with it a natural incentive to share it with others. Make your purpose a desire to share something that has meant a great deal to you, or that you are intensely interested in at the moment.

In speaking, your *purpose* furnishes a wise guide. It will indicate the type of reaction desired from your audience. If you merely wish to inform them, it is only necessary that they understand your message. If you wish to convince them of the value or truth of your message, that requires proof and evidence. And if you wish them to take specific action because of your message, you must supply them with the necessary emotional stimulation. Ask yourself, "What result do I wish to get from my audience?" The answer will streamline your energies and guide your efforts. It will reveal your aim in speaking and indicate the best means to be used.

4. *Be friendly.* So important did the Greeks and Romans consider the attitude of friendliness between speaker and audience that they decreed it the primary function of the beginning of any speech. The purpose of the exordium was to render the listeners well wishing and attentive (*benevolus et attentus*). Both of these are achieved through a communication of feeling. Consider the audience as a group of friends gathered to enjoy with you an interesting experience. When Queen Marie of Rumania was asked the secret of her great popularity, she responded simply, "I like people." In the same manner, the good speaker likes people, and the audience instinctively feels it.

*Assignment*

Your assignments have been graded from the simple to the more complex. You will find them easy hurdles pleasantly taken with a little effort. Your first assignment is a challenging one. You are to introduce a member of your class to the group. In turn, your partner will introduce you.

Make this an exciting event. Search out the interesting things in your classmate's life and present him or her to the class with novelty and interest. For example, has your classmate traveled, has he or she a particular talent, a unique ambition, a strong conviction, or an exciting point of view? Search out the interesting aspects of personality that make this individual unique.

After you have attained your information, you are ready to arrange it in terms of interest to the audience. Don't just tell the things you have learned, but set yourself the goal of presenting a real personality. Select your items as you would if you were introducing a celebrity on the air. Be gracious, informative, and entertaining. Make the person you introduce justly proud of a portrait generously drawn.

*Sample Communication Outline*

Speaker _____ Class _____ Date _____

  I. Name of student interviewed _____
 II. Purpose of speech.
III. Speech.
     *A.* Introduction: gain attention by. . . .
     *B.* Theme or central idea: Elaboration or development by instances.
     *C.* Conclusion: Presentation of classmate.

*Questions for Critical Discussion of Performance*

  1. Was the speaker direct?
  2. Did he seem interested in making the speech?
  3. Was his purpose clear and evident?
  4. Was he friendly with the audience?
  5. Did he adjust his presentation to the audience's interests?
  6. Had he secured sufficient information to make an interesting presentation?
  7. Did he achieve novelty by capturing interesting events and details?
  8. Was the portrait generously drawn?
  9. Did he communicate easily?
 10. What was the high point of interest in this speech?

*Developing Semantic Skill*

The basis of semantic skill is an effective vocabulary. Throughout the term you can establish a habit of vocabulary building by following faithfully the instructions in each project. It is a scheme to use your word-learning experiences in all your college courses. To help you establish this worth-while habit, the form of each of these exercises will remain the same. First, you will be given words encountered in the speech text; second, you will be given words that are commonly mispronounced; and third, you should add a small number of words (at least three) from your experiences in other courses or outside activities. You may write these words out on cards, as indicated in the Foreword. Remember, you really know a word only when you can use it at will, understand its meaning precisely, and are confident that your pronunciation is acceptable. Constant review of words previously learned will ensure your command over them.

I. Words used in the speech text:

| *Word* | *Pronunciation* | *Meaning* |
|---|---|---|
| 1. phonetic | | |
| 2. semantic | | |
| 3. situation | | |
| 4. strata | | |

II. Words commonly mispronounced:
   1. again
   2. antarctic
   3. aquatic

III. Words from your own experience.

## REFERENCES

BLOOMFIELD, LEONARD, *Language*, Chap. II, "The Use of Language," pp. 21–41.

BRITTON, KARL, *Communication: A Philosophical Study of Language.*

FIRTH, J. R., *Speech*, pp. 5–11.

———, *The Tongues of Men*, Chap. I, "Adam, the Speaking Animal," "Origins," pp. 19–28.

GRAY, G. W., and C. M. WISE, *Bases of Speech*, Chap. I, pp. 1–5, 42–55; and Chap. VI, pp. 312–326.

JESPERSEN, OTTO, *Language: Its Nature, Development and Origin*, pp. 320–322, 328–332, 432–442.

MALINOWSKI, BRONISLAU, "The Problem of Meaning in Primitive Languages," *The Meaning of Meaning* by OGDEN and RICHARDS, pp. 451–470; also pp. 296–337, 337–357, 471–510.

MENCKEN, H. L., *The American Language*, pp. 556–574.

O'NEILL, J. M., and A. T. WEAVER, *Elements of Speech*, Chap. II, pp. 13–24.

## Chapter 2

# THE SPEECH SITUATION

Think all you speak; but speak not all you think;
Thoughts are your own; your words are so no more.
—DELAUNE

Your social skill will in large part determine your success or failure in professional life. If you acquire the skill of handling people, you are headed for success. John D. Rockefeller said, "I will pay more for the ability to deal with people than for any other ability under the sun." Even in the realm of research this ability is priceless. Charles F. Kettering, vice-president in charge of research for General Motors, wrote, "Research is just about 10 per cent experiment and 90 per cent knowing how to get along with the fellows you are working with." In the papers of President Roosevelt, President Harry Truman found this undelivered speech: "We are faced with the pre-eminent fact that, if civilization is to survive, we must cultivate the science of human relationships—the ability of all people, of all kinds, to live and work together, in the same world, at peace." When Mr. Truman commented on this speech, he said, "When we have learned these things, we shall be able to prove that Hiroshima was not the end of a civilization, but the beginning of a new and better world."

Can this valuable skill be developed? Most assuredly it can. It consists of knowing the elements operating in the situations of daily life and being able to participate effectively in those situations. It requires that you become conscious of the basic motivations that guide human actions and that you possess the skills of communication and direction. This chapter will give you vital insights into the nature of the situation and the factors that determine your success in the situation. In no other human activity is it more true that knowledge is power. So, study this chapter carefully and refer to it throughout the course.

14

## THE SPEECH SITUATION

What is a speech situation? Whenever two or more people come together to exchange ideas and feelings, to clarify their thinking, to make a plan, or to enjoy mutually an aesthetic experience, a speech situation occurs. It is a speech situation because the medium of speech makes it possible. Speech is the means whereby these activities are brought to satisfactory conclusions. The number and form of such situations are beyond conjecture. Each is unique. Yet certain elements recur so regularly that we can isolate them as recurring variables. For instance, every situation has a purpose, participants, ideas, a more or less accepted way of thinking, an environment, and an emotional set. All these vary from situation to situation. They are constant, however, because they will be found in every situation. Hence, they provide a means of studying the nature of speech situations.

### Factors in the Situation

Six fundamental elements determine the nature of speech situations.

1. The purpose of the situation.
2. The participants in the situation.
3. The ideas held in common by the participants.
4. The pattern of succession of ideas, or mental habits.
5. The emotional set of the group due to preceding or succeeding situations.
6. The physical and physiological conditions in the situation.

These factors never occur in the exact order listed, nor are they ever in complete harmony. An ideal situation would necessitate that (1) the purpose be clear, known to, and agreed upon, by all; (2) the participants be alike in temperament, education, religion, race, sex, and age; (3) the ideas be shared in common; (4) the thinking patterns be at once direct and obvious to all; (5) the mood of the moment be shared with equal intensity; and (6) the environment be conducive to the physical comfort of each individual participant. Such situations are rare if at all possible. A sharper insight is gained if we phrase these elements in specific questions, and examine each in turn:

1. Why is this group assembled?
2. Who are they?
3. What do they think about?
4. How do they habitually think?
5. What is their social and economic condition?
6. What is their physical condition?

### Purpose of the Situation

In answer to question 1, there are four general purposes for human gatherings:

1. To share information.
2. To make a decision.
3. To move to action.
4. To entertain.

If the group has come together to share information about a problem, their purpose is to achieve understanding. Once you realize this purpose, you can operate more intelligently because you have an objective in common with your audience. Similarly, if the group's purpose is to make a decision or to take some action, you can more readily assist them by being conscious of their desires. On the other hand, if you have the wrong purpose in mind, you will be embarrassed and your efforts ineffective. Misunderstanding of the purpose on the part of any member of a group leads to friction. For example, suppose a group wants to learn about a certain subject through discussion; if one member insists on trying to get the group to act, friction will arise, and the situation may turn into an argument. The result is misunderstanding and personal bickering.

Again, suppose a salesman takes a prospective buyer to lunch. The purpose of the situation is good-fellowship, an aesthetic experience. It calls for levity, conversation, and mutual enjoyment. The true purpose of the situation should be to gain good will. But if the salesman tries to sell his product at the luncheon, he defeats the purpose of the situation. Instead of an enjoyable experience, all the buyer gets is indigestion. Such mistakes are called tactlessness, but most often they are simply instances of failure on the part of a participant to realize the purpose of the situation.

We have all had the misfortune of meeting earnest people who continually violate the purpose of the situation. Consider the occasions of fellowship when you have gathered with friends to "just talk." Into this pleasant exchange of opinions comes the arguer. He proceeds not only to give his opinion but to indicate the nature of your intelligence. However casual your remarks, he proceeds to inquisition you until you regret that you came. Finally, you find yourself enmeshed in an argument or so embarrassed that you seek escape. The worst part of such social menaces is that they are usually correct in their facts. The next time you plan an evening of fellowship, this encyclopedic biped is omitted for the sake of everyone— yet all he did was to ignore the purpose of the situation.

## Participants

It is easily conceivable that two people can more readily understand a problem than can three or four. Numbers affect people. Psychologists indicate that people's dispositions change once they become members of a group. Individuals in a group are swayed by emotional appeals much more readily, are quicker to act, and are impatient with logical distinctions. That is why the multimillion audiences of radio require a leveling down to simple thoughts simply expressed. This furnishes a cue to the skilled speaker, namely: *The larger your audience, the more simply your message must be presented. Draw your picture in broader strokes as your audience increases.*

However, the number of people in a situation is of only slight importance compared with the complexities arising from a group's varied educational and experiential backgrounds. The things people are interested in determine what they consider important. The information they have gathered, the assumptions they have accepted, and the affiliations they have formed are not only unique but must be respected. They form the basis of the participants' thinking and furnish a guide to their likely reactions. Therefore, it is wise to discover as much as you can about every group in your environment.

This human-interest technique is invaluable in political and public service. It is the essence of diplomacy. William H. Stoneman points it out as the secret of the success of Trygve Lie, secretary-general of the United Nations. "Trygve Lie actually works at the job of learning as much as he possibly can about everyone with whom he has dealings—the foreign minister of a country, his chauffeur, or members of his office staff. He is a student of people, and as a result never 'works blind' when he deals with another person. This fact has enriched his own life and is largely responsible for his outstanding success in negotiations." Remember, the more you know about the participants in a situation, the more intelligently you are likely to act.

### Participants' ideas

The communication of ideas is a difficult process. People take comfort in the ideas they already have and object to new ones. When the ideas are numerous, unfamiliar, or subtle, your task triples in difficulty. But you can add to people's ideas if you proceed cautiously. Be mindful that the human mind can attend to only one idea at a time. So be wary when your purpose is to transmit more than one idea. The best advice in handling ideas is to make haste slowly. Expect resistance, but continue patiently to insinuate your thought. Make the audience feel that the idea you have just given them is one they have had since infancy. This is no more than what every artist must do. If his work merely reflects his ideas, it is valueless. It must have within it the power to suggest a similar idea to those who behold it. If it does not, others are uninterested and it is neglected. However, if it provides for a restimulation of the creative process in others, if it gives them an idea, they will swear by it. They will go out of their way to prove that they see more in it than the artist. They will become his advocates. So it is with your ideas. You must make them part of the thinking pattern of the participants in the situation. As Mohandas Gandhi observed, "God Himself dare not appear to a hungry man except in the form of bread."

Don't become discouraged at the amount of time it takes to communicate an idea. A new idea must be understood to be accepted; it must fit into the sum total of previous experience. If a series of unfamiliar ideas comes rapidly, comprehension diminishes. This danger is recognized in schoolwork, and therefore elementary and advanced courses are arranged in most subjects. In business and professional situations, the uninitiated are prevented from participation until they have acquired a working knowledge of the basic ideas. In every situation there is some degree of unfamiliarity with certain ideas among the participants. Be careful not to pass over these ideas too quickly. Remember that situations are complicated by the number, precision, and familiarity of the ideas involved.

*Participants' succession of ideas*

The succession of ideas can either mar or make a situation. Modes of thought, like modes of action, vary considerably with individuals. When the sequence of ideas fails to follow a mutually acceptable pattern, complications arise. The man with the "one-track mind" permits no deviation; the "inductive leaper" springs to generalization with the agility of a trapeze artist; the impressionist has no use for logic; the intuitionist knows and is impatient; the "assumer" accepts hypotheses as facts; and the *"post hocer"* exclaims, "It followed, did it not? That's proof enough for me." Fortunately, these types are not encountered all at once; yet every situation seems to include at least one of them. To arrive at an acceptable pattern of thought sequence in any group, therefore, requires great skill.

*Participants' emotional condition*

The emotional condition of the participants permeates the whole situation. If a person is involved in a serious emotional upheaval, it is almost impossible for him to react normally in social situations. Even so slight a thing as a scheduled trip to the dentist will condition responses. Strongest of all emotional conditioners are the feelings that are so habitual as to be called "prejudices." Prejudice plays such an important part in our thinking that we find ourselves marshaling arguments in favor of a point of view that we really don't understand. While we make up our minds very readily, we do not change them without a great struggle. Somehow *our* feelings, *our* thoughts, *our* opinions are unduly enhanced, and while it is easy to see the error in another's thinking, it is difficult to suspect ourselves of error; in fact, the most difficult utterance yet discovered is "I was wrong."

Make a habit of observing the tensions stirring the people around you. On your next trip to the movies, notice the group reactions to scenes of horror, anger, pathos, tenderness, and love. Then, when you come before an audience, make an effort to direct their feelings. As you practice this you will gradually perceive that you can affect their feelings. And it is only by experiencing how human beings react that you can learn to control their reactions. It is an exciting and intriguing study.

## Participants' physical environment

As every wise executive knows, there is great value in arranging the proper physical environment. People react as they are expected to react when the situation is set. Bruce Barton, the world's most famous advertising executive, conceived a novel way of decorating his office so that the environment assists him in thinking of his clients' needs. He has a large photographic mural covering the entire wall of his New York office. It is a scene of the Atlantic City boardwalk jammed with people. "Those are the people," says Barton, "that we must keep in mind. That is the market we must reach. It's what they want, not what we want, that counts. That picture helps us keep them in mind."

Become conscious of the environment in which you must operate. Interviews, discussions, recitals, and entertainments usually require different arrangements for their success. The size of a room has a very definite effect on the reactions of people. You cannot feel very chummy in a large auditorium. Even the arrangement of furnishings may create an inappropriate feeling. The stubbornness of a participant is sometimes caused by as slight an irritation as a glare in his face. Time spent in surveying the actual place of meeting is well invested. Even the appearance of the group itself can lead to harmony or friction. Not only should the word and the action suit the situation, but the dress of the participants should be in harmony with the occasion.

## Summary

All these factors do not affect the situation equally, yet any one of them is powerful enough to destroy the purpose of the situation. Awareness of the factors operating, and the degree to which each factor is dominant, helps to ensure intelligent action in the situation. When you know what all the variables are, your action is bound to be more valuable than an action in which there are unknown factors operating. Constant observation of the elements at work will result in ready perception of these forces.

### SITUATION ANALYSIS CHART

The following chart has been designed to include the factors that move men to action. It serves a double purpose: It is a check for the speaker as he studies the audience he is to address and it furnishes an insight to the speech situation. It may be used best by isolating the most probable answer to each of the four main questions: (1) Why are they there? (2) Who are they? (3) What and how do they think? (4) What is their social, economic, and physical condition? Study the chart with a view to adjusting it to your own community environment. As it is easier to talk with friends than with strangers, so is it easier to talk with an audience you know. You can know your audience if you ask these pertinent questions about them.

*Participants' Purpose* (Why are they there?):

1. To clarify or exchange ideas; seek information.
2. To plan a future procedure—organize a campaign or decide a present issue.
3. To persuade—move to action; to sell.
4. For fellowship—the joy of being together; for entertainment.

*Participants* (Who are they?):

| | |
|---|---|
| Sex | Age |
| Education | Nationality |
| Religion | Race |

*Participants' Ideas* (What do they think? How do they think?):

| | |
|---|---|
| Intellectual level | Habits of thought |
| Prejudices | Views on national politics |
| Persuasions | Views on economic situation |
| Knowledge of subject | Artistic inclinations |

*Condition of Participants* (What is their social, economic, and physical condition?):

| | |
|---|---|
| Standard of living | Present psychological tensions |
| Occupation (office worker, laborer, professional) | Physical comforts in present situation |
| Recreation | Source of income |
| Community interests | Health |
| Social strata | Wealth |
| Location of community | Cosmopolitan interests |
| Issues currently motivating community | Civic pride |

## Projects

*Assignment 1*

To make the factors in the speech situation more real, let us cooperate on a group assignment for the next class. Each member will prepare a two-minute speech on the topic "How to Make This a Better College." You are in a situation. You are a student at college. How can you study this situation and intelligently present to your colleagues a single idea which will improve your college life? This is a challenge.

Is there something in the library arrangement, the dormitories, the cafeteria, the student council, or the college paper that could be improved? If there is, make that the point of your talk; suggest a remedy, give an illustration, and conclude by advocating the change you suggest.

In preparing this speech seek three simple things:

*a. Make your point clearly.* People seldom hear things the first time a speaker says them. So tell them in the very beginning what you want them to do. Then repeat it several times in your talk—and end with it. Remember, a clear statement carries ten times the conviction a confused one does, and a short statement has more punch than a long one. So make your point dynamic and direct.

*b. Be specific, vivid, and concrete.* Don't talk in generalities. Pious advocations to do better are next to useless. Tell your audience *one* specific thing that can be done, and they may do it. Tell them a whole program, and they will do nothing. So in your plea to better the college, select *one* point and illustrate it with several examples. The more examples a speaker has at his command, the more forceful he is likely to be.

*c. Close your speech on a high note!* The last sentence you utter is frequently the only sentence the audience remembers. So, if you would influence their thinking, make that final statement a strong, clear, and vigorous plea. As Lord Chesterfield advised, "Be very modest in your beginning, and as strong as you can be in your ending." As the old adage says, "Start low, go slow, rise higher, and catch fire." If you are interested, your audience will be interested; if you are enthusiastic, they will be, too. But remember, "Dead men tell no tales"—especially on a public platform. So, be clear, be specific, and be dynamic.

*Assignment 2*

Start a file of interesting items from your experience and your reading. Follow the simple principle that whatever interests you is likely to interest others. Such a file will enhance your writing and speaking because it will supply you with accurate observations, with a fund of illustrations, and with a ready stock of human-interest incidents.

W. Somerset Maugham kept such a file in a series of notebooks. In 1949, he published the results under the title *A Writer's Notebook*.[1] In the Preface of that book he enumerates the advantage of such a practice:

"By making a note of something that strikes you, you separate it from the incessant stream of impressions that crowd across the mental eye, and perhaps fix it in your memory. All of us have had good ideas or vivid sensations that we thought would one day come in useful, but which, because we were too lazy to write them down, have entirely escaped us. When you know you are going to make a note of something, you look at it more attentively than you otherwise would, and in the process of doing so the words are borne in upon you that will give it its private place in reality."

Your file or notebook will become an invaluable personal possession and help make you a more interesting person. Remember, knowledge is a perishable commodity, and you need a method of preserving it. This is a delightful and rewarding hobby.

*Sample Speech Situation Outline*

Speaker _____ Class _____ Date _____

I. Topic.
II. Purpose of speech (to inform, to entertain, to convince, to move to action).
III. Source of materials (personal experience).
IV. Organization of material.
   A. Introduction: Arouse interest.
   B. Body: Present illustration of your point.
   C. Conclusion: Repeat your point.

*Questions for Critical Discussion of Performance*

1. Was the speaker's point clearly made?
2. Was it a reasonable point?
3. Did he present it in specific, vivid, and concrete proposals?
4. Was the analysis of the audience accurate?
5. Was his purpose evident?
6. Did he contact the audience by apt analogies, by well selected gestures, and by his reasonable attitude?
7. Was his manner convincing?

[1] Maugham, W. Somerset, *A Writer's Notebook*. New York: Doubleday & Company, Inc., 1949.

8. Was he negative?
9. Did he present a better plan than the *status quo?*
10. Did he illustrate his proposal?

*Developing Semantic Skill*

Add to your word cards the following:

I. Words used in the speech text:

| *Word* | *Pronunciation* | *Meaning* |
|--------|-----------------|-----------|
| 1. proximity | | |
| 2. symbol | | |
| 3. synchronize | | |
| 4. technique | | |

II. Words commonly mispronounced:
   1. adult
   2. alias
   3. ally
III. Words from your own experience.

*Chapter 3*

# PERSONAL FACTORS IN THE SPEECH SITUATION

> Considered as the last finish of education, or of human culture,
> worth and acquirement, the art of speech is noble, and even divine;
> it is like the kindling of a Heaven's light to show us what a glorious
> world exists, and has perfected itself, in a man.
>
> —CARLYLE

Your appearance is a powerful factor in your success or failure in
speech situations. Your posture, your gestures, and your facial expressions all communicate ideas to your listeners. If you appear at
ease, your audience will be at ease; if you appear nervous and jittery,
your audience will feel the same way. The wise speaker gives an
air of confidence and poise, and the audience accepts him in that
role. If you have any unpleasant mannerisms, slouchy posture, a
waddling or mincing gait, this is the time to eliminate such liabilities.
This chapter can help you make the most of your physical appearance. It can enable you to present yourself as an alive and dynamic
person. Any person who walks, sits, and stands properly commands
respect and attention.

The first essential for good platform presence is good posture.
Gelett Burgess has written a book, *Look Eleven Years Younger*, in
which he shows by means of photographs the difference in appearance which poor habits of standing, sitting, and walking can make.
For you as a speaker the importance of looking awake and alive cannot be overestimated. The response you awaken when you approach
your audience with zest and vitality is stimulating. And nowhere is
it more true than on a platform that "Dead men tell no tales."

*Standing*

What is meant by good posture? The human body works as a system of levers. If you throw one part of your body out of line, other
parts are thrown out of line. When you stand properly, you set the

conditions for maximum efficiency and health. Posture control centers in the abdominal muscles. Don't try to achieve a good standing position by jerking the shoulders back. Stand tall, feet together, with the weight directly over the instep. Pull in on the muscles around the abdomen. As you pull in on these muscles you will notice that the chest automatically rises. Keep the chin on a line parallel to the floor or at right angles to the backbone. Stand lightly, gracefully. Feel the sense of control this posture gives. Now let your muscles sag, your stomach protrude, your shoulders droop. Notice the difference in appearance these bad habits make. You look discouraged, tired, worn-out. Learn to stand properly and to carry yourself well, and you have the first essential for success, not only in speaking but in other activities as well.

### Sitting

Most business firms recognize the importance of good posture. They purchase office equipment which makes for maximum efficiency. Notice the importance attached to good posture in the training courses given to secretaries and typists. Recently a series of exercises was prepared for business men and women to be done at their desks. The improvement in health and appearance which comes from assuming the correct sitting position is doubly important for the speaker whose position of prominence on the platform makes faults even more apparent to the audience.

Place a chair in front of a long mirror. Walk to the chair and watch yourself in the mirror as you sit down. Did you sit twice? Did you lower yourself to the chair and then slump? You should lower yourself into the chair in one movement. Your whole thigh should rest on the seat of the chair. Your back, from the waist up, should be straight. Your two feet should be on the floor, one slightly in front of the other. Sit up tall. Pull in on the abdominal muscles and notice your chest come into line as it should. Do not lean back on the base of your spine. This is really not a comfortable position. It produces strain. Practice walking up to a chair, sitting properly, rising from the chair effortlessly, and walking away from it properly.

### Walking

Avoid an awkward, ungainly walk by learning to walk properly. Remember, you walk with your legs, not with your shoulders or arms. Queer mannerisms in walking not only make you look ludicrous but tend to tire you easily. Assume the correct position for good posture. Stand tall. Pull in on the abdominal muscles. Walk gracefully, moving the legs freely from the hips. Do not take tiny, mincing steps. Avoid a stride. Lift your feet from the floor. Do not drag or shuffle them. Walk in a straight line. An experienced actor says, "A good walk is a series of interrupted falls." This means that you should keep the sensation of moving forward. Keep the shoulders free. Don't jerk them as you walk. A good walk is one of the most profitable forms of exercise. The ability to walk across the stage with ease and grace contributes much to the initial impression the speaker makes upon his audience. You can learn to appear confident, energetic, and vital by acquiring correct walking posture.

## Gestures

The experienced speaker has his audience with him before he begins to speak. The inexperienced speaker betrays his nervousness by facial grimaces and ineffective gestures. You must learn to look at the audience. Do not look over their heads or out the window. Staring at the floor or at one particular member of the audience is equally inappropriate. You can gain much from watching the facial expressions of your listeners. Avoid mannerisms such as frowning or biting your lips as you speak. Playing with a ring, twisting a key chain, or clasping your hands tightly behind your back rob you of effectiveness. A well-timed gesture can help you carry your point. Let the thought precede the gesture and concentrate on getting the message to the audience. You will find the study of pantomime profitable because through pantomime you learn that every pose, every movement, every facial expression carries a meaning to your audience. Since this is so, it is well to make your gestures and facial expressions convey just the meaning you want to express.

There are three phases in the preparation of a pantomime: observation, practice, and presentation. The experience of working out a complete pantomime stimulates your imagination, forces you to concentrate on the ways in which emotion can be expressed by bodily movement, and *thus* helps you to acquire better bodily control. Each pantomime should tell a story for your audience. Begin to *plan* your pantomime about a simple life situation. Decide upon the character you wish to represent in this situation. *Work out* the action. *Rehearse* the action at home. *Come prepared* to interpret your pantomime before the class.

Here are some situations which you might select: a jeweler selecting a watch; a stamp collector arranging his favorites; a sports fan watching an exciting game. Working out the pantomime will stimulate your powers of observation. The necessity for portraying emotion without using words should help you to develop flexibility. Notice particularly the effect of timing. The preparation of the pantomime should help you realize the importance of the personal factors in the speech situation. The way to acquire control over these factors is to practice correct standing, sitting, and walking positions. You will gain confidence by synchronizing these factors in actual public-speaking situations. The feeling of power which adequate bodily control gives will inspire you to face future speech situations with assurance.

## PROJECTS

*Assignment*

Prepare a pantomime or tell a short story which requires the use of gestures. Make it brief. It should not exceed two minutes in length. Here is a sample with the gesture words italicized.

> Yesterday I visited a *huge* box factory located on a *high hill.* Running *all around* this building was a *picket fence* about *this high.*
>
> I went *up* the hill, *threw open* the door of the factory, *walked in* and found myself in a *long hallway.*
>
> At the *far end* of the hallway was a *spiral staircase.* At the *top of it* stood a *tall* man with a *Vandyke beard,* which *reached down to here.* I cautiously walked up the *spiral* staircase to a *flat* landing with a sliding door. The man had *disappeared* into *thin air. Sliding* the door open, *inch* by *inch,* I found a *big* room, piled *high with boxes.* There were *big boxes, middle-sized boxes,* and *very small boxes.*
>
> Suddenly, the boxes started *to tumble down around my head.* I woke up with a start—*yawned, stretched,* and *went back to sleep.*

Remember, your purpose in this assignment is to gain bodily control on the platform. As you enact your pantomime or story note the effect of your gestures and facial expressions on the audience. Sometimes the slightest movement creates the most telling effect. Make your body muscles talk.

Here are a few suggestions for topics:

1. Demonstrate to a beginner how to swing a golf club for a drive down the fairway, for a putt, for getting out of the rough.

2. Demonstrate the proper technique for bowling, for batting, for putting the shot, or any other sport.

3. Demonstrate the proper and improper way to do ballroom dancing.

4. Demonstrate the fundamental steps of the ballet, the technique of leading an orchestra, or the cheerleader on the playing field.

5. Demonstrate how several people sit down, get in and out of a car, climb stairs, or walk in a parade.

Keep your pantomime or story interesting and alive. But don't let the reactions of the class disturb you. This is a serious assignment and if you do it well, it will give you a new sense of physical freedom on the platform.

### PERSONAL FACTORS CHART

Make out a check list for yourself to encourage effective use of the personal factors in the speech situation. The important precept to be remembered is that daily practice is essential. Correct one thing each day. It is only applied knowledge that becomes power.

Rate yourself on a three-point basis: 1, sometimes; 2, usually; 3, always.

| *Standing* | 1 | 2 | 3 |
|---|---|---|---|
| I stand tall. . . . . . . . . . . . . . . . . . . . . . . . . . . . . . . . . . . . . . . . . . . |  |  |  |
| I pull in on the abdominal muscles. . . . . . . . . . . . . . . . . . . . |  |  |  |
| I stand on both feet with one foot slightly in front of the other and with the weight directly over the instep. . . . . . . |  |  |  |
| I look alert and interested, not bored or indifferent. . . . . . . |  |  |  |
| I keep my chin on a line parallel to the floor. . . . . . . . . . . . |  |  |  |
| I maintain a feeling of ease and confidence. . . . . . . . . . . . . . |  |  |  |
| I look at the audience, not out of the window or over their heads or at the floor. . . . . . . . . . . . . . . . . . . . . . . . . . . . . . . . |  |  |  |
| I avoid nervous mannerisms such as frowning, biting my lips, etc. . . . . . . . . . . . . . . . . . . . . . . . . . . . . . . . . . . . . . . . . |  |  |  |

[*Continued on next page.*]

| *Sitting* | 1 | 2 | 3 |
|---|---|---|---|
| I sit tall............................................... | | | |
| I rest the full length of my thighs on the chair and do not slump down into it..................................... | | | |
| I keep both feet on the floor, not crossing my knees or putting my feet on the rungs of the chair................ | | | |
| I rise easily from the chair without leaning on the arms.... | | | |

| *Walking* | 1 | 2 | 3 |
|---|---|---|---|
| I walk from the hips................................. | | | |
| I move forward, not waddling from side to side........... | | | |
| I take good steps, neither mincing nor striding........... | | | |
| I walk quietly, not scuffing my feet.................... | | | |

| *Gestures* | 1 | 2 | 3 |
|---|---|---|---|
| I avoid ineffective movements such as playing with a ring, twisting a key chain................................ | | | |
| I let the thought precede the gesture................... | | | |
| I keep hands ready to gesture, not clasped behind back or thrust into pockets................................ | | | |
| I suit the word to the action, the action to the word....... | | | |
| I gesture with my whole body, thus giving unity, purpose, and coordination to my gestures..................... | | | |

*Developing Semantic Skill*

Add to your word cards the following:

I. Words used in the speech text:

| Word | Pronunciation | Meaning |
|------|---------------|---------|
| 1. apathetic | | |
| 2. environment | | |
| 3. pantomime | | |
| 4. posture | | |

II. Words commonly mispronounced:
1. arraign
2. athlete
3. aviation

III. Words from your own experience.

# PART II. SEMANTIC SKILL

The study of social skill has shown you how human relationships become alive in speech situations. It revealed the function of speech as a useful and necessary social skill and made you conscious of the value of improving your personal assets. The second valuable skill to be acquired is your semantic skill, *i.e.*, the ability to use symbols called "words" in meaningful patterns. This requires that you understand the nature of linguistic forms, that you become aware of the problems of meaning, and that you develop precision in the use of words. In addition, it implies that you acquire a sufficient variety of word symbols to enable you to express your thoughts with clarity, force, and beauty. This skill will enable you to think more effectively and to perceive the thinking patterns of others more readily. As you acquire it, you will notice that you are thinking more clearly and expressing your thoughts in a more satisfying manner.

Harry S. Truman, President of the United States, is an extraordinary example of how much a person can improve his speaking ability. When President Truman succeeded the superb speaker Franklin D. Roosevelt his delivery was weak and his speech lacked variety. However, he developed a straightforward and sincere style which is convincing and pleasant to hear. Notice his skillful use of audience contact and his sense of communication as he addresses the Congress of the United States. At appropriate moments he is jovial, grim, and profound. President Truman's speaking skill is an inspiration to every American youth.

*Chapter 4*

# THE PROBLEM OF MEANING

Language is called the Garment of Thought: however it should
rather be, Language is the Flesh-Garment, the Body of Thought.
—CARLYLE

There is a children's story that tells of two kings who were friends
until one sent this request:

"Send me a blue pig with a black tail or else—" To this the other king
replied, "I haven't got one; and if I had—" Upon receiving this answer,
the first king flew into a rage and declared a long and weary war against
his former friend. After some time the war ended as usual at the conference table.

"What did you mean," said the first king, "by saying, 'Send me a blue
pig with a black tail or else—'?"

"Why," he answered, "I meant a blue pig with a black tail or else some
other color. But what did you mean by threatening me with your message,
'I haven't got one; and if I had—'?"

"My meaning was simple enough; for, of course, if I had had such a pig,
I should have sent it."

This simple story illustrates the confusion that can arise without
intention. People can say what they mean, but that is no assurance
that it will mean the same thing to others. Language, being a practical tool, loses its exactness. During the Second World War, this situation was so flagrant that the *Associated Press* issued the following
glossary of red-tape officialese in wartime Washington:

Concur generally—"I haven't read the document and don't want to be
bound by anything I might say."

In conference—"I don't know where he is."

Passed to higher authority—"Pigeonholed in a more sumptuous office."

Appropriate action—"Do you know what to do with it? We don't."

Giving him the picture—"A long, confusing, and inaccurate statement
to a newcomer."

Under active consideration—"We have never heard of it. However, we'll try to find it in the files."

Has received careful consideration—"A period of inactivity covering a time lag."

Have you any comments?—"Give me some idea what it's all about?"

That project is in the air—"I am completely ignorant of the subject."

You will remember—"You have forgotten, or never knew, nor do I."

Transmitted to you—"You hold the bag a while, I'm tired of it."

It is recommended—"We don't think it will work, but you go ahead and stick your neck out and try it."

It is estimated—"This is my guess—now you guess."

For compliance—"Sure it's silly, but you gotta do it anyhow."

For necessary action—"We don't know what they want, so you do it."

For immediate action—"We have stalled it long enough, now you do something about it."

For signature—"I thought it up, but you sign it and take the rap."

Another example of the problem of meaning is the tendency of professions to speak in their own peculiar jargon. The following instance was reported in *The Pleasure of Publishing:*

*Medicalese:* "The patient, who previous to the onset of his disability obtained his source of livelihood from the manipulation of the exterior keys of the pianoforte so as to form a consistent and harmonious arrangement of musical impressions, suffered a bilateral digital amputation as a result of maljuxtaposition with a provender bearing vehicle. Resultant from this disability is a diminution of digital dexterity requisite to the execution of his vocational patterns, the end product of same being a severe limitation of the patient's preoperative ability at livelihood acquisition."

*English translation:* "The patient, who used to be a piano player, lost two fingers after bumping into a grocery truck. Since he can't play the piano as well as he used to, he doesn't make so much money anymore."

Such examples illustrate that there is a basic need for understanding the nature of language. Whence came this confusion? What created this modern Tower of Babel? In essence, it is the result of the human inability to communicate meanings effectively. To solve the problem of meaning there is only one sure cure: an understanding of the basic nature and purpose of language. How do men learn to speak and how do they translate their thinking into symbols called "words"? To understand this problem it is necessary to go back to the simplest element involved: man's first use of words.

## The Word

During the first year of life the child makes a variety of noises as part of his reaction to his environment. Such activities have no linguistic counterpart. Gradually, however, between the ninth and sixteenth month, the child discovers that external objects have names. This is not an abrupt discovery, but rather a slow realization of a more effective mode of action. He discovers that a certain sound produces a desired result more quickly than other sounds. Speech, then, becomes for him a manner of acting in which a sound symbol is used to attain some external object. He realizes that special sounds are magical servants. The phonetic outburst, or words, have the power to bring desired gratifications. This is the beginning of the sound-symbol substitution for action. Words now begin to replace crying because they are more efficient tools.

While the child remains in this stage, words have meaning only as attached to external objects. There is only a slight problem of meaning, as there is a direct physical counterpart for each symbol used. The following diagrams will help make clear how this process of substitution of symbols for objects begins and finally permeates thinking and acting situations.

Diagram 1 represents the identity of the symbol and the external object in the nominative stage. No distinction is made by the child

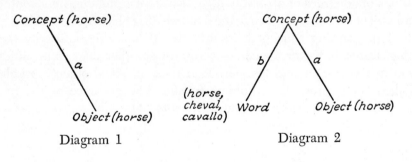

Diagram 1          Diagram 2

between the thing and the word. The process that actually takes place, however, is that shown in diagram 2. Through sense perception, the mind has come in contact with the object and formed a concept, which, in turn, has been expressed through a symbol. Hence, the concept is causally connected with the external object but is only nominally connected with the symbol. Between the thing and the symbol there is no real connection except as the mind confers it. For that reason, the base of the triangle has been left out.

To be sure the meaning of the above is clear, let us view it in another way: In diagram 2, the line *a* refers to the direct connection existing between the concept and the external thing; the line *b* refers to the accidental connection between the concept and the symbol (word) selected. If the external object were horse, the *concept* would be of *horse* necessarily, while the symbol selected might be "horse," "*cavallo*," or "*cheval*," depending on whether the person were American, Spanish, or French. Hence, the connection signified by *a* is casual; the connection *b* is accidental.

In the *nominative* stage, meaning depends upon the adequacy of the symbol to reveal the concept, and the acceptance of the symbol as a substitute for the external object. Before the second year, however, the child advances to a different stage of development. He begins to inquire about the relation of things, to ask, "Why is a moon?" etc. This is a sign that he is comparing, inferring, and discovering new relationships in things. These relationships are called "judgments" and are expressed in sentences. The simple sentence "The dog is white" means that two concepts have been juxtaposed in the mind and a relationship noted. In other words, it is an indication that the *speculative* stage has been reached.

The child's mental activity in this stage may be explained in terms of "degrees of abstraction." For instance, the child encounters an object and discovers that the symbol "dog" has been attached to it. The resulting concept is identified with one dog, and only that dog. Later, however, he comes across three other dogs quite different in size, shape, and manner. That these physical objects are also called "dog" presents a problem to him. The presence of the four separate objects supplies four concepts. The discovery of great similarity in the concepts occasions a comparison and the forming of a new concept. This new concept refers to no one dog in particular but to "dogness" in general. Finally, the essence "dogness" is applied to a similar object (*i.e.*, another dog) when next encountered. In the above, three degrees of abstraction have taken place: (1) the abstracting of similarities among the four concepts, (2) the forming of the general concept, and (3) the applying of the general concept to new objects when encountered.

In regard to the problem of meaning, the formation of the general concept is of great significance. *It is the source of abstract words.*

For example, in explaining the speculative stage, the abstract word "dogness" was used. This symbol has no physical counterpart. It expresses a relationship between concepts in the mind. To crystallize for ourselves and to communicate to others, a symbol for the relationship must be agreed upon by all. And so it is that "dogness" is arbitrarily selected. How involved the problem becomes is evident when we try to define exactly what is meant by such abstract words as "liberty," "democracy," "faith," "truth," and "justice."

The following diagram designates the entire process of abstractions and should furnish an insight into the relationship between

### WORDS

### (Symbols)

| | *Concrete* | | | |
|---|---|---|---|---|
| | 1 | 2 | 3 | 4 |
| Source of concrete symbols | Physical reality | Act of sense perception | Formation of concept | Selection of symbol |

| | *Abstract* | | | |
|---|---|---|---|---|
| | 1 | 2 | 3 | 4 |
| Source of abstract symbols | Discovery of similarity in concepts | Formation of general concept (universal) | Selection of symbol expressing relationship | Application of abstract symbol to include new objects |

| | *Relationships of universals* | | |
|---|---|---|---|
| | 1 | 2 | 3 |
| | | | Intellective memory |
| | Reflection | Syntheses | |
| Source of abstract reasoning symbols | Act of mind contemplating its own acts and states | Analysis comparison | Act of recognizing past operations |

DIAGRAM 3. Three sources furnish the degrees of abstraction inherent in word symbols. Concrete symbols act as substitutes for actual objects perceived by the senses. Abstract symbols express universal groups in terms of likenesses and express relationships between such groupings. Finally, what may be termed abstract reasoning symbols arise because of the power of the mind to remember, reflect, synthesize, and analyze. This is the realm of reason and the basis of all philosophic notions and systems.

thinking and linguistic forms. A reasonable amount of study will reward you with a deeper understanding of the problem of meaning in human intercourse. You will realize that to record and communicate effectively, a system of symbols as intricate as the thought process itself is required. Moreover, a careful review of the diagram will make you conscious of the many abstract words you use without an accurate conception of their true meaning.

In the instance of a concrete symbol, it was indicated that there were only two sources of possible misunderstanding of meaning. Further, these misunderstandings could be cleared up by actual reference to the thing symbolized. With the introduction of abstract words, however, the diagram reveals how varied the meanings may be and how liable to misinterpretation. As no symbol is capable of complete representation, even of a physical object, how much more so is this true of abstract relationships. It was the contemplation of this that made Stevenson point out in his *Truth of Intercourse* that even with the best intentions it is well-nigh impossible to say entirely what we mean.

Up to this point we have assumed that no false concepts or symbols have entered into the process described. Yet this is far from true. People are continually basing their actions on false conceptions. As the process described in the last diagram is continually being enacted to some degree with every new experience and thought, it can readily be seen that we all possess areas in which our thinking proceeds with rather faulty material. Add to that the number of times we use words without a full realization of their meaning. All these factors combine in every speech situation in forms more complicated than it is possible to describe. All help create the problem of meaning.

Projects

*Assignment*

The next class will be an imaginative exercise. Suppose the entire population were to be wiped out by an atomic weapon which struck only those over two years of age. Assume, further, that most of the two-year-olds lived to be twenty. What kind of a language would they possess? What technical skills would they have? How long would it take them to arrive at a civilization comparable to the present? Would their civilization be anything like the present one? What social situations would they develop?

Let your imagination roam freely in solving this problem. Jot down a few notes on the linguistic features of this future society. Select a discussion leader and enjoy the experience of many minds solving an imaginative problem.

In your discussion, try to cover the following questions:

1. How would they most likely communicate?
2. Would sign language precede the spoken word?
3. Could they make use of any of the records left by us?
4. Would speech be only a system of danger signals?
5. Would thousands of new languages grow up?
6. How long would it take them to learn to write?
7. How would they name the animals, the birds, and each other?
8. What abstract symbols would they develop?
9. How long would it take them to develop fears, prejudices, and hatreds?
10. What religious concepts would guide their lives?

*Developing Semantic Skill*

Add to your word cards the following:

I. Words used in the speech text:

| *Word* | *Pronunciation* | *Meaning* |
|--------|-----------------|-----------|
| 1. culture | | |
| 2. custom | | |
| 3. nominative | | |

II. Words commonly mispronounced:
   1. bade
   2. blatant
   3. bouquet
III. Words from your own experience.

### REFERENCES

BLOOMFIELD, LEONARD, *Language*, Chap. IX, "Meaning," pp. 139–157, and Chap. XXIV, "Semantic Change," pp. 425–443.

CHASE, S., *Tyranny of Words*, Chap. VII, pp. 96–116.

FIRTH, J. R., *Speech*, Chap. V, "The Problem of Meaning," pp. 38–45.

GRAFF, WILLIAM L., *Language and Languages*, Chap. II, "Meaning," pp. 71–93.

GRAY, LOUIS H., *Foundation of Language*, Chap. II, "What Is Language," pp. 12–44, and Chap. IX, "Semantics: The Changing Meaning of Words," pp. 249–276.

GRAY and WISE, *Bases of Speech,* Chap. VI, pp. 296–307.

LEWIS, M. M., *Infant Speech,* Chap. II, pp. 5–18; Chap. VIII, pp. 124–142; and Chap. XI, pp. 189–209.

OGDEN, C. K., and I. A. RICHARDS, *The Meaning of Meaning,* Chap. I, pp. 1–18.

PILLSBURY and MEADER, *The Psychology of Language,* Chap. IX, "Thought and Language: Words and Their Meaning," pp. 152–186.

*Chapter 5*

# UNDERSTANDING SEMANTICS

A word fitly spoken is like apples of gold in networks of silver.
—PROVERBS

The science which deals with meaning is called "semantics." It seeks to classify the changes that have taken place in the meanings attached to words. These changes have taken place through such phenomena as connotative use, expansion of meaning, specialization, and ease of production. To catalogue the changes in language and trace its historical forms is to practice a *science*. The *art* of semantics is another matter. The art seeks to practice in actual situations the formulation of meanings; it deals with the use of symbols and not the study of their origin and classification. Hence, semantics is an art used in the speech situation to help solve the problems of meaning. Semantics goes beyond mere knowledge of formal changes and demands that there be skill in the use of symbols. It demands creative action through being more sensitized to the forms meaning assumes. The semantic artist is one who is attuned to the slightest nuance of thought because of his acquaintance with meanings in all guises.

There are four understandings necessary in the analysis of semantics:

1. Understanding the thought behind the symbol.
2. Understanding the variety of symbols needed to express thought.
3. Understanding the power of the symbols to color the thought.
4. Understanding the dependency of the thought on the symbol and vice versa.

These understandings do not constitute semantic skill but are necessary in the sense that they aid intelligent acquisition of that skill. Each understanding is really an avenue of approach to semantic skill, so it is valuable to consider briefly their nature.

Realization that there is a thought behind the symbol should make us skeptical of the symbol. It shows that, at best, the symbol is a mere approximation of a more vital reality—thought. Thought, in turn, is the expression of a relation between two concepts in the mind. This relation is a judgment. The means of communicating such a relationship is called a "proposition" and is expressed in symbols called "words." Hence, it is not words that are significant but the thought behind the words, the meaning or relationship, that is intended. It is the thought that is to be communicated, not the words. The words are but means to an end, and less significant than the thought. This truth should caution against the abuse of semantic skill, for words without thought are as "sounding brass and tinkling cymbals," signifying nothing.

The problem of meaning exists because symbols are inadequate to convey the complete thought. Stuart Chase in *The Tyranny of Words* illustrates this fact copiously. To mention a single instance, assume you possess a worth-while thought. To crystallize it for yourself and to communicate it, you seek to phrase it in words. Your first attempt is not satisfactory because it is not clear enough. You must seek for more precise symbols, ones that will appeal more directly to the intellect. Your second attempt achieves the clarity you desire; the thought is quite clear, but it lacks the forcefulness that it deserves. You try again. After much labor you attain a clear and forceful symbolization of the thought. Yet it is not completely the thought you had in mind. True, it is exact and vivid in its present language, but you are not satisfied. The present expression is cruder than the thought you possess. The thought deserves better clothing. You search for more aesthetic symbols and finally reach an expression which conveys the complete thought. It is obvious that such a process requires the possession of a wide variety of symbols.

The power of the symbol to influence thought is a vital consideration in semantic relationships. Recall the comments current in political discussions. What one side considers sound and practical policy, the opposition party describes as "crackpot politics," "raw-deal visions," "sheer fantasy," and "Un-American." War reports carry similar instances of "bravery" on our side and "butchery" on the enemy's part. In personal discussion, the word "firm" can be declined as follows: I am firm, you are obstinate, he is pigheaded. We are likely to ignore this third understanding if we acquire the habit of using symbols in our thinking which color the thought process. All forms of propaganda seek to implement the thinking of the people with emotionally charged symbols. How intricately linguistics works with emotion is exhibited in the story of the baseball umpire. In an intercollegiate contest the daylight started to fade on a tie score. As soon as one team got ahead, the umpire called the game. In the inevitable protest that followed, the coach of the losing team accused the umpire of favoritism. The response of the umpire was, "The trouble with you is that you're just sore because *we* won." The two colleges don't play baseball any more.

This power of the symbol to influence the thought is carried on without the thinker's knowledge unless he perceives the extent to which the symbol has developed emotional meaning. Almost every word carries a slight emotional value or connotation. In primitive people, an extreme example is found in their magic phrases. In our own society, taboos are placed on certain words because their emotional suggestion is too forceful. To think continually in terms of highly charged symbols inevitably leads to slipshod and wishful thinking. It further leads to a narrowness of concept which ultimately results in prejudice toward any varying interpretation. Hence, the discipline of checking the thought process through its emotionally charged tools is essential to clear thinking. Mark how Shakespeare describes Cleopatra sitting in her barge on the Nile with attendants trying to stir up a breath of air.

> The barge she sat in, like a burnished throne,
> Burn'd on the water: the poop was beaten gold;
> Purple the sails, and so perfumed that
> The winds were love-sick with them, the oars were silver,
> Which to the tune of flutes kept stroke, and made
> The water which they beat to follow faster,
> As amorous of their strokes. For her own person,
> It beggar'd all description: she did lie
> In her pavilion—cloth-of-gold of tissue—
> O'er-picturing that Venus where we see
> The fancy outwork nature: on each side her
> Stood pretty dimpled boys, like smiling Cupids,
> With divers-colour'd fans, whose wind did seem
> To glow the delicate cheeks which they did cool,
> And what they undid did.

There are two main reasons why words arouse extraneous feelings:

1. Words leave their original references and carry over some old shades of meaning.
2. Words have numerous meanings.

Both factors add to the confusion as you try to describe the thoughts you possess. But the fact that you understand that this problem of meaning exists gives you an insight to its solution. Hence, it is wise to review these two tendencies in detail.

First, note the tendency of words to leave their original reference. Instances of this are abundant in a complex society such as ours. For example, the young bride who asked her mother what part of the cow a "leg of lamb" came from is not unusual. To her the "leg of lamb" referred to a type of meat that was served on the table, and she never had associated it with any part of a lamb. On telling this story to my butcher, he told me that the day before a girl had inquired if one should ask for a leg or a shoulder of tongue. The study of the etymology of words will reveal amazing stories of the shift of references that are being made. Originally, "curfew" meant the covering of a fire at night; "bedlam" was a madhouse called Bethlehem in London of the thirteenth century; "neighbor" is the old Anglo-Saxon for "near-by farmer"; "congregation" meant a herdsman and his flock; and "*capella*" was not a chapel or a choir, but a short cloak or hood. Note the interesting etymology of "gossip," "silly," "knave," "pedagogue," etc. Such linguistic histories will give you a new insight into the problem of using symbols to make yourself understood.

Second, do not be satisfied with one meaning for a word; it probably has many. Let us take one of the first words children usually learn: "cat." On the surface, there seems to be nothing involved in understanding the word "cat." Upon investigation, however, we find the following possible meanings attached to that one symbol:

1. A carnivorous quadruped kept as a domestic pet.
2. A wicked or spiteful woman.
3. The fur or pelt of the cat.
4. The corn god in folklore.
5. A double tripod having six feet, on three of which it rests, however placed.
6. The part of the first coat of plaster going between laths.

7. A game, called "tipcat"; one old cat, two old cat (one a-cat).
8. A spare hand in playing cards.
9. A movable defensive structure used in medieval warfare.
10. A boat.
11. To flog with a cat-o'-nine-tails.
12. To fish for catfish.

The above meanings are not exhaustive; they are merely the ones that have become so generally used and recognized that they deserve a place in the dictionary. The use made of the symbol in vulgar or common speech, in colloquial references, and in dialects of English can only be conjectured.

To take another example, consider the word "game." Dr. Irving Lorge, in his interesting article "The English Semantic Count," indicates the following meanings that are frequently attached to that single-syllable word:

1. Amusement.
2. Diversion.
3. A diversion of the nature of a contest.
4. Such games played in ancient Greece and Rome, *e.g.*, Olympian games.
5. Proper method of play.
6. A proceeding; intrigue followed up like a game.
7. A person's policy.
8. A definite portion of play.
9. Position or advantage in play.
10. The quarry.
11. The flesh of wild animals used for food.
12. Spirited.
13. Lame.
14. To play, sport, jest.
15. To gamble for a prize or stake.

While this word is somewhat unusual, there are many like it, and the average word has not less than four or five meanings. Thus, in a connected sentence using five such words, there is the possibility of 15,625 combinations of meanings. This, it must be remembered, deals only with situations in which the word is used in an accepted sense. What the changes of interpretation are when words are wrongly or carelessly used can hardly be estimated.

These two tendencies of words, namely, to lose original references and to have many meanings, make your problem in communication more difficult—for you must remember that the problem of making your meaning clear is your personal responsibility. The more clearly you can deliver a message, the easier it is for an audience to understand. The more direct and incisive your attitude, your imagery, and your words, the more directly your message hits its target. It is like pounding a nail into a board: you hit it and hit it, again and again, and when it gets loose you pound it some more. Your ideas are nails, and your words are the hammer strokes. Use the hammer to drive the nail home. Make your words precise strokes, and you will drive home your ideas.

One caution must be mentioned in the study of semantic skill. DO NOT USE WORDS FOR THEIR OWN SAKE. It is a temptation of youth to fall in love with words for their sound and length. And it is a temptation of age to amuse itself with such flourishes of language. Avoid this double evil by striving for simplicity and directness. Use words purposively. Let them remain tools to serve you. Always realize that the function of language is to communicate thought. Language is an auxiliary skill acquired for the more fundamental purpose of communicative meaning. As an end in itself it has limited value.

Shakespeare has bequeathed us a classic example of semantic skill run riot. When Polonius attempts to tell the King and Queen that he has recovered a letter from Hamlet, he begins thus:

POLONIUS: My liege, and madam, to expostulate
    What majesty should be, what duty is,
    Why day is day, night night, and time is time,
    Were nothing but to waste night, day and time.
    Therefore, since brevity is the soul of wit,
    And tediousness the limbs and outward flourishes,
    I will be brief. Your noble son is mad:
    Mad call I it; for, to define true madness,
    What is't but to be nothing else but mad?
    But let that go.
QUEEN: More matter, with less art.
POLONIUS: Madam, I swear I use no art at all.
    That he is mad, 'tis true: 'tis true 'tis pity,
    And pity 'tis 'tis true: a foolish figure;

But farewell it, for I will use no art.
Mad let us grant him then: and now remains
That we find out the cause of this effect,
Or rather say, the cause of this defect,
For this effect defective comes by cause:
Thus it remains, and the remainder thus.
Perpend.
I have a daughter—have while she is mine—
Who, in her duty, and obedience, mark,
Hath given me this: now gather, and surmise. (*Reads letter*)

What Polonius has said in 23 lines and about 184 words is: "Your majesties, Hamlet is mad; here's the proof." While extremely useful to the dramatist seeking to portray a prating old man, such verbosity should be shunned like the plague. Semantic skill aims not at volume but at brevity and precision in language. When asked how long he could speak on a subject, an old preacher sagely replied, "If I'm not prepared, one hour. If I am prepared, fifteen minutes." Strive to say what you mean exactly, and to say exactly what you mean.

Finally, you must realize that the task of understanding meanings is not easy. In fact, the Supreme Court is continually trying to determine the exact meanings of pieces of legislation and their constitutionality under the basic law. An editorial in the New York *World-Telegram and Sun* describes how complicated this can become.

A 5 to 4 decision of the United States Supreme Court holds that the Standard Oil Co. of California violated the antitrust laws by making exclusive contracts with independent gasoline dealers in seven Western states.

Justice Jackson, in a dissenting opinion signed also by Chief Justice Vinson and Justice Burton, observes:

"If the courts are to apply the lash of the antitrust laws to the backs of businessmen to make them compete, we cannot in fairness also apply the lash whenever they hit upon a successful method of competing. That . . . appears to be the case before us."

Far be it from us to take sides in this controversy among the learned justices. But it reminds us of a plaintive observation recently published in a business newsletter:

"Apparently a businessman now—

"1. Is guilty of collusion if he sells at the same price as his competitors.

"2. Is guilty of profiteering if he raises his price to avoid the charge of collusion.

"3. Is guilty of cut-throat competition if he lowers his price to avoid the charge of profiteering."

This chapter has sought to demonstrate that there is great need for deeper understanding of the problem of meaning. The next chapter will assist you in developing skill in word usage which is the wisest solution to the problem. The development of semantic skill will assist you in expressing yourself and in understanding the expressions of others. Moreover, it will furnish your mind with more effective instruments for clear thinking. Work diligently for this prized goal.

## PROJECTS

### Assignment

The greatest value of semantics is to make you aware that you are influenced by the way events are related to you. You are continually battered with daily reports in the papers, by books selected for your reading, by accounts of national and international events, and by interpretations of events via the radio. To acquire the skill of discernment you must become aware of the use that is made of words to influence your thinking. Virtually all the information you receive will have been interpreted by someone. Even though that person may be sincere, he cannot help but be partisan to his own thought patterns and convictions. And frequently information is colored for a purpose. As Lincoln Steffens shrewdly observed, "Nobody can read a newspaper every day and not be influenced by it; we 'read' our papers in our quiet, relaxed moments, when we might be thinking, and thus unwittingly let the editors form our minds."

This assignment will make you a keener observer of the world of propaganda in which we all must live. Be wary of what you read in a single account or a single book. Check all sources and their purposes. Watch for oversimplifications, repetitions, and emotionally charged words; they frequently distort facts. Recollect that for more than twelve years the minds of the German people were clouded by Paul Joseph Goebbels, Nazi Minister of Propaganda and National Enlightenment. How did he do it? On Jan. 29, 1942, the satanic "Little Doktor" wrote the secret in his personal diary:

"Propaganda must always be essentially simple and repetitious. In the long run only he will receive basic results in influencing public opinion who is able to reduce problems to the simplest terms, and who has the courage to keep forever repeating them in this simplified form—despite the objections of the intellectuals."

Such a revelation should make you wary of the power propaganda has in your life.

Let's engage in an intellectual detective hunt. For the next class meeting take the accounts of any action appearing in two or three different newspapers. Pick papers with opposing policies and points of view. Note how they differ in observation of details: how they use different kinds of emotionally charged words; how they express an attitude toward a situation. Then select a specific story, cut out the different versions, and present your analysis to the class. Don't be content with simply reading the stories, but select two or three items and mold your talk around them. Make it alive with examples.

*Sample Semantic-skill Outline*

Speaker _____ Class _____ Date _____

  I. Topic.
 II. Purpose of speech.
III. *Arouse interest:* Highlight the vital differences in the two versions of your selections.
IV. *Make your point:* Indicate how various views can create different impressions.
 V. *Illustrate by quoting specific instances:* Quote direct contrasts in words, in details emphasized, and instances of attitude coloration.
VI. *Advise audience:* Make a vivid connection between your illustrations and the caution intelligent people should exercise when viewing printed versions of the news.

*Questions for Critical Discussion of Performance*

   1. Was the selection of newspaper accounts well chosen?
   2. Did the speaker make his point clearly?
   3. How did he highlight the semantic differences?
   4. What were the emotionally charged words?
   5. Can you suggest synonyms for these charged words?
   6. How skillfully was the contrast in the different versions indicated?
   7. Was the presentation reliable?
   8. Was the speaker's semantic skill adequate?
   9. Was the speaker poised and confident?
  10. What means could be used to improve this presentation?

*Developing Semantic Skill*

Add to your word cards the following:

I. Words used in the speech text:

| Word | Pronunciation | Meaning |
|------|---------------|---------|

    1. copiously
    2. medieval
    3. pedagogue
    4. tripod

II. Words commonly mispronounced:
    1. façade
    2. fazer
    3. lyric

III. Words from your own experience.

### REFERENCES

COOPER, LANE, *The Rhetoric of Aristotle*, Bk. 3, Chaps. 1, 3, 6, 7.

EISENSON, JON, *The Psychology of Speech*, Chaps. 6, 7, 8, 9, pp. 72–134.

GRAY, LOUIS H., *Foundations of Language*, Chap. IV, "Language and Thought," pp. 88–114.

HOLMES, ROGER W., *The Rhyme of Reason*, "The Logician and Why He Uses Symbols," pp. 1–28.

MILLER, CLYDE R., *The Process of Persuasion*, Chap. VI, "The Word and Its Meaning," pp. 87–106.

OGDEN, C. K., and I. A. RICHARDS, *The Meaning of Meaning*, Chap. II, "The Power of Words," pp. 32–132.

RICHARDS, I. A., *The Philosophy of Rhetoric*, Chap. IV, "Some Criteria of Words," pp. 69–86.

WILLIS, GEORGE, *The Philosophy of Speech*, Chap. III, "Speech and Thought," pp. 41–49, and Chap. X, "Thought without Words," pp. 198–205.

## Chapter 6

# HOW TO DEVELOP SEMANTIC SKILL

His words, like so many nimble and airy servitors, trip about him at command.

—MILTON

President Eliot of Harvard University once said that there were only four steps in thinking: "One, observing accurately; two, recording correctly; three, comparing, grouping, and inferring justly; and four, expressing the results of these mental operations." Three of the four steps are directly concerned with your ability to use words. This is important because you think in terms of the symbols you possess. If you possess a series of accurate symbols (words), your thinking will have a more accurate base. If you possess a series of slipshod symbols, your thinking will be slipshod. You will find difficulty in reasoning and speaking because you are forcing the mind to use dull tools. Moreover, if your vocabulary is limited, you are limiting the activity of your mind. So do the wise thing and devote some time to gaining a command of words.

Command over words is a skill everyone must possess to a certain degree. Increase the degree of skill you possess, and you increase your effectiveness as a speaker and thinker. *Every study of successful businessmen reveals that top executives have large vocabularies.* This is quite natural, for a thinking mind requires a wide knowledge of words.

This chapter is aimed to help you establish a method of gaining control over words. Such control is the result of a habit pattern which requires constant practice. It is not easily acquired, but the process will unfold pleasures that will lighten the task and prove a source of continued interest. You will soon find that words are magical keys unlocking the gates to the realm of thought.

There are many ways of studying words:

1. Read the works of good writers. They are masters in choice of words. Here you meet words in their natural habitat. You acquire a feeling for a word and a knowledge of how to use it.

2. Read the daily papers to become familiar with words in their current usage.

3. Take any short passage and study it carefully. Look up each word, if necessary. Then reread the selection until you have become so thoroughly acquainted with the meaning and use of each word that it becomes part of your own vocabulary.

4. Study the histories of words. Trace their development through successive changes.

5. Study the various denotations of words. You must meet a word many times before you can understand all the uses to which the word may be put. In this course we have used the word "pitch." To you, the word may mean the highness or lowness of a sound. To a baseball fan, the word would have a meaning pertinent to sports terminology. To a roofer, it would mean the black substance used in repairing roofs. A word has meaning according to the context in which it is used. It is not enough to know a dictionary definition of a word.

6. Study antonyms and synonyms for the word. If you can give a term which means the exact opposite of the word in question, you can be sure you know the meaning of the word. Moreover, because English has borrowed from many languages, it contains many synonyms. You gain in power to express shades of meaning as you gain in the discriminative use of synonyms.

In addition to these seasoned ways of building a vocabulary, there is a modern approach of word lists, such as Thorndike's list of frequency words. Thorndike made a study of writing words and tabulated the frequency for 20,000 words. You can begin work on your vocabulary as measured by this test list of frequency words. It will enable you to begin at the natural starting place for your own purpose and furnish a scientific guide to the most practicable words for you to acquire.

One of the best ways to learn words is to take part in situations in which the words are used. The person who flies learns aviation terminology; the industrial engineer learns manufacturing terminology; the lawyer learns legal terminology; and the doctor learns medical terms. It may be that you cannot take actual part in bridgebuilding, dress designing, building construction, or aviation, yet your business may require that you talk intelligently with people in all these fields. You can acquire an understanding of a wide variety of terms and learn to use them intelligently by the following exercise.

Supply yourself with a pack of small index cards. Each day, read at least one interesting article in a magazine devoted to some activity, *e.g.*, *Etude* for music; *Town and Country* for sports; *Time* for current events. As you read the article, you will come across terms which are not familiar to you. Don't interrupt your reading by stopping to look up the words. Copy the sentence in which the word occurs on the card and underline the word. When you have finished reading the article, look up the word in an unabridged dictionary; read the sentence over again, saying the word aloud.

You will be surprised how quickly you can acquire a technical vocabulary for a wide variety of interests. Keep reading over these cards in your leisure moments. The advantage of the exercise is that you learn how to use the word as the expert uses it. You avoid the mistake of using the word improperly, for dictionary definitions are often misleading. You can profit tremendously from making this exercise a stimulating hobby. The good conversationalist sets himself the job of drawing the other fellow out, and command of the vocabulary of the other fellow's hobby is an excellent help in this respect. Good salesmen say that they find a knowledge of hobbies the best approach to their prospects. This way of adding to your vocabulary is both interesting and profitable.

## Projects

*Assignment*

Since you have been given several means of developing your semantic skill, let us go a step further in this assignment. Let us analyze the role that language plays in preparing your mind for the acceptance of various points of view. Let us catch the cues that warn us that the writer or speaker is preparing our minds to accept his views. We'll call these cues semanticues. Semanticues are symbols which suggest that what is to be proved has been proved and must be accepted. Or they suggest that unless the hearer or reader accepts their point of view that person is very foolish, idiotic, or immoral.

Such a wholesale attempt at persuasion is one of the props of every propagandist. Whether his cause is good or bad, he uses these cues. Noting these cues warns us that this is the moment for clear thinking. Whenever you hear or read one of these phrases, be sure to put your thinking cap right on your head, for the theory behind these cues is that few people follow arguments alertly. Most people wait until the communicator draws his conclusions, and then they accept the conclusions as proved facts. A vital part of your college education consists in making you skeptical of such acceptances. In other words, higher education seeks to teach you to think for yourself.

Here are 40 such "semanticues":

1. There is adequate criteria to judge that. . . .
2. We may be certain that. . . .
3. There is an abundance of evidence to show. . . .
4. There is every reason to assume. . . .
5. This is no assumption. . . .
6. Undeniably. . . .
7. A conclusion which no open-minded person can fail to ignore. . . .
8. Thinking men must admit. . . .
9. No fair mind will disagree. . . .
10. There is ground for identifying. . . .
11. No one would challenge. . . .
12. Therefore. . . .
13. For obvious reasons. . . .
14. It follows that. . . .
15. It would be an insult to ask you to believe. . . .
16. Science has established that. . . .
17. The whole history of the world shows. . . .
18. How much more so is it true. . . .
19. No one has ever questioned that. . . .
20. Modern man has discovered that. . . .
21. We must admit that. . . .
22. So, as is well known. . . .
23. From this we see that. . . .
24. So, it must be concluded. . . .
25. We are justified in believing that. . . .
26. It is nonsense to suppose that. . . .
27. This shows that. . . .
28. Consequently. . . .
29. Even a journeyman logician could prove that. . . .
30. Who could be so dense as to think that. . . .
31. It is indeed a fallacy based on no logic at all. . . .
32. And from the foregoing we see. . . .
33. One would have to be deprived of God-given intelligence to. . . .
34. A child could see that. . . .

35. We, who love liberty, know that. . . .
36. Only a savage mind could conceive that. . . .
37. A half minute of real thought will convince you that. . . .
38. The thought of all ages reveals that. . . .
39. Every moral fiber cries out that. . . .
40. In like manner. . . .

The persuasive power of these cues is that they insinuate the thought into our minds. They arrange for its reception by creating a mood of acceptance. Obviously, the above list is not complete. For our next assignment, suppose each one brings in a sample of a new "semanticue," or an old one, and the argument that follows it. Read the cue to the class and then discuss how it prepares the audience for the acceptance of the thought. You may wish to point out bad cues that alienate the good will of the audience. "Listen, you dope!" is one often heard on campuses before the fight starts. Search out editorials, textbooks, and propaganda leaflets for these cues. Don't rely on your memory, but bring the clipping to class. It will be an interesting session.

*Developing Semantic Skill*

Add to your word cards the following:

I. Words used in the speech text:

| *Word* | *Pronunciation* | *Meaning* |
|--------|-----------------|-----------|
| 1. empirical | | |
| 2. speculative | | |
| 3. process | | |
| 4. eloquence | | |

II. Words commonly mispronounced:
1. catch
2. chameleon
3. clangor

III. Words from your own experience.

# PART III. VOCAL SKILL

You have now acquired two valuable skills: the social skill and the semantic skill. The next four chapters and projects will assist you in acquiring vocal skill, *i.e.*, the ability to use your voice effectively to convey thought and emotion. This is the most personal of all skills because it concerns your most characteristic feature: your mode of expression. It requires that you learn to use your vocal mechanism as a delicate instrument. It requires that you understand the elements that fashioned your voice and that you learn to use your voice effectively. This means practicing to acquire a full, resonant voice capable of interpreting the finest shades of meaning and feeling. This skill is attained by achieving correct posture, proper pitch and volume, pleasant quality, and sufficient force and emphasis for your speech needs. As you acquire these abilities you will function more effectively in your speech situations.

*Wide World Pho*

General Dwight D. Eisenhower smiles and frowns as he speaks. The general typifies the old maxim, "Dead men tell no tales." This is especially true on a platform. The enthusiasm and vitality of the speaker are directly reflected in the audience. As Emerson observed, "Wooden minds, wooden voices." The driving energy of the man who created the greatest military force in history is revealed in these pictures. No one comes within his hearing who is not influenced by his deep convictions and his dynamic delivery. His voice trumpets his convictions as calls to truth.

*Chapter 7*

# STUDY AND PRACTICE OF VOCAL CHARACTERISTICS

Lord, what an organ is human speech, when played on by a master.
—MARK TWAIN

Your voice is an expression of your personality. A dynamic person has a lifelike voice, a confident person an assuring voice, and a charming person a pleasant voice. In short, your voice reveals you. If you have a personality problem, your voice is likely to reveal it. The voice of the shrew, for example, comes sharp and shrill in unmistakable quality, and the voice of the whiny person drags along with screeching telltale effect. Such difficulties cannot be remedied without changing the attitude of the person.

The kind of person you are is a basic question in voice training. The richer the personality, the greater the possibility of a vibrant, warm, expressive voice. You cannot give what you do not possess. Your voice is the most sensitive instrument known. It reveals your whole person more clearly than an infrared camera, and it detects your feelings more graphically than a lie detector. So resolve to make your voice a pliant instrument revealing your assets and the cultural advantages you have enjoyed.

In order to improve your voice it is necessary to concentrate on certain aspects of vocal training. Your voice is not merely pitch or quality or tempo; it is all of these things in one complete process. However, to train your voice you must isolate certain features and work on these individually. Note how the engineer concentrates on separate forces and stresses, and then combines these in the final engine, bridge, or building. The dress designer does the same thing. She considers fabrics, patterns, and design before combining them in a costume. The football coach concentrates on separate aspects of athletic training such as exercises for general health, exercises for the arm muscles, exercises in tackling, etc. Then he combines all of these with practice in scrimmage against scrub teams. Similarly, you

CHART OF VOCAL CHARACTERISTICS

| Term | What is it? | Upon what does it depend? | Varieties | What can speaker do about characteristics of voice? |
|---|---|---|---|---|
| Pitch | Highness or lowness of tone; pitch is our reaction to frequency, *i.e.*, the number of double vibrations per second produced by the vocal cords. | The production of pitch depends upon the length, thickness, and tension of the vocal cords. The perception of pitch depends upon sensitivity of hearing. | High<br>Medium<br>Low | Concentrate on ear training; practice reading aloud selections which demand changes in pitch; strive to use varied inflections in your daily speech; select a vowel sound and run up and down the scale with it. |
| Volume | Loudness or softness of tone; it is our reaction to amplitude and the degree of reinforcement given sound. | Depends on breath control and resonance. Perception of volume depends upon sensitivity of hearing, size of room, position from speaker, presence of acoustic qualities in room, etc. | Loud<br>Medium<br>Soft | Learn to project your tones; be conscious that the seat of power for voice is at the diaphragm, not at the throat; strive for good posture; and become aware of the acoustic properties of the rooms in which you speak. |
| Quality (Timbre Clang) | The distinguishing feature differentiating one musical instrument from another; it is the result of a combination of pitch and resonance. | Depends upon size and shape of resonating cavities, the health or resiliency of the mechanism, and the use to which it is put. It is determined by the kind or form of vibratory motion, *i.e.*, fundamental tone and partials. Control depends on clear attack, relaxation, firm steady support, and proper combination of resonators. | Head<br>Orotund<br>Pectoral<br>Faulty qualities are:<br>Breathy<br>Husky<br>Harsh<br>Strident<br>Nasal<br>Denasal<br>Thin<br>Flat | Be certain that your voice is being freely and easily produced; listen discriminately to determine if your voice has one of the irritating qualities; determine if there is an emotional condition in your life that is fashioning a strained quality; discover the points of fatigue when you must speak at length; hum on the nasal sounds to establish proper resonance; and, finally, sustain a single note on an open vowel. |

| | Definition | Description | Types | Practice |
|---|---|---|---|---|
| Stress | Is force applied to a word or syllable; force is the amount of energy or intensity used. | Use depends upon rules of usage in regard to a syllable, and upon sentence meaning in regard to a word. | Strong<br>Secondary | Observe the rules of good usage; learn the accepted stress forms in pronunciation; examine all your expressions for their true meaning; realize that the accent in a word is similar to the stress of the word in the sentence; and, finally, train your hearing to discriminate degrees of stress. |
| Inflection | Use of pitch change on a single syllable. | Depends upon change in pitch caused by tension of vocal cords. | Rising<br>Falling<br>Circumflex | Strive to convey different implications by a change of inflection; practice the falling, rising, and especially the circumflex patterns on single syllables, then on words, and finally in phrases; repeat a sentence with a monotone pattern, then add variety by changing the inflections. |
| Emphasis | Any means used to draw attention to the thought expressed. | Change in pitch, rate, force, quality, facial expression, gesture, etc. | According to agent used | Search for the meaning and seek means to present it as forcefully as possible; practice using different agents to reinforce your point; note how you can focus the audience's attention by different means. |
| Enunciation | Clearness of speech pattern. | Correct articulation of sounds in pattern. | Clear<br>Slovenly | Learn to make all sounds precisely and clearly; study the phonetic basis of each sound you have difficulty with and learn a set of practice materials to use at your leisure; review continually. |
| Pronunciation | Conformance of articulation—production of sounds—to rules of good usage. | Depends upon use of articulators, acuity of hearing, training, and background. | Standard<br>Local<br>Slovenly<br>Pedantic | Listen to educated speakers; check your pronunciation with theirs, and refer to a good pronouncing dictionary. |

must separate the elements of the vocal process and concentrate on each element so that the complete process may become more effective.

The Chart of Vocal Characteristics explains each element of voice in brief form. When you know these characteristics, you are then ready to practice them individually. Always remember that each element is but a part of the total process of voice production.

All the above vocal characteristics have contributed to the development of your voice. If you have any definite vocal difficulty, such as nasality, stridency, or hoarseness, you need a program of remedial training to overcome it. Your instructor will refer you to helpful individual exercises. Since all students do not have difficulties, the following exercises offer ways to *improve* vocal quality when no definite vocal shortcomings exist. Following is a summary of practical suggestions for your use.

1. *Be dynamic toward the undertaking.* Determination and confidence in your own ability to achieve the desired result will help you overcome any difficulty.

2. *Be systematic in your plan for voice improvement.* Have a record made of your voice. Listen to it critically. Ask your professor to analyze it for you. Decide just what is right about your voice and just what is unsatisfactory. Start working toward a definite goal.

3. *Work for one thing at a time.* Suppose you have a weak, monotonous voice. Work for variety first; then, when your voice has become flexible enough to express a variety of emotions, you can begin to work for volume and power.

4. *Make your study of voice fit your needs.* The young man who is preparing to become a brief lawyer does not have to have the skill in public address that the trial lawyer must possess. If you are going to have to appear in public you should find some club in school or in the community in which you can begin to speak before groups. Experience of this kind will teach you a great deal more than reading aloud in your room at home.

5. *Arrange definite times for your practice periods.* A little time given daily to the task of improving your voice is more fruitful than sporadic efforts at odd times.

6. *Check your progress.* Make a record each month. Use the same selection you read for your first recording. The improvement you have made, no matter how slight, will encourage you.

7. *Do each exercise carefully to improve quickly.* Find an exercise which interests you and work on it until you have achieved the result

you wish. Remember individual initiative is vitally necessary, for no instructor can give you a good voice. You must do the work yourself. The most valuable accomplishment you can gain from a speech course is the ability to judge your own efforts. If you can tell when you have accomplished your purpose and what factors contributed to your success, then you have the key to improvement and can work ahead without guidance.

8. *Remember that your voice is a delicate instrument.* Train, never strain! Be sure you are practicing correctly. If you are not, then you are merely setting the errors you have been making. Relax the vocal mechanism before you begin. Listen for signs of tension. Stop if you feel even the slightest strain.

## Posture and Voice

Posture is important in voice production. You can practice standing and sitting properly at every moment of the day, whether you are at business, traveling, or at home. The seat of control for posture is in the abdominal muscles.

Lie down comfortably on a bed. After a while you will notice the muscles which are just below the waistline expanding and relaxing. Place your hands palms down over these muscles. Stand erect, pull in on these abdominal muscles, and note the automatic raising of the chest. Stand tall. The old actors used to recommend a unique device for assuming correct standing position: Imagine your head is suspended against the clouds. Your chin should be on a line parallel with the floor. Weight should be on the balls of the feet.

Raise arms shoulder height, palms down; describe an arc with the arms; relax. Raise arms shoulder height; bring hands in to chest, palms down; pull back at the elbows; relax. Stretch muscles by tensing and relaxing. Do this every night and morning.

Exercises to be done at the desk during the day: Sit correctly, chest up, back straight not humped, feet on the floor not draped around the desk or the chair. Put hands behind back; clasp hands together, palms out. Twist hands until the palms are turned front and the shoulders have been pulled back thereby raising the chest. Put arms around the back of the chair, forcing yourself up to a straight good sitting position.

## Pitch

The first vocal characteristic to be considered is that of pitch. The relation between pitch and emotion is vividly summarized in the current joke: "Excited? Who's excited?" screamed in high-pitched tones by the person who claims he is not excited. A high pitch generally indicates excitement. A low pitch indicates seriousness of purpose or solemnity of thought. Consider for a moment the effect of the low tones of the organ as contrasted with the effect of high notes played by wind instruments in jazz bands. As a speaker you need to be able to control the pitch of your voice. For example, in anger the voice tends to rise in pitch; yet, circumstances may make it imperative that you conceal this anger. At such moments it is useful to be able to control the pitch consciously. Such control will enable you to keep your voice low in pitch, and with a soft answer turn away wrath.

A most effective way of acquiring control over pitch is to begin to listen critically to the pitch of your own voice and to that of other voices. If you listen to a new song often enough, you will soon find yourself singing it. The judges who listen to voices of applicants for radio positions find that the process of listening critically has resulted in improvement of their own voices. You can improve your voice by discriminate listening. This is an exercise you can be doing at many otherwise idle moments during the day.

Study the voices of radio speakers. Is the pitch of the minister on Sunday-morning programs lower or higher than the pitch used by the announcer of the sports events? Does your favorite news commentator vary his pitch in announcements? Are they similar? Why do Bob Burns, Gracie Allen, and Charlie McCarthy use the pitch patterns that are characteristic of them?

Learn to listen critically to the pitch of people's voices at times when you do not have to listen to what they are saying. After several days of this, you should notice an improvement in your ability to discriminate between pitches of different voices.

The second step in acquiring pitch control is to concentrate on improving your pitch directly. Once your ear has been trained to distinguish variations in pitch you have the key to intelligent self-direction. The following exercises are indicative of lines along which to work. Make up exercises of your own built upon the same principles as these.

1. As your mood changes, the pitch of your voice should change. Say the word "wait" to portray the following commands:

a. As you would to a messenger in a matter-of-fact way.
b. As you would to a child about to step off the curb at a dangerous crossing.
c. As you would to a student, meaning wait till I get you outside.
d. As you would repeat the word if someone told you to wait and you knew that this was impossible.
e. As the soldier bidding his sweetheart good-by as he goes off to war.

2. Imitate the pitch pattern of a wide variety of types. The following are indicative of the variety of patterns used:

a. The lady lecturer who flutters from one pitch level to another indiscriminately.
b. The auctioneer in his final "Fifty. Do I hear seventy-five? Seventy-five. Do I hear a hundred? A hundred. Going at a hundred, a hundred, going, sold for a hundred to. . . ."
c. The pitch used by the tobacco auctioneer in his chant at the tobacco auction.
d. The pitch used for the phrase "Hi-yo, Silver," which sets the tone of excitement for the program.
e. The low, unvaried pitch of the minister.
f. The forced overvaried pitch of the radio advertiser who says such inane phrases as "Ladies, do you find your pies flat and tasteless?" in a pitch pattern suited for heavy emotional material.

3. To acquire variety in pitch, read aloud selections which have contrasting emotional connotations. For example:

a. The pitch for the Psalm should be low for reverence and for the solemnity of the thought.

"The earth is the Lord's and the fulness thereof;
the world, and they that dwell therein."

Or

"The Lord is my shepherd; I shall not want."

b. The pitch for Antony's speech changes as he gains control over the mob. Practice his phrase "Brutus is an honorable man" as he says it, first sincerely and then gradually more insinuatingly.
c. The pitch for the speeches of the witches in *Macbeth* should be high to give the eery, unnatural feeling to the lines.

First Witch: When shall we three meet again
In thunder, lightning, or in rain?

SECOND WITCH: When the hurlyburly's done
When the battle's lost and won.
THIRD WITCH: That will be ere the set of sun.
ALL: Fair is foul, and foul is fair:
Hover through the fog and filthy air.

4. Sometimes you can get very good results from taking one very emotional line and rendering it as the speaker would have done. The pitch must vary for the contrast in mood. The following are examples:

a. Pippa, the gay young girl, says joyously,

"The year's at the spring"

b. Hamlet, outraged, says,

"It is the cause, it is the cause, my soul:"

c. Lady Macbeth goads her husband by her sarcastic

"Fie, my lord! Fie! a soldier and afeard?"

d. Ko-Ko, in deep disgust, says,

"The flowers that bloom in the spring, tra la,
Have nothing to do with the case."

5. Keep a small notebook in which you record the effect of your attempts to use pitch effectively in situations, e.g., saying "good morning" in a pitch which will provoke laughter, or in one that will make the hearer ask you if something is the matter, or in one that will make the listener think you're angry, etc. Record your attempt and the effect it produced.

## Inflection

Alarm clocks are usually annoying things. Did you ever stop to think why? Someone said because they go off when you are asleep. But even in the daytime the clang-clang-clang is stopped quickly. The real reason they annoy is that there is no pitch or tempo variation to the sound. The bell rings on the same note at equal intervals, and this jars your nervous system.

Not long ago a manufacturer of clocks decided he would change all this. He invented a clock that played a little tune instead of ringing. Many people bought his clocks. But do you know what happened? After the first few days, they slept right through the alarm. The alarm clock wasn't annoying, and the people weren't irritated.

If the clock rang in the day, they just listened to the melody. In fact, when company came, people played their clocks to amuse the guests. Everyone likes a melody; nobody likes irritation.

Voices are like alarm clocks, they either irritate, and make you feel you want to turn them off, or they please you. How about your voice? Does it irritate because you're a "Johnny-One-Note"? Do you have a melody in your speech, or is it a clang-clang-clang that annoys people? Remember, people don't rush home to listen to the alarm clock. The alarm is a necessary evil and is turned off as soon as it annoys us enough to get up. Then the radio is turned on because it has melody, variations in pitch. You can have a pleasant radio voice instead of an alarm-clock monotone.

The difference between a man's voice and a woman's voice is mostly one of pitch. Men usually have low-pitched voices, while women have higher pitched voices. The reason for this lies in the vocal cords. A man's vocal cords are thicker, longer, and wider than a woman's vocal cords. When the heavier cords vibrate, they produce a lower tone, just as a thick rubber band produces a deeper tone than a thin one. The difference in tone is called "pitch." Pitch, then, describes the highness or lowness of a tone.

A change of pitch on a single syllable is called "inflection." There are three kinds of inflection: rising, falling, and circumflex. The voice may begin low and go high ‹. This is called "rising inflection." The voice may begin in a high pitch and then go to a low pitch. This is called "falling inflection" ›. The voice may combine these, and may go low-high-low ∩; or, high-low-high ∪.

What happens when you say, "Yes" ‹? Your listener waits to hear more for he knows you haven't finished. The rising inflection indicates an incomplete thought. Say "Yes" ›. Your listener knows you've completed your thought. There is no indecision in your voice this time, but a definite complete "yes" ›.

Say "Yes" ∪ or ∩. These indicate complex thought, doubt, or surprise. When you wish to express an incomplete thought, you must use the rising inflection. When the thought is complete, you use falling inflections. The falling inflection indicates this for your listener. If you wish to tease someone (or to express any other complex thought or emotion), you should use the circumflex inflection. Can you change the pitch of your voice for these inflections? Try them. Say "Ah" ‹, "Ah" ›, "Oh" ∩, "Oh" ∪.

Practice:

| Sentence | Meaning |
|---|---|
| 1. I went home 6. | Oh, you must be wrong. |
| 2. I went home 9. | Don't contradict me, I did go home. |
| 3. I went home ʊ. | You dared me to, and I did! You couldn't, but I did. |

*Exercises for inflection*

Select a partner. You take the statement and let him take the answer. Be sure to make your voice follow the pattern indicated by the symbols: up 6, down 9, down-up-down Ω, up-down-up ʊ.

| Statement | | Answer | |
|---|---|---|---|
| 1. They want me. (puzzled, doubtful) | 6 | 1. Yes! (definite) | 9 |
| 2. You went with him. (teasing) | Ω | 2. I did not. (definite, indignant denial) | 9 |
| 3. I went to the door. (excited, thought incomplete) | 6 | 3. Yes. (Do go on, I'm interested.) | 6 |
| 4. No. (You can't go.) | 9 | 4. Oh, please, Dad. (still pleading) | 6 |
| 5. I'm going to the movies. (Don't you dare say I can't go.) | 9 | 5. Oh, you are! (We'll see about that.) | 6 |
| 6. I've won. (excited over victory) | 6 | 6. Congratulations! (equally thrilled at friend's success) | Ω |
| 7. It's raining! (on the morning of the picnic) | Ω | 7. Ah. (also disgusted and disappointed) | 9 |
| 8. Tomorrow's Saturday! (the day of the big game) | 6 | 8. Who cares. (I can't go anyway.) | 9 |
| 9. Excuse me. (annoyed, saying the word unduly) | 9 | 9. Certainly. (sarcastic) | ʊ |
| 10. Good morning. (happy, genuine) | 6 | 10. Morning. (What's good about it? I feel rotten.) | 9 |

The following is an excellent example of the use of rising and falling inflection. Hamlet is questioning the guards about the appearance of his father's ghost. All his inflections are rising while their inflections are falling. Hamlet's final statement falls to close the scene.

HAMLET: Indeed, indeed, sirs. But this troubles me.
    Hold you the watch to-night?
MARCELLUS: } We do, my lord.
BERNARDO:
HAMLET: Arm'd, say you?
MARCELLUS: } Arm'd, my lord.
BERNARDO:
HAMLET: From top to toe?
MARCELLUS: } My lord, from head to foot.
BERNARDO:
HAMLET: Then saw you not his face?
HORATIO: O, yes, my lord; he wore his beaver up.
HAMLET: What, look'd he frowningly?
HORATIO: A countenance more in sorrow than in anger.
HAMLET: Pale, or red?
HORATIO: Nay, very pale.
HAMLET: And fix'd his eyes upon you?
HORATIO: Most constantly.
HAMLET: I would I had been there.
                        *—Hamlet,* Act I, Scene 2

## Volume

A student who had been playing the piano for years in a city apartment was surprised to find she had ruined her technique for concert work. She was afraid to use the amount of force necessary for certain parts of the compositions because she had practiced in subdued tones out of deference to the people in other apartments. A skillful speaker knows how to adjust his volume to the size of the room, the number of people present, the distance from him to the audience, the acoustic qualities of the room, etc. Public speakers trained in the old school find it difficult to adjust to the microphone for radio speech. A good way to acquire control over volume in speaking is to place yourself deliberately in situations which call for use of different volumes. For example, speak to a group in one section of an office so that your voice does not disturb others who are working in another part of that office, or address a group of people in a small auditorium with good acoustics. Then talk to a group on a street corner against the roar of an elevated train.

The danger to be avoided in these exercises is excessive strain. If you use the mechanism incorrectly, you will find yourself hoarse after speaking. This difficulty can be avoided if you keep the tone free. Be mindful that power for the voice comes from deep breathing and firm support for the tone, rather than from straining at the delicate mechanism in the larynx. Experienced voice teachers say, "Activity at the diaphragm; passivity at the throat." Deep, well-controlled breathing should furnish the source of power. Yawn before you begin speaking. This will relax the whole vocal tract. Let the tone come forth loud but free. If you feel a sense of strain, stop immediately. The reason you are hoarse after you have been shouting at a football game is not because you shouted, but because you shouted when you were excited. The tension at the larynx strained the vocal mechanism at its weakest part. The physical-education instructor shouts instructions to large groups daily for hours at a time without producing this unfortunate effect. He has learned to produce a loud voice without straining at the larynx.

Modern loud-speaking equipment is eliminating the need for such masterful skill, but if you do much public speaking you will sooner or later be obliged to speak in a room with poor acoustics. The ability to increase or decrease volume as the situation demands is an indispensable asset. The person who shouts everything he says is annoying. The person who whispers everything in a weak Caspar Milquetoast type of voice is equally annoying. Control over volume is an asset for the speaker in public or private speaking. The following exercises suggest ways in which you can acquire this control:

1. Speak in different-sized rooms with widely differing acoustics.
2. Take a common word like "stop" and say it as you would if:
    a. You were calling a child about to jump from a high limb of a tree a good distance away from you.
    b. You were speaking to your small brother at the breakfast table.
    c. You were commanding a mob gathered out of doors.
    d. You were speaking over the radio.
3. Imitate the characteristic volume of such types as:
    a. Caspar Milquetoast.
    b. Joe Humphreys.
    c. Physical-education instructor to a large class.
    d. The elocutionist who rants even when speaking in a drawing room.

*e.* The intimate radio speaker or the commercial announcer.

*f.* A street peddler vending his wares.

## Stress

The next vocal characteristic to be considered, stress, is related to the question of volume and force. Stress is force applied to a word or syllable to give it greater prominence. The accented syllable in the word gets the stress. In the sentence, the words which carry the meaning get the stress. The beginner in public speaking usually makes the mistake of trying to stress everything. He sounds ludicrous, because all his ideas are not equally important. A good principle in any art process is to select one main idea and give it emphasis by subordinating all other ideas to it.

The use of stress varies with the speech situation. There are some situations which call for the use of a great many stressed words. Generally, the speaker who faces a hostile audience and attempts to change their attitude by sheer force uses more stress forms than the speaker who addresses a friendly audience. However, the use of a great many stressed forms excites your audience. You have undoubtedly had the experience of finding yourself in essential agreement with a speaker who persisted in stressing all his words as though he had to convince you. This is a waste of energy and may even be annoying. *Do not use stress unless you need it.* The following exercises give suggestions for your practice in the use of stress:

1. Experiment with the different effects obtained by changing the important word. In every case, note the change in meaning.

   Í am going to college.
   I ám going to college.
   I am góing to college.
   I am going tó college.
   I am going to cóllege.

2. Note the effect of change in the accustomed stress pattern of words:

   car-pén-ter for cár-pen-ter
   di-ffí-cul-ty for díff-i-cul-ty
   syl-lá-ble for sýl-la-ble

3. Take an ordinary phrase and stress it as you might in a variety of situations, *e.g.*, "Fellows, listen."
   *a.* To a group of friends gathered at your home.
   *b.* To a group of laborers about to go out on strike.
   *c.* To a group who are hostile to your plans.
4. Imitate the stress pattern of radio speakers who have impressed you.
5. Imitate the stress pattern of such types as:
   *a.* The person who stresses everything.
   *b.* The person who stresses nothing.
   *c.* The person who uses good variety in stress pattern.
6. An advertisement reads, "So much for so little." Say this meaning a bargain, and meaning no bargain.

## PROJECTS

### Assignment

Select one exercise for each of the following and be prepared to read it effectively in class: pitch, inflection, volume, and stress.

More than one session will be devoted to this project. As a second assignment you can have an interesting time trying to see how many of the following types of voices you can imitate. Listen critically to the radio and to the voices of people in motion pictures and newsreels. You will be surprised how many characters depend on individuality of voice for their effects.

Which of these 20 qualities can you demonstrate and explain?

| | |
|---|---|
| 1. mellow or rich | 11. throaty |
| 2. metallic | 12. nasal |
| 3. dull or dead | 13. resonant |
| 4. sharp | 14. vibrant |
| 5. shrill | 15. smooth |
| 6. blatant | 16. melodious |
| 7. whining | 17. mild |
| 8. piercing | 18. thin |
| 9. hollow | 19. rasping |
| 10. flat | 20. guttural |

Make this class session valuable by trying to explain what distortion of the proper use of the vocal mechanism creates these vocal oddities. Another fascinating item in the discussion is the relationship between types of voices and types of people who have such voices. For example, how does the radio doctor, the shrew, the child bride, the homely philosopher, the warm and tender grandfather, the villain, or the gangster use vocal effects to achieve believability? Come prepared to do three things, namely, to imitate the vocal distortion, to describe the character most likely to have such vocal quality, and to tell how it occurs.

*Developing Semantic Skill*

Add to your word cards the following:

I. Words used in the speech text:

| Word | Pronunciation | Meaning |
|------|---------------|---------|
| 1. pitch | | |
| 2. quality | | |
| 3. stress | | |
| 4. volume | | |

II. Words commonly mispronounced:
1. data
2. decorous
3. dishabille

III. Words from your own experience.

## References

AVERY, E., J. DORSEY, and V. A. SICKELS, *First Principles of Speech Training,* Chap. III, pp. 48–72.

BARBER, SARA M., *Speech Education,* Chaps. V–X, pp. 15–62.

DAVIS, ESTELLE H., and EDWARD W. MAMMEN, *The Spoken Word in Life and Art,* Chap. V, "Voice Training," pp. 60–97.

KARR, HARRISON M., *Your Speaking Voice,* Chaps. II–IV, pp. 11–144.

MURRAY, ELWOOD, *The Speech Personality,* Chap. X, "Vocal Quality," pp. 139–155.

SARETT, LEW, and W. T. FOSTER, *Basic Principles of Speech,* Chap. VII, "The Voice," pp. 192–227.

VAN DUSEN, C. R., *Training the Voice for Speech.*

WINANS, JAMES ALBERT, *Public Speaking,* Chap. XVII, "Voice Training," pp. 497–512.

*Chapter 8*

# YOUR VOICE AND ITS EMOTIONAL EFFECT

Her voice was like the voice the stars
Had when they sang together.
D. G. ROSSETTI

It is important for you as a speaker to realize that the effect you
have upon your listeners affects your own attitude. The speaker
whose voice is pleasant and vibrant enjoys the enthusiastic response
of his hearers. This audience reaction inspires him to greater eloquence, and he accomplishes his purpose. The speaker with a monotonous voice wearies his hearers. They may conceal their boredom
if they are a trained audience, but the speaker does not experience
the stimulation which comes from feeling that the audience is "with"
him.

A student whose aggressive manner and positive tone of voice
piqued all who heard him, made enemies instead of friends throughout his school career. Just before graduation, he asked one of his
professors to tell him what was wrong with him. "You know," he
said, and for once he wasn't so cocksure, "I'm leaving here tomorrow, and there isn't one person either among the professors or among
the students whom I can call my friend." The professor explained
that his rough, aggressive manner had affected his human relations.
He advised the student to stop speaking in such abrupt, positive
tones, and to cultivate a quiet, confident manner.

A friendly greeting generally gets a friendly response, a harsh
manner, a harsh retort. You probably know at least one person who
has a reputation for gruffness who is really a rather friendly personality. People say of him, "Oh, his bark is worse than his bite." Sometimes other valuable characteristics make his associates overlook his
rough manner; but it is better not to develop personality traits which
make it difficult for others to work with you.

In these days of keen competition, it is important to develop

satisfactory ways of dealing with people. The busy executive interviews many applicants for a position, and you will have very few
minutes in which to impress him. Recently, a director of personnel
made a statement that the young people his firm employed did not
need speech training. "Because," said he, "if their speech isn't satisfactory, we don't hire them." He later stated that before anyone was
advanced he was called in for an interview to convince the executive
that he was able to meet the requirements for the raise in rank. The
shy, hesitant person, unable to speak for himself, never got ahead
with this firm.

## Quality

In the preceding chapter, you studied the factors that fashion a
pleasant voice. You studied and practiced the four features of pitch,
inflection, volume, and stress. Now review the Chart of Vocal Characteristics for the treatment of quality. Quality is the distinguishing
feature of your voice and is the result of a combination of pitch and
resonance. You can improve the quality of your voice by increasing
your resonance and attaining more variety in pitch. The very first
truth to remember is that the human voice is a pleasant musical instrument when used properly. You have a good voice, but you are
likely to mar it if you have acquired the habit of rasping, growling,
shouting, or abusing your vocal cords by tensing the mechanism.
The best practice for all, therefore, is to learn to relax the vocal tract.
The yawn is the best vocal drill ever devised for good quality. It
removes the tension from the entire mechanism.

For good quality there must be good resonance. The chief reso-
nators are the mouth and the nasal passages. For greater nasal resonance hum on the three nasal sounds "m," "n," and "ng." You can
do this drill up and down the scale for variety. Next, select the low
back vowel "ä," and hold "ah" as long as possible without straining.
With these two simple drills Dr. Richard R. Hutcheson has achieved
remarkable results in his District Speech Clinic in Washington, D.C.
You can do the same thing with this drill:

> Hum: Ah ma-pa ma-ah-n-ah m-ah-ng
>
> Me may-my more-moon moan-mine ming
>
> Oh m-ah n-oh ng-ah m-oh n-ah-ng

Say the following, prolonging the nasal sounds:

| | |
|---|---|
| zoom, zoom, zoom | din, din, din |
| boom, boom, boom | spring, spring, spring |
| sing, sing, sing | ding, ding, ding |
| clang, clang, clang | ring, ting-aling |

Another approach to gaining good quality is by practicing selections with varied emotional content. For example, you may easily gain variety by capturing the mood of the following:

1. (*Loneliness*)

Alone, alone, all, all alone;
Alone on a wide, wide sea.
—COLERIDGE

2. (*Action*)

Awake, awake!
Ring the alarm-bell. Murder and treason!
—SHAKESPEARE

3. (*Pensive mood*)

The day is done, and the darkness
Falls from the wings of Night,
As a feather is wafted downward
From an eagle in his flight.
—LONGFELLOW

4. (*Confidence*)

The Lord is my shepherd; I shall not want.
—Psalm 23

5. (*Courage*)

Dare to be true;
Nothing can need a lie;
The fault that needs one most
Grows two thereby.
—HERBERT

An excellent example of how quality of voice carries emotional effect is given by John Masefield in his poem "Cargoes." Note how you must change your feeling and your quality of voice as you capture the spirit of the gorgeous gracefulness of the ancient quinquireme rowing into Palestine; then the majesty and wonder of the Spanish galleon with pride riding at the mast; and, finally, the rasping quality you must take on to describe the cheapness of the dirty coaster butting the choppy channel waves. Underline the words that the poet stresses to get these three varied effects. So skillfully has he selected these sound symbols that you will find yourself instinctively changing the quality of your voice as you read.

Quinquireme of Nineveh from distant Ophir,
Rowing home to haven in sunny Palestine,
With a cargo of ivory,
And apes and peacocks,
Sandalwood, cedarwood, and sweet white wine.

Stately Spanish galleon coming from the Isthmus,
Dipping through the Tropics by the palm-green shores,
With a cargo of diamonds,
Emeralds, amethysts,
Topazes, and cinnamon, and gold moidores.

Dirty British coaster with a salt-caked smoke stack,
Butting through the Channel in the mad March days,
With a cargo of Tyne coal,
Road-rails, pig-lead,
Firewood, iron-ware, and cheap tin trays.
—JOHN MASEFIELD,[1] "Cargoes"

## Tempo

The final vocal characteristic that can bring effectiveness to your voice is tempo. Tempo is the rate at which you speak. It carries emotional overtones so forceful that it may change the entire meaning of your utterance. Say, "I am going to go home" with a rapid tempo. Now try the same sentence with a slow and deliberate tempo, leaving long pauses between each word: "I . . . am . . . going . . . to . . . go . . . home. . . ." Have you ever noticed the dignity of the processions held in church and on solemn occasions? Such processions would lose all their meaning if they were done hurriedly. Commencements use "Pomp and Circumstance" in order to achieve a sense of dignity. The same is true of your speaking: you must use a slow tempo for serious thought and a lively one for gaiety.

[1] From *Poems*, selected by Canby, Pierce, and Durham, 1927, by permission of The Macmillan Company, publishers.

Contrast the following four selections:

1. Full fathom five thy father lies;
   Of his bones are coral made . . .

2. Blow, blow, thou winter wind!
   Thou art not so unkind
      As man's ingratitude. . . .
                —SHAKESPEARE

3. Heigh ho! heigh ho! unto the green holly:
   Most friendship is feigning, most loving mere folly:
      Then, heigh ho, the holly!
      This life is most jolly.

4. Merrily, merrily shall I live now,
   Under the blossom that hangs on the bough.
                —SHAKESPEARE

To get a vivid sense of what tempo can really do, read the following limerick solemnly and then with rapid tempo:

> There was a young lady from Niger,
> Who smiled as she rode on a tiger.
>     They came back from the ride
>     With the lady inside,
> And the smile on the face of the tiger.

## PROJECTS

*Assignment*

Demonstrate the flexibility of your voice by showing at least two contrasting moods. Awaken the appropriate emotional response in your hearers by giving any two of the following selections adequate interpretation in class. The young Hamlet speaks with a different quality of voice from the old man Capulet. Othello, the Moor, speaks with different quality and tempo when he is pleading with the Senators from the voice he uses when he is enraged over the fighting of the guards, which has been instigated by Iago deliberately to anger him. Take two selections which show contrast either in type of person or in mood. Practice each selection until you have the desired effect. Memorize your assignment.

1. *Romeo and Juliet,* Act II, Scene 2

ROMEO (the young, noble lover) speaks: But, soft! What light through yonder window breaks?

It is the east, and Juliet is the sun.
Arise, fair sun, and kill the envious moon,
Who is already sick and pale with grief
That thou, her maid, art far more fair than she.

.   .   .   .   .   .   .   .   .

It is my lady, O, it is my love!
O, that she knew she were!

.   .   .   .   .   .   .   .   .

See, how she leans her cheek upon her hand!
O, that I were a glove upon that hand,
That I might touch that cheek!

2. *Othello*, Act I, Scene 3

OTHELLO (to Senators) pleads: Her father lov'd me; oft invited me;
    Still question'd me the story of my life
    From year to year, the battles, sieges, fortunes,
    That I have pass'd.
    I ran it through, even from my boyish days
    To the very moment that he bade me tell it;
    Wherein I spoke of most disastrous chances,
    Of moving accidents by flood and field,
    Of hair-breadth scapes i' th' imminent deadly breach,
    Of being taken by the insolent foe
    And sold to slavery, of my redemption thence
    And portance in my travel's history;
    Wherein of antres vast and deserts idle,
    Rough quarries, rocks, and hills whose heads touch heaven,
    It was my hint to speak,—such was the process. . . .

3. *Othello*, Act II, Scene 3

OTHELLO (enraged by the fighting): Why, how now, ho! from whence
    ariseth this?
    Are we turn'd Turks, and to ourselves do that
    Which Heaven hath forbid the Ottomites?
    For Christian shame, put by this barbarous brawl.
    He that stirs next to carve for his own rage
    Holds his soul light; he dies upon his motion.
    Silence that dreadful bell; it frights the isle
    From her propriety. What is the matter, masters?
    Honest Iago, that looks dead with grieving,
    Speak, who began this? On thy love, I charge thee.

### 4. *Romeo and Juliet,* Act IV, Scene 3

JULIET (alone at last, speaks her fears before taking the strange drug):
     Farewell! God knows when we shall meet again.
   I have a faint cold fear thrills through my veins,
   That almost freezes up the heat of life.
   I'll call them back again to comfort me.
   Nurse!—What should she do here?
   My dismal scene I needs must act alone.
   Come, vial.
   What if this mixture do not work at all?
   Shall I be married then to-morrow morning?
   No, no; this shall forbid it. Lie thou there.
   (*Laying down her dagger.*)
   What if it be a poison, which the friar
   Subtly hath minist'red to have me dead,
   Lest in this marriage he should be dishonour'd,
   Because he married me before to Romeo?
   I fear it is; and yet, methinks, it should not,
   For he hath still been tried a holy man.

### 5. *Twelfth Night,* Act I, Scene 1

ORSINO, DUKE OF ILLYRIA (melancholy over his unrequited love): If
     music be the food of love, play on!
   Give me excess of it, that, surfeiting,
   The appetite may sicken, and so die.
   That strain again! It had a dying fall.
   O, it came o'er my ear like the sweet sound
   That breathes upon a bank of violets,
   Stealing and giving odour. Enough! no more!
   'Tis not so sweet now as it was before.
   O spirit of love, how quick and fresh art thou,
   That, notwithstanding thy capacity
   Receiveth as the sea, naught enters there,
   Of what validity and pitch soe'er,
   But falls into abatement and low price
   Even in a minute! so full of shapes is fancy
   That it alone is high fantastical.

### 6. *Romeo and Juliet,* Act I, Scene 1

PRINCE ESCALUS (rage): Rebellious subjects, enemies to peace,
     Profaners of this neighbour-stained steel,—
     Will they not hear?—What, ho! you men, you beasts,

That quench the fire of your pernicious rage
With purple fountains issuing from your veins,
On pain of torture, from those bloody hands
Throw your mistemper'd weapons to the ground,
And hear the sentence of your moved prince.

### 7. *Merchant of Venice*, Act V, Scene 1

LORENZO (the lover speaks to Jessica): How sweet the moonlight sleeps
    upon this bank!
Here will we sit and let the sounds of music
Creep in our ears. Soft stillness and the night
Become the touches of sweet harmony.
Sit, Jessica. Look how the floor of heaven
Is thick inlaid with patines of bright gold.
There's not the smallest orb which thou behold'st
But in his motion like an angel sings,
Still quiring to the young-ey'd cherubins.
Such harmony is in immortal souls;
But whilst this muddy vesture of decay
Doth grossly close it in, we cannot hear it.

### 8. *Romeo and Juliet*, Act III, Scene 5

CAPULET (angrily berating Juliet's disobedience): Hang thee, young bag-
    gage! disobedient wretch!
I tell thee what: get thee to church o' Thursday,
Or never after look me in the face.
Speak not, reply not, do not answer me!
My fingers itch. Wife, we scarce thought us blest
That God had lent us but this only child;
But now I see this one is one too much,
And that we have a curse in having her.
Out on her, hilding!

### 9. *Romeo and Juliet*, Act I, Scene 5

CAPULET (joyfully greeting his guests): Welcome, gentlemen! Ladies that
    have their toes
Unplagu'd with corns will walk a bout with you.
Ah, my mistresses, which of you all
Will now deny to dance? She that makes dainty,
She, I'll swear, hath corns. Am I come near ye now?
Welcome, gentlemen! I have seen the day
That I have worn a visor and could tell

A whispering tale in a fair lady's ear,
Such as would please; 'tis gone, 'tis gone, 'tis gone.
You are welcome, gentlemen! Come, musicians, play.
A hall, a hall! give room! and foot it, girls.

### 10.  *Hamlet*, Act III, Scene 4

GHOST (appearing to Hamlet): Do not forget! This visitation
Is but to whet thy almost blunted purpose.
But, look, amazement on thy mother sits.
O, step between her and her fighting soul.
Conceit in weakest bodies strongest works.
Speak to her, Hamlet.

### 11.  *Antony and Cleopatra*, Act II, Scene 5

CLEOPATRA (impatient, betrays her eagerness in questioning messenger):
(*Enter a Messenger.*)
O, from Italy!
Ram thou thy fruitful tidings in mine ears,
That long time have been barren.
MESSENGER: Madam, madam,—
CLEOPATRA: Antonio's dead!—If thou say so, villain,
Thou kill'st thy mistress; but well and free,
If thou so yield him, there is gold, and here
My bluest veins to kiss; a hand that kings
Have lipp'd, and trembled kissing.
MESSENGER: First, madam, he is well.
CLEOPATRA: Why, there's more gold.
But, sirrah, mark, we use
To say the dear are well. Bring it to that,
The gold I give thee will I melt and pour
Down thy ill-uttering throat.
MESSENGER: Good madam, hear me.
CLEOPATRA: Well, go to, I will.
But there's no goodness in thy face; if Antony
Be free and healthful, why so tart a favour
To trumpet such good tidings? If not well,
Thou shouldst come like a Fury crown'd with snakes,
Not like a formal man.

### 12.  *The Taming of the Shrew*, Act IV, Scene 3

KATHERINA (the shrew vents her rage against Petruchio): The more my
wrong, the more his spite appears.

What, did he marry me to famish me?
Beggars, that come unto my father's door,
Upon entreaty have a present alms;
If not, elsewhere they meet with charity;
But I, who never knew how to entreat,
Nor never needed that I should entreat,
Am starv'd for meat, giddy for lack of sleep,
With oaths kept waking and with brawling fed;
And that which spites me more than all these wants,
He does it under name of perfect love,
As who should say, if I should sleep or eat,
'Twere deadly sickness or else present death.
I prithee go and get me some repast;
I care not what, so it be wholesome food.

*Developing Semantic Skill*

Add to your word cards the following:

I. Words used in the speech text:

| *Word* | *Pronunciation* | *Meaning* |
|--------|-----------------|-----------|
| 1. neurological | | |
| 2. officious | | |
| 3. paramount | | |
| 4. reciprocal | | |

II. Words commonly mispronounced:
   1. elm
   2. ennui
   3. eschew
III. Words from your own experience.

*Chapter 9*

# VARIETY: A COMBINATION OF VOCAL SKILLS

Let your speech be always with grace, seasoned with salt.
—COLOSSUS

Variety is not only the spice of life it is the spice of interest in speaking. A voice which has variety is interesting, and a voice that sounds like a "Johnny-One-Note" is annoying. Audiences usually make a simple judgment: As you sound, so you are. This may not be a fair judgment, but it is the one that people will make if your voice is flat and uninteresting. They will suspect that your life is as humdrum as your expression. So it is important that you achieve variety in your reading and speaking. You must charm and intrigue your listeners through your ability to interpret mood, feeling, and character.

Consider the actors and actresses you like to hear on the stage and radio. Notice their use of volume, of pausing, of inflection, of emphasis, and pitch changes. You will perceive that their interesting personalities are founded in their skillful use of the full gamut of their vocal abilities. They have their voices under complete control and easily play upon the emotional content of their lines. Note also the effect produced when celebrities in all walks of life appear in newsreels and television programs. They are alive and dynamic. Their voices reflect the excitement of a life filled with adventure.

You are an interesting person and you should desire to make your voice a true reflection of your personality. This is not a natural skill but one that must be acquired through effort and more effort. You can capture the quality of excitement in your voice if you will devote some time to the selections in this assignment. You have now studied the factors that create interesting voices, and you have had some practice in discovering your own qualities of voice. This is an opportunity to formulate all you have learned in a total pattern. Try to see the relationship between the characteristics of vocal control and their actual use in the best examples of literature. Do not expect perfection at first but be willing to practice patiently on one selection for a considerable length of time. It is better to master one selection than to have a haphazard notion of how to read many selections.

In preparing this assignment, spend some time analyzing the meaning of the selection. Remember, there is no expression without impression. So read the selection over several times. Ask yourself if you can express the meaning in your own words. Then check the exact phrasing the playwright has given each thought. Finally, fit all these into the total pattern, or over-all effect, that the passage is intended to communicate. You are now ready to start your first oral reading of the lines. Your first reading will be as barren as the bare structure of a new building. That is to be expected. You have yet to put the ornaments in place. You have yet to give the building character. It is in this task that your vocal skill comes into play.

In this assignment you can spend endless time on the details of vocal improvement. For this reason it is wise to plan definitely what you desire to gain in each practice session. Set yourself a goal and then bring all your techniques to bear in achieving that goal. For example, these selections require a variety of vocal inflections, a change of mood, volume and pausing, changes of pitch, and variety of rate. Analyze your selection from a vocal point of view. As a radio commentator divides his script into the various pauses he will take, the change of pace he will use, the emphasis he will deliver, and the timing of his entire broadcast, so you should evolve a working chart similar to the blueprint of a building for your vocal guidance. Take the judgment of the sentence, then write the exact vocal technique that will most skillfully communicate that meaning. Draw lines between words for pauses; underline words and phrases for emphasis; and group words that must be expressed rapidly in close order. Your first attempts may be slow but they will increase your vocal skill quickly.

The following exercises have been chosen because they have been the training materials of generations of great speakers. Moreover, they are of such literary quality that you may practice them again and again and not lose interest. Each time you will be enriched with new discoveries of meaning and you will grow to appreciate the worth while in literature.

## PROJECTS

*Assignment*

Select one of the following, or any other famous speech. Come prepared to demonstrate your vocal power in rendering the selection. Memorize the lines so that you can display your ability to arouse emotional response by your command of vocal skills.

1. *The Merchant of Venice*, Act IV, Scene 1

PORTIA: The quality of mercy is not strain'd.
It droppeth as the gentle rain from heaven
Upon the place beneath. It is twice blest:
It blesseth him that gives and him that takes.
'Tis mightiest in the mightiest; it becomes
The throned monarch better than his crown.
His sceptre shows the force of temporal power,
The attribute to awe and majesty,
Wherein doth sit the dread and fear of kings;
But mercy is above the sceptred sway;
It is enthroned in the hearts of kings;
It is an attribute to God Himself;
And earthly power doth then show likest God's
When mercy seasons justice.

2. *Cyrano de Bergerac*, "The Nose Speech" [1]

CYRANO: Ah, no, young sir!
You are too simple. Why, you might have said—
Oh, a great many things! Mon dieu, why waste
Your opportunity? For example, thus:—

AGGRESSIVE: I, sir, if that nose were mine,
I'd have it amputated—on the spot!

FRIENDLY: How do you drink with such a nose?
You ought to have a cup made specially.

DESCRIPTIVE: 'Tis a rock—a crag—a cape—
A cape? say rather, a peninsula!

INQUISITIVE: What is that receptacle—
A razor-case or a portfolio?

[1] From *Cyrano de Bergerac*, by Edmond Rostand, Brian Hooker translation, copyright, U.S.A., 1923, by Henry Holt and Company. Reprinted by permission.

KINDLY: Ah, do you love the little birds
So much that when they come and sing to you,
You give them this to perch on?

INSOLENT: Sir, when you smoke, the neighbors
Must suppose your chimney is on fire.

CAUTIOUS: Take care—a weight like that
Might make you topheavy.

THOUGHTFUL: Somebody fetch my parasol—
Those delicate colors fade so in the sun!

PEDANTIC: Does not Aristophanes
Mention a mythological monster called
Hippocamp-elephanto-camelos?
Surely we have here the original!

FAMILIAR: Well, old torchlight! Hang your hat
Over that chandelier—it hurts my eyes.

ELOQUENT: When it blows, the typhoon howls,
And the clouds darken.

DRAMATIC: When it bleeds—the Red Sea!

ENTERPRISING: What a sign for some perfumer!

LYRIC: Hark—the horn of Roland calls
To summon Charlemagne!—

SIMPLE: When do they unveil the monument?

RESPECTFUL: Sir, I recognize in you
A man of parts, a man of prominence—

RUSTIC: Hey? What? Call that a nose? Nay!
I be no fool like what you think I be—
That there's a blue cucumber!

MILITARY: Point against cavalry!

PRACTICAL: Why not a lottery
With this for the grand prize?

Or—parodying Faustus in the play—
"Was this the nose that launched a thousand ships
And burned the topless towers of Ilium?"

These, my dear sir, are things you might have said
Had you some tinge of letters, or of wit
To color your discourse. But wit,—not so,
You never had an atom—and of letters,
You need but three to write you down—an Ass.
　　　　　　　　　　—EDMOND ROSTAND

## 3. *Macbeth*, Act V, Scene 1

LADY MACBETH: Out, damned spot! out, I say!—One: two: why, then 'tis time to do't.—Hell is murky!—Fie, my lord, fie! a soldier, and afeard? What need we fear who knows it, when none can call our pow'r to account?—Yet who would have thought the old man to have had so much blood in him?

．　　．　　．　　．　　．　　．　　．　　．　　．　　．　　．　　．

The thane of Fife had a wife; where is she now?—What, will these hands ne'er be clean?—No more o' that, my lord, no more o' that; you mar all with this starting.

．　　．　　．　　．　　．　　．　　．　　．　　．　　．

Here's the smell of the blood still: all the perfumes of Arabia will not sweeten this little hand. Oh, oh, oh!

．　　．　　．　　．　　．　　．　　．　　．　　．

Wash your hands, put on your nightgown; look not so pale.—I tell you yet again, Banquo's buried; he cannot come out on's grave.

．　　．　　．　　．　　．　　．　　．　　．　　．

To bed, to bed! there's knocking at the gate. Come, come, come, come, give me your hand. What's done cannot be undone.—To bed, to bed, to bed!

## 4. *Hamlet*, Act III, Scene 1

HAMLET: To be, or not to be: that is the question.
　　　Whether 'tis nobler in the mind to suffer
　　　The slings and arrows of outrageous fortune,
　　　Or to take arms against a sea of troubles,
　　　And by opposing end them. To die; to sleep;
　　　No more; and by a sleep to say we end
　　　The heart-ache and the thousand natural shocks
　　　That flesh is heir to. 'Tis a consummation
　　　Devoutly to be wish'd. To die; to sleep;—
　　　To sleep? Perchance to dream! Ay, there's the rub;
　　　For in that sleep of death what dreams may come,
　　　When we have shuffl'd off this mortal coil,

Must give us pause. There's the respect
That makes calamity of so long life.
For who would bear the whips and scorns of time,
The oppressor's wrong, the proud man's contumely,
The pangs of dispriz'd love, the law's delay,
The insolence of office, and the spurns
That patient merit of the unworthy takes,
When he himself might his quietus make
With a bare bodkin? . . .

5. I am a very model of a modern major-general,
    I've information vegetable, animal, and mineral,
    I know the kings of England, and I quote the fights historical
    From Marathon to Waterloo, in order categorical;
    I'm very well acquainted too with matters mathematical;
    I understand equations, both simple and quadratical;
    About binomial theorem I'm teeming with a lot of news—
    With many cheerful facts about the square of the hypotenuse; . . .
    I'm very good at integral and differential calculus;
    I know the scientific names of beings animalculous;
    In short, in matters vegetable, animal, and mineral,
    I am the very model of a modern major-general.
                                                —W. S. GILBERT

6. *As You Like It*, Act III, Scene 5

PHOEBE: Think not I love him, though I ask for him;
    'Tis but a peevish boy; yet he talks well.
    But what care I for words? Yet words do well
    When he that speaks them pleases those that hear.
    It is a pretty youth; not very pretty;
    But, sure, he's proud, and yet his pride becomes him.
    He'll make a proper man. The best thing in him
    Is his complexion; and faster than his tongue
    Did make offence his eye did heal it up.
    He is not very tall; yet for his years he's tall.
    His leg is but so so; and yet 'tis well.
    There was a pretty redness in his lip,
    A little riper and more lusty red
    Than that mix'd in his cheek; 'twas just the difference
    Betwixt the constant red and mingled damask.
    There be some women, Silvius, had they mark'd him
    In parcels as I did, would have gone near
    To fall in love with him; but, for my part,

I love him not nor hate him not; and yet
I have more cause to hate him than to love him,
For what had he to do to chide at me?
He said mine eyes were black and my hair black;
And, now I am rememb'red, scorn'd at me.
I marvel why I answer'd not again.
But that's all one; omittance is not quittance.
I'll write to him a very taunting letter,
And thou shalt bear it; wilt thou, Silvius?

7. *Macbeth*, Act II, Scene 2

MACBETH: Go bid thy mistress, when my drink is ready,
She strike upon the bell. Get thee to bed. [*Exit Servant.*]
Is this a dagger which I see before me,
The handle toward my hand? Come, let me clutch thee.
I have thee not, and yet I see thee still.
Art thou not, fatal vision, sensible
To feeling as to sight? or art thou but
A dagger of the mind, a false creation,
Proceeding from the heat-oppressed brain?
I see thee yet, in form as palpable
As this which now I draw.
Thou marshall'st me the way that I was going,
And such an instrument I was to use.
Mine eyes are made the fools o' th' other senses,
Or else worth all the rest. I see thee still,
And on thy blade and dudgeon gouts of blood,
Which was not so before. There's no such thing.
It is the bloody business which informs
Thus to mine eyes.

8. *Henry the Eighth*, Act III, Scene 2

WOLSEY: Farewell! a long farewell, to all my greatness!
This is the state of man: to-day he puts forth
The tender leaves of hopes; to-morrow blossoms,
And bears his blushing honours thick upon him;
The third day comes a frost, a killing frost,
And, when he thinks, good easy man, full surely
His greatness is a-ripening, nips his root,
And then he falls, as I do. I have ventur'd,
Like little wanton boys that swim on bladders,
This many summers, in a sea of glory,

But far beyond my depth. My high-blown pride
At length broke under me, and now has left me,
Weary and old with service, to the mercy
Of a rude stream that must forever hide me.

9. *The Merchant of Venice,* Act V, Scene 1

PORTIA: That light we see is burning in my hall.
How far that little candle throws his beams!
So shines a good deed in a naughty world.
NERISSA: When the moon shone, we did not see the candle.
PORTIA: So doth the greater glory dim the less.
A substitute shines brightly as a king
Until a king be by; and then his state
Empties itself, as doth an inland brook
Into the main of waters. Music! Hark!
NERISSA: It is your music, madam, of the house.
PORTIA: Nothing is good, I see, without respect;
Methinks it sounds much sweeter than by day.
NERISSA: Silence bestows that virtue on it, madam.
PORTIA: The crow doth sing as sweetly as the lark
When neither is attended, and I think
The nightingale, if she should sing by day,
When every goose is cackling, would be thought
No better a musician than the wren.
How many things by season season'd are
To their right praise and true perfection!

10. *Richard the Second,* Act III, Scene 2, "Richard's Trust in Heaven"

RICHARD: Discomfortable cousin! know'st thou not
That when the searching eye of heaven is hid
Behind the globe, that lights the lower world,
Then thieves and robbers range abroad unseen
In murders and in outrage boldly here;
But when from under this terrestrial ball
He fires the proud tops of the eastern pines
And darts his light through every guilty hole,
Then murders, treasons and detested sins,
The cloak of night being pluck'd from off their backs,
Stand bare and naked, trembling at themselves?
So when this thief, this traitor, Bolingbroke,
Who all this while hath revell'd in the night,
Whilst we were wand'ring with the antipodes,

Shall see us rising in our throne, the east,
His treasons will sit blushing in his face,
Not able to endure the sight of day,
But, self-affrighted, tremble at his sin.
Not all the water in the rough rude sea
Can wash the balm off from an anointed king;
The breath of worldly men cannot depose
The deputy elected by the Lord.
For every man that Bolingbroke hath press'd
To lift shrewd steel against our golden crown,
God for his Richard hath in heavenly pay
A glorious angel; then, if angels fight,
Weak men must fall, for Heaven still guards the right.

11. *Hamlet*, Act III, Scene 2

HAMLET: Speak the speech, I pray you, as I pronounc'd it to you, trippingly on the tongue; but if you mouth it, as many of your players do, I had as lief the town-crier spoke my lines. Nor do not saw the air too much with your hand, thus, but use all gently; for in the very torrent, tempest, and, as I may say, whirlwind of passion, you must acquire and beget a temperance that may give it smoothness. O, it offends me to the soul to see a robustious periwig-pated fellow tear a passion to tatters, to very rags, to split the ears of the groundlings, who for the most part are capable of nothing but inexplicable dumb-shows and noise. I could have such a fellow whipp'd for o'erdoing Termagant. It out-herods Herod. Pray you, avoid it. . . .

Be not too tame neither, but let your own discretion be your tutor. Suit the action to the word, the word to the action; with this special observance, that you o'erstep not the modesty of nature. For anything so overdone is from the purpose of playing, whose end, both at the first and now, was and is, to hold, as 'twere, the mirror up to nature; to show virtue her own feature, scorn her own image, and the very age and body of the time his form and pressure. Now this overdone, or come tardy off, though it make the unskillful laugh, cannot but make the judicious grieve; the censure of the which one must, in your allowance, o'erweigh a whole theater of others. O, there be players that I have seen play, and heard others praise, and that highly, not to speak it profanely, that, neither having the accent of Christians nor the gait of Christian, pagan, nor man, have so strutted and bellowed that I have thought some of Nature's journeymen had made men and not made them well, they imitated humanity so abominably.

12. *Henry the Fifth,* Act II, Scene 2, "Henry V's Sentence on the Conspirators"

HENRY: Hear your sentence.
  You have conspir'd against our royal person,
  Join'd with an enemy proclaim'd, and from his coffers
  Receiv'd the golden earnest of our death;
  Wherein you would have sold your king to slaughter,
  His princes and his peers to servitude,
  His subjects to oppression and contempt,
  And his whole kingdom into desolation.
  Touching our person seek we no revenge;
  But we our kingdom's safety must so tender,
  Whose ruin you have sought, that to her laws
  We do deliver you. Get you therefore hence,
  Poor miserable wretches, to your death,
  The taste whereof God of his mercy give
  You patience to endure, and true repentance
  Of all your dear offences! Bear them hence.

*Developing Semantic Skill*

Add to your word cards the following:

I. Words used in the speech text:

| Word | Pronunciation | Meaning |
|------|---------------|---------|
| 1. theater | | |
| 2. lighting | | |
| 3. aesthetic | | |
| 4. tempo | | |

II. Words commonly mispronounced:
  1. fiancé
  2. film
  3. forehead

III. Words from your own experience.

## Chapter 10

# VOCAL HECKLING SESSION

There was speech in their dumbness, language in their very gesture.

—SHAKESPEARE

It is a rare speaker who will not sometime encounter an antagonistic audience. When great issues are at stake, feelings run high. At such times, the speaker will need a ready wit to hold his audience, and a good share of vocal force to control malcontents. The speaker whose voice lacks power will shortly be ridiculed off the platform. Any vocal weakness in the speaker is quickly mimicked by a heckler, and he is easily made to appear ludicrous. Hence, it is important for you to have the experience of being heckled. It may reveal some weakness you will want to correct.

Heckling is of two varieties: verbal and vocal. The verbal heckler depends upon his ready use of wit to throw the speaker from his purpose. For instance, recently in Ireland an advocate was urging young men to join the army. After all other appeals had gotten little response, he appealed to the Irishmen's love of adventure and ended with "Join the Army and see the world." A wit in the crowd ruined his climax by adroitly observing, "You mean see the *next* world."

The speaker usually has the advantage over the heckler if he is prepared for the situation. For example, in a political campaign a speaker was centering his attack on a local political boss. One of the boss's henchmen was in the crowd, and at the psychological moment inquired why this speaker was so vehement against one man. He wanted to know why he didn't attack the other politicians. Rising to the occasion, the speaker responded with great dignity, "When I'm killing a mad dog, don't bother me with the fleas on his back."

The one-cause heckler is a variety that must be handled carefully. He will continuously ask the speaker if the cause of all these things is not so-and-so. Usually so-and-so refers to the present administration, some official, or some current movement. The heckler's purpose is to waste the speaker's time in answering foolish objections. If the speaker slights him for too long, the audience is likely to sympathize with the heckler and believe the speaker is concealing something. Therein lies the speaker's cue: tolerate the annoyance until the audience is with you; then, if possible, answer the charge briefly and clearly.

The worry-type heckler is the most crafty and treacherous. He seeks to give the speaker a problem other than the present speech. He demands that the speaker tell about the "1937 Affair." By repeating his entreaty with growing earnestness he starts to worry the speaker. A timid speaker will try to ignore the charge, not knowing what to expect. Should the speaker say he doesn't know what the heckler's talking about, the retort charges him with a convenient memory. Sometimes such a technique is carried through a whole campaign.

The vocal heckler attempts to match his volume with the speaker's. This is a lower type of heckling than the verbal, but it is quite frequently encountered. If the speaker tries to outshout the heckler, a riot ensues. At times, a dignified pause is effective, but every situation varies with the type of audience and occasion. The inebriated heckler is usually merely vocal and is sometimes stopped by a kind retort.

Sincerity is the only perfect response to heckling.

### PROJECTS

*Assignment*

Select some national or campus issue. Be certain that it is of vital interest to the group. Present your point of view despite all opposition. Attempt to mingle the vocal skill you have been acquiring with your native wit and spontaneity of response.

*Sample Heckling-Project Outline*

Name _____ Class_____ Date _____

*Speech:*
1. What is the purpose of your speech?
2. Why must you move this audience to fulfill this purpose?

3. What is the best approach to this audience? (Will you intimidate hearers, anger them, compliment them?)

*Voice* (getting effects with your voice):
1. What can you do to gain attention by voice?
2. What can you do to arouse interest by voice?
3. In what way will you present your plan?
4. How will you create emotional reaction to plan?
5. Will you build to climax, leave audience at crucial point?

During this speech you must watch the effect of your voice on your audience. Plan your attack before you approach hearers, but it is well to be able to adjust your attack to their reactions. Do not weary your hearers by using one type of voice pattern. There are many ways to accomplish a purpose. Charm your hearers with the variety of your attack. Play with the audience, sway it, build powerfully to a climax. Don't leave until you have gained your end. You must know an audience before you can rule it. Plan your speech to fit the group. If you find your attack is producing the wrong effect, be ready to adjust to the situation.

## Developing Semantic Skill

Add to your word cards the following:

I. Words used in the speech text:

| Word | Pronunciation | Meaning |
|------|---------------|---------|
| 1. adroitly | | |
| 2. climax | | |
| 3. intimidate | | |
| 4. pattern | | |

II. Words commonly mispronounced:
1. gesture
2. gondola
3. gratis

III. Words from your own experience.

# PART. IV. PHONETIC SKILL

The acquisition of phonetic skill completes the four essential skills needed for an effective speech personality. The next four chapters and projects treat articulation and pronunciation of the basic speech sounds. The material is arranged in the form of a drill manual, as you are more interested in acquiring a skill than in theoretical knowledge. After you have had an analysis made of your present phonetic pattern, work out a program geared to the specific sounds you wish to improve. Copious material is provided to ensure sufficient drills for each sound. As you gain phonetic skill, you will acquire confidence and poise in the assurance that your speech is acceptable in all social groups.

## PHONETIC AND DIACRITICAL SYMBOLS

| Key Word | Phonetic Symbol | Diacritical Mark |
|---|---|---|
| 1. bee | [i] | ē |
| 2. bit | [ɪ] | ĭ |
| 3. bet | [ɛ] | ĕ |
| 4. bear | [ɛə] | â |
| 5. bat | [æ] | ă |
| 6. bask | [a] | à |
| 7. bird | [ɝ] | û |
| 8. butter | [ə] | ē |
| 9. bunch | [ʌ] | ŭ |
| 10. boot | [u] | o͞o |
| 11. book | [ʊ] | o͝o |
| 12. boat | [ou] | ō |
| 13. brought | [ɔ] | ô |
| 14. Bob | [ɒ] | ŏ |
| 15. bark | [ɑ] | ä |
| 16. bay | [eɪ] | ā |
| 17. buy | [aɪ] | ī |
| 18. boy | [ɔɪ] | oi |
| 19. bout | [aʊ] | ou |
| 20. bier | [ɪə] | ē̦ (r) |
| 21. bear | [ɛə] | â (r) |
| 22. boor | [ʊə] | o͝o (r) |
| 23. boar | [ouə] | ō (r) |
| 24. peep | [p] | p |
| 25. bib | [b] | b |
| 26. maim | [m] | m |
| 27. toot | [t] | t |

| Key Word | Phonetic Symbol | Diacritical Mark |
|---|---|---|
| 28. deed | [d] | d |
| 29. noon | [n] | n |
| 30. cook | [k] | k |
| 31. gig | [g] | g |
| 32. sing | [ŋ] | ng |
| 33. ether | [θ] | th |
| 34. either | [ð] | th |
| 35. fife | [f] | f |
| 36. valve | [v] | v |
| 37. cease | [s] | s |
| 38. zones | [z] | z |
| 39. mission | [ʃ] | sh |
| 40. vision | [ʒ] | zh |
| 41. church | [tʃ] | ch |
| 42. judge | [dʒ] | j |
| 43. rear | [r] | r |
| 44. lull | [l] | l |
| 45. hail | [h] | h |
| 46. wail | [w] | w |
| 47. whale | [hw] | wh |
| 48. you | [j] | y |

Throughout the phonetic drill section the word lists will give continual practice on virtually all sound combinations. You will notice that each consonant is given with all the vowels and diphthongs in simple word combinations. In the same manner each vowel and diphthong is combined with all the consonants in simple word combinations. This assures you of the widest variety of drill material.

*Wide World Ph*

One of the historical moments in our lifetime occurred when Franklin Delano Roosevelt took the oath of office for his fourth term as President of the United States. In his inaugural address he issued his final challenge for total victory. Roosevelt's understanding of people, his intimate attitude in the famous "Fireside Chats," and his skillful use of analogy made him one of the great speakers of modern times. Worn by the responsibility of a global war, he still carried the banner of his country. Note his vigor in the picture on the left as he stresses the need for total victory; center, his poise as he reads his script; and right, the traditional sense of timing as he awaits an audience reaction. He might well be described as "he from whose lips divine persuasion flows." No small part of his persuasive power was his perfected phonetic skill. As a visiting linguist observed, "His every public utterance raised the speech standard of the nation."

*Chapter 11*

# HOW TO MAKE THE CONSONANTS

Speak the language of the company that you are in; speak it purely
and unlarded with any other.

LORD CHESTERFIELD *Letters*

Articulation is the process by which the voice is molded into speech
sounds. It refers particularly to the way in which the consonants
are made. Every speaker can profit from a study of his articulation.
Careless articulation results in delay, irritation, and annoyance.
Moreover, poor articulation indicates a lack of training and background and proves a definite handicap. On the other hand, clear
articulation lends effectiveness to speech and facilitates daily contacts with others.

You can get the most benefit from speech training if you understand the factors which have influenced your speech pattern. Speech
sounds are acquired by the process of imitation. You have copied
the models you have heard most frequently; therefore, some of your
sounds may be acceptable and others unacceptable. Simple words
like "going" and "better" may be giving you difficulty because you
have not acquired the proper way of saying these words. "Goin"
and "bedder" are not acceptable. You can eliminate such errors in
articulation, and this chapter will show you how to do so.

Realize that you imitate the sounds you hear about you. Train
yourself to discriminate between the sounds which you should use
and the ones you have been using. Next, read over the description of
the ways in which the speech sounds are made. Concentrate particularly on the characteristic features of the sounds you have been
slighting. Then, read over the word lists to give yourself oral drill
on the sounds. Read aloud the sentences which give practice on the
sounds. Practice simple expressions which you use in ordinary conversation. Go over these several times every morning and evening
until you have established the pattern you wish. Read aloud as often

as possible, noting particularly the sounds which you wish to improve.

Remember that most of the speakers whom you admire have practiced long and faithfully to acquire the articulatory habits which make their speech clear and forceful. In Shaw's play *Pygmalion*, the struggle of the lowly flower girl to acquire the type of speech used by a "lady" emphasizes the amazing changes which can be made by motivated practice. The patient efforts of people like Helen Keller, who achieved speech despite the handicap of loss of hearing, should prove an inspiration. It is not an affectation to speak well. Indeed, it is indispensable for successful participation in business, professional, and social life.

### The Way to Study

Choose a partner and arrange to work two half-hour periods, with a rest between. Then proceed as follows:

1. Read carefully the instructions for making each sound under the heading "How to Make the ――― Sounds." Be sure that you understand the directions.

2. Study each picture of the speaker and check the position of your own speech mechanism (lips, tongue, etc.) with a small hand mirror.

3. Make each sound by itself. Have your partner listen to you and repeat the sound. You and your partner should make criticisms and suggestions whenever necessary. Continue until each of you is satisfied that the other is saying the sound accurately.

4. Take turns reading the words given in lists for each sound. As one reads the list of words slowly, the other should make suggestions and corrections whenever the sounds are not correct. Remember, accuracy depends largely upon clear and precise production of sounds.

5. Each one, in turn, should read the "sound-loaded" sentences aloud. Attentive listening will train and improve your hearing. Remember that receiving the sound correctly is just as important as making it correctly. And—if you hear a sound correctly, you will learn more quickly to make it correctly.

6. At this point take a recess of ten minutes.

7. Review the instructions at the start of each section. Being sure that you understand will help you remember them. Produce the sound again by itself and review the word lists and sentences.

8. Each of you should memorize a sound-loaded sentence for your most

troublesome sounds. Repeat these sentences to yourself at odd moments during the day.

9. Rehearse in actual situations. *Remember* that constant practice in daily conversation will perfect your speech forms.

### THE PLOSIVE SOUNDS

The simplest speech sounds are the plosive sounds. They are called "plosives" because they furnish the short pauses in the flood of sound that makes your speech. Say them: "b-p," "d-t," "g-k." Notice that they are short sounds made with a slight explosive effect. These "stop" sounds give life and clarity to speech patterns. They are the staccato notes that make your speech stand out clearly. Practice these sounds until they resemble the sharp, clear tapping of the Morse code.

### *HOW TO MAKE THE PLOSIVES "b" [b] AND "p" [p]*

— "b" as in bee, bit, bet, bear —

Put your lips together, then gently blow them apart as you vibrate the vocal cords. Check on yourself by placing your index finger and thumb on your Adam's apple and feeling the vibrations of the cords. Say "Bumble bees bite black bears." Now just say the first sound of each word: "B—b—b—." Look into a hand mirror as you feel the vocal

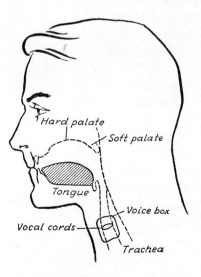

**THE SPEAKER SAYS "b" AND "p"**

Notice how he sounds "b" as in "bet" and then how he makes "p" as in "pet." He puts his lips together and blows them apart. The vocal cords vibrate for "b" but not for "p."

cords vibrating and you will sense the two requirements for making this sound: The lips will be separating and the vocal cords will be vibrating.

### — "p" as in pea, pit, pet, pear —

Put your lips together, then gently blow them apart. The only difference between "b" and "p" is that for "p" the vocal cords do not vibrate. Hence it is called a "voiceless" or a "breathed sound." Say "Paul's presence pleased Polly." Now say the first sound of each word: "P–p–p–p." Note that the vocal cords do not vibrate.

Read the following words aloud:

| | | | | | |
|---|---|---|---|---|---|
| bee | pea | bunch | punch | buy | pie |
| bit | pit | boot | pool | boys | poise |
| bet | pet | book | put | broke | poke |
| bear | pear | boat | pole | bout | pout |
| bat | pat | brought | pawn | bier | peer |
| bask | past | Bob | pop | bear | pear |
| bird | pert | bark | park | boor | poor |
| butter | putter | bay | pay | boar | pore |

### Drills for "b," Phonetic Symbol [b]

Read aloud:

1. Better to bear with a boor than to be bothered with a black bigot.
2. The babbling brook bubbled by the boulders near the bank.
3. The bold bachelor's breezy byplay bored Barbara.
4. Betty Botta bought a bit of bitter butter.
5. Whereat, with blade, with bloody blameful blade,
   He bravely broached his boiling bloody breast. . . .
                  **—SHAKESPEARE**
6. The barge she sat in, like a burnish'd throne,
   Burn'd on the water: the poop was beaten gold—
                  **—SHAKESPEARE**

### Drills for "p," Phonetic Symbol [p]

Read aloud:

1. Please pass the patties on the pink platter, Polly.
2. Past experiences often prove practical precepts.
3. The peacock preened its plumage with pride.
4. It's poor policy to rob Peter to pay Paul.
5. Piping down the valleys wild,
   Piping songs of pleasant glee,

On a cloud I saw a child,
  And he laughing said to me:

"Pipe a song about a lamb!"
  So I piped with merry cheer.
"Piper, pipe that song again."
  So I piped: he wept to hear.
    —BLAKE, "The Piper"

## HOW TO MAKE THE PLOSIVES "d" [d] AND "t" [t]

### — "d" as in dee, dill, dell, dare —

Raise the tip of the tongue to the gum ridge behind the upper front teeth and make a voiced sound as you quickly lower it. The secret of getting a clear-cut "d" sound is to use just the tip of the tongue. Do not use the whole front of the tongue or put the tongue on the teeth as this will blur the sound. Train your hearing by listening as you practice. Once you can hear yourself say the sound correctly, the rest is easy.

### — "t" as in tea, till, tell, tear —

Raise the tip of the tongue to the gum ridge behind the upper front teeth and make a voiceless sound as you quickly lower the tongue. The "t" sound is not voiced and in this way differs from "d." Mistakes come from using the "d" sound for the "t" sound. Be careful. Make the sound end cleanly; do not follow it with a stream of breath. Remember, it is a short plosive sound.

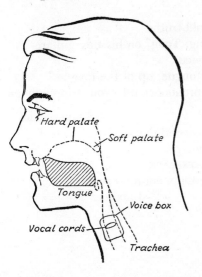

Hard palate

Soft palate

Tongue

Voice box

Vocal cords

Trachea

### THE SPEAKER SAYS "d" AND "t"

Notice how he presses the tip of the tongue lightly against the upper gum ridge just behind the upper front teeth as he makes a voiced sound for "d" and a voiceless sound for "t."

Read the following words aloud:

| | | | | | |
|---|---|---|---|---|---|
| dee | tea | done | ton | dime | time |
| dill | till | Duluth | tool | doily | toil |
| dell | tell | dole | toll | down | town |
| dare | tear | dawn | torn | deer | tier |
| Dan | tan | dock | tog | dare | tear |
| dance | trance | dark | tart | durable | tour |
| dirt | turf | day | tail | door | tore |

### Drills for "d," Phonetic Symbol [d]

Read aloud:

1. The delicate dame dropped the dainty damask dinner napkins.
2. The Reverend Dan Deedle was ordained the Reverend Dan Deedle, D.D.
3. The desperado destroyed the damaging document.
4. Doing duties daily deserves dividends.
5. When the devil was sick, the devil a Monk would be;
   When the devil was well, the devil a Monk was he.
   —RABELAIS
6. Let us, to the end, dare to do our duty as we understand it.
   —LINCOLN
7. These are the dead, the debt is due;
   Dust claims dust, and we die too.
   —SHELLEY

### Drills for "t," Phonetic Symbol [t]

Read aloud:

1. Take time to test; testing tells untold truths.
2. Tippy Tippy Tim went "Ting, Tang, Tong" on his tiny guitar.
3. *Twice-Told Tales* tells tales told twice.
4. Tillie told him to say, "Tip of the tongue, tip of the tongue."
5. Speak the speech, I pray you, as I pronounce it to you: trippingly on the tongue.
   —SHAKESPEARE
6. Night's candles are burnt out, and jocund day
   Stands tiptoe on the misty mountaintops.
   —SHAKESPEARE
7. Temperance is a tree which has contentment for a root.
   —BUDDHA

## HOW TO MAKE THE PLOSIVES "g" [g] AND "k" [k]

### — "g" as in green, grit, get, garish —

Raise the back of the tongue toward the soft palate and then quickly lower it as you make a voiced sound. The sound is made by the tongue stopping the breath by pressing against the roof of the mouth and then releasing the breath while vibrating the vocal cords. Make the release quickly to get a crisp, clear-cut sound.

### — "k" as in keen, kin, ken, Karo —

Raise the back of the tongue toward the roof of the mouth and then quickly lower it, making a voiceless sound. Make "k" very lightly, easily, and quickly, like the other voiceless plosives. Note that "k" is made exactly as "g" but is voiceless. For this reason these sounds are called cognates, *i.e.*, originating in the same place.

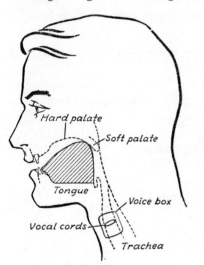

### THE SPEAKER SAYS "g" AND "k"

As he says the "g" in gate, and the "k" in Kate, he raises the back of the tongue to the soft palate and then quickly lowers it. The vocal cords vibrate for "g" but not for "k."

Read the following words aloud:

| | | | | | |
|---|---|---|---|---|---|
| green | keen | gut | cut | guide | cried |
| grin | kin | goose | cool | goiter | coy |
| get | ken | good | could | gold | cold |
| garish | Karo | goat | coat | gout | cow |
| gap | cap | gawky | caught | gear | clear |
| grass | cast | got | cot | glare | care |
| girt | curd | guard | card | guerdon | cure |
| goer | curler | gay | Kay | gore | core |

*Drills for "g," Phonetic Symbol* [g]

Read aloud:

1. The gifted girls gained greater glory.
2. Great-Great-Grandmother Grace's gown gave Gertrude a glorious golden garb for the costume ball.
3. Tags, our dog, plagued the poor ragged, hungry beggar.
4. Go get the bag for the rags.
5. Good is no good, but if it be spend,
   God giveth good for none other end.
   —SPENSER
6. Gifts are as gold that adorns the temple;
   Grace is like the temple that sanctifies the gold.
   —LONGFELLOW

*Drills for "k," Phonetic Symbol* [k]

Read aloud:

1. The kitten cavorted comically on the crazy quilt.
2. The creaking caravan crashed through the cactus thicket.
3. The children's chorus sang Christmas carols for cakes, crackers, and candy.
4. The archduke rebuked the castle keeper for careless work.
5. He packed his bike with kodaks, clocks, chemicals, chromium, a wicker stick, and other bric-a-brac.
6. . . . . for you are call'd Kate,
   And bonny Kate, and sometimes Kate the curst;
   But Kate, the prettiest Kate in Christendom;
   Kate of Kate-Hall, my super-dainty Kate,
   For dainties are all Kates: and therefore, Kate,
   Take this of me, Kate of my consolation.
   —SHAKESPEARE

## THE NASAL SOUNDS

The nasal sounds are three: "m," "n," and "ng." These give resonance and carrying power to your speech and make it possible to be heard despite surrounding noises. Hence, they enable you to make yourself heard at a distance. A voice without resonance is easy to drown out. Lack of resonance on these three sounds produces a husky voice. You can achieve resonance by sustaining your nasal tones over long periods. Hum your favorite tune on one of the nasal sounds. You can actually feel the resonance by lightly holding the bridge of your nose. Try it.

### HOW TO MAKE THE NASALS "m" [m], "n" [n], AND "ng" [ŋ]

— "m" as in mead, mid, met, Mary —

Press your lips together and send a voiced sound out through your nose. This is the sound you make when you are hungry and see a sizzling steak: "Mmmmm." Be careful, do not let this sound slide back into your throat and get an empty, moaning sound. Bring it forward by holding the bridge of your nose to feel the resonance as the sound passes through. Remember, the more resonance, the more carrying power.

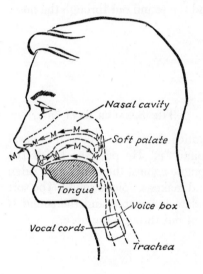

THE SPEAKER SAYS "m"

Notice how he makes the nasal sound "m." He puts his lips together and makes a long, voiced sound. The soft palate is lowered and the sound is sent out through the nose.

Read the following words aloud:

| mead | mat | much | Mall | my | mere |
| mid | mask | moon | mob | moist | mare |
| met | mirth | Moor | mark | mole | Moore |
| Mary | manor | moat | May | mound | more |

### Drills for "m," Phonetic Symbol [m]

Read aloud:

1. Mean men make miserable companions.
2. Mary crammed madly for myriad exams by the calm Cam.
3. Martin Mulligan's murmur might mean many mysterious things.

4. Five miles meandering with a mazy motion
   Through wood and dale the sacred river ran,
   Then reached the caverns measureless to man
   And sank in tumult to a lifeless ocean.
   —COLERIDGE

5. Myriads of rivulets hurrying thru' the lawn,
   The moan of doves in immemorial elms,
   And murmuring of innumerable bees.
   —TENNYSON

— "n" as in need, nil, net, near —

Recall how you made the sounds "d" and "t"? You raised the tip of your tongue to the gum ridge. Do that again. Now instead of releasing it quickly, hold the tongue there and send the sound out through the nose. This will give you the sound "nnnnnn."

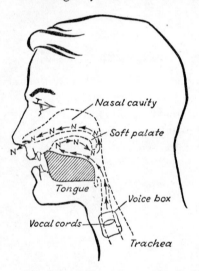

### THE SPEAKER SAYS "n"

Notice how he makes the nasal sound "n." He puts the tip of the tongue against the upper gum ridge and makes a voiced sound. The soft palate is lowered and the sound is sent out through the nose.

Read the following words aloud:

| | | | | | |
|---|---|---|---|---|---|
| need | gnat | none | naught | nigh | near |
| nil | nasty | noon | knob | noise | ne'er |
| net | nurse | nook | Narcissus | nose | newer |
| nares | neurotic | note | neigh | noun | Noah |

### Drills for "n," Phonetic Symbol [n]

Read aloud:

1. Nat had a nasty, neurotic nurse who knew naught of medicine.
2. The knave knelt on his knees knowing the Lord was nigh.

3. Nan Newman was fined nine hundred and ninety-nine dollars.
4. None, none descends into himself to find
   The secret imperfections of his mind:
   But everyone is eagle ey'd to see
   Another's faults, and his deformity.
                                        —DRYDEN
5. It was many and many a year ago
     In a kingdom by the sea,
   That a maiden lived, whom you may know
     By the name of Annabel Lee.
                                        —POE

— "ng" as in learning, ring, netting, faring —

In the same manner as you made "g" and "k," raise your tongue toward the rear roof of the mouth and hold the tongue there as you make a voiced sound through the nasal passages. Be certain to make this a single sound, *not* two sounds. It is a single sound though spelled with two letters.

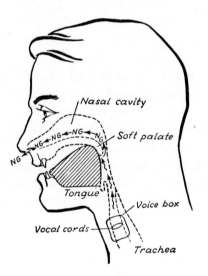

**THE SPEAKER SAYS "ng"**

Notice how he makes "ng." He raises the back of the tongue toward the soft palate while making a voiced sound. The soft palate is lowered so that the sound is sent out through the nose.

Read the following words aloud:

| being | sang | lung | dawning | dining | peering |
| ring | basking | blooming | bobbing | toying | glaring |
| netting | nursing | booking | guarding | doting | touring |
| airing | rotting | noting | staying | pouting | pouring |

*Drills for "ng," Phonetic Symbol* [ŋ]

Read aloud:

1. Anything worth having is worth working and waiting for.
2. Joking, laughing, and singing, we were driving along the winding road.
3. Religion binds you to things—believing things, doing things.
4. Like young Shakespearian kings, He won the adoring throng,
     And, as Apollo sings, He triumphed with a song;
     Triumphed, and sang, and passed along.

—LIONEL JOHNSON

5. A drop of ink may make a million think.

—BYRON

6. Kentish Sir Byng stood for the King,
     Bidding the crop-headed Parliament swing;
     And, pressing a troop unable to stoop
     And see the rogues flourish and honest folk **droop,**
     Marched them along, fifty-score strong,
     Great-hearted gentlemen, singing this song.

—BROWNING

## THE SIBILANT SOUNDS

The sibilant, or hissing, speech sounds are "z" as in zeal, "s" as in seal, "zh" as in rouge, "sh" as in ship, "j" as in judge, and "ch" as in church. *These sounds cause the most mistakes in messages transmitted by electrical devices.* Quite often the spelling form of these sounds is misleading. The sound "z" tends to become "s" when in final position. In careless speech, his becomes hiss; eyes may become ice, or lies, lice. Good articulation requires exact speech sounds. Moreover, since these sounds are the most frequently used in our language special care should be taken to make them accurately. The sibilants are not pleasant sounds but are less irritating when properly produced.

### *HOW TO MAKE THE SIBILANTS "z"* [z] *AND "s"* [s]

— "z" as in zeal, zip, zest —

Say "z" as in zeal. Notice that the tip of the tongue is raised high in the mouth; the sides of the tongue are raised slightly so that the breath is sent out in a steady flow through the opening between the front teeth, making a voiced "z."

— "s" as in seal, sip, set —

Say "s" as in seal. Notice that this sound is made exactly the same way as the "z" sound except that it is not voiced.

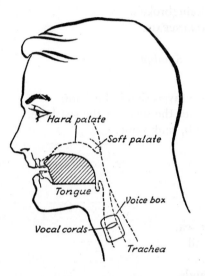

THE SPEAKER SAYS "z" AND "s"

Notice how he makes these sounds by raising the tongue high in the mouth, grooving the sides of it and sending the breath out in a steady stream over the center of the tongue. For "z" as in zeal, the vocal cords vibrate; for "s" as in seal the vocal cords do not vibrate.

Read the following words aloud:

| zebra | zoo | xylophone | sap | soak | so |
|-------|-----|-----------|-----|------|-----|
| zip | Zukor | Zoroaster | staff | stalk | spout |
| zest | zone | zero | skirt | spot | sear |
| Zachary | zorofic | sea | sir | star | stair |
| Xavier | zorro | sip | sulk | say | sewer |
| Xerxes | czar | set | sue | sigh | sower |
| Zuider Zee | zany | spare | stood | soil | |

*Drills for "z," Phonetic Symbol* [z].

Read aloud:

1. Basil Razzle-dazzle was razzed to a frazzle by Erasmus Fraser.

2. Mr. Zimms gave me zero for my examination in zoology.

3. Did you ever find a cozy lizard in a blizzard? Prize lizards sizzle in a drizzle, but lazy lizards are wizards with scissors.

4. Those are pearls that were his eyes. . . .

—SHAKESPEARE

5. Of comfort no man speak:
　Let's talk of graves, of worms and epitaphs;
　Make dust our paper and with rainy eyes
　Write sorrow on the bosom of the earth;
　Let's choose executors and talk of wills:
　And yet not so, for what can we bequeath
　Save our deposed bodies to the ground?
　Our lands, our lives, and all are Bolingbroke's.

—SHAKESPEARE

### Drills for "s," Phonetic Symbol [s]

Read aloud:

1. Selwyn stole a stack of silver that we saved simply for Sam.
2. Sarah could have spoken to Sally after the scene at the seashore.
3. Ensign Mason signaled, "Sighted sub, sank same."
4. Swiftly, swiftly flew the ship,
　　Yet she sailed softly too:
　Swiftly, swiftly blew the breeze—
　　On me alone it blew.

—COLERIDGE

5. This precious stone set in the silver sea,
　Which serves it in the office of a wall
　Or as a moat defensive to a house,
　Against the envy of less happier lands,
　This blessed plot, this earth, this realm, this England.

—SHAKESPEARE

6. When to the sessions of sweet silent thought
　I summon up remembrance of things past,
　I sigh the lack of many a thing I sought,
　And with old woes new wail my dear times' waste.

—SHAKESPEARE

7. Persuasive speech, and more persuasive sighs,
　Silence that spoke, and eloquence of eyes.

—HOMER

### HOW TO MAKE THE SIBILANTS "zh" [ʒ] AND "sh" [ʃ]

— "zh" as in rouge, azure, measure, leisure —

— "sh" as in sheer, share, sure, shore —

Say "zh" as in pleasure. Notice that the tip of the tongue is raised high in the mouth toward the hard palate and just a bit farther back than for "z." A broad stream of voiced breath is sent out against the teeth. The sound "sh" as in ship is made in exactly the same way except that it is voiceless so the vocal cords do not vibrate in its production. There are two other sibilant sounds which are combinations of the sounds already studied. They are "j," which is a combination of "d" and "zh" as in judge, and "ch" which is a combination of "t" and "sh" as in church.

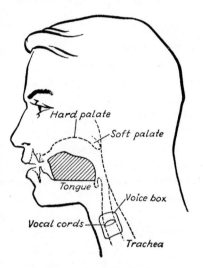

### THE SPEAKER SAYS "zh" AND "sh"

Notice how he raises his tongue high in his mouth, but not quite so far forward as for "z," and spreads the breath out across the upper teeth, while slightly rounding the lips. The "zh" is voiced and the "sh" is voiceless.

Read the following words aloud:

| | | | | | |
|---|---|---|---|---|---|
| sheen | cheek | shun | chum | shy | chide |
| shrill | chill | shoot | choose | | choice |
| shell | chest | should | | show | choke |
| share | chair | shoulder | chosen | shout | chow |
| shall | chat | short | chaw | sheer | cheer |
| shaft | chaff | shot | chop | share | chair |
| shirk | church | sharp | charm | sure | |
| shudder | chapel | shade | chain | shore | chore |

*Drills for "zh," Phonetic Symbol* [ʒ]

Read aloud:

1. It was a pleasure to tread a measure.
2. The explosion created an illusion of grandeur.
3. Usually leisure and pleasure come only on occasion.
4. The usual sometimes seems bizarre.
5. To the old, long life and treasure;
   To the young, all health and pleasure.
   —BEN JONSON

6. Rich the treasure,
   Sweet the pleasure,—
   Sweet is pleasure after pain.
   —DRYDEN

### Drills for "sh," Phonetic Symbol [ʃ]

Read aloud:

1. Shivering Charlotte shook her shining shillings.
2. Shortie shifted shortly, shunning the sharp-shooter.
3. She sells short shirts and shells in the shop near the shore.
4. The shady shoal by the shallow shore shielded his shabby shirt.
5. A shining shaft of light shone on his face.
6. My shame will not be shifted with my sheet:
   No; it will hang upon my richest robes
   And show itself, attire me how I can.
   —SHAKESPEARE
7. Conscience is a blushing, shamefaced spirit.
   —SHAKESPEARE

### Drills for "j," Phonetic Symbol [dʒ]

Read aloud:

1. Jonathan Jones jumped in his jeep.
2. Jack and Jill joined the general jamboree.
3. Come to college to gather knowledge.
4. Judge not, ye collegians, lest ye be judged.
5. A joyous heart makes a joyous face.
   —PROVERB.

### Drills for "ch," Phonetic Symbol [tʃ]

Read aloud:

1. The speech teacher coached the preacher to reproach cheaters.
2. Chunky Chester Charles chopped cheap chipmunks for witch sandwiches.
3. "Teach, preach, or screech, but you'll not reach me," chimed the wretch as he fetched the teacher's sketch.
4. The cheap chap threw chips in the church basket.
5. To sit in solemn silence in a dull, dark dock,
   In a pestilential prison, with a lifelong lock,
   Awaiting the sensation of a short, sharp shock,
   From a cheap and chippy chopper on a big black block.
   —W. S. GILBERT

6. Chippy, chippy chirio,
   Chippy, chippy chirio,
   Not a man in Dario
   Can catch a chippy, chippy chirio.
                          —BURROUGHS

## THE CONTINUANT SOUNDS

The sounds of "w" as in wear, "wh" as in where, "v" as in van, "f" as in fan, "th" as in these, "th" as in thin are called "continuants." These sounds are called continuants because the sound is not stopped as in the plosives, but passes out without interruption. You can test this by trying to prolong the plosive sounds. Plosives cannot be prolonged. But the above sounds depend for their existence on the fact that they are acceptably made only when continued. Hence, phoneticians have called this group of sounds "continuants."

## HOW TO MAKE THE CONTINUANTS "w" [w] AND "wh" [hw]

— "w" as in we, wit, wet, wear —

— "wh" as in whee, whim, whet, where —

Say "w" as in we. Notice that the lips are rounded for this sound. The back of the tongue is raised high in the mouth as for "oo." The vocal cords vibrate for "w." Now say "wh" as in the word where. This sound is made in exactly the same way as "w" except that the vocal cords do not vibrate. It is voiceless.

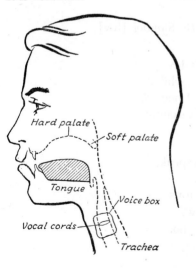

Hard palate
Soft palate
Tongue
Voice box
Vocal cords
Trachea

### THE SPEAKER SAYS "w" AND "wh"

Notice how he says "w" as in wait, and "wh" as in white. He brings his lips together, rounds them slightly, and sends the breath out through the small opening between them. The back of his tongue is raised toward the soft palate; "w" is voiced, "wh" is voiceless.

Read the following words aloud:

| we    | whee  | were | whisper    | way       | whey      |
|-------|-------|------|------------|-----------|-----------|
| wit   | whim  | won  | whereunder | wife      | whine     |
| wet   | whet  | woo  | whereunto  |           |           |
| wear  | where | wood | whew       |           |           |
| way   | whale | woe  | whoa       | water boy | Wiltshire |
| waft  |       | warp | wharf      | willow    | wore      |
| worse | whirl | watt | what       | wound     | wineglass |

### Drills for "w," Phonetic Symbol [w]

Read aloud:

1. We won the war, and we will win the peace.
2. We were slowly wending our way toward the water.
3. "Worse and worse," wailed the woeful woman.
4. Water, water, everywhere,
       And all the boards did shrink;
   Water, water, everywhere,
       Nor any drop to drink.
                              —COLERIDGE
5. Into this Universe, and *Why* not knowing
   Nor *Whence*, like Water willy-nilly flowing;
       And out of it, as Wind along the Waste,
   I know not *Whither*, willy-nilly blowing.
                              —FITZGERALD
6. She is a woman, therefore may be woo'd;
   She is a woman, therefore may be won.
                              —SHAKESPEARE

### Drills for "wh," Phonetic Symbol [hw]

Read aloud:

1. Which witch he witched which witch?
2. Which whale swallowed Jonah for awhile?
3. White whistled on the wharf while I hooted.
4. Such whirling and whistling was deafening.
5. If wisdom's way you wisely seek,
       Five things observe with care:
   To whom you speak, of whom you speak,
       And how, and when, and where.
                              —ANONYMOUS
6. Whether it rains, or whether it snow,
   We shall have weather, whether or no.
                              —OLD SPANISH PROVERB

## HOW TO MAKE THE CONTINUANTS "v" [v] AND "f" [f]

— "v" as in veal, villa, vest, vet —

— "f" as in feel, fill, fell, fare —

Say "v" as in volunteer. Notice that the lower lip is pressed against the upper front teeth so that the voiced breath is sent out in a narrow stream between the lips and teeth. Say "f" as in feel. It is made exactly the same way as "v" except that the vocal cords do not vibrate—"f" is the voiceless cognate of "v."

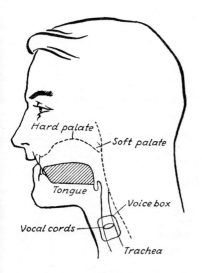

### THE SPEAKER SAYS "f" AND "v"

Notice that his lower lip is placed against the edge of the upper front teeth as he makes a voiceless sound for "f" and a voiced sound for "v." The sound is made by friction as the air passes between the teeth and lower lip.

Read the following words aloud:

| | | | | | |
|---|---|---|---|---|---|
| feel | veal | ferment | virility | fight | vie |
| filler | villa | fun | vulcan | foil | voice |
| fell | velvet | fool | voodoo | folk | vocal |
| fare | varied | foot | vulnerable | frown | vowel |
| fan | van | foe | vote | fear | veer |
| fast | vast | fault | vault | fair | vary |
| first | virgin | flop | volume | furor | velour |
| farce | varsity | fail | veil | floor | vortex |

### Drills for "v," Phonetic Symbol [v]

Read aloud:

1. Velour is vastly more valuable than velvet.
2. The vicious are often victims of their own viciousness.

3. Variety is the very spice of life.
4. Violence begets violence, virtue begets virtue.
5. To overcome evil with good is good, to resist evil with evil is evil.

—MOHAMMED

### Drills for "f," Phonetic Symbol [f]

Read aloud:

1. Fight fear by facing the thing you fear fearlessly.
2. Fly with the finest, fittest, fightingest air force.
3. Forty-five farmers acted as fire fighters at the film-factory fire.
4. A flea found a fly in a flue
   And neither knew what to do.
     "Let us fly," said the flea;
     "Let us flee," said the fly.
   So they flew through a flaw in the flue.

   —ANONYMOUS

5. The fair breeze blew, the white foam flew,
   The furrow followed free.

   —COLERIDGE

## HOW TO MAKE THE CONTINUANTS "th" [ð] AND "th" [θ]

— "th" as in these, this, then, that —

— "th" as in thin, thing, thick, thistle —

Say "th" as in these. Notice that the tongue touches the edge of the upper front teeth lightly as the voiced stream of breath is sent forth; "th"

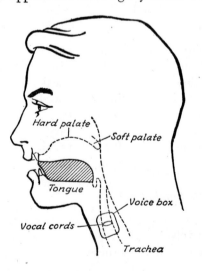

Hard palate

Soft palate

Tongue

Voice box

Vocal cords

Trachea

**THE SPEAKER SAYS "th" AND "th"**

Notice how he presses the tip of his tongue against the upper front teeth as he makes a voiced sound for "th" and a voiceless sound for "th."

as in thin is made in exactly the same way except that it is voiceless. The vocal cords do not vibrate for its production. Most difficulties arise from substituting a "d" for th and a "t" sound for "th." Remember, these are long sounds. Do not make them as plosives.

Read the following words aloud:

| | | | |
|---|---|---|---|
| these * | thereinafter * | throw | thyroid |
| this * | thirst | thaw | throne |
| them * | thatcher | thereafter * | thou * |
| there * | thumb | they * | theater |
| that * | threw | thought | their * |

(In words marked * the "th" is voiced.)

### Drills for "th," Phonetic Symbol [ð]

Read aloud:

1. The weather tossed them hither and thither.
2. Though the weather withered their clothes, they went further and further.
3. This is that, but it isn't so much that as it's this.
4. Seething southern heat makes breathing difficult.
5. Thou'st not thyself
   For thou exist'st on many thousand grains
   That issue out of dust. Happy thou art not;
   For what thou hast not, still thou striv'st to get,
   And what thou hast, forget'st.
   —SHAKESPEARE

### Drills for "th," Phonetic Symbol [θ]

Read aloud:

1. Think thoughtfully, think thoroughly, think through.
2. Ethyl gas makes all earthly things thrillingly thin.
3. A thousand brave deaths thwarted the enemy's thrusts.
4. I'll example you with thievery:
   The sun's a thief, and with his great attraction
   Robs the vast sea; the moon's an arrant thief,
   And her pale fire she snatches from the sun;
   The sea's a thief, whose liquid surge resolves
   The moon into salt tears; the earth's a thief
   That feeds and breeds by a composture stolen
   From general excrement, each thing's a thief.
   —SHAKESPEARE

5. And thought leapt out to wed with thought,
Ere thought could wed itself to speech.

—TENNYSON

## THE SEMI-VOWEL SOUNDS

### *HOW TO MAKE THE SEMI-VOWELS* "l" [l], "r" [r], *AND* "y" [j]

#### — "l" as in led, lid, lead, lair —

Make the "l" sound by raising the tip of the tongue to the gum ridge and letting a voiced sound escape over the sides of your tongue. The tip of the tongue is in the same position as for "d" and "t." Instead of dropping the tip of the tongue, hold it and emit the sound over the sides. Say "d—l," "t—l." Now say "idle, little." Check the three elements of this very important sound: (1) tip of the tongue position; (2) vibration of the vocal cords; (3) sound sent over sides of the tongue. Because the sound goes over the side of the tongue, "l" is called the "lateral sound." It is the only one so made.

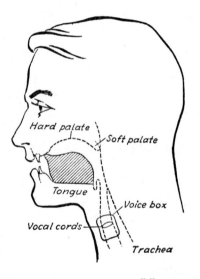

Hard palate

Soft palate

Tongue

Voice box

Vocal cords

Trachea

### THE SPEAKER SAYS "l"

Notice how he raises the tongue tip to the ridge behind the upper front teeth and lets his breath escape over the sides of his tongue. This is a lateral sound.

#### — "r" as in reed, rid, red, rare —

Say "Robert Rawley rolled the round rock round." The beginning sound is the sound "r." Make it by curling the tip of the tongue back toward the hard palate (roof of the mouth) while you make a voiced sound. Be careful that the tip of the tongue is turned back but doesn't quite touch the roof of the mouth. To get the position, try to trill the "r" as a Scotchman might do in reading R-R-Robert R-R-R-Rawley r-r-r-r-rolled, etc. Repeat it, lengthening and smoothing the "r" sound. Do you feel your tongue tip easily turning back? Practice it until you hear it and feel it at the same time.

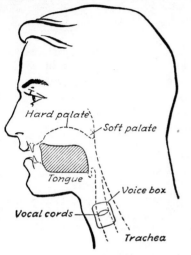

### THE SPEAKER SAYS "r"

Notice how he curls the tip of his tongue back as he makes a voiced sound for "r" as in red.

— "y" as in yeast, yet, yeah, yak —

Say "Yell, young yellers, yell!" The sound "y" begins each word. You made the sound by raising the front, not the tip, of the tongue until it nearly pressed against the roof of the mouth while you made a voiced sound. This sound is easily made at the beginning of a word. But it is

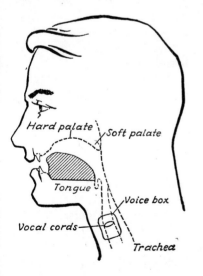

### THE SPEAKER SAYS "y"

Notice how he raises the front of his tongue until it nearly touches the hard palate as he says "y" as in yet.

often omitted by careless speakers when it does not appear in the spelling, as for example, in duty, beauty, and tube. It is important that beauty should not be pronounced as booty and vice versa, nor that feud becomes food, nor use ooze. Be mindful of this sound when it does not appear in the spelling form of the word.

Read the following words aloud:

| | | | | | |
|---|---|---|---|---|---|
| lead | reed | yeast | law | wrought | yawl |
| lid | rid | Yiddish | lot | rob | yacht |
| let | red | yet | lark | raja | yarn |
| lair | rare | yeah | lay | ray | yea |
| latch | rat | yak | lie | rye | Yuletide |
| last | rascal | | loyal | royal | |
| learn | rehearse | yearn | low | rope | yeoman |
| letter | require | yodler | lout | rout | yowl |
| lunch | run | young | lear | rear | year |
| loot | root | use | lair | rare | |
| look | rook | | lure | rural | hewer |
| loaf | road | yoke | lower | roar | yore |

### Drills for "l," Phonetic Symbol [l]

Read aloud:

1. Silly Sally still sells silver shells.
2. Lilting lines liven light lyrics.
3. Little Lillian laughed lightly.
4. Lie lightly on her, gentle earth,
   Her step was light on thee.
   —EPITAPH
5. Why so pale and wan, fond lover?
   Prithee, why so pale?
   Will, when looking well can't move her,
   Looking ill prevail?
   Prithee, why so pale?
   —SIR JOHN SUCKLING

### Drills for "r," Phonetic Symbol [r]

Read aloud:

1. Round the rough and rugged rock, the ragged rascal ran.
2. Rows of ripe berries grow near the forest.
3. Travel by train provides rich experiences for roving riders.
4. Robert Rowley rolled a round roll round,
   A round roll Robert Rowley rolled round;
   Where rolled the round roll Robert Rowley rolled round?

5. Great rats, small rats, lean rats, brawny rats,
   Brown rats, black rats, gray rats, tawny rats.
   Grave old plodders, gay young friskers. . . .
   —BROWNING.

6. Reading maketh a full man, conference a ready man, and writing an exact man.
   —BACON

## Drills for "y," Phonetic Symbol [j]

Read aloud:

1. The huge human sat mute in the pew.
2. Feuds are disputes which abuse human security.
3. The youngster yearned to yodel to advertise Yankee yeast.
4. What ye gave, ye have;
   What ye spent, ye had;
   What ye left, ye lost.
   —EPITAPH
5. Youth is full of sport, age's breath is short;
   Youth is nimble, age is lame;
   Youth is hot and bold, age is weak and cold;
   Youth is wild, and age is tame.
   —SHAKESPEARE

## PROJECTS

*Assignment*

This is an opportunity to analyze your own articulation, and to discover which sounds you need to improve. If your speech lacks crispness and precision, work on the plosive sounds. If your speech lacks color, work for full, rich resonance on the three nasal sounds. If you need a general brush-up, make the distinction between the voiceless "wh" and the voiced "w" in such pairs of words as "where," "wear." Make your sibilants short and clear. Be careful not to unvoice the voiced "z" in such words as "is," "has," "does." Give the liquid "l" sound its full beauty.

Do some practice on all sounds. Everyone can improve his or her articulation. Concentrate on the sounds which your instructor indicates are especially difficult for you. Be prepared to demonstrate your skill in the following activities:

1. Be able to produce the sound in isolation.
2. Be able to describe how the sound is made by your vocal mechanism.
3. Be able to read the lists with accuracy and precision. The lists provide practice of the sound in combination with all the vowels and diphthongs.

4. Be able to recite from memory one or two of the sound-loaded sentences.

5. Be able to recite one of the selections from literature which highlights the individual sound.

6. Bring in a short selection from a newspaper or current magazine. Underline the sounds you are striving to perfect. Read your selection aloud to the class.

These six requirements illustrate the simplest method of gaining control over speech sounds. Work on one sound at a time. A good plan is to copy the drills on a piece of paper and keep the paper handy. This will remind you of your articulation problem and assist you in carrying over your drill to your daily speech. While drillwork is tedious, it produces amazing results. Patience and persistence will produce results.

Continue this assignment as long as your instructor deems it necessary. Use the same pattern until all your articulation defects have been given special attention.

Do the drills diligently. There is no better advice than this: *Invest in yourself.*

### Developing Semantic Skill

Add to your word cards the following:

I. Words used in the speech text:

| Word | Pronunciation | Meaning |
|------|---------------|---------|
| 1. assimilation | | |
| 2. controversial | | |
| 3. diphthong | | |
| 4. shaft | | |

II. Words commonly mispronounced:
   1. idea
   2. indict
   3. Italian

III. Words from your own experience.

*Chapter 12*

# HOW TO MAKE THE VOWELS

Mend your speech a little,
Lest it may mar your fortunes.
—SHAKESPEARE

In order to improve your speaking voice, it is essential to know how the sounds of speech are produced. This knowledge serves as a valuable guidepost for purposeful practice. Moreover, a knowledge of the phonetic basis of speech is a vital part of your liberal education. For you cannot be truly educated if you do not understand the nature of your mother tongue. But understanding is not enough. The cultured person possesses skill in the spoken and written forms of his language. These are the indelible marks of an educated man. As you experience more and more cultural advantages, see that your speech reflects these advantages. Make use of the same plan that you followed in the study of the consonant sounds. You will be gratified at the improvement in your speaking personality.

There are two distinct types of sounds in your speech: vowels and consonants. As you now realize, the consonants are made by the obstruction of energized air in its passage from the lungs. This is done by the various positions of the tongue and articulators as they create a variety of different resonating cavities in the mouth and the nasal passages. Unlike the plosive, nasal, hissing, and fricative interruptions creating consonants, the vowels flow freely. As you will notice, it is the position of the tongue that in large part controls the formation of the vowel sounds. For this reason, the position of the tongue determines the classification of the vowels into front, middle, and back vowels. In like manner, because the "l," "r," and "y" [l], [r], and [j] sounds were only slightly impeded, they were referred to as semi-vowels.

Another distinction of tongue activity creates the group of sounds called "diphthongs." A diphthong is a speech sound changing continuously from one vowel sound to another on the same syllable and with a single pulse of utterance. In other words, the tongue moves from the position for one vowel to another related vowel in a glide so quickly made that the resultant sound is identified as a single phonetic unit, *i.e.,* one distinguishable sound. For example: "ā" is in reality a combination of "ĕ" as in pet and a quick glide of the tongue to the position of "ĭ" as in it; and hence producing the diphthong "ā". Diphthongs are further classified as rising or falling diphthongs. When the tongue position goes from a lower to a higher point, the diphthong is rising; and when it goes from a higher to a lower position, the diphthong is falling.

These groupings of sounds are merely means of classification intended to facilitate your understanding. They are set for the purpose of making your approach to the study of sounds as scientifically accurate as possible and as the simplest means of making the vast array of sounds intelligible. Once you can identify a sound by its place of production, its characteristic quality, and the symbol used to describe it, you have achieved a working knowledge of that sound. You are then ready for the true task of using this knowledge to improve your speech pattern. To speak with the assurance of knowledge gives poise and confidence to the speaker. For this reason, you are asked to seek first the understanding of the scientific basis of each sound, and then to practice assiduously the graded material. This procedure will establish intelligent habits that will be part of your speaking personality all your life. It will endow you with an assurance otherwise unattainable.

### The Front-vowel Sounds

#### *HOW TO MAKE THE VOWEL "ē" [i]*

— "ē" as in bee, pea, deal, tea —

Say "Three police chiefs seek the fleeing thief." Watch your tongue make the same sound in three, police, chiefs, seek, fleeing, and thief. This vowel is written in diacritical markings as "ē" and in phonetics [i]. To utter it, the front part of the tongue should be high up in the mouth toward the hard palate, or roof of the mouth. The lips are spread tensely in a long, thin, narrow opening. Listen to the sound several times. In your study of speech sounds you must be ear-minded rather than eye-minded. Say words aloud to discover the vowel sound. The sound "ē" has many spellings: sometimes it is written "ee" as in fleet, free, see, meet; or it may be written "ie" as in piece, field, grieve, thief; or, perhaps as "ea" in meat, meal, deal; as "e" in be, me, key; and even as "ei" in ceiling, receive.

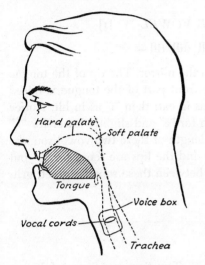

**THE SPEAKER SAYS ē [i]**

Notice how the speaker says ē as in "he" by raising the front of the tongue high, keeping the tip of the tongue behind the lower front teeth and making a voiced sound. His lips are spread and both lips and tongue are tensed. The soft palate is raised and the sound is sent out through the mouth.

Read the following words aloud:

| | | | | |
|---|---|---|---|---|
| bee | keen | sea | wheel | theme |
| peel | mead | liege | heel | lead |
| deal | need | sheen | veal | read |
| tea | evening | cheek | feel | yeast |
| greet | zebra | we | thee | |

*Drills for "ē," Phonetic Symbol* [i]

Read aloud:

1. The sea seems free and so do we;
   But only by the Lord's decree.
2. Mean people lead uneasy lives.
3. These green leaves are easy to see at eve.
4. Wheat freely feeds the body heat.
5. The only steel Achilles could feel was in his heel.
6. My Mary's asleep by the murmuring stream,
   Flow gently, sweet Afton, disturb not her dream.
   —BURNS

7. There was a Door to which I found no Key:
   There was a Veil past which I could not see:
   Some little Talk awhile of Me and Thee
   There seemed—and then no more of Thee and Me.
                                        —FITZGERALD

## HOW TO MAKE THE VOWEL "ĭ" [ɪ]

— "ĭ" as in bit, pill, dill, till —

Say "ĭ" as in it. Watch your tongue in the mirror. The tip of the tongue stays behind the lower front teeth. The front part of the tongue is raised toward the roof of the mouth. Say "ē" as in eat; then "ĭ" as in hit. Notice that the front part of the tongue is high for "ē" and slightly lower for "ĭ." Say bead, bid. Notice the difference in length of these two vowel sounds: "ē" is long and "ĭ" is short. The tongue and the lips are tense for "ē" but relaxed for "ĭ." Listen to the difference between these sounds: greet, grit; heat, hit; meat, mit; neat, knit; feel, fill.

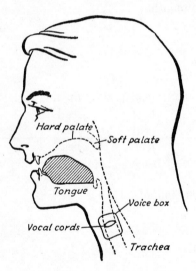

### THE SPEAKER SAYS ĭ [ɪ]

Notice how he says ĭ as in "hit." The front of the tongue is raised, but not quite as high as for ē. The tip of the tongue is behind the lower front teeth. Lips and tongue are lax, not tense. The vocal cords vibrate, the soft palate is raised and the sound is sent out the mouth.

Read the following words aloud:

| | | | |
|---|---|---|---|
| bit | mill | shrill | fill |
| pill | nil | chill | this |
| dill | ring | wit | thistle |
| till | zip | whip | lid |
| grit | sit | hill | rid |
| kin | religion | villain | Yiddish |

*Drills for "ĭ," Phonetic Symbol* [ɪ]

Read aloud:

1. Humidity hinders visibility for motorists.
2. Persistence! This is the thing which will win.
3. The little blimp signaled the dirigible with its blinker system.
4. Thin griddle cakes fill the bill on chill mornings.
5. A little learning is a dangerous thing;
   Drink deep, or taste not the Pierian spring:
   There shallow draughts intoxicate the brain,
   And drinking largely sobers us again.
   —POPE
6. The Moving Finger writes; and, having writ,
   Moves on: nor all your Piety nor Wit
     Shall lure it back to cancel half a Line
   Nor all your Tears wash out a Word of it.
   —FITZGERALD
7. Fib, and Nib, and Pick and Pin,
   Tick, and Quick, and Jill, and Jim,
   Tit, and Nit, and Wap, and Win,
   The train that wait upon her.
   —SHAKESPEARE

## HOW TO MAKE THE VOWEL "ĕ" [ɛ]

### — "ĕ" as in bet, pet, debt, Ted —

Say "Ted fed Heddy." As you say the vowel sound in each word, the front of your tongue rises to a position slightly lower than for the sound "ĭ" as in hit. Notice that the tongue is gradually lowering for each succeeding vowel. Say "Eve hit Heddy." Notice the lowering of the tongue as "ē," "ĭ," and "ĕ" are said: "ē" and "ĭ" are so-called "high" sounds; "ĕ" is called a "half-high" sound. As you try to become ear-minded rather than eye-minded note the variety of spelling combinations that indicate "ĕ": "a" as in many, any; "ai" as in said; "ea" as in weather; "ie" as in friend; "ue" as in quest; and "e" as in led.

Read the following words aloud:

| | | | |
|---|---|---|---|
| bet | met | shell | fell |
| pet | net | chest | them |
| debt | netting | wet | theft |
| tell | zest | whelm | let |
| get | set | helm | red |
| ken | ledge | velvet | yet |

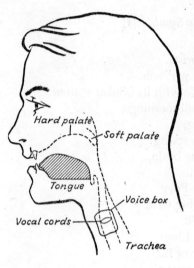

**THE SPEAKER SAYS ĕ [ε]**

Notice how he says ĕ as in "head" by raising the front of the tongue to a half-high position and keeping the tip behind the lower front teeth. The vocal cords vibrate; the soft palate is raised so that the sound is sent out through the mouth.

*Drills for "ĕ," Phonetic Symbol* [ε]

Read aloud:

1. Cedric fell pell-mell off the edge of the ledge.
2. Well-fed men went West in quest of wealth.
3. "Get ready for vengeance, men," the message read.
4. Fred read his text with good intent but never knew his lesson.
5. Ken led Heddy, the pet red hen, into the pen.
6. I do not love thee, Doctor Fell,
   The reason why I cannot tell;
   But this I know, and know full well:
   I do not love thee, Doctor Fell.
   —BROWN
7. The bell invites me.
   Hear it not, Duncan; for it is the knell
   That summons thee to heaven or to hell.
   —SHAKESPEARE

## HOW TO MAKE THE VOWEL "ă" [æ]

— "ă" as in bat, pat, Dan, tan —

Say "The fat cat sat on the black mat." The vowel "ă" is made with the tip of the tongue behind the lower front teeth, and the front of the tongue is low in the mouth. Of the four vowels studied this is the lowest tongue position. Repeat these four vowel sounds as you watch your tongue: "ē," "ĭ," "ĕ," "ă." Note how the front of the tongue gradually lowers.

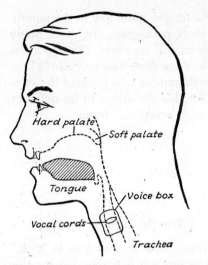

Hard palate

Soft palate

Tongue

Voice box

Vocal cords

Trachea

## THE SPEAKER SAYS ă [æ]

Notice how he says ă as in "cat." The front of the tongue is low in the mouth and the tip is behind the front teeth. This is the lowest front sound of the four studied.

Read the following words aloud:

| | | | | | |
|---|---|---|---|---|---|
| bat | gap | sang | chat | van | rat |
| pat | can | strap | wag | fan | |
| Dan | mat | shall | whang | that | |
| tan | Nat | badge | hat | latch | |

### Drills for "ă," Phonetic Symbol [æ]

Read aloud:

1. That man is a bad man. He sat on my black hat.
2. The Yankee band played at the annual banquet.
3. Man is a sad animal. That's a fact.
4. And malt does more than Milton can
   To justify God's ways to man.
                    —A. E. HOUSMAN
5. As with my hat upon my head
   I walk'd along the Strand,
   I there did meet another man
   With his hat in his hand.
                    —SAMUEL JOHNSON

## HOW TO MAKE THE VOWEL "à" [a]

— "à" as in bask, pass, staff, last —

This is a very controversial vowel. It is a sound midway between the "ă" as in man and the "ä" as in art. As such, it is the lowest of the front vowels and is made with the front of the tongue quite low in the mouth. Many speakers use it in words like ask, shaft, path, grass, last, glass. Many other speakers do not use "à," but rather use "ă" for them. The important point about the use of this vowel is to be consistent. You may use "ă" for all of them if you wish. A safe rule is to determine which sound the educated speakers in your community prefer. Do not strive to be different in your speech, but do strive to use the most acceptable forms.

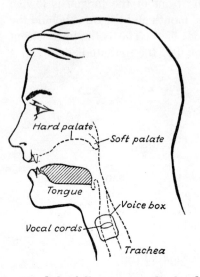

THE SPEAKER SAYS à [a]

Notice how he says à as in "task." The lips are half rounded for this sound, and the tongue is low but forward in the mouth.

Read the following words aloud:

| | | | |
|---|---|---|---|
| bask | grasp | basking | vast |
| pass | castle | staff | fast |
| dance | mast | shaft | last |
| task | nasty | waft | rascal |

*Drills for "à," Phonetic Symbol* [a]

Read aloud the following exercises with either "ă" or "à" in the italicized words:

1. It was a *task* to *pass* the *glass* around the *class* as we were *asked.*
2. The *master's last gasp* held the *class* in a *trance.*
3. The *class passed* out *laughing.*
4. He who *laughs last laughs* best.
5. It was her *last chance* to *dance* at her *aunt's castle* in *France.*
6. Knowledge *advances* by slow steps with a *staff,*
   And not by an easy *path.*

                                        —MACAULAY

7. *Dance, laugh* and be merry.
   For tomorrow you may die.
   —ANONYMOUS

8. Man thinks, and at once becomes the *master* of the *class* that does
   not think.
   —BUFFON

9. Others import yet nobler arts from *France,*
   Teach kings to fiddle, and make senates *dance.*
   —POPE

10. A thousand *dancing* flowers
    Amid the dewy *grass*
    *Glance* at you with *laughter*
    And greet you as you *pass.*
    —ANONYMOUS

### THE BACK-VOWEL SOUNDS

There are four back vowels. As the name indicates, they are placed
in the back of the mouth.

### HOW TO MAKE THE VOWEL "ōō" [u]

— "ōō" as in boot, pool, tool, goose —

This is the highest back vowel. Say "ooooooooo," the sound the wind
makes. Watch your lips in the mirror. They should be rounded so that

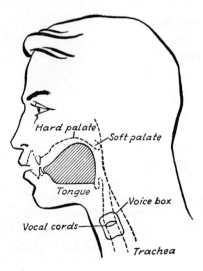

### THE SPEAKER SAYS ōō [u]

Notice how he says ōō as in "who,"
by raising the back of the tongue
toward the soft palate and keeping
the tip of the tongue behind the
lower front teeth. The vocal cords
vibrate; the soft palate is raised so
that the sound is sent out through
the mouth. The lips are quite
rounded.

the opening is a small round hole about the size of an ordinary lead pencil. It is very important to round the lips for the back vowels. If you want to see what happens to the tongue as you make this sound, open your mouth wide and say who. You will see that the tip of the tongue remains behind the lower front teeth, and the back of the tongue is raised high in the mouth.

Read the following words aloud:

| boot | goose | zoo | choose | Voodoo | root |
|------|-------|-----|--------|--------|------|
| pool | cool | sue | woo | fool | |
| Duluth | mood | shoot | whew | threw | |
| toot | noodle | Scrooge | hoop | loot | |

### Drills for "ōō," Phonetic Symbol [u]

Read aloud:

1. Cool troops moved the crude enemy to doom.
2. Sue's crooning soon dispelled the room's gloom.
3. Who is using the crude tools in the workroom?
4. The new moon floods the room and soothes the moody groom.
5. The crew chuted as the balloon looped the loop in the monsoon.
6. She left the web, she left the loom,
   She made three paces through the room,
   She saw the water-lily bloom,
   She saw the helmet and the plume.
   —TENNYSON
7. Sir, I admit your genial rule,
   That every poet is a fool,
   But you yourself may serve to show it,
   That every fool is not a poet.
   —POPE

## HOW TO MAKE THE VOWEL "ŏŏ" [ʊ]

— "ŏŏ" as in hook, put, pudding, took —

The next back vowel is shorter and less tense than "ōō." Say "He took the good book to the brook." Watch your lips as you say "ŏŏ." They are rounded, but they are less tense than for "ōō." Your tongue should be just slightly lower than for "ōō." Listen to the sound of each of these two high back vowels. Say "ōō" as in who, and "ŏŏ" as in hood; cooed, could; shoe, should. Be sure to round your lips or your "ŏŏ" may sound like up, and your "book" will sound like buck. Round the lips, raise the back of the tongue toward the soft palate, and make a voiced sound as in pull, could, would, should. The sound "ŏŏ" may be spelled as "o" in wolf; "ou" in could; "u" in pull; "oo" in good.

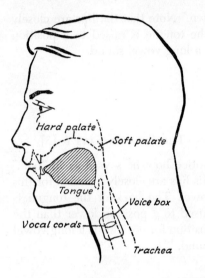

Hard palate

Soft palate

Tongue

Voice box

Vocal cords

Trachea

### THE SPEAKER SAYS ŏŏ [ʊ]

Notice how he says ŏŏ as in "hood" by raising the back of his tongue high toward the soft palate, keeping his tongue tip behind the lower front teeth. The lips are rounded, the vocal cords vibrate. The soft palate is raised and the sound is sent out the mouth.

Read the following words aloud:

| | | | | | |
|---|---|---|---|---|---|
| book | took | moor | Zukor | wood | foot |
| put | good | nook | stood | whoosh | thereunto |
| pudding | could | mooring | should | hood | look |
| | | | | | rook |

### Drills for "ŏŏ," Phonetic Symbol [ʊ]

Read aloud:

1. Woods, the cook, could cook good pudding, couldn't he?
2. Put the booklet on the bulletin board.
3. Could you look for the book you took? You could! Good!
4. The rookie's bullet hooked the hooded hoodlum in the foot.
5. The wolf pulled the wool over Red Riding Hood.
6. Good night, good night! parting is such sweet sorrow,
   That I shall say good night till it be morrow.
   —SHAKESPEARE

7. My only books were women's looks
   And folly all they taught me.
   —BYRON

8. And with a child's undoubting wisdom look,
   On all those pages of God's book.
   —LOWELL

## HOW TO MAKE THE VOWEL "ô" [ɔ]

*— "ô" as in ball, Paul, drawl, tall —*

Say "Paul caught a haul of fish at dawn." Note that the lips are closely rounded for this vowel. The back of the tongue is raised to a position lower than the position for "ŏŏ." This is a long vowel sound.

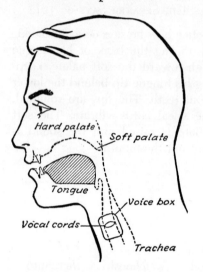

Hard palate

Soft palate

Tongue

Voice box

Vocal cords

Trachea

### THE SPEAKER SAYS ô [ɔ]

Notice how he says ô as in "ball." His lips are closely rounded for this vowel. The back of the tongue is raised to a position lower than the position for ŏŏ. This is a long vowel sound.

Read the following words aloud:

| brought | gawky | yawning | wharf | thaw |
|---------|--------|---------|--------|------|
| pawn | caught | resort | haunt | law |
| dawn | morbid | stalk | vault | yawl |
| taught | naught | warn | fault | |

### Drills for "ô," Phonetic Symbol [ɔ]

Read aloud:

1. All ought to obey the Lord's law.
2. The law ought to be the embodiment of all that is good.
3. The nautical outlaw yawned awkwardly.
4. The fall brought raw winds and awful storms.
5. A damsel with a dulcimer
   In a vision once I saw:
   It was an Abyssinian maid,
   And on her dulcimer she play'd,
   Singing of Mount Abora.
   —COLERIDGE

6. The wrinkled sea beneath him crawls;
   He watches from his mountain walls,
   And like a thunderbolt he falls.
   —TENNYSON, "The Eagle"

## HOW TO MAKE THE VOWEL "ŏ" [ᴅ]

— "ŏ" as in Bob, pot, dot, tot —

Say "Bob got a lot of jobs." Your lips are not quite so rounded as for the "ô" in all. This is a shorter sound. The back of the tongue is raised to a position slightly lower than the position for "ô" as in orb. Sometimes Americans use the "ä" as in art for this sound. Make the sound shorter than the "ä" sound and it will produce a sharper effect.

Notice that Webster gives the symbol "ȯ" to indicate that the speaker may say "ŏ" or "ô" for words like off, loft, soft, coffee, offer, etc.

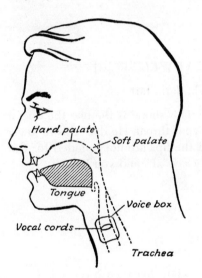

**THE SPEAKER SAYS ŏ [ᴅ]**

Notice how he says ŏ as in "pot." The lips are not quite rounded as for the ô in "all." This is a short sound. Make it shorter than the à sound as in "ask."

Read the following words aloud:

| | | | |
|---|---|---|---|
| Bob | mop | lodge | flop |
| pot | not | chop | throng |
| dock | bobbing | watt | lot |
| top | Zombi | what | rob |
| got | stop | hot | yacht |
| cot | shop | volume | |

*Drills for "ŏ," Phonetic Symbol* [ɒ]

Read aloud:

1. A fox terrier was offered as a watchdog.
2. Don didn't care a jot about the lot.
3. John got a lot of spots on his cotton blouse.
4. Boswick scoffed at the loss of a dog.
5. Robert tossed rocks at the log in the bog.
6. A weapon that comes down as still
      As snowflakes fall upon the sod;
   But executes a freeman's will,
      As lightning does the will of God.
        —JOHN PIERPONT, "The Ballot"
7. The raging rocks
   And shivering shocks
   Shall break the locks
     of prison-gates.
        —SHAKESPEARE

## HOW TO MAKE THE VOWEL "ä" [ɑ]

— "ä" as in bark, park, dark, tart —

Say "Charles darted into the market." This sound is the one the doctor asks you to make in order to look down your throat. He does this to lower your tongue in your mouth. Notice that the lips are not rounded for this sound and that it is a long sound. Simply say "ah" and you have it.

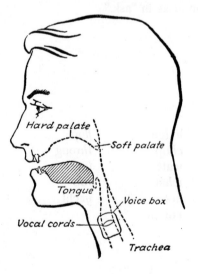

THE SPEAKER SAYS ä [ɑ]

Notice how he says ä as in "bark." The vowel is made low in the mouth. The lips are not rounded for this sound. It is a long sound.

Read the following words aloud:

| | | | |
|---|---|---|---|
| *b*ark | *m*art | *sh*arp | *f*arce |
| *p*ark | *gn*arl | *ch*arm | *th*ereafter |
| *d*ark | *b*ar*k*in*g* | *w*ineglass | *l*ark |
| *t*art | *cz*ar | *wh*arl | *wr*ath |
| *g*uard | *s*tar | *h*eart | *y*arn |
| *c*art | lar*ge* | *v*arsity | |

### *Drills for "ä," Phonetic Symbol* [ɑ]

Read aloud:

1. The sergeant was startled at the large armada of armed guards.
2. Arthur darted into the market with Carl and Charles.
3. Father marveled at the artistry of Martha's bargains.
4. Barbara charmed and disarmed the guards in the park.
5. Sunset and evening star,
     And one clear call for me!
   And may there be no moaning of the bar,
     When I put out to sea.
                                      —TENNYSON
6. Two men looked out from prison bars,
   And one saw mud, the other saw stars.
                                      —ANONYMOUS
7. Once more; speak clearly if you speak at all;
   Carve each word before you let it fall:
   Don't, like a lecturer or dramatic star,
   Try overhard to roll the British R.
                                      —HOLMES

## THE MID-VOWEL SOUNDS

There are three main mid-vowels. As the name indicates, they are made by raising the middle of the tongue. They are commonly heard in the words tub, sofa, herd.

### *HOW TO MAKE THE MID-VOWEL "û"* [ɝ]

— "û" as in bird, pearl, dirt, twirl —

Say "û" as in herd. If you live in a section of the country in which "r" is pronounced before consonants, you will notice that the middle of the tongue is raised for the "û" and the tip of the tongue turned up immediately after it. If the people in your community do not pronounce "r" before consonants, you will notice that your mid-vowel sound is long and made with the middle part of the tongue raised. Say "Pearl turned as she heard the third word." Be careful not to confuse this sound with the diphthong "oi."

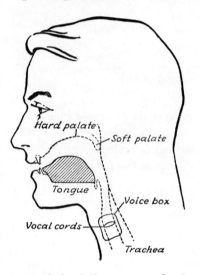

THE SPEAKER SAYS û [ɝ]

Notice that the middle of his tongue is raised for the first sound of û, after that the tip turns upward immediately. This is a long sound.

Read the following words aloud:

| | | | | |
|---|---|---|---|---|
| bird | girt | earning | whirl | thirst |
| purge | curd | surly | herd | learning |
| dirt | merge | shirt | virgin | rehearse |
| turf | nurse | worse | first | yearn |

*Drills for "û," Phonetic Symbol* [ɝ]

Read aloud:

1. The early bird catches the worm that squirms in a perfect circle.
2. The third girl in the third row had curly hair.
3. A perfect nurse turned to serve the burned girl.
4. Personnel first learned to observe and then to certify.
5. The alert colonel heard every word.
6. Errors, like straws, upon the surface flow;
   He who would search for pearls must dive below.
   —SHAKESPEARE
7. O blithe New-comer! I have heard,
   I hear thee and rejoice.
   O Cuckoo! shall I call thee Bird,
   Or but a wandering Voice?
   —WORDSWORTH

8. Quit, quit for shame! this will not move,
   This cannot take her;
If of herself she will not love,
   Nothing can make her:
   The Devil take her!
                    —SIR JOHN SUCKLING

## HOW TO MAKE THE MID-VOWEL ē, ȧ, ă, ĕ, ŏ, ŭ [ə]

— ē, ȧ, ă, ĕ, ŏ, ŭ as in maker, abhor, sofa, jewel, occur, circus —

Say "er . . . er . . . er . . . er . . . er," as though you were reaching
for a word. This is the sound called the "neutral vowel." It is so called
because the tongue hangs naturally in the mouth. Under the influence
of the linguistic principle of ease of production most vowels tend to become neutral vowels. However, the spelling form of the word does not
change and so the "a" in sofa, the "e" in jewel, the "o" in occur, and the
"u" in circus are still spelled the same but pronounced as a neutral vowel.
Hence, the sound is represented by a single phonetic symbol [ə], but by
six different diacritical marks. This is precisely where the principles of
phonetics and diacritical markings differ. The phonetic rule is that the
sound is the symbol and the symbol is the sound; while diacritical markings attempt to keep the pronouncing aid as close to the original spelling
form as possible. An easy way to remember the different markings is to
note that with the exception of ē they are all cast in italics.

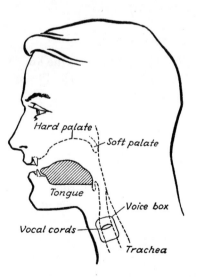

### THE SPEAKER SAYS ȧ [ə]

Notice how he says ȧ as in "sofa."
This sound is called the neutral
vowel. Most frequently it is used
in unstressed syllables.

Read the following words aloud:

| | | | | |
|---|---|---|---|---|
| about | against | among | achievement | afar |
| apart | akin | sofa | await | athwart |
| data | amaze | aspersion | avoid | alarm |
| atop | anon | ashamed | awhile | aroma |

*Drills for ē, à, ă, ĕ, ŏ, ŭ, Phonetic Symbol* [ə]

Read aloud:

1. The speaker's ideas about the circus were awful.
2. Lydia was awarded a medal for scholarship.
3. The giant cannon sounded a national salute.
4. In the midst of the fountain of wit there arises something bitter, which stings in the very flowers.

—LUCRETIUS

5. The moon on the one hand, the dawn on the other:
   The moon is my sister, the dawn is my brother.
   The moon on my left hand and the dawn on my right,
   My brother, good morning; my sister, good night.

—HILAIRE BELLOC

6. Ah, Love! could you and I with Him conspire
   To grasp this sorry Scheme of Things entire,
       Would not we shatter it to bits—and then
   Re-mould it nearer to the Heart's Desire!

—FITZGERALD

## HOW TO MAKE THE MID-VOWEL "ŭ" [ʌ]

— "ŭ" as in bunch, punch, dunce, ton —

Say "A tub of butter is too much for lunch." The sound "ŭ" is the lowest of the three mid-vowels. *It occurs in stressed syllables only.* The lips are unrounded in producing it, and the vocal cords vibrate.

Read the following words aloud:

| | | | | |
|---|---|---|---|---|
| bunch | gulp | lung | chum | fun |
| punch | cut | buzz | won | thumb |
| dunce | money | sulk | whuff | lunch |
| ton | none | shun | hull | run |
| | | judge | vulgar | young |

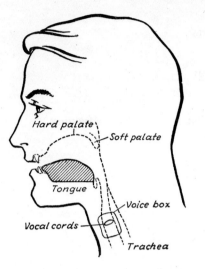

### THE SPEAKER SAYS ŭ [ʌ]

Notice how he says ŭ as in "but." This is the lowest of the three mid-vowels. It occurs in stressed syllables only. The lips are rounded for it and the vocal cords vibrate.

*Drills for "ŭ," Phonetic Symbol* [ʌ]

Read aloud:

1. A tub of butter is much too much.
2. The juggler tumbled in the mud near the pump.
3. Chubby youngsters sulked with thumbs in mouths.
4. The vulgar bunch gulped the punch like dunces.
5. Avoid extremes; and shun the faults of such
   Who still are pleased too little or too much.
   —POPE
6. Double, double, toil and trouble;
   Fire burn, and cauldron bubble.
   —SHAKESPEARE
7. For freedom's battle, once begun,
   Bequeath'd by bleeding sire to son,
   Though baffled oft, is ever won.
   —BYRON
8. If all the world and love were young,
   And truth in every shepherd's tongue,
   These pretty pleasures might me move
   To live with thee, and be thy love.
   —RALEIGH

PROJECTS

*Developing Semantic Skill*

Add to your word cards the following:

I. Words used in the speech text:

| Word | Pronunciation | Meaning |
|------|---------------|---------|
| 1. controversial | | |
| 2. monsoon | | |
| 3. dulcimer | | |
| 4. horologue | | |

II. Words commonly mispronounced:
   1. holocaust
   2. hidalgo
   3. hierarchy

III. Words from your own experience.

*Chapter 13*

# HOW TO MAKE THE DIPHTHONGS

The manner of speaking is full as important as the matter, as more
people have ears to be tickled, than understanding to judge.
—Lord Chesterfield

Diphthongs are made by blending two vowels into one sound. They
require accurate production. The blend must be smooth and complete. Although two vowels are blended, there is only one diphthong.
The sound starts in the position of one vowel and ends in the position
of another. Both vowels will be given for identification of the sound,
but remember that the glide from one position to the other is a very
vital part of the diphthong. You have been using these diphthongs
in your daily speech and probably have considered them as single
sounds. Hence, you should have no trouble in thinking of them as
single sounds. They are separated so you will understand their
nature, and as an aid to clear production.

## HOW TO MAKE THE DIPHTHONG "ā" [eɪ]

— "ā" as in bay, pay, day, tail —

Say "The rain made the train remain in the station." Listen to the vowel
sound in rain, made, train. The combination of two vowel sounds is called
a "diphthong." Watch your tongue in the mirror as you say "ā." The tongue
first says "ě" as in get, then quickly moves to "ĭ" as in it. The result is
"ā" as in gate. These diphthongs are all voiced sounds. The vocal cords
vibrate while producing them.

Read the following words aloud:

| | | | | |
|------|------|--------|--------|------|
| bay  | gay  | saying | change | fail |
| pay  | cake | zany   | chain  | hay  |
| day  | may  | say    | way    | lay  |
| tail | neigh| shade  | veil   | ray  |
|      |      |        |        | yea  |

149

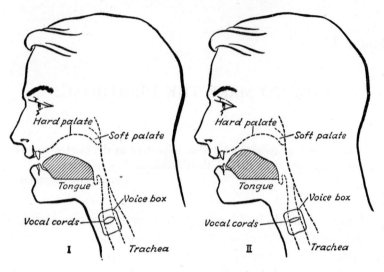

THE SPEAKER SAYS ā [eɪ]

Notice how he says ā as in "hail." In I, the tip of the tongue is behind the lower front teeth; the front of the tongue is raised to the position for ĕ in "head." In II, the front of the tongue is raised higher: as for ĭ in "hit." The diphthong ā is the sound which results as the tongue glides from position I to position II. The vocal cords vibrate. The soft palate is raised and the sound is sent out through the mouth.

*Drills for "ā," Phonetic Symbol* [eɪ]

Read aloud:

1. The train remained in the station all day.
2. In Spain the rain remains mainly in the plains.
3. They say the lady with the jade bracelet always leads the way.
4. Ray baked the steak in the grate.
5. Too late! Too late! The knave exclaimed in despair.
6. Some are born great, some achieve greatness, and some have greatness thrust upon them.

—SHAKESPEARE

7. I knew a black beetle, who lived down a drain,
   And friendly he was, though his manners were plain;
   When I took a bath he would come up the pipe,
   And together we'd wash and together we'd wipe.

—CHRISTOPHER MORLEY

8. A Moment's Halt—a momentary taste
   Of BEING from the Well amid the Waste—
      And, Lo! the phantom Caravan has reach'd
   The NOTHING it set out from— Oh, make haste!
                                        —FITZGERALD

## HOW TO MAKE THE DIPHTHONG "ī" [aɪ]

— "ī" as in pie, buy, dine, tie —

Say "High." Listen to the diphthong. Watch your tongue as you say "ī."
The tip of the tongue stays behind the lower front teeth, and the front part
of your tongue starts low as for "ȧ" in ask and then glides higher to "ĭ" as
in hit. The resulting diphthong is "ī" as in my, sty, Clyde. Keep your
tongue forward for this sound.

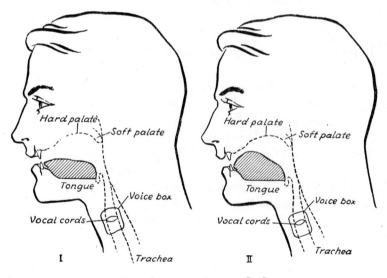

THE SPEAKER SAYS ī [aɪ]

Notice how he says ī as in "high." In I, the front part of his tongue is low
as for ȧ in "ask." In II, the front part of the tongue is high as for ĭ in
"hit." The diphthong ī results, as his tongue glides from I to II. The vocal
cords vibrate for all diphthongs. The soft palate is raised and the sound
is sent out through the mouth.

Read the following words aloud:

| | | | | |
|---|---|---|---|---|
| *buy* | *kite* | *sigh* | *white* | *lie* |
| *pie* | *my* | *shy* | *vie* | *rye* |
| *d*ine | *n*igh | *j*ibe | *fight* | |
| *t*ie | di*n*ing | *ch*ide | *thy* | |
| *g*uide | *x*ylophone | *w*ife | *th*ine | |

### *Drills for "ī," Phonetic Symbol* [aɪ]

Read aloud:

1. "Time flies, and tides rise," cried the lighthouse keeper.
2. The diver sighed as he dived through the white ice.
3. The knight was wise and kind.
4. I tied my tie twice.
5. Five Flying Tigers survived ninety-nine night flights.
6.          Hail to thee, blithe spirit!
         Bird thou never wert—
      That from heaven or near it
      Pourest thy full heart
   In profuse strains of unpremeditated art.


      Higher still and higher
         From the earth thou springest,
      Like a cloud of fire;
         The blue deep thou wingest,
   And singing still dost soar, and soaring ever singest.
                              —SHELLEY

7. I said to Heart, "How goes it?" Heart replied:
   "Right as a Ribstone Pippin!" But it lied.
                              —HILAIRE BELLOC


## HOW TO MAKE THE DIPHTHONG "ō" [oʊ]

— "ō" as in broke, poke, dote, token —

Say "Oh, no, don't go." Listen to the diphthong in "Oh, no." Notice what happens as you say the sound. The lips are rounded and it is hard to see that the back part of the tongue starts to say "ō" as in obey, then glides quickly to "o͞o" as in book. These two vowel sounds make the diphthong "ō." The vocal cords vibrate and the diphthong is voiced.

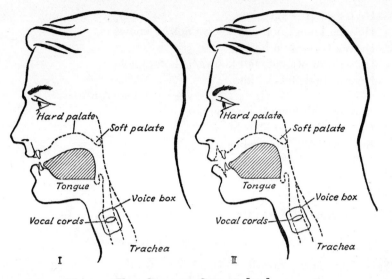

THE SPEAKER SAYS ō [ou]

Notice how he says ō as in "oh!" In I, the back of the tongue is raised to the position for ō as in "obey." In II, the back of the tongue is raised higher as for ŏŏ in "book." The diphthong ō results as the tongue glides from position I to position II. The vocal cords vibrate, the soft palate is raised so that the sound is sent out through the mouth.

Read the following words aloud:

| broke | go | doting | show | low |
| poke | cold | Zoroaster | choke | rope |
| dote | Moses | so | vocal | yeoman |
| token | nose | loges | folk | |

### Drills for "ō," Phonetic Symbol [ou]

Read aloud:

1. He sewed his radio code in his old coat.
2. Lowell, the noted poet, wrote folio after folio.
3. Joe's nose is cold; Joe's toes are cold; in fact, Joe's froze.
4. The colt broke the rope and bolted down the open road.
5. "Oh, no, don't go, Joe," moaned the moldy ghost.
6. He who knows, and knows he knows,—
   He is wise—follow him.
   He who knows, and knows not he knows,—

He is asleep—wake him.
He who knows not, and knows not he knows not,—
He is a fool—shun him.
He who knows not, and knows he knows not,—
He is a child—teach him.

—PROVERB

7. And up and down the people go,
Gazing where the lilies blow
Round an island there below,
    The island of Shalott.

—TENNYSON

## HOW TO MAKE THE DIPHTHONG "ou" [aʊ]

— "ou" as in bout, pout, doubt, town —

Say "How now, brown cow?" Listen to the diphthong in "how." Watch yourself as you say it. Notice how the lips begin, unrounded, then round for the final element. The tongue begins in the position for "à" as

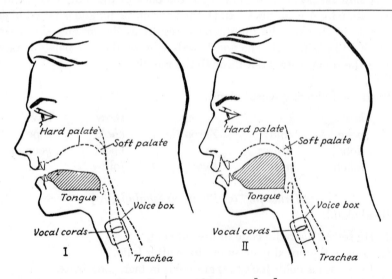

THE SPEAKER SAYS ou [aʊ]

Notice how he says ou as in "how." In I, the back of the tongue is low in the mouth as for à in ask. In II, the back of the tongue is raised high to the position for ŏŏ in "book." The diphthong ou results as the tongue glides from I to II. The vocal cords vibrate, and the soft palate is raised so that the sound is sent out through the mouth.

in ask and then glides to "o͝o" as in book. The combination of these two vowel sounds gives the diphthong "ou." Be sure you begin with the vowel sound as in ask for the first sound in this diphthong.

Read the following words aloud:

| | | | | |
|---|---|---|---|---|
| *b*out | *g*out | *dr*owni*ng* | *ch*ow | *th*ou |
| *p*out | *c*ow | *s*ound*s* | *w*ound | *l*out |
| *d*oubt | *m*ound | *sp*out | *v*owel | *r*out |
| *t*own | *n*oun | *sh*out | *f*rown | *y*owl |

### Drills for "ou," Phonetic Symbol [aʊ]

Read aloud:

1. "How now, brown cow?" browsed Mrs. Brown.
2. How the scouts howled when they found the town.
3. We counted a thousand mounds outside the grounds.
4. And lo! from the assembled crowd
   There rose a shout, prolonged and loud.
                    —LONGFELLOW
5. The owl looked down with his great round eyes
   At the lowering clouds and the darkening skies,
     "A good night for scouting," says he,
   "With never a sound I'll go prowling around,
   A mouse or two may be found on the ground
     Or a fat little bird in a tree."
   So down he flew from the old church tower,
   The mouse and the birdie crouch and cower,
   Back he flies in half an hour,
     "A very good supper," says he.
                    —ANONYMOUS
6. Doubt thou the stars are fire;
     Doubt that the sun doth move;
   Doubt truth to be a liar;
     But never doubt I love.
                    —SHAKESPEARE

## HOW TO MAKE THE DIPHTHONG "oi" [ɔɪ]

— "oi" as in boy, poise, doily, toy —

Say "Noisy boys." Listen to the diphthong "oi." Use a mirror and notice what happens as you say "oi" as in oyster. The lips are first rounded, then spread. The back of the tongue begins in position for "ô" as in orb, and then the front of the tongue rises to "ĭ" as in ill. The resulting diphthong is "oi" as in boy, a combination of the two vowel sounds. Be certain not to confuse "û," as in nurse, with this diphthong.

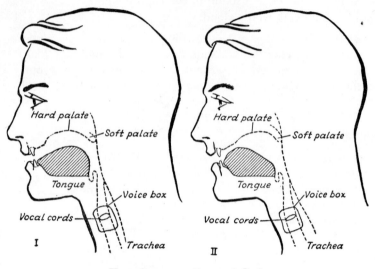

THE SPEAKER SAYS oi [ɔɪ]

Notice how he says oi as in "boy." In I, the back of the tongue is raised high as for ô in "orb." In II, the front of the tongue is raised high as for ĭ in "it." The diphthong oi results as the tongue glides from position I to position II. The vocal cords vibrate and the soft palate is raised so that the sound is sent out through the mouth.

Read the following words aloud:

| | | | | |
|---|---|---|---|---|
| boy | goiter | toying | water boy | thyroid |
| poise | coy | soil | hoist | loyal |
| doily | moist | adjoin | voice | royal |
| toy | noise | choice | foil | |

*Drills for "oi," Phonetic Symbol* [ɔɪ]

Read aloud:

1. What noise annoys an oyster? A noisy noise annoys an oyster.
2. The royal envoy was annoyed by the rejoicing employees.
3. The destroyer loitered near the convoy.
4. The devil has not, in all his quiver's choice,
   An arrow for the heart like a sweet voice.

—BYRON

5. Joy is the sweet voice, joy the luminous cloud.
   We in ourselves rejoice!

—COLERIDGE

## HOW TO MAKE THE DIPHTHONG "ȩ̄ (r)" [ɪə]

— "ȩ̄" as in bier, pier, deer, tear —

Say "here." Watch your tongue in the mirror. In British speech, the front part of the tongue begins in position for "ĭ" as in it and quickly glides to the position for the off-glide represented by *à* as in sofa. This latter sound is the one you make when you say "er-er-er"; the middle part of the tongue is raised. In the Eastern and Southern parts of the United States, this diphthong consists of the "ĭ" followed by the off-glide "*à*." However, in the West, the diphthong begins with the "ĭ," as in it, but lengthened, and finishes with tonguetip curled back for "r" as in red. Watch your tongue in the mirror. Which pronunciation of the diphthong do you see?

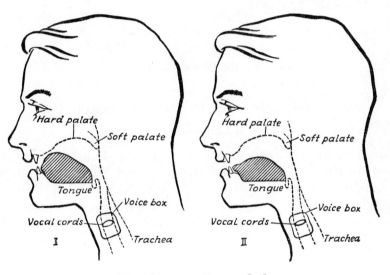

THE SPEAKER SAYS ȩ̄ [ɪə]

Notice how he says ȩ̄ as in "tear." The front of the tongue begins in the position of ĭ as in "it," as seen in diagram I, and quickly glides to the neutral vowel *à* as in "sofa." As in all diphthongs the vocal cords vibrate.

Read the following words aloud:

| | | | | |
|---|---|---|---|---|
| bier | gear | peering | cheer | theater |
| peer | clear | zero | Wiltshire | lear |
| deer | mere | sear | veer | rear |
| tear | near | sheer | fear | year |

*Drills for "ē̤ (r)," Phonetic Symbol* [ɪə]

Read aloud:

1. I fear it's sheer folly to swim too near the pier.
2. The theater is good this year. And it's quite near here.
3. I hear "The Fierce Bluebeard" is a weird picture.
4. The Peers shouted, "Hear! Hear! Hear! Hear!"
5. "Oh, dear! I feel quite queer," said she in tears.
6. Reflected in a mirror clear
   That hangs before her all the year,
   Shadows of the world appear;
   Here she sees the highway near
   　Winding down to Camelot.
   　　　　　　　—TENNYSON
7. Gold pays the worth of all things here;
   But not of love—that gem's too dear—
   　　　　　　　—WILLIAM COWPER

## HOW TO MAKE THE DIPHTHONG "â (r)," [ɛə]

— "â" as in bear, pear, dare, tear —

Say "â" as in air. Watch your tongue in the mirror. In British speech, the tip of the tongue remains behind the lower front teeth; the front part raises to the position halfway between the vowel position "ĕ" as in bed and "ă" as in hat, and then glides quickly to the position for "à" as in sofa. This is the way Easterners and Southerners make the diphthong. In the West, the tonguetip may be curled back for "r" as the second tongue position in making this diphthong.

Read the following words aloud:

| | | | | |
|---|---|---|---|---|
| bear | glare | glaring | wear | lair |
| pear | care | stair | varied | rare |
| dare | mare | share | fair | |
| tear | ne'er | chair | their | |

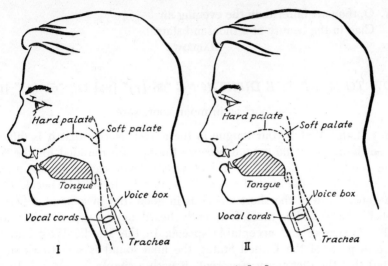

### THE SPEAKER SAYS â [ɛə]

Notice how the speaker says â as in "bear." The front part of the tongue raises to a position between ĕ as in "bed" and ă as in "hat," and then quickly glides to the position of ȧ as in "sofa." Be mindful that both positions produce a single diphthongal sound.

### *Drills for "â (r)," Phonetic Symbol [ɛə]*

Read aloud:

1. Beware! Take care! Don't dare go there!
2. The daring bear at the fair did not care for the damp **air**.
3. Claire stared and glared at the fair-haired mare.
4. "Fair is fair," the soothsayer declared.
5. 'Tis rare to share a chair with one so **fair**.
6. Shall I, wasting in despair,
   Die because a woman's fair?
   Or make pale my cheeks with **care**,
   'Cause another's rosy are?

   Be she fairer than the day,
   Or the flowery meads in May,
     If she be not so to me,
     What care I how fair she be?
            —WITHER

7. O, thou art fairer than the evening air
   Clad in the beauty of a thousand stars.

                  —MARLOWE

*HOW TO MAKE THE DIPHTHONG* "ŏŏ (r)" [ʊə] *OR* "ōō (r)" [uə]

— "ŏŏr" as in moor, tour, sure —

Say "tour." Watch your tongue in the mirror. Notice that it is difficult to see the back of the tongue because the lips are rounded for the "ŏŏ" as in good, or for the "ōō" as in loot, but that you can easily see it as it quickly glides to the neutral vowel "*å*" as in sofa. In British speech, there is a general use of the short vowel as in good, but in general American speech, this sound is more frequently heard nearer the sound in loot. Either is correct and acceptable speech. In the Middle West and the western parts of the United States, the final sound is sometimes so inverted that the dictionary represents it with a simple "r" symbol. In the East, this is only heard when the following word begins with a vowel or diphthong.

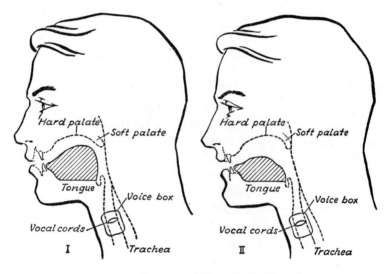

THE SPEAKER SAYS ŏŏr [ʊə]

Notice how the speaker says ŏŏr as in "tour." The speaker is using the first vowel position of the ŏŏ in "good." He may readily use the longer sound ōō as in "loot" by simply raising the tongue high in the back position. In either case the tongue then glides quickly to the neutral vowel *å* as in "sofa." Like all failing diphthongs this sound ends in the neutral vowel.

Read the following words aloud:

| | | |
|---|---|---|
| *b*oor | *c*ure | *f*uror |
| *p*oor | *t*ouri*ng* | *l*ure |
| *d*uration | *s*ure | *r*ural |
| *t*our | *v*elour | |

*Drills for "ŏŏ (r)," Phonetic Symbol* [ʊə]

Read aloud:

1. Surely you will want to tour the moor.
2. He had the furor of a rural boor.
3. The lure of an enduring cure endured for centuries.
4. To be sure and feel secure: INSURE!
5. The rural lass appeared demure and pure to the tourist.
6. She is so proper and so pure
   Full steadfast, stable and demure.
   There is none such, ye may be sure,
     As my swete sweting.
                                      —OLD SONG
7. To the pure all things are pure.
                                      —SHAKESPEARE

## *HOW TO MAKE THE DIPHTHONG* "ō (r)" [oʊə] *OR* "ô (r)" [ɔə]

— "ōr" as in more, core, four —

Say "core." Watch your tongue. Notice whether it begins in a position for "ô" as in awe, or whether it begins in a position of "ō" as in no, and then glides to the neutral vowel "ȧ." Many speakers do not use this diphthong. They say "core" as "kō" and not as "kôĕ." Other speakers say the diphthong with the final tongue position for "r." All forms are acceptable in various localities.

Read the following words aloud:

| | | | | |
|---|---|---|---|---|
| *b*oar | *g*ore | *p*ori*ng* | *v*ortex | *y*ore |
| *p*ore | *c*ore | *sh*ore | *f*loor | |
| *d*oor | *m*ore | *ch*ore | *l*ore | |
| *t*ore | *n*or | *w*ore | *r*oar | |

*Drills for "ō (r)," Phonetic Symbol* [oʊə] *or* [ɔə]

Read aloud:

1. Fourscore and more were gored by the wild boar.
2. The vortex roared around the shores of the Azores.

3. There is nothing but more chores, and more chores.
4. He pored over the gory story of forgotten lore.
5. The floor wore more by the door.
6. Helen, thy beauty is to me
     Like those Nicæan barks of yore,
That gently, o'er a perfumed sea,
     The weary, wayworn wanderer bore
     To his own native shore.

—Poe

7. Let knowledge grow from more to more.

—Anonymous

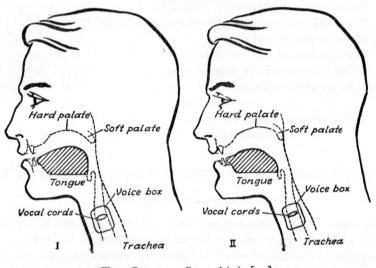

THE SPEAKER SAYS ô(r) [ɔə]

Notice how he begins with ô as in "awe," and then glides to the neutral vowel à. The combination creates the falling diphthong as in "more," "core," "four."

## PROJECTS

*Assignment*

Make a careful analysis of the speech of a prominent radio personality. Come to class prepared to give a talk on the speech sounds used, including articulation of consonants as well as production of vowels and diphthongs. Attempt to weave the technical information into an interesting, informative speech.

*Developing Semantic Skill*

Add to your word cards the following:

I. Words used in the speech text:

| Word | Pronunciation | Meaning |
|------|---------------|---------|
| 1. enunciation | | |
| 2. discriminate | | |
| 3. paradoxical | | |
| 4. pronunciation | | |

II. Words commonly mispronounced:
   1. height
   2. heinous
   3. hiccough

III. Words from your own experience.

## Chapter 14

# STUDY OF PRONUNCIATION

> Words were given us to communicate our ideas, and there must
> be something inconceivably absurd in uttering them in such a manner
> that people cannot understand them or will not desire to understand
> them.
>
> —Lord Chesterfield

Pronunciations are acquired by a process of imitation. You have not
noticed the way you have been pronouncing words because you
have been more concerned with expressing your ideas or feelings.
You have used sounds merely as a means to an end. However, since
many differences in pronunciation exist, the question of preference
arises.

Whether or not America will ever establish a standard speech is
a question of vital concern to language scholars. Increased means
of communication, such as the radio and the motion pictures, are
tending to increase the possibility that it will. Systematic attempts
at teaching a standard used by the educated classes are being made
in order to eliminate the social handicaps certain pronunciations
create. Even popular songs express the dilemma of two people whose
speech indicates the difference in their social background. One uses
the type of pronunciation of one set of speakers and the other uses
the type of pronunciation used by a different set. As a college student, you will be wise to acquire the forms used by the educated
speakers in your community.

Every speaker uses several styles of speaking. These vary from
your most careful style to your most familiar style. The difficulty
arises when your most careful style is not suitable for your purpose.
For example, the college graduate who takes a job with day laborers
must adjust to their way of speaking if he is to get along with them.
Usually, however, you are concerned with the problem of improving
your most careful style of pronunciation so that it will meet the

standards set by professional and social groups. These are the groups with which you desire to associate easily and freely.

Before you can begin a study of pronunciation, you must know something about the nature of language. Language is living and changes from one generation to the next. Originally, spelling attempted to provide a written picture for the oral form of the word. Yet most spellings are inadequate for this purpose as alphabets do not represent the sounds of the word accurately. Once the word is written down, the spelling tends to influence the pronunciation, and we have what is called a "spelling pronunciation." This is particularly true of place names as pronounced by people who have never heard the name but have seen its written form. Such spelling pronunciations tend to become the standard, and the original pronunciation of the word may drop out. The study of changes in pronunciation, and the factors that influence them, is fascinating. The student of language understands the relationship of dialect to the standard form and realizes that the standard is merely the particular dialect which has been preferred by the majority of cultured speakers.

As most people are influenced greatly by the written form of the word, they tend to think of this form as the word itself. When they begin to improve their pronunciation, they study the word with the idea that each letter must be sounded. As a matter of fact, the unphonetic English alphabet is almost totally inadequate as a guide to pronunciation; e.g., key and quay are pronounced alike, although the spelling would lead the reader to believe they had different sounds. The late George Bernard Shaw was so struck with this problem that he left the bulk of his estate to the cause of evolving a new phonetic alphabet for the English language.

In any systematic study of pronunciation, it is necessary, therefore, to devise some method of making the written form represent the oral form more accurately. The most commonly used devices to achieve this are: (1) the system of phonetic respelling by means of diacritical markings, as used in most dictionaries, and (2) the use of a phonetic alphabet such as the I.P.A., in which each symbol represents one sound and each sound has but one symbol. The phonetic alphabet is preferred to the diacritical markings because each symbol stands for a sound with definite acoustic properties. The production of a vowel can be described by reference to a neutral-vowel on a cardinal-vowel scale, and the production of a consonant by accurate descriptions of the movements of the vocal organs. The diacritical markings, on the other hand, are generally defined by the use of sample or key words, *e.g.*, "a" as in p*a*le, g*a*te, p*a*y, etc. The person who mispronounces the key word would automatically mispronounce the word he had looked up in the dictionary; *e.g.*, "oi" as in oil and noisy would be read as erl and nersy by a speaker with local dialect. As a matter of fact, the dictionary does describe the production of each of the sounds in the introductory section under "Pronunciation," but very few people who use the dictionary are aware that they need to learn how to make certain sounds correctly.

The treatment of "Pronunciation" given in the Introduction to *Webster's New International Dictionary* (second edition) should be read, for it is the best compact description of the topic you can find. The list of words with their stressed and unstressed forms found on p. xxxviii should be studied. The greatest danger in the conscious attempt to improve pronunciation is the tendency to overlook the fact that in English one form is used when a word is stressed, and several forms are used when the word is not stressed. All words listed in the dictionary are given the pronunciation they would have if stressed, and it is necessary in speaking to use the proper form, whether stressed or unstressed, according to the meaning intended. For this reason, it is well to listen to the speech of the most careful speakers, as well as to check your pronunciation with that recorded in the dictionary. Remember always that the purpose of speech is communication, and avoid unusual pronunciations which detract from the power of the message you intend to convey.

## Projects

### Student Preparation

The following words are listed in order to draw your attention to certain errors commonly made in pronouncing them. Read each word aloud. Determine whether you use the correct or incorrect form. Check the form you use ( $\sqrt{}$ ). If you find you have been using incorrect forms, you may appeal to the instructor who has additional practice material planned to solve your particular difficulty.[1]

---

[1] For all articulation difficulties refer to practice material in Chaps. 11 and 12.

## SUBSTITUTIONS OF ONE SOUND FOR ANOTHER

| n for ng | | d for t | | oi for ɚ | |
|---|---|---|---|---|---|
| doin | doing | liddle | little | nois | nurse |
| comin | coming | twendy | twenty | goil | girl |
| runnin | running | pardy | party | thoid | third |

| ERRONEOUS INSERTIONS | | ERRONEOUS OMISSIONS | |
|---|---|---|---|
| athaletic | athletic | pom | poem |
| filum | film | amist | amidst |
| acrosst | across | duke | djuke |
| forehead | foread | histry | history |
| umberella | umbrella | evning | evening |
| often | ofen | factry | factory |
| subtle | sutle | famly | family |
| ekscape | escape | reconize | recognize |

### MISPLACEMENT OF ACCENTUATION [2]

On which syllable do you accent the following:

| | | | |
|---|---|---|---|
| adult | corral | inquiry | vagary |
| address | formidable | mischievous | grimace |
| finance | despicable | adept | irremediable |
| financial | theater | ribald | irreparable |
| romance | advertisement | apotheosis | antipode |
| research | ignoble | aspirant | antipodes |
| influence | ally | desultory | ineffable |
| robust | defects | impotent | recondite |
| secretary | irrevocable | incomparable | askance |
| dictionary | indissoluble | inclement | concomitant |

*Assignment 1*

The universal use of radio and talking motion pictures in our country has led certain phoneticians to believe that America may attain a standard speech. Other speech authorities claim such a thing is too distant to talk about and probably will never happen. *Do you think the radio and cinema are fashioning a standard American speech?*

[2] Some words are accented differently when used as different parts of speech, *e.g.*, "frequent" or "frequent," the adjective and the verb.

Select a chairman and three student speakers to prepare a panel discussion. Each panel member will present a three-minute speech on some aspects of the question. The panel will be then allowed a ten-minute discussion period. Following this, the meeting will be opened to audience participation under the direction of the chairman.

*Assignment 2: Pronunciation Bee*

The pronunciation bee adds zest to the study of words and provides a stimulating final oral drill. It can be conducted like the old-fashioned spelling bee. If the class is large, an elimination contest may be held to select the ten best contestants. Students line up around the room. Each student pronounces a word from the list in turn. If a student mispronounces a word, the class calls out "down," and he takes his seat. The word is passed on to the next student until it has been correctly pronounced. It is wise to use one authority, such as Webster. The bee continues until only one student remains. Another possibility is to divide the class into two teams and to have the members of the teams alternate in pronouncing words from the list. As a member fails to pronounce the word correctly, he takes his seat. The team with the most members left at the end wins.

### WORD LIST FOR PRONUNCIATION BEE

| | | |
|---|---|---|
| 1. abdomen | 20. askance | 39. canine |
| 2. absorb | 21. aspirant | 40. casualty |
| 3. acclimate | 22. aunt | 41. catch |
| 4. adage | 23. aviator | 42. cello |
| 5. address | 24. azure | 43. chasm |
| 6. adult | 25. bacillus | 44. chimera |
| 7. aerial | 26. bade | 45. chiropodist |
| 8. again | 27. badinage | 46. clandestine |
| 9. agile | 28. banquet | 47. clique |
| 10. alias | 29. bequeath | 48. coiffure |
| 11. alien | 30. bestial | 49. column |
| 12. ally | 31. bibliophile | 50. combatant |
| 13. almond | 32. bicycle | 51. comely |
| 14. amateur | 33. blasé | 52. condolence |
| 15. amenable | 34. blatant | 53. conjugal |
| 16. apparatus | 35. bourgeois | 54. contemplative |
| 17. Arctic | 36. bravado | 55. conversant |
| 18. arraign | 37. brochure | 56. credulity |
| 19. ask | 38. candelabra | 57. culinary |

58. cynosure
59. data
60. deaf
61. debris
62. debut
63. decade
64. decorum
65. definitive
66. demise
67. depot
68. despicable
69. diamond
70. dirigible
71. disputant
72. divan
73. docile
74. dossier
75. dramatis
    personae
76. draught
77. duty
78. ego
79. elm
80. ennui
81. entree
82. ephemeral
83. epitome
84. epoch
85. exemplary
86. exquisite
87. extant
88. facile
89. falcon
90. fetish
91. fiancé
92. fifth
93. film
94. flaccid
95. forehead
96. fragile
97. fungi
98. gala

99. gallant
100. genuine
101. gesture
102. ghoul
103. gibbet
104. gist
105. gondola
106. government
107. grandeur
108. gratis
109. grimace
110. height
111. herculean
112. homeopathy
113. hygiene
114. ignoramus
115. importune
116. inchoate
117. inclement
118. inexorable
119. inexplicable
120. infantile
121. inquiry
122. inveigle
123. iodine
124. iron
125. irrevocable
126. just
127. juvenile
128. lamentable
129. language
130. larynx
131. laugh
132. leisure
133. lenient
134. lethal
135. literature
136. loathe
137. longevity
138. lyceum
139. mausoleum
140. memoir

141. miniature
142. mirage
143. mischievous
144. museum
145. naïve
146. nomenclature
147. oasis
148. obligatory
149. often
150. orchestra
151. orgies
152. orotund
153. otiose
154. parquet
155. pediatrics
156. penal
157. percolator
158. peremptory
159. persiflage
160. philatelist
161. pianoforte
162. picture
163. piquant
164. plebeian
165. plethora
166. poem
167. poignant
168. poinsettia
169. posthumous
170. precedent
171. precocious
172. premier
173. presage
174. prestige
175. program
176. protégé
177. psalm
178. pseudonym
179. puerile
180. qualm
181. quay
182. quintuplets

| | | |
|---|---|---|
| 183. raillery | 200. strata | 218. vagary |
| 184. recipe | 201. strength | 219. valet |
| 185. rendezvous | 202. subtle | 220. vase |
| 186. reputable | 203. suggest | 221. vaudeville |
| 187. research | 204. suite | 222. verbatim |
| 188. résumé | 205. surveillance | 223. vignette |
| 189. rout | 206. tepid | 224. visa |
| 190. route | 207. theater | 225. vis-à-vis |
| 191. sagacious | 208. tomato | 226. voluminous |
| 192. saline | 209. toward | 227. vowel |
| 193. salutary | 210. travail | 228. wholly |
| 194. schism | 211. trough | 229. wont |
| 195. secretary | 212. trousseau | 230. wraith |
| 196. senile | 213. truths | 231. youths |
| 197. sinecure | 214. turgid | 232. zephyr |
| 198. slough | 215. turquoise | 233. zoological |
| 199. status | 216. ultimatum | 234. zwieback |
| | 217. umbrella | |

*Developing Semantic Skill*

Add to your word cards the following:

I. Words used in the speech text:

| *Word* | *Pronunciation* | *Meaning* |
|---|---|---|
| 1. associate | | |
| 2. diacritics | | |
| 3. dilemma | | |
| 4. influence | | |

II. Words commonly mispronounced:
 1. juvenile
 2. lamentable
 3. length

III. Words from your own experience.

### REFERENCES

BARROWS, SARAH T., and ANNA D. CORDTS, *The Teachers' Word Book of Phonetics.* Boston: Ginn & Company, 1926.

KENYON, JOHN SAMUEL, *American Pronunciation*, 6th ed., rev. Ann Arbor: George Wahr, 1937.

KNOTT, THOMAS A., "How the Dictionary Determines What Pronunciation to Use," *Quarterly Journal of Speech*, Vol. XXI, No. 1, February, 1935.

KRAPP, GEORGE P., *English Language in America*, 2 vols. New York: D. Appleton-Century Company, 1925.

LOUNSBURY, THOMAS R., "Linguistic Causes of Americanisms," *Harper's Magazine*, Vol. 127, June, 1913.

McLEAN, MARGARET P., *Good American Speech*, rev. ed. New York: E. P. Dutton & Co., Inc., 1935.

MENCKEN, H. L., *The American Language*, 4th ed. New York: Alfred A. Knopf, Inc., 1936.

RIPMAN, WALTER, *Good Speech*. New York: E. P. Dutton & Co., Inc., 1924.

SAPIR, EDWARD, *Language*. New York: Harcourt, Brace and Company, Inc., 1921.

SWEET, HENRY, *A Primer of Spoken English*. Oxford: Clarendon Press, 1890.

# PART V. PUBLIC SPEAKING

Human activities tend to develop into forms. The nature of such forms depends upon recurring elements in the activities. Thus, in literature, the forms of poetry, drama, and prose arose, and within these forms more specific patterns evolved. In speaking situations there is an analogous growth. From simple person-to-person communications there gradually arose an act called "public speaking." Let us look at the reasons which impel men to speak publicly.

One member of a group had an unusual experience. The experience was realized only when he could share it with his fellow men. The frequency of such situations led to a pattern of speaking called the *informative speech*.

The sharing of happy moments adds enrichment to life. Human interest and enjoyment are spread when one transmits his experience to others. So universal was this desire to share pleasant moments that there arose a second pattern of speaking situations called *fellowship situations*.

Again, one man perceived that a certain action was essential to the well-being of his community. Like Demosthenes, he sought to arouse his audience to take definite action. If a man foresees the doom of his country, he cannot rest until he has moved his fellow men to take action. The recurrence of such situations led to the third major type of speech situation, namely, the *persuasive situation*.

Finally, the discovery of truth comes first to an individual and then is communicated to a people. Picture the struggle for the acceptance of the germ theory or the importance of the vitamin. When the discovery deals with future actions such truths are more difficult to have accepted. Yet so common have been the efforts of the discoverer to transmit truth that a pattern of situations has developed called the *deliberative* or *convincing situation*.

These, therefore, constitute the four general aims of public speaking: *information, fellowship, persuasion, deliberation*.

Warren Austin, United States Ambassador to the United Nations, is noted for his deliberate manner of speaking and his keen perception of fallacies in the opposition. Notice the energy with which he denounces a statement made in the Security Council of the United Nations. His gestures are an eloquent language in themselves.

*Chapter 15*

# HOW TO PREPARE A SPEECH

> In my library are about a thousand volumes of biography—a rough calculation indicates that more of these deal with men who talked themselves upward than with all the scientists, writers, saints, and doers combined. Talkers always have ruled. They will continue to rule. The smart thing is to join them.
>
> —BRUCE BARTON

## THE INTRODUCTION

There are three purposes of a good introduction: to establish friendliness, to arouse interest, and to provide necessary information. It is the speaker's responsibility to render the audience friendly, interested, and informed. Since these three requisites are true of all public-speaking situations, they are worth considering at some length.

### Establishing Friendliness

Speak to your audience as you would speak to a group of friends. The basis of friendly relations is mutual respect, and you dignify your audience by the respect you show them. Shakespeare gives an example of such dignity in *Hamlet* when Hamlet asks Polonius how he will treat the wandering players.

HAMLET: Good, my lord, will you see the players well bestow'd.
POLONIUS: My lord, I will treat them according to their desert.
HAMLET: God's bodykins, man, better. Use every man after his desert, and who should scape whipping? Use them after your own honour and dignity. The less they deserve, the more merit is in your bounty.

Never talk down to an audience. This is a public declaration of their inferiority and invariably meets with resentment. Rather seek to establish a mood of fellow human beings sharing common problems. Remember, it is the compatibility of interests that creates

175

friendship. If you respect the interests of the audience, you respect the professed desires of that audience.

### Identify Yourself with Your Cause

The speaker who feels above his cause will fail to contact his audience. Long before a speaker gets to his point the audience has made up its mind to believe or to disbelieve him. When Richelieu cried "I am France," he epitomized the devotion of all great men to great causes. There is an enthusiastic response on the part of an audience when brought face to face with sincere devotion. To be truly eloquent you must identify yourself with your cause. Only such sincerity moves men.

Have confidence in yourself and in your audience. Their friendliness is shown by their willingness to listen; your friendliness is shown by your desire to tell your story. Friendliness is the attitude which wins the audience, and sincerity keeps their good will.

### Arousing Interest

Interest is basic to every part of a speech. Think of the three principal parts of your speech as:

Beginning ..................... gaining interest
Middle ...................... sustaining interest
End .......................... crystallizing interest

There are four linguistic principles that can assist you in arousing interest. These are valuable because they specifically indicate means of making any message interesting. The four principles are: epigrams, alliteration, antithesis, and balance.

An *epigram* or slogan is an apt expression of a professed truth. Every cause must be refined into a slogan to have lasting coinage. People act on slogans; nations go to war for slogans; and civilizations survive by their devotion to a conceived truth expressed in an apt way. Slogans epitomize the control of emotion over reason. They are lasting indexes of men's faith in shibboleths. Hence, you must beware of them, see through them, and be ready to use them persuasively in the interest of a true cause.

*Alliteration* is the repetition of initial sounds in two or more closely related words or stressed syllables. It is helpful in slogans as the repetition heightens the meaning. Advertisers use it frequently, as "cream of the crop," "heading home for Hoffman," "music in the modern manner," "melody-masters and their magic music." It should not be used too frequently, however, or it loses its effect.

*Antithesis* is a figure of speech characterized by strongly contrasting words, clauses, sentences, or ideas. As a seasoning in your talk, antithesis can give point and vigor to your views. Used sparingly, it aids in making distinctions, as "man proposes, God disposes," or to point observations, as "We hate the sin, but love the sinner," or,

> The hungry judges soon the sentence sign,
> And wretches hang that jurymen may dine.
> —Pope

*Balance* is the technique of arranging clauses or sentences so as to emphasize contrast in meaning. Balance is an effective structure in speaking as it leads to applause and is remembered. When an epigram has balance it carries a grace note of effectiveness. Consider the balance of

> It's not the hours you put in,
> But what you put into the hours.

or

> The memory of other authors is kept alive by their works
> But the memory of Johnson keeps many of his works alive.
> —Macaulay

## Informing the Audience

The audience must know what you propose to prove. If it is confused on this point, there can be nothing but further confusion as you offer your proof. It is your duty to make it as easy as possible for the audience to follow you. Make a clear statement of the proposition. This may require that the wording of the proposition be defined, or the meaning made clear by analogy, or the point at issue be sharply focused. An audience refuses to set itself in a receptive mood until it knows which side of a question the speaker favors. Only when your position is unpopular is it wise to keep the audience in suspense.

It is not enough simply to announce the proposition. An audience has too many distractions at the beginning of a speech to grasp the proposition. You must tie the proposition to the occasion and reiterate it in various forms. The surest way to inform the audience is to *state* the proposition; *show* its relation to the audience, to the occasion, and to the day; *fashion* it into a metaphor; *paraphrase* it; and finally *give a specific instance.*

Informing the audience is sometimes the most difficult step. Often you are too impetuous to get on with the proof, too eager to establish your convictions. The young lawyer makes the same mistake. But watch an experienced lawyer gain an admission from a witness. He never asks a blunt question, gains an admission, and files away his evidence. Rather he seeks to use that evidence to make the best impression on the jury. With the patience of the gods on Olympus who have eternity before and after them, he proceeds to get as many varied admissions as possible. Start your speech effectively by using the same technique. Repeat your point in a variety of ways until you are certain the audience understands your point of view.

### Body of the Speech

The form of a speech is determined by the purpose of the situation. For example, if the audience is simply to be *informed,* you need only relate clearly what you are talking about; if they are assembled to be *entertained,* you need only seek to tickle their risibility. If, however, they are to be *convinced,* the problem becomes more involved: They must understand; they must see one side as preferable to another; and they must form a judgment. If they are to be *persuaded,* they must not only be convinced but moved to action.

To assist you in analyzing the basic purpose of your talks the Four Function Form has been designed. It summarizes the principal parts of speechmaking. Use it as a guide in the preparation of your talks.

### Four Function Form

I. To gain audience attention by rendering audience
   A. Friendly.
   B. Interested.
   C. Well informed.
II. To state and elaborate the nature of your proposition by
   A. Explaining its uniqueness.
   B. Its relation to the *status quo.*
   C. Its particular difference with opposition (issue).
   D. The need for its acceptance.

III. To convince or persuade the audience by
    A. Reasoning logically from general principles.
    B. Reasoning logically from particular instances.
    C. Furnishing evidence to substantiate your position by
        1. Testimony—statements of authority.
        2. Circumstances—factors surrounding the situation which strengthen your position.
IV. To recapitulate vitally what you have established by
    A. Summary of main points established by reiteration in succinct form.
    B. Use of an epigram or slogan.
    C. Repetition of proposition as conclusion.

## CONCLUSION

Most beginning speakers neglect the conclusion. They feel that all they have to do is to state their case. Do not make that mistake. Many times, the only part of the talk that the audience remembers is the conclusion. Be certain you let the audience know *exactly* what you want them to do. If you ask them to do nothing, that is exactly what they will do. But if you make your conclusion a definite, specific action, your audience is likely to follow your suggestion.

The most recent validation of this principle of final suggestion was reported by Horton & Henry, the New York sales consultants. They conducted a hidden-microphone survey on the effectiveness of 600 jewelry salesmen. This unique method enabled the Sterling Silversmiths Guild of America to eavesdrop on salesmen in a typical business day. It showed:

1. About half the time the salesmen made no effort to close the sale but waited for the customer to make up his mind.

2. Some 10 per cent used a negative sales method, suggesting that maybe the customer ought to think it over and come back later.

3. Where the salesmen used good closing methods, the sales were made in 70 per cent of the cases; the negative approach yielded not a single result.

The conclusion provides you with an added opportunity to present your case briefly to the audience. Its force consists in reminding the audience that you have proved your point. Further, the conclusion is valuable as a final plea for action. Quickly reviewing the main arguments, you can form them into a more believable pattern leading to your proposal. If possible, fashion a slogan which summates your case.

### GATHERING MATERIAL

The most important step in the preparation of your speech is the gathering of the material. The value of a speech depends upon the quality of the material presented. You may secure the material from your own experience, the experiences of others obtained from personal interviews with them, group discussions, or by letters and questionnaires. Books, newspaper articles, journals, pamphlets, and encyclopedias will give you a wealth of information that will give your talks variety, interest, and authority.

When you begin to prepare your speech, determine its purpose. Study your audience.[1] Make a tentative outline and then begin to gather your material. Do not slight your own experiences. Material from personal experience is vivid and concrete and gives color to your talk. Your experiences camping will prove more entertaining to the audience than some other person's if you can draw upon a wealth of unique details. The facts you present will be real and vital. If you have been to a scientific exhibit or to a showing of paintings, you can more easily describe the event to your audience. Moreover, when you speak from experience, you have confidence and assurance. So do not hesitate to draw upon your own experiences as material for your speeches.

You can give scope to your speech by turning to other sources of information to supplement your own experiences. Much can be learned from interviews with other members of the community. When properly approached, people are usually quite willing to give you the results of their experience with your subject. It takes tact and ability to draw others out, but the results are worth the effort involved. Be careful to quote accurately all those whom you interview.

Give your speech variety and timeliness by using the wealth of printed materials available on your topic. Note your material and

[1] Review Chap. 2. Refer to the Situation Analysis Chart.

its source on small cards. Such a system gives you flexibility in arranging material and reveals the part of your speech which needs additional research.

## USE OF OUTLINES

Speech is the interchange of thought and feeling between two or more persons by the use of symbols called "words." When the thought or feeling is simple, there is little difficulty in its communication. When it is complex, difficulty arises. For instance, the idea "stop" can be readily and effectively communicated by a single word. Yet this word cannot indicate the manner of stopping, nor which part of an intricate process is meant, nor intermittent stopping and starting. In other words, the more complicated an operation becomes, the more need exists for some method of arrangement. Hence, there is a vital need for arranging what you intend to communicate to your listeners.

The primary element of a good outline is orderly arrangement: the placing of each item of information in relation to the other facts at your disposal. This orderly placing reveals the connections between facts. It enables you to discard unimportant material and to strengthen the connection between important facts.

As in the framework of a building, order in your outline determines the form of the structure that is to be erected. A weak connection in an outline is like a skyscraper with a weak third floor. A gap in the thought pattern in your outline is like a building without a third floor. Such mistakes lead to vagueness and misunderstanding, so make your outline represent the framework you wish to imprint on the mind of your listeners.

The value of an outline is that it presents to your mind the connection between the parts of your speech. You use words and sentences to communicate some order or pattern of thought to your audience. How often have you said to yourself, "I wish I could make this clear to you. I see it all in perfect order." At such times, you were experiencing failure to communicate an outline of your thought. Whether you speak to one person or five thousand, the problem of transmitting your pattern of thought is present. The clearer it is in your mind, the easier the task of communication.

Make your outline serve this double purpose: to secure organization of your own thought, and to aid in the transmission of that thought.

### Types of Outlines

Outlines are of different types. Chief among these are: (1) the topical, (2) the sentence, (3) the paragraph, and (4) the précis. Each type has a special advantage, so strive to become proficient in the use of all of them.

### Topical outline

The topical type consists of blocking out the organization by the use of topics. This arrangement aids in gaining effective subordination. This outline is used chiefly as a means to determine the over-all picture. The danger in its use is that it tends to become diffuse and it lacks connectives.

### Sentence outline

The sentence-type outline is known in the legal profession as a "brief." It is a plan of connected sentences logically related in light of some stated proposition. It deals with the connection of the judgments expressed in sentences. It provides for the inclusion of statements and evidence as well as the main contentions. Its value is that it reveals the logical relationship between your proposition and your proof, and provides for accurate expression in sentence form. Make your headings in complete sentences. A safeguard for your logical arrangement is to add the word "because" or "for" after main sentences. The sentence-form outline is best for all types of exposition and argumentation.

### Paragraph outline

The paragraph type is popularly known as the "writing-it-out-of-you stage." Some speakers have found it successful to put on paper all their thoughts about a subject. Generally, this is done without regard for the connections between the ideas. It represents the order in which the ideas come to mind. This has advantages when the subject has many ramifications, or when aspects are little understood and likely to escape notice. It must, however, be followed by some method of arrangement.

*Précis outline*

The précis form of outline is used to summarize the work of another. It consists in giving an epitome of the essential points covered. It is brief, yet complete. Its chief use is in organizing the contents of a writing or speech. This form is significant for you because it develops the ability to discern and remember essentials.

The above types are neither exclusive nor exhaustive. Any combination found suitable by you is a valid type of outline. Moreover, you may find it convenient to use some features of each. Before the artist finally evolves a style of his own, he goes through a period of imitation and random improvisations. Consider your outlines as instruments for imitation and improvisation. Imitate them on principle, master their use, and change them to your convenience.

## PROJECTS

*Assignment*

The purpose in this part of your course is to teach you how to speak publicly. To do this, a simple routine has been established. Information and principles are given, and a series of graded experiences suggested. These projects have a unique quality: They demonstrate every speech you are required to give. They ask you to follow the examples of men who have succeeded in influencing human behavior, and, as Coleridge recommended, "to imitate them on principle." This is a proved technique.

Your first assignment is to read the two speeches following and study carefully the analyses given. In the next class meeting, your instructor will discuss the speeches with you and resolve any difficulties encountered.

### DON'T DIE ON THIRD!

### By W. J. Cameron

Tonight, the students of Greenfield Village and the Edison Institute are present as guests and participants in the program. Last year, on a similar occasion, we told a story. We shall attempt to tell a story—a true story—tonight.

It was 25 years ago, when the Detroit Tigers were playing the team from Cleveland. The score was a tie. It was the last half of the ninth, and two men were out. The fate of the game rested with Moriarty, the white-bloused figure that shuttled back and forth at third base. As the decisive moment approached, Tigers and Naps stood up at their benches, and

18,000 spectators bent forward in tense expectancy. Moriarty was on third.

He had come there in the ordinary way. At bat he had hit the ball and run to first. The next batter had bunted and sacrificed to move Moriarty on to second. Then a "long fly" had advanced him to third. There he stood, alert in every nerve, his powerful running legs, his quick eye and quicker brain holding the hazard of the game.

Much as it meant to have advanced that far, third base runs are not marked up on the scoreboard. Third base is not a destination—it is the last way station on the road "home." The world is full of third bases. To leave school, to earn your college degree, to enter a profession, is only to start toward third base. To get the job you want, even to become the head of your business, is merely to reach third base. Third base is opportunity, and opportunity is not arrival, it is only another point of departure. Attain the White House itself, and you have only got as far as third base. The test of all you have is yet to come. No time for self-applause at third— many a promising run has died there. And there stood Moriarty. If he failed it was not alone, the team failed with him. Concentrated on him at that moment were the hopes and fears of thousands who seemed to hold their breath, and so still was the great park that even the breeze seemed forgetful to blow.

One way to get off third is to wait for someone to bat you off. Another is to get away on your own initiative—Moriarty chose *that*. He knew his game. He knew the catcher's signals called for a ball thrown high to Mullin, who was now at bat. He knew that a runner might duck low to touch the home plate while the catcher's mitt was in the air for a high ball. He knew that in throwing high, pitchers "wind up" in a certain way. He knew also that pitchers have a way of "winding up" when they don't intend to throw. He knew, moreover, that *this* pitcher, being left-handed, could not keep watch on third while delivering the ball—the runner might safely take a longer lead. *Moriarty knew all the ins and outs of his job.* Luck might lie in the lap of the gods, but preparation, knowledge, judgment *and initiative* were with the player.

Had Moriarty waited for Mullin to bat, Mullin might have failed him, ending the inning. One opening remained: make "home" between the moment the pitch was begun past all recall, and the moment the ball struck the catcher's mitt—make "home" in the fraction of time Mullin's hit or miss hung in futurity. That would be a contest in speed between a five-ounce ball delivered with all the force of a superb pitching arm and the 170-pound body of Moriarty! An unequal contest, for the pitched ball travels only 60 feet while the runner from third must hurl his body over a distance of 90 feet.

Moriarty is on third. He builds his prospective run as an engineer builds a bridge across a torrent, with infinite pains. Now the Cleveland pitcher is poising himself for a throw. Moriarty is crouched like a tiger ready to spring—*Now!* There is a white streak across the field! A cloud of dust at the home plate! The umpire stands over it with hands extended, palms down. That old baseball park echoes and re-echoes with a thunderous roar of acclaim, which bursts forth again and again in thrilling electric power. Every eye strains toward the man who is slapping the dust from his white uniform. *Moriarty is Home!*

It was only a run made in the course of a baseball game; but it has been saying to us these many years—*Don't die on third.* You may be put out, but it need not be by your inaction. If the run must die, let it die *trying.* All of us are on bases. Some of us are waiting for someone to bat us further. Suppose he misses! Mullin missed the ball that day—had Moriarty waited, he would not have scored. It would not be right to say that all the world's a baseball diamond—it *does* offer us the ever-present choice between indolence and initiative, but life's rules are fairer. In life there is an inner scoreboard where every effort is credited to your record. Many a valiant run is lost, but the valor of it builds the soul. So, while there's one thing yet to do, and there's always one thing yet to do, or a fraction of time to do it in, *don't die on third.* Study conditions, learn all you can, use all you learn, summon your strength and courage, defy luck— and then, bold player—just by doing this, *you have already scored.* Something great is strengthened within you. The run may fail, but *you* have not, and there's another game tomorrow.

*Outline*

I. Introduction.
   A. The speaker greets the audience.
   B. Detroit vs. Cleveland game is on.
   C. Moriarty is on third.
II. Discussion.
   A. Third base is not a destination.
   B. Moriarty knew his game.
   C. Moriarty challenges a pitched ball.
   D. Moriarty runs.
III. Conclusion.
   A. Don't die on third.
      1. Keep on trying.
      2. Life credits effort.
      3. There's another game tomorrow.

*Analysis*

*Introduction.* Cameron wins the *friendship* of his audience by a personal reference in his welcome. He uses the occasion and the event of his guests' former visit to establish kinship and praises them tactfully. He arouses *interest* by selecting a story, a traditional means of interest, but selects it wisely since the audience is of baseball age, and the time is the beginning of the baseball season. Purposely, the speaker delays *informing* his audience of the proposition. Instead, he creates the setting for his story and personalizes the outcome by describing his central character, Moriarty.

*Discussion.* Cameron delays the statement of his proposition by the skillful use of two digressions and by a dramatic description. This is necessary because the simple recital of the fact that Moriarty stole home would be uninteresting unless the audience felt they knew Moriarty and wanted him to win. Cameron awakens affections for Moriarty by a recital of his worth, and then treats the audience to a dramatic "photo finish." The first digression, *a passage helping the speaker's purpose but not directly proving his proposition,* occurs in paragraph four when the speaker generalizes about the third bases of life. He develops his digression by a contrast, "third is not a destination," and by a series of metaphors, *implied likenesses between things in different categories.* Cameron cast his metaphors in a fiction, *an imaginative device expressing a message in a novel and attractive form,* by comparing the journey to third base with the normal progress of life. He returns to his central character, Moriarty, and by an apt use of circumstance brings the audience back to the ball park, recapturing suspense by personifying the breeze in a hyperbole, *a fanciful exaggeration.*

The second digression is an encomium on skill and is developed by iteration, *insistence on the same truth in varied ways.* The speaker reiterates the factors which constitute skill. He gains credence by the constant repetition of "he knew" followed by each element of skill. This is done six times. Finally, he sums up these factors as the unique possessions of Moriarty and concludes the comparison of initiative and skill with a cliché, "luck might be in the lap of the gods."

A graphic description sets the scene for the climax. First, Moriarty's dilemma is revealed: Will he run or won't he? and this is developed by circumstance and contrast. A parallel structure heightens the unevenness of the contest. The speaker's language sharpens the contrast of a "five-ounce ball" versus "170-pound body" and "the pitched ball travels only 60 feet" versus "while the runner from third must hurl his body over a distance of 90 feet." Cameron brings the audience back to the scene by a statement of fact: "Moriarty is on third." Again sympathy is thrown to Moriarty by a simile comparing his skill to the careful planning of an engineer. Then the speaker builds suspense by referring to the dramatic circumstances surrounding the run while he delays the result for a smashing climax: "Moriarty is home."

*Conclusion.* Cameron crystallizes his proposition in a proverb, *a brief epigrammatic saying or a popular byword:* "Don't die on third!" He elaborates his conclusion by contrasting Mullin's failure to hit with Moriarty's success. He strengthens his analogy, *a relation of likeness between two things,* between baseball and life by emphasizing the fairness of life. He maintains the baseball figure by calling character "an inner scoreboard." He enters a final plea by reiterating his proposition and culminates his proof by reference to an undeniable truth: "there's another game tomorrow."

### "WHICH KNEW NOT JOSEPH"

### By Bruce Barton

There are two stories—and neither of them is new—which I desire to tell you, because they have a direct application to everyone's business. The first concerns a member of my profession, an advertising man, who was in the employ of a circus. It was his function to precede the circus into various communities, distribute tickets to the editor, put up on the barns pictures of the bearded lady and the man-eating snakes, and finally to get in touch with the proprietor of some store and persuade him to purchase the space on either side of the elephant for his advertisement in the parade.

Coming one day to a crossroads town, our friend found that there was only one store. The proprietor did not receive him enthusiastically. "Why should I advertise?" he demanded. "I have been here for twenty years. There isn't a man, woman or child around these parts that doesn't know where I am and what I sell." The advertising man answered very promptly (because in our business if we hesitate we are lost), and he said to the proprietor, pointing across the street, "What is that building over there?" The proprietor answered, "That is the Methodist Episcopal Church." The advertising man said, "How long has that been there?" The proprietor said, "Oh, I don't know; seventy-five years probably." "*And yet,*" exclaimed the advertising man, "*they ring the church bell every Sunday morning.*"

My second story has also a religious flavor. It relates to a gentleman named Joseph, who is now deceased.

Those of you who were brought up on the Bible may have found there some account of his very remarkable business career. Those of you who have not read that book may have heard of Joseph through the works of Rudyard Kipling.

Said Mr. Kipling:

> "Who shall doubt the secret hid
> Under Cheops' pyramid
> Was that the contractor did
> Cheops out of several millions
> And that Joseph's sudden rise
> To comptroller of supplies
> Was a graft of monstrous size
> Worked on Pharaoh's swart civilians."

The account of Joseph in the Old Testament is much more complete and to his credit. It tells how he left his country under difficulties and, coming into a strange country, he rose, through his diligence, to become the principal person in the state, second only to the King. Now, gentlemen, the Biblical narrative brings us to that point—the point where Joseph had public relations with all the other ancient nations, while his private relations held all the best-paying jobs—it brings us up to the climax of his career and then it hands us an awful jolt. Without any words of preparation or explanation, it says bluntly:

"And the king died, and there arose a new king in Egypt which knew not Joseph."

I submit, gentlemen, that this is one of the most staggering lines which has ever been written in a business biography. Here was a man so famous that everybody knew him and presto, a few people die, a few new ones are born, and *nobody* knows him. The tide of human life has moved on; the king who exalted the friends of Joseph is followed by a king who makes them slaves; all the advertising that the name "Joseph" had enjoyed in one generation is futile and of no avail, *because that generation has gone.*

Now, what has all that to do with you? Very much indeed. When we gathered in this room this afternoon, there were in this country, in bed, sick, several thousand old men. It perhaps is indelicate for me to refer to that fact, but it is a fact, and we are grown up and we have to face these things. On those old men you gentlemen collectively have spent a considerable amount of time and a considerable amount of money. It is to be supposed that you have made some impression upon them regarding your service and your purposes and your necessities. But in this interval, while we have been sitting here, those old men have died and all your time and all your money and whatever you have built up in the way of good-will in their minds—*all* your labor and investment have passed out with them.

In the same brief interval, there have been born in this country several thousand lusty boys and girls to whom you gentlemen mean no more than the Einstein theory. They do not know the difference between a Mazda lamp and a stick of Wrigley's chewing gum. Nobody has ever told them that Ivory Soap floats or that children cry for Castoria, or what sort of soap you ought to use if you want to have a skin that people would like to touch. The whole job of giving them the information they are going to need in order to form an intelligent public opinion and to exercise an intelligent influence in the community has to be started from the beginning and done over again.

So the first very simple thing that I would say to you is that this business of public relations is a very constant business, that the fact that you told your story yesterday should not lead you into the delusion of supposing that you have ever told it. There is probably no fact in the United States that is easier to impress upon people's minds than that Ivory Soap floats, and yet the manufacturers of Ivory Soap think it is not inconsistent or wasteful to spend more than a million dollars a year in repeating that truth over and over again.

Cultivating good-will is a day-by-day and hour-by-hour business, gentlemen. Every day and every hour the "king" dies and there arises a new "king" to whom you and all your works mean absolutely nothing.

Now, the second very simple thing which I might say to you is that in your dealings with the public, in what you write and say, you must be genuine.

When I came to New York a great many years ago I had a lot of trouble with banks. It was very hard to find any bank that would be willing to accept the very paltry weekly deposit that I wanted to make. Finally I discovered one which was not as closely guarded as the others, and I succeeded for a period of three years in being insulted by the teller every Saturday. At the end of three years when I came to draw out my money I had an audience with the vice-president who wanted personally to insult me. I said to myself, If I live and grow old in this town, some day I think I would like to take a crack at this situation.

And so as the years passed (as they have the habit of doing), and I lived and grew old, one day a bank official came in to us and said he would like to have us do some advertising for him. I said to this banker, "Now you go back to your office and shave off all the side-whiskers that there are in your bank and you take all the high hats and carry them out into the back yard of the bank and put them in a pile and light a match to the pile and burn them up, because I am going to advertise to people that you're human, and it may be a shock to have them come in and find you as you are."

So he went back to his bank and I wrote an advertisement which said:

"There is a young man in this town who is looking for a friendly bank; a bank where the officers will remember his name and where some interest will be shown when he comes in," etc.

It was very successful. It was *too* successful. It was so successful that we could not control it, and all over the country there broke out a perfect epidemic, a kind of measles, of "friendly banks." Bankers who had not smiled since infancy and who never had had or needed an electric fan in their offices suddenly sat up and said, "Why, we are friendly."

Well, our bank dropped out. The competition was too keen. But it culminated, I think, in a letter which I saw and which was mailed by the president of a really very important bank in a large city. I won't attempt to quote it verbatim, but it was to this effect:

"Dear Customer: As I sit here all alone in my office on Christmas Eve thinking of you and how much we love you, I really wish that you and every other customer could come in here personally so I could give you a good, sound kiss."

Well, that is a trifle exaggerated, but the fact is this—if you don't feel these things you can't make other people feel them. Emerson said, as you will remember, "What you are thunders so loud I cannot hear what you say." Unless there is back of this desire for better public relations a real conviction, a real genuine feeling that you are in business as a matter of service, not merely as a matter of advertising service—unless there is that, then it is very dangerous, indeed, to attempt to talk to the public. For as sure as you live the public will find you out.

The third very simple thing, and the last thing that I suggest is this: In dealing with the public the great thing is to deal with them simply, briefly, and in language that they can understand.

Two men delivered speeches about sixty years ago at Gettysburg. One man was the greatest orator of his day, and he spoke for two hours and a half, and probably nobody in this room can remember a single word that he said. The other man spoke for considerably less than five minutes, and every school child has at some time learned Lincoln's Gettysburg Address, and remembers it more or less all his life. Many prayers have been uttered in the world—many long, fine-sounding prayers—but the only prayer that any large majority of people have ever learned is the Lord's Prayer, and it is less than two hundred words long. The same thing is true of the Twenty-third Psalm, and there is hardly a Latin word in it. They are short, simple, easily understood words.

You electric light people have one difficulty. I was in Europe this spring, and I rode a great deal in taxicabs. In England I sat in a taxicab and watched the little clock go around in terms of shillings. Then I flew over to Amsterdam and watched it go around in terms of guilders. Then I went down to Brussels and it went around in terms of francs. Then I went to France and it went around in terms of francs of a different value.

I would sit there trying to divide fifteen into one hundred and multiply it by seven, and wonder just where I was getting off, and I have no doubt now that really I was transported in Europe at a very reasonable cost, but because those meters talked to me in terms that were unfamiliar I never stepped out of a taxicab without having a haunting suspicion that probably I had been "gypped."

In a degree you suffer like those taxicab men. You come to Mrs. Barton and you say, "Buy this washing machine and it will do your washing for just a few cents an hour." She says, "Isn't that wonderful!" She buys it, and at the end of a month she sits with your bill in her hands and she says, "We have run this five hours and that will probably be so and so." Then she opens the bill and finds that she has not run it five hours; that she has run it 41 kw. and 11 amp. and 32 volts, and that the amount is not so-and-so but it is $2.67.

Well, that is a matter that I suppose you will eventually straighten out.

Asking an advertising man to talk about advertising at a convention like this is a good deal like asking a doctor to talk about health. I have listened to many such addresses and they are all about the same. The eminent physician says, "Drink plenty of water. Stay outdoors as much as you can. Eat good food. Don't worry. Get eight hours sleep. And if you have anything the matter with you, call a doctor."

So I say to you that there is a certain technique about this matter of dealing with the public, and if you have anything seriously the matter with you—whether it be a big advertising problem or merely a bad letterhead (and some of you have wretched letterheads)—there probably is some advertising doctor in your town who has made a business of the thing, and it may be worth your while to call him in. But in the meantime, and in this very informal and necessarily general talk, I say to you, "Be genuine, be simple, be brief; talk to people in language that they understand; and finally, and most of all, be persistent." You can't expect to advertise when you are in trouble, or about to be in trouble, and expect to get anything in that direction. It is a day-by-day and hour-by-hour business. If the money that has been thrown away by people who advertised spasmodically was all gathered together it would found and endow the most wonderful home in the world for aged advertising men and their widows. Don't throw any more of that money away. If advertising is worth doing at all, it is worth doing all of the time. For every day, gentlemen, the "king" dies, and there arises a new "king" who knows not Joseph.

*Outline*

I. Introduction: Two stories apply to everyone's business.
  A. Church-bell story.
  B. Which knew not Joseph.
II. Body: Public relations must be persistent, genuine, simple.
  A. Public relations must be persistent.
    1. Several thousand men died this afternoon.
    2. Several thousand lusty boys and girls were born this afternoon.
    3. The "king" dies every hour and every day.
  B. Public relations must be genuine.
    1. Fiction of a friendly bank.
    2. Emerson's dictum.
  C. Public relations must be simple.
    1. Brevity: Lincoln's "Gettysburg Address."
    2. Simplicity: the Lord's Prayer, the Twenty-third Psalm.
    3. Language easily understood: European currency, Mrs. Barton's electric bill.
III. Conclusion: Final plea—proposition restated.
  A. Analogy: doctor and advertising man.
  B. Restatement of message.
  C. Completion of extended analogy: Which knew not Joseph.

*Analysis*

Bruce Barton constructed an excellent persuasive speech for a fellowship situation. He set himself the difficult task of delivering a serious message in a humorous and enjoyable manner. His deft use of anecdote, fiction, contrast, and analogy produced an unforgettable framework for his message. He wisely wove the pattern of his speech with the material the occasion presented. Realizing the men were at a convention for social and business contacts, he made the situation pleasurable while deliberately stressing his proposition. By the use of a Biblical story, he graced his message with an association not easily forgotten. He divided his proposition into three main points, and through copious illustrations and instances climactically entered his final plea.

*Introduction.* The speaker achieves the purpose of his introduction by concentrating on the simple functions of an effective opening. He arouses audience *interest* by the use of an anecdote and two versions of a Biblical story. The contrast in the two versions of the Biblical story allows repetition and invites interest through the novelty of the approach. The modernity of the Kipling version of Joseph adds further interest.

The audience is *informed* of the coming message by a process of insinuating the necessity for continual contact. Indeed, the business tragedy of Joseph is stated, "a few people die, a few new ones are born, and nobody knows him." This is heightened by the climactic order of its presentation as it occurs at the end of the introduction. It potently suggests the coming main argument.

The audience is rendered *friendly* by the situation, the humorous approach to the topic, and the novelty of the Biblical interpretation. Joseph as a businessman who, while in office, takes care of his relatives makes history current gossip. This is vivified by the play on the terms, "public relations" and "private relations." Finally, by an apt analogy, the speaker completely modernizes Joseph by assuming his name is an advertising symbol. In selecting the framework and title of Joseph's story, the speaker associates Biblical lore with current business practice and adds a sense of dignity to his business advice. Hence, the speaker has aroused interest, insinuated the topic to be discussed, and won the good will of the listening audience.

*Body of the Speech.* The speaker's proposition is *public relations must be persistent, genuine, and simple.* He divides this message into three main arguments and proceeds to prove each separately. Since the three main parts are not of equal importance, he places *persistency* first and uses the bulk of his introduction to prepare the audience for this argument. Having selected persistency as his strongest argument, the speaker makes use of the situation as a vivid gauge to measure the rapidity with which the old men are passing on and the young men are being born. He interprets his findings in terms of audience interest, and points up his message as identical with their interest. These old men are not just old men passing on, they are the vested interests of the audience. For these vested interests, the advertising men must be willing to build new bonds, constantly renewed for the public—for public relations must be persistent. This leads to a repetition of the need for persistency and an outstanding example of its successful use. He concludes this argument by reference to the keynote analogy of Joseph's story. Hence, he develops the thought by comparison, situational similarity, concrete examples, and reiteration.

The speaker's second argument, *public relations must be genuine,* is developed by an anecdote ideally suited to the situation. It mirrors the struggle of the speaker toward success and thus establishes kinship with the audience. The human role played by the speaker in the anecdote extols him without pretense. The use of fiction, *an imaginative device illustrating a point in a novel manner,* is coupled with hyperbole, *an exaggerated statement,* to form the humorous letter of the friendly bank executive. While this provokes laughter, a useful factor in reception, the speaker is wise enough to dignify his message. This he does by a quotation from Emerson. The deft turning of the pleasantness of the situation to the realization of the proposition is reminiscent of the axiom of Henry Ward Beecher: "Open their mouths with laughter—and shove in the facts."

The speaker's final argument, *public relations must be brief, simple, and expressed in language easily understood,* is a composite proposition, *i.e.,* one subject (public relations) and three predications (brief, simple, and easily understood). The proof offered in support of the proposition falls into the same three divisions: *Brevity* is illustrated by authority of the "Gettysburg Address," *simplicity* by the authority of the Lord's Prayer and the Twenty-third Psalm. Both items are high-lighted by contrast with their opposites. Two anecdotes of common experience furnish the proof of his third argument.

It is worthy of notice that the situation was one which did not require statistical or accurate proof, but achieved its purpose by reference to common experience and knowledge.

*Conclusion.* With the protest that general things are all that can be said in a brief speech, the speaker again repeats his proposition. Comparing his advice with that of the doctor, he claims for public-relations counsel an equal professional competency. He enters his final plea with a short résumé of his arguments, a terse statement of the major proposition, and a concluding reference to the analogy of Joseph's story in Egypt. His final plea reveals the emphasis of the speech. It is with the nature of *persistency* that he begins his speech, the necessity of *persistency* that he forms his main argument, and the advisability of *persistency* that he enters his final admonition. The compactness of the speech adds a sense of "truth well demonstrated" that engenders acceptance.

*Chapter 16*


# INFORMATIVE SITUATIONS


Words are the signs of thoughts and thoughts make history.
—GREENOUGH


All speaking situations may be said to have one of four general purposes: information, fellowship, persuasion, or deliberation. Information is the purpose of speaking when one seeks to (1) impart knowledge, (2) establish relationships between things, (3) explain a process, (4) interpret an agreement or expound a writing. These are informative situations because each seeks to make meanings clear. For example, to impart knowledge is an essential function of all college lectures. What the instructor understands is to be communicated to the students. However, a simple statement of new facts is not sufficient. All the devices of persuasion must be used to make the students realize the nature of the facts presented. Hence, a class lecture is a speech situation whose aim is understanding in general and the imparting of information in particular.

Informative speeches rely on five basic sources:

1. Experiences to be related—such as, travels, adventures, romances.
2. Processes to be explained—such as, the making of a book, mixing pigments for colors, photographing sound.
3. Writings to be expounded—such as, the meaning of the Constitution, the philosophy of Plato.
4. Ideas to be exposited—such as, the meaning of aesthetics, etc.
5. Instructions to be delineated—such as, how to play chess, how to build a boat, etc.

The appeal in informative situations is intellectual rather than emotional. You attempt to place things in some easily discernible order. To do this, make frequent use of comparison, contrast, genus, species, and definition. Thus, the question of what a thing is may be answered by placing it in relation to known things, showing its likeness (comparison) or unlikeness (contrast); by placing it in a class more readily known (genus); or by telling its parts (definition). Your approach may be *deductive,* saying about members of a class what is true of a class, or *inductive,* abstracting from particulars a general relationship. The aim of information is accomplished when your message is fully known, *i.e.,* conceived in relation to the audience's previous experience and knowledge.

Take the attitude that your information is interesting and that your audience is desirous of hearing it. Feel that you are imprinting on the mind of your audience the clear concepts in your mind. Remember that all uses of language, such as contrast, analogy, comparison, and definition, are aids to communicating your thoughts to the audience. To inform, you must first seek clarity. If your information lacks unity, or if you ramble, the audience will have to supply order to your talk. This they may not care to do. You can achieve a lively contact with your audience by noting changes in facial expressions as each succeeding link in your message is revealed. Your listeners, if you look directly at them and talk with them, will tell you with a frown, or uneasiness, or a puzzled expression just what part is difficult. If your message is complicated, use graphic material to aid in clarifying each step. The construction of a figure on the blackboard, point by point, is an excellent technique. Do not draw the complete figure and then begin your talk, but construct it as you go.

In relating an experience, follow an easily perceived order. The most readily followed order is that of time. Human experiences occur in this order, and it needs no elucidation. The order of cause to effect is most helpful when the "why" of your information is the aim. In explaining a process, follow the order of operation. Finally, adjust your material to the occasion. William Lyon Phelps relates the incident of an alumnus asking him about the future of American poetry on the way to a football game. Dr. Phelps was annoyed by the question, and in that situation he was right. The situation demanded fellowship and excitement and not academic concern over the future of American poetry. To a lesser degree, many of us commit this blunder daily. Because you know a fact is no justification for relating it every time an ear appears. Be certain that the situation is one demanding information before you tell your story.

While all situations can be grouped in a set of four general aims, the particular aim in each situation differs slightly. Thus, under the classification "informative," we may group such recognizable situations as:

1. Lecture
2. Travelogue
3. Announcement
4. Report
5. Instruction
6. Description of a scene
7. Nomination
8. Eulogy
9. Anecdote
10. Story

PROJECTS

*Assignment 1*

Read the three short speeches given as examples. You will notice that while each one has the purpose of communicating information, each makes use of situations, each makes use of incidents, each makes use of significant details. To forcefully transmit facts of any kind, the speaker must dress those facts in their most appealing garb. He must make them palatable to the audience. In doing this, the power of narrative is unquestioned. Any audience will pause to hear a story. Any audience will be more receptive if the information is dramatized for them. Merely to tell about an incident is only half as powerful as to narrate it in the present tense, to make the hearers feel that they are actually witnessing the event itself.

Relating events in their most dramatic form frightens beginning speakers. They are afraid to take time to dramatize events, to relate fragments of conversations, to build gradually to a climax, to create suspense, and to enact the characters in a situation. Yet, these are the very things that create interest.

This assignment is a challenge to your imagination. It asks you to furnish yourself with the materials of your talk and then to seek ways of arranging that material in dramatic form. Take the facts of O'Connell's life, for example. They might have been very prosaically portrayed by barren repetitions, but Wendell Phillips casts them into incidents that make the information as current as gossip. In like manner, Mr. Wiles gives the dramatic force of actually seeing Pershing and his troops march through the Arc de Triomphe. And Hanlon touches us with the immediate story of a simple incident.

Study these speeches carefully; then determine which is the best way to make your speech interesting. Remember that interest is the one thing that must characterize the speech to inform. People learn what they want to learn. That is the challenge to the speaker. He must make his message something that the audience wants to know. So beware of making a too-scientific exposition of your story. If you cut it down to skeletal proportions it will be as uninteresting as a skeleton. It is the warmth of flesh that creates interest, not the barrenness of bones. So be warm, be human, be simple, and understanding, and the audience will react in the same way.

Select one of the forms of situations suggested and come prepared to deliver a three- to four-minute talk which will inform the audience. Strive to find something within the core of human experience. Do not seek the bizarre. Rather seek to tell the common things of life uncommonly well. This is the height of the art of narration. Let it be your goal.

*Assignment 2*

The most frequent informative speech is the "chalk talk." Business calls this type of informative talk a "chart presentation." The value of this presentation is realized when you consider that knowledge is obtained through our five senses in the following ratios:

| | | |
|---|---|---|
| Sight | 85% | ⎱ 95% |
| Hearing | 10% | ⎰ |
| Touch | 2% | |
| Smell | 1½% | |
| Taste | 1½% | |

Supporting your talk with charts increases the effectiveness by adding sight to hearing, thus giving a potential of 95 per cent reaction and attention. This can be achieved if you learn to use your chart by skillfully reading it and adding comments adroitly. Five simple rules can assist you:

1. Always stand with the chart on your left.
2. Turn the page only when ready to read it.
3. Read the whole page before starting commentary.
4. Face the audience.
5. Draw listeners from chart by stepping away from it.

Prepare an informative talk on a subject of your interest and present it graphically to the class. Use a chart which high-lights your main points and embeds them in the minds of the audience.

### O'CONNELL

### By Wendell Phillips

I think I do not exaggerate when I say that never since God made Demosthenes has He made a man better fitted for a great work than O'Connell.

You may say that I am partial to my hero; but John Randolph of Roanoke, who hated an Irishman almost as much as he did a Yankee, when he got to London and heard O'Connell, the old slaveholder threw up his hands and exclaimed, "This is the man, those are the lips, the most eloquent that speak English in my day!" and I think he was right.

Webster could address a bench of judges; Everett could charm a college; Choate could delude a jury; Clay could magnetize a senate, and Tom Corwin could hold the mob in his right hand; but no one of these men could do more than this one thing. The wonder about O'Connell was that he could out-talk Corwin, he could charm a college better than Everett, and leave Henry Clay himself far behind in magnetizing a senate.

It has been my privilege to hear all the great orators of America who have become singularly famed about the world's circumference. I know what was the majesty of Webster; I know what it was to melt under the magnetism of Henry Clay; I have seen eloquence in the iron logic of Calhoun; but all three of those men never surpassed and not one of them ever equaled the great Irishman. I have hitherto been speaking of his ability and succss, I will now consider his character.

To show you that he never took a leaf from our American gospel of compromise, that he never filed his tongue to silence on one truth fancying so to help another, let me compare him to Kossuth, whose only merits were his eloquence and his patriotism. When Kossuth was in Faneuil Hall, he exclaimed, "Here is a flag without a stain, a nation without a crime!" We abolitionists appealed to him, "O, eloquent son of the Magyar, come to break chains, have you no word, no pulse-beat for four millions of negroes bending under a yoke ten times heavier than that of Hungary?" He exclaimed, "I would forget anybody, I would praise anything, to help Hungary!" O'Connell never said anything like that.

When I was in Naples I asked Sir Thomas Fowell Buxton, "Is Daniel O'Connell an honest man?" "As honest a man as ever breathed," said he, and then he told me the following story: "When, in 1830, O'Connell first entered Parliament, the antislavery cause was so weak that it had only Lushington and myself to speak for it, and we agreed that when he spoke I should cheer him up, and when I spoke he should cheer me, and these were the only cheers we ever got. O'Connell came with one Irish member to support him. A large party of members (I think Buxton said twenty-seven) whom we called the West India interest, the Bristol party, the slave party, went to him, saying, 'O'Connell, at last you are in the House with one helper—if you will never go down to Freemason's Hall with Buxton and Brougham, here are twenty-seven votes for you on every Irish question. If you work with those abolitionists, count us always against you.'

"It was a terrible temptation. How many a so-called statesman would have yielded! O'Connell said, 'Gentlemen, God knows I speak for the saddest people the sun sees; but may my right hand forget its cunning and my tongue cleave to the roof of my mouth, if to help Ireland—even Ireland—I forget the negro one single hour.'

"From that day," said Buxton, "Lushington and I never went into the lobby that O'Connell did not follow us."

And then, besides his irreproachable character, he had what is half the power of a popular orator, he had a majestic presence. In youth he had the brow of Jupiter, and the stature of Apollo. A little O'Connell would have been no O'Connell at all. Sydney Smith says of Lord John Russell's five feet, when he went down to Yorkshire after the Reform Bill had passed, the stalwart hunters of Yorkshire exclaimed, "What, that little shrimp, *he* carry the Reform Bill!" "No, no," said Smith, "he *was* a large man, but the labors of the bill shrunk him." You remember the story that Russell Lowell tells of Webster when we in Massachusetts were about to break up the Whig party. Webster came home to Faneuil Hall to protest, and four thousand Whigs came out to meet him. He lifted up his majestic presence before that sea of human faces, his brow charged with thunder, and said, "Gentlemen, I am a Whig; a Massachusetts Whig; a Revolutionary Whig; a Constitutional Whig; a Faneuil Hall Whig; and if you break up the Whig party, where am *I* to go?" "And," says Lowell, "we all held our breath, thinking where he *could* go." "But," says Lowell, "if he had been five feet three, we should have said, 'Confound you, who do you suppose cares where you go?'" Well, O'Connell had all that, and then he had what Webster never had, and what Clay had, the magnetism and grace that melt a million souls into his.

When I saw him he was sixty-five, lithe as a boy. His every attitude was beauty, his every gesture grace. Why, Macready or Booth never equaled him.

It would have been a pleasure even to look at him if he had not spoken at all, and all you thought of was a greyhound. And then he had, what so few American speakers have, a voice that sounded the gamut. I heard him once in Exeter Hall say, "Americans, I send my voice careening like the thunderstorm across the Atlantic, to tell South Carolina that God's thunderbolts are hot, and to remind the negro that the dawn of his redemption is drawing near"; and I seemed to hear his voice reverberating and re-echoing back to London from the Rocky Mountains.

And then, with the slightest possible flavor of an Irish brogue, he would tell a story that would make all Exeter Hall laugh, and the next moment there were tears in his voice, like an old song, and five thousand men would be in tears. And all the while no effort—he seemed only breathing.

"As effortless as woodland nooks
Send violets up and paint them blue."

### HOW GENERAL PERSHING SYMBOLIZED AMERICA

#### By G. M. Wiles

The recent death of General Pershing took me back to a day in Paris many years ago. It was Bastille Day, July 14, 1919, and the French were staging their Victory Parade. That day I stood for five hours watching French troops parade through the Arc de Triomphe. It was the first time since 1871 that French troops had been permitted to parade through the arch. In that year it had been decreed that no French soldiers could ever again march through until they first had avenged the humiliating defeat by the Germans.

There were contingents from all of their fighting units in the parade. Middle-aged men and youngsters trooped along in their badly worn and patched up uniforms with almost no attention being paid to cadence or military bearing. It was a pathetic, yet stirring sight—it told far better than words can of the great toll that the war had taken of France.

Suddenly there was a great shout. The crowds went wild. Down the street came General Pershing astride a handsome horse—riding as only Pershing could ride. Behind him came his Composite Regiment.

Immediately after the Armistice, Pershing realized that he would be expected to appear in the various European capitals before returning home. He decided to use that opportunity to symbolize America to the world. He ordered our one and one half million combat troops in France screened and 4,750 of the best soldiers selected and sent to a special camp to be drilled in close-order formations for six months. There never has been a better looking or finer marching regiment. New equipment—new uniforms—not a detail was overlooked. It was magnificent. To the French, those boys typified America—strength—hope.

No one who witnessed that sight failed to get its significance. Pershing had symbolized for the world—America. America the strong—the champion of freedom—the hope of the world.

#### SALLY

#### By Harry J. Hanlon

Upon reaching home after my day's work, a few years ago, I heard a commotion at the rear of the house. I found my oldest son, who was then five years old, playing with a little dog.

They were having a grand time. The little dog was racing about barking and thoroughly enjoying herself. Upon inquiry it developed that "Sally" belonged to a neighbor and followed my little boy home.

Sally was a "Black and Tan." Her eyes were very bright and her pointed ears stood up quite erect. She was most intelligent and became more affectionate as we became better acquainted.

Before long we had a visitor, who turned out to be our neighbor, the owner of Sally. After a few minutes our neighbor departed with Sally, leaving much gloom in her place.

Within a few minutes, however, Sally returned and made such joyous ado that we welcomed her once more into our home. Fortunately our neighbor did not return to claim Sally, and we adopted her as our family pet.

She also adopted us and was most faithful and devoted to all of us. She had natural ability as a watch-dog, and gave a warning before any visitors arrived. As she grew from puppy-hood, she developed great agility in her slender legs. She would take great pleasure in chasing birds, and if they flew close to the ground Sally would leap several feet into the air in an effort to catch them.

While driving through the country one summer day, Sally leaped from the car as a bird flew from the roadside. I picked her up dazed and bleeding and after dressing her wounds secured her so that she could not repeat the performance.

One morning as I left to go to business, Sally was tied up to prevent her from following me. As a tradesman arrived shortly after, however, she slipped through her bonds, darted from the house, and, as she trailed me, was struck by a car. It happened so suddenly that Sally never knew what struck her.

The sorrow this caused still remains and no "Black and Tan" that I have seen since has Sally's bright and smart appearance. I have one consolation, that is the satisfaction that we were always kind to Sally. Won't you too be kind to animals?

*Sample Informative Outline*

Speaker _____ Class _____ Date _____

  I. Topic.
 II. Purpose of speech: Indicate specific aim.
III. Audience analysis: Weigh carefully audience's previous knowledge of subject. Consult Situation Analysis Chart, Chap. 2.

IV. Organization of material.
  A. Introduction: Establish friendliness; arouse interest; and state the proposition.
  B. Body: Establish most conducive order for unfolding your message.
  C. Conclusion: Restate main ideas briefly.

*Questions for Critical Discussion of Performance*

1. Was the subject interesting?
2. Did the speaker communicate his interest in the subject?
3. Was each point illustrated by an incident or illustration?
4. Did the speaker make use of specific details to clarify important points?
5. Were word pictures powerful enough to create images in the minds of the audience?
6. Was a simple order followed?
7. Was the speaker's manner pleasant and ingratiating?
8. Was the speaker's organization evident and easily perceived?
9. Did the speaker show good critical judgment in developing his presentation?
10. How could the speaker improve his information speeches?

*Developing Semantic Skill*

Add to your word cards the following:

I. Words used in the speech text:

| *Word* | *Pronunciation* | *Meaning* |
|--------|----------------|-----------|
| 1. dogmatic | | |
| 2. enmeshed | | |
| 3. fellowship | | |
| 4. inquisition | | |

II. Words commonly mispronounced:
  1. often
  2. orgy
  3. orthoëpy

III. Words from your own experience.

*Chapter 17*

# FELLOWSHIP SITUATIONS

Let your spakin' be light and airy.
—Mr. Dooley

No more pleasurable human activity has been devised than group entertainment. There is something about being happy together that outdistances private joy. Human experiences are intensified through sharing. Nowhere is this more true than in fellowship situations. The participants desire a speaker to epitomize in mood, thought, and action the feelings of the group. For the speaker, this challenge determines his attitude, his material, and his delivery. All three should echo friendliness and enhance the mutual feelings of the group. Friendliness should be the keynote, and the pleasure of being together should be the specific purpose.

The most common means of securing a feeling of fellowship is through entertaining speeches. To entertain is to amuse with that which is pleasant. Create a mood of gaiety by rollicking in the pleasure of being a member of this group. Aim at simple, humorous, and human incidents. At times, a deeply moving instance of human virtue is not amiss, but the tone of the entire speech should be uplifting and enjoyable. The most frequent medium for such requirements is the art of storytelling.

## Telling Stories

Realize how much of your speaking time is spent in recounting what has happened to you or to someone you know. The act of relating the particulars of a previous occurrence is called "storytelling." It is the rehearsing of a scene that has taken place in the past but is so linked with the situation of the moment that its recital will give pleasure. Such recountings can be very entertaining if proper care is taken to arrange specific details in a cumulative order of climax.

The climax depends in large part upon the kinship between the purpose of using the story and its similarity to the present instance.

Climax and situational similarity characterize interesting stories. Even when the purpose is solely entertainment, the story is more easily told if the situation itself has set the scene. Use all the help the situation offers. Avoid being guilty of pointless, uninteresting rambling. Be conscious of the purpose of the gathering, the purpose of your account, the mood of the moment, and the pertinence of your climax. *Don't try to tell a story merely because other people do.* If your story does not contribute to the occasion, dispense with it immediately. Only those stories which you feel must be told should be told.

## Anecdote

Etymologically, *anecdote* simply meant "not published." Basically, it is a personal story not widely known in detail. Webster's brief description sums up its essential features: "A narrative, usually brief, of a separable incident or event of curious interest, told without malice and usually with intent to amuse or please, often biographical and characteristic of some notable person, especially of his likable foibles." For example, during one of his campaign speeches, Theodore Roosevelt was continually interrupted by a heckler who kept shouting, "I am a Democrat."

Finally, Roosevelt had to do something. With disarming gentleness, he inquired, "May I ask the gentleman why he is a Democrat?"

"My grandfather was a Democrat," replied the heckler. "My father was a Democrat. And I am a Democrat."

"And suppose," continued Roosevelt, "that your grandfather had been a jackass, and your father had been a jackass, what would you be?"

The heckler shouted back, "*A Republican!*"

## Short story

A short story is told in one mood and usually makes use of suspense. It revolves about a single action with no extraneous asides or plots. The action rises gradually and is concluded at the crisis, or point of highest interest. In common with all stories, heavy emphasis should be placed on characterization. No event can be related which is not enhanced by clear, believable characters. You read of thousands killed in far countries and are little moved, yet if the man next door is injured, you feel vitally concerned. Take care of the characters, and the characters will take care of the story.

Storytelling is an art, and its effectiveness depends upon the perfection of certain techniques. You can acquire skill in this art by constant practice. Get into the habit of reading stories aloud. Learn to enliven your discourse with choice anecdotes and stories. Before beginning to tell the story, you must have all the necessary details in mind. Then, create atmosphere, arouse interest, sustain suspense, and clinch your story with a powerful ending. Omit unnecessary detail. Use vivid imagery. The experience of holding a group enthralled as you tell a particularly good story is a sensation no speaker should miss. It is well worth the effort it takes to develop this skill.

### Humor

Aristotle described humor as that which gives mental pleasure by painless incongruity. The elements therein are simple: It gives pleasure, it is mental, it is painless to the observer, and its basis is incongruity. Yet humor is easier to analyze than to create. Its creation requires continual practice in observing the incongruous in men's action. Further, it requires effective expression and the absence of any likelihood that the audience may be caught in a similar plight. A person laughs at another's fall, feeling that it couldn't happen to him. To help you acquire a sense of humor and appreciate its nature, the following types are illustrated.

### Humor of words

The humor of words centers around the expression of some incongruity. The most frequent type is the *pun*. No one is above making a pun, but the perpetual pun maker is a nuisance. The pun is a seasoning to be used with caution—like English mustard. Shakespeare fashioned his advice on punning in "A pun should be punished." While this pun has some intellectual pleasure in analyzation, the other type, such as the story of the two Greek tailors "Euripidies and Eumendidies," only produces a groan. In the use of puns, remember the dictum for all humor in speaking: *The best humor comes unsought.*

Irony in the use of words forms a basis for humor. For example, "He *talks* a good game of golf," or the expression used by one of the dictator's lieutenants when asked how the people felt about war. He replied, "Oh, they can't complain." Irony is sometimes used skillfully by a speaker in an extended manner by picturing the incongruous results of following an opponent's argument.

A wealth of humor is at your hand in the pronunciation, word confusion, and dialects common to regions and classes. For instance, the speaker who was trying to increase the membership of his club but unfortunately pronounced the word "roster" as if it were "rooster."

## Humor of thought

If the humor resides in the words, then the humor is lost when the expression changes. If, however, the humor persists despite change of expression, it resides in the thought. Three main types of humor of thought are useful: false expectation, hyperbole, and caricature.

*False expectation* leads the audience to expect one reaction and then furnishes a connected, but unexpected, finish, as the remark that: "Everything seems to go wrong—and then—when everything seems blackest—all of a sudden—everything gets—worse."

*Hyperbole* creates humor by exaggeration. The story is told of two Irishmen:

PATRICK: I tell you I saw a man jump halfway across the river Shannon, and seeing that he couldn't make it when halfway, he turned back.

MICHAEL: What are you trying to tell me? No man could go halfway across and then turn back. He'd drown in the middle of it.

PATRICK: Well, 'tis easy for you to say that, and it was your own son Timothy that did it.

MICHAEL: Sure, great God Almighty, why didn't you say it was Timothy? Imagine the strength of him doing a thing like that.

*Caricature* emphasizes some salient characteristics and presents a distorted, but recognizable, picture. It can add vividness to your descriptions of people, as the description of a person as "a small man who always went through the door first."

All forms of humor should be used by the speaker with discretion. The speaker who resorts to humor too often becomes known as a "wit," and people refuse to take him seriously. This jeopardizes his chances as an effective speaker when he has something vital to say.

Use humor as a means to an end, to lighten up the long stretches, or to help people enjoy situations devoted to fellowship.

## Occasions for the Fellowship Speech

If a gift is to be given, a building dedicated, a dinner held, a new member of the group welcomed or an old one bid farewell, an anniversary celebrated, a new series begun, an award made, or special commendations administered, a speech is in order. These are occasions in which common feelings are crystallized and expressed by the speaker for the group. The essence of the situation is in sharing beliefs held in common. Liberty of expression, freedom from strain, felicitations, and an easy good humor should permeate your talk. The following are the most easily recognized types:

Speech of welcome
Speech of farewell
Presentation speech
Response speech
Commencement address
Afterdinner talk
Anniversary speech
Entertainment speech
Eulogy

### PROJECTS

*Assignment*

Select one of the above types of speech. Tell the class the occasion and ask the class to act as the audience for that occasion. Pay particular attention to the purpose of fellowship and use all the means of attaining interest. Do not be satisfied with your first preparation of this speech because it will gain in interest as you practice it. This is a challenge to your imagination.

George Foster's interesting talk called "Waiting at the Church" provides an excellent example of how specific instances can produce a humorous speech. Notice how he opens with a direct situation, explains his point, proceeds directly to give eight different examples, and concludes with a statement of his point in the words of a well-known psychologist. A great deal of the interest of the talk resides in the famous people chosen as examples. Anecdotes are usually interesting, and when told about famous people they have added zest. In your humorous talk, select an amusing theme and document it with instances from famous people's lives. Biographies and autobiographies abound with such instances.

## WAITING AT THE CHURCH

### By George Foster

The caterers, the musicians and the florists had been engaged. Eight bridal attendants and 15 ushers were looking forward to the big event.

Then, the happy date only 12 days away, the announcement came that Joan Farquhar Hadden, New York City post-debutante, and Louis Bell Baker, of Wynnewood, Pa., were calling off their wedding.

The only explanation given was that the marriage plans had been canceled by "mutual consent."

Such embarrassing situations often occur—but sometimes there is no forewarning, no formal cancellation. Sometimes, the bride or the bridegroom just fails to show up at the appointed time and place.

There have been a number of celebrated instances of that sort.

Ulysses S. Grant, Jr., son of the famed Civil War General and President, was engaged to fabulously rich Jennie Flood. They were to be wed atop a mountain at Summit, Colo. Jennie waited there in her private railroad car for two days. Ulysses never arrived.

James Gordon Bennett, Jr., son of the famous publisher, was scheduled to become a bridegroom in a Paris ceremony. When it became evident that he would not arrive, the wedding was called off.

Hannah More, 19th century English educator and authoress, was left waiting at the church—in the words of a contemporary writer—by a "gentleman who receded from his promise. He subsequently renewed his offer, and on being refused made all the reparation in his power by securing her an annual sum."

Picturesque Davy Crockett, fabulous frontiersman, imbibed too much and missed his wedding. When he sobered up and sought to regain the favor of his jilted bride, he found she had wed another on the rebound.

General Ambrose Burnside, after whom burnside whiskers were named, walked to the altar and dutifully said his "I do." The bride-to-be, however, refused to say hers. The marriage was called off.

Later the same girl became engaged to an Ohio lawyer. On their wedding day he showed her a revolver. "You come home from church either a bride or a corpse," he said. She came home a bride.

There was, in more recent times, the famous case of John Jacob Astor, 3d, scion of wealth who was engaged to Eileen Gillespie, New York society girl. Ushers and bridesmaids had been named, young Astor had presented his fiancée with a $100,000 engagement ring and purchased a $200,000 Newport, R.I., villa for a wedding present.

A few weeks before the event, which all society awaited with bated breath, Eileen's parents announced the engagement had been broken. There was no official reason given, but several months later Astor, returning from a world cruise that was to have been a bridal journey, explained:

"We would have been all right but for her parents. They even planned to go with us on our honeymoon."

Seven hundred guests had gathered in the town of Fremont, Neb., for the nuptials of Althea Marr, Fremont's prettiest girl, and John Windsor Norris, of Syracuse, N.Y., the son of a wealthy manufacturer.

The wedding party was in the church for a last-minute rehearsal when Althea's aunt marched in and announced: "The wedding will not take place now nor at any other time."

It was recalled that Willard "Dutch" Witte, Nebraska University football hero and college friend of Althea's, had called her on the phone a few hours before her sudden renunciation of Norris. Shortly afterward, Althea and Witte were married.

King Zog of Albania promised to marry Mlle. Tiranje Verlatsi, daughter of Verlatsi Ahmed Beg, powerful Albanian chieftain, in return for the chieftain's support in putting him on the throne.

At the last minute, when details of the wedding were all arranged, Zog coldly jilted Mlle. Verlatsi and wed half-American Countess Geraldine Apponyi of Budapest. Chief Verlatsi swore revenge.

When Mussolini invaded Albania, Verlatsi aided the dictator in his speed conquest and helped rout Zog from the country.

David Ridgway, ex-Navy officer, and Emily Moran Peter, of Detroit, were about to leave the Peter home for a pre-wedding party when the phone rang. It was long-distance for Ridgway.

"Don't take the call, darling," said Emily. "We're late now." "But, Honey, it's probably from my uncle. I want to take it," said Ridgway. "Apparently your family means more to you than I do," said Emily, stamping her foot. "If you take that call, David, the wedding is off!" David took the call. Emily waited until he was through, then called a Detroit newspaper. "I have an item for you," she said. "I'm not going to be married." And she wasn't.

What is the psychological explanation of suddenly terminated marriage plans? "In every case," said Donald A. Laird, well-known psychologist, "there is some particular reason, which usually is not revealed. Sometimes the bridegroom or the bride has a last-minute apprehension that he or she might not make a good mate. Sometimes the person who backs out at the last minute wasn't in love from the start and never really wanted to get married but kept hoping that love might be awakened during the engagement period. Sometimes there's another party in the picture."

*Sample Fellowship Outline*

Speaker _____ Class _____ Date _____

   I. Topic.
  II. Purpose of speech: Indicate specific aim.
 III. Audience analysis: Consider audience's interests. Consult Situation Analysis Chart, Chap. 2.
 IV. Introduction: Establish friendliness and arouse interest.
  V. Theme of entertainment: Indicate means of interest leading to climax.
 VI. Conclusion: Apply theme to audience or occasion if possible.

*Questions for Critical Discussion of Performance*

  1. Did the speaker create a mood of fellowship?
  2. Was his material interesting?
  3. How appropriate was his material?
  4. Did he create suspense?
  5. Did the story have a climax?
  6. Was the purpose of the speech evident?
  7. Was the speech sufficiently humorous?
  8. Were the speaker's vocal and semantic skills adequate?
  9. Were his timing and pauses accurate?
10. How could this speech be improved?

*Developing Semantic Skill*

Add to your word cards the following:

  I. Words used in the speech text:

| Word | Pronunciation | Meaning |
|------|---------------|---------|
| 1. deductive | | |
| 2. genus | | |
| 3. inductive | | |
| 4. species | | |

 II. Words commonly mispronounced:
    1. larynx
    2. library
    3. lyceum
III. Words from your own experience.

*Chapter 18*

# PERSUASIVE SITUATIONS

> Persuasion is the art of implanting motives which lead to consequent free action.
>
> —ARISTOTLE

Persuasion is your aim when you desire action. It presents to the audience the desirability of performing a single act or pursuing a certain course of action. Such actions may be the accepting of a point of view, the adoption of a set of principles, or the act of carrying out such tasks. The appeal is mostly emotional. It presents to the will motives for acting in a desired way. When action cannot be had without conviction, then argumentation presents proofs to the intellect for judgment. When understanding is necessary to secure action, exposition and description present clear concepts of the meanings involved. These processes, however, are mere stepping-stones to the real end of securing action.

Sometimes the reasons for following a course of action are evident and yet not followed, for knowledge is not always causally connected with action. People do not follow their judgments so readily as they do their feelings. A college student who was trying to decide whether or not to get married attempted to be very scientific about the matter. He drew a straight line and labeled one side "arguments for" and the other side "arguments against." After a thorough examination of conscience and long weighing of the assets and liabilities involved, the chart contained 23 good "arguments against" and one "argument for." This made up his mind. He tore up the chart and got married. Whether true or not, the story illustrates that it is not sufficient when action is desired simply to reveal the reasons for a suggested action.

*To secure action, the will of the person must be aroused to conceive of the action as desirable.*

An audience has been persuaded when they freely resolve upon the action desired by the speaker. They do this when they feel that the proof is sufficient to warrant action, when they have been brought to see the desired action as worthy and good, and when an impelling motive has been implanted by the speaker. In summary, your threefold task is to offer reasonable proof, present that proof attractively, and furnish an adequate motive for action.

## Emotional Appeal

Audiences are moved to action by emotional appeals. The shortest route to their hearts is through their feelings. Last spring a blind man startled passers-by with an appeal to the pity of his fellow men by carrying a sign reading, IT IS MAY—AND I AM BLIND. In one of my classes the mother of a blind boy told how she was worried because her son was always getting lost. Then she discovered the reason. Whenever he was on his own he would take off the sign I AM A BLIND BOY. This reveals how powerful the emotional appeal is in all our lives.

The fundamental appeal of all speakers is the personal appeal. No audience is convinced or persuaded unless they have faith in the character of the speaker. This feeling of his worth is vital to all forms of appeal. When the audience feel that he is what Quintilian called a *"bonus vir docendi dicendi"* (a good man skilled in speaking), they are willing to give their assent to his appeal. The absence of this feeling makes all skill seem affectation.

The impelling motives for any audience are the things that they hold to be sacred. This does not mean that they are conscious of their feelings as such. Often they are persuaded without a direct knowledge of why and how persuasion took place. Every analysis that has been made, however, has found that the following basic appeals were used in moving the group to action. Man moves to action when his self-preservation is attacked, when his property is in danger, when his power is questioned, when his reputation is besmirched or disregarded, when his affections are slighted, and when his tastes are ignored.

But more often man moves to action when his desire is aroused, when he pictures some gratification to himself. This may be a noble cause such as the protection of his family, the saving of his country, or the defense of his character, but most frequently it is some simpler drive that arouses him. For instance, the electric company admonishes: "Eyesight is priceless; light is cheap"; and the toothbrush company assures you that this brush gets between the teeth and thus prevents decay. The airline measures life in terms of hours and reminds you of the more abundant life it provides. The motorcar companies feature safety glass and improved brakes for your protection. These are all appeals to the basic instinct of self-protection.

These are practical motivators of human action. Do not scorn them for they constitute the moving forces of daily American life. People are seldom called upon to make world-shaking decisions, but they are buying and selling every day. Merely to study the speeches of epoch-making events is to become academic and impractical. Persuasion is an integral part of everyday life, and your skill in its use will determine in large part the effectiveness of your college education.

Schwab and Beatty, the famous New York advertising agency, after years of research, suggests these seven ways to get action through basic appeals:

1. *Make an offer*—offer "hook"; offer booklet, sample, free trial, premium, introductory price, or other extra inducement.

2. *Time limit*—give time limit on your offer, if such is bonafide.

3. *Limited supply*—if selection or supply of product is limited, stress this fact.

4. *Guarantee*—if product is guaranteed, point out that this assurance removes cause for delay or inaction.

5. *Price going up*—if price is to be raised, emphasize that fact, giving specific date if possible.

6. *Price reduced*—if so, say so; point out desirability of taking advantage of it at once.

7. *Gain or loss*—stress what your reader gains by purchasing product immediately, or what he loses daily by not owning it.

For twenty years an annual experiment was conducted at Queens College and Fordham University in which classes were asked to isolate the appeals in advertising and then to vote on the basis of effectiveness. The aim was to determine which appeal was most effective in securing action. A tabulation of the responses of over 6,000 college students reveals the following order of effective human appeals:

1. Social acceptance
2. Better health
3. Product's success
4. Greater popularity
5. Improved appearance
6. Saving money
7. Romance
8. Novelty
9. Sex
10. Personal success
11. Adventure
12. More leisure
13. Security
14. Pride
15. Honor

Do not suppose that these are all the human appeals, nor assume that these appeals will be effective in the order suggested. The fact is that proposals identified with these appeals are most fruitful in securing human action. Hence, to make your idea more effective, show people how it will increase their mental, physical, emotional, or spiritual satisfaction, their well-being or security; or how it will decrease their fear of poverty, illness or accident, discomfort or boredom, and the loss of business or social advantage or prestige. The magic of appeal must never be forgotten. It is the item that decides human beings more forcefully than any rhetoric known. Capture the right appeal and your cause is half won. More than that, the right appeal can win impossible causes.

Sir Ernest Shackleton had an idea that was impossible to sell to the English public in 1900. He wanted men to share the worst possible hardships in the Antarctic. He wanted them to leave home and hearth and go on an adventure that seemed insane. The possibility of survival was scant. All his friends advised against attempting the adventure and guaranteed that he could never persuade anyone to go with him. But Lord Shackleton was undaunted. He placed this "ad" in the London papers:

Men Wanted for Hazardous Journey. Small wages, bitter cold, long months of complete darkness, constant danger, safe return doubtful. Honor and recognition in case of success—
                                            —SIR ERNEST SHACKLETON

The response was overwhelming. Sir Shackleton's appeal was to the spirit of adventure and social acceptance. Should this venture succeed, all their dreams would come true. And for their dreams the responders were willing to suffer bitter cold, darkness, danger, small wages—and even the possibility of no return. Such is the power of the right appeal.

*Specific Instances*

The most persuasive force in speaking is the use of specific instances. Generalities inform but they do not inspire action. The listener frequently believes in the wisdom of a proposed cause, but fails to carry that belief into action. He is content to acknowledge a truth, but he is not motivated to take any course of action because of his belief. Hence, if you desire action, you must present vivid imagery, actual details and descriptions that appeal or frighten. Your audience must sense the necessity of doing something. You must be specific in language, in analogy, and in examples.

The persuasive power of graphic illustrations is immeasurable. Such instances remove the personal basis of the transfer of ideas. You are no longer telling the audience to do something, you are merely telling them a story, and they are making up their own minds. Their critical powers are not being called forth, but their imaginative powers are. They are reading between the lines; they are inferring; they are deciding. You are an architect unfolding plans, and the audience is freely determining its own reactions. Such a process comes nearest to Aristotle's definition of persuasion: "Persuasion is the art of implanting motives that lead to consequent free action." To assist you in gaining this skill, let us study examples of the three indispensable means of gaining specificity.

An example of specificity in language is given by Shakespeare in *Henry the Fifth*. The citizens of Harfleur are reluctant to capitulate because of a sense of civic pride. In order to secure action, the specific details of assault are presented to them in compelling vividness:

> If I begin the batt'ry once again,
> I will not leave the half-achieved Harfleur
> Till in her ashes she lies buried.
> The gates of mercy shall be all shut up,
> And the flesh'd soldier, rough and hard of **heart,**
> In liberty of bloody hand shall range
> With conscience wide as hell, mowing like grass
> Your fresh fair virgins and your flow'ring infants.
> . . . Therefore, you men of Harfleur,
> Take pity of your town and of your people,
> Whiles yet my soldiers are in my command . . .
> If not, why, in a moment look to see
> The blind and bloody soldier with foul **hand**

Defile the locks of your shrill-shrieking daughters;
Your fathers taken by the silver beards,
And their most reverend heads dashed to the walls;
Your naked infants spitted upon pikes,
Whiles the mad mothers with their howls confus'd
Do break the clouds, as did the wives of Jewry
At Herod's bloody-hunting slaughtermen.
What say you? Will you yield, and this avoid,
Or, guilty in defense, be thus destroy'd?
                    —SHAKESPEARE, *King Henry the Fifth*,
                                        Act III, Scene 3

An example of the skillful use of specificity in an analogy was used recently by Kidder, Peabody & Company when they tried to create interest in Mutual Fund Investing:

Many years ago Chinese merchants shipped goods down the Yangtze River on heavily laden skiffs. All would go well until the skiffs reached the rapids. Here many a merchant's fortune was dashed on the rocks.

One day when 100 skiffs were ready to sail a wise old Chinaman suggested that each merchant divide his shipment into 100 bundles and put one on each skiff. Five skiffs were lost in the rapids but 95 got through safely, and all the merchants profited.

                                        —OLD CHINESE STORY

When the Norfolk and Western Railroad tried to interest people in the romantic story of building that amazing road, they used an example which truly depicted the appeal of romance and adventure. This is the way they started their national advertising campaign:

HE FOUND THE CITY MEN SAID NEVER EXISTED

As a boy, Heinrich Schliemann developed a passionate interest in the ancient city of Troy, which scholars of his time said never existed. He fiercely resented this belief, and was convinced that the remains of the city could be found, but only after years of study and search, and the expenditure of vast sums of money. He began his struggle for learning and wealth as a grocer's boy. By 1870 he had accumulated both, and began excavation in Asia Minor, near the spot where the Hellespont flows into the Aegean Sea. Explorations continued for more than 20 years and disclosed nine distinct towns, one above the other. In 1893, after Schliemann's death, the sixth city from the bottom, a city which had perished in flames some 1200 years before Christ, was proven to be Homer's ancient city of Troy.

The appeal of adventure specifically drawn from an instance in life captured the attention of the readers and made them read the advertisement. No matter what the proposition you desire to leave in the minds of your hearers, you must follow Nature's way to the mind. You must give them definite sensuous experiences which will impress the mind. Simply to state a fact, no matter how true, is not sufficient. You must reveal the same thought in varied ramifications. For example, when Edward Everett wanted to express the simple truth that "there are occasions in life in which a great mind lives years of rapt enjoyment in a moment," he supported his statement with these specific instances:

I can fancy the emotions of Galileo when, first raising the newly constructed telescope to the heavens, he saw fulfilled the great prophecy of Copernicus, and beheld the planet Venus, crescent like the moon. It was such another moment as that when the immortal printers of Metz and Strasbourg received the first copy of the Bible into their hands—the work of their divine art; like that, when Columbus, too, through the gray dawn of the 12th of October, 1492, beheld the shores of San Salvador; like that when the law of gravitation first revealed itself to the intellect of Newton; like that when Franklin saw by the stiffening fibres of the hempen cord of his kite, that he held the lightning within his grasp; like that when Leverrier received back from Berlin the tidings that the predicted planet was found.

—EDWARD EVERETT

The persuasive force of a series of events all tending to prove a single point is almost irresistible to an audience. Such instances break down the resistance of unbelief and skepticism. People question the single happening, but when a thing occurs again and again, the cumulative effect is overpowering. The evidence offered is mute testimony of reality, and it is not sane to question reality. The wise speaker, therefore, seeks to establish his case by searching out an abundance of instances that bear out his case. Not only do such instances persuade but they add interest during the process of persuasion.

The psychological basis of persuasion can be summed up in a single word—repetition. Few minds are capable of resisting an idea which is continually presented. One of the greatest orators of all time, Daniel O'Connell, stated this truth in these words:

It is not by advancing a political truth once or twice, or even ten times, that the public will take it up and adopt it. Incessant repetition is required to impress political truths upon the mind. Men, by always hearing the same thing, insensibly associate them with truisms. They find the facts at last quietly reposing in a corner of their minds, and no more think of doubting them than if they formed a part of their religious beliefs.

Such technique requires that you envision your message in specific terms, and that you search for instances in which that message has operated. This is not as difficult as would be supposed. In fact, it is one of the exciting experiences in preparing for your talk. It has all the adventure of a detective hunt as you browse through events in human lives that typify your idea. As you find a number of such instances you become more convinced of the value of your message and gain assurance of its truth. This conviction on your part engenders conviction in your audience.

## EXAMPLES

The following three examples have been selected because they have proved effective persuasive speeches. They have actually moved audiences to action and have been constructed on the same principles that this chapter advocates. One is a brief speech such as you will be required to make in this project, and two are longer talks which will reveal how to extend the length of your speech when that is necessary. Each speech will be briefly analyzed, and your assignment will contain exact descriptions to guide you in preparing your talks.

The first speech, "What Makes America Tick?" by E. E. Caspell, was delivered to a high-school audience and follows the simple pattern of gaining attention by use of a dramatic incident, stating the point directly, supporting that point with two examples, and then restating the point as a final plea.

### WHAT MAKES AMERICA TICK?

### By E. E. Caspell

Everyone is yelling his head off. Our band is blaring. The girl just behind me has just knocked my hat off. But wait! The coach is sending in a substitute. A hush comes over the crowd and everyone waits expectantly to see what play will be called now. What is the coach's advice when it comes to a crucial moment like this? Just one simple rule—"Don't forget how you got down there!"

Like the coach's instructions for a touchdown play, what is it that "makes America tick"? For America is *your* business. You must have been born under a lucky star. The chances were 15 to 1 against you, but somehow the stork left you in America—the land of opportunity. You live in a land of marvelous opportunities; yet you are in a land of indifference, surrounded by a moat of ignorance.

Nearly sixty years ago, a Virginia state legislator introduced a bill to change the value of "pi" from 3.14159 plus to an even 3. He said, "If everyone pretended it was an even three, it would work. Also, it would make things much easier for high school math students." But unfortunately it didn't work. You smile at this example of ignorance. Yet, here is illustrated a simple formula: you can't legislate something for nothing. It just doesn't work.

How did we get where we are today? Meet "Slinky." "Slinky" is simply a coil of high-carbon steel wire, 78 feet long, wound into 92 coils like a bed spring. But "Slinky" can do things. You can put him on the top step of a staircase, flip his top coil of wire over, and "Slinky" will coil over and roll step by step down the stairs like a snake. Dick James, the 31-year-old marine engineer who invented "Slinky," has sold two and a half million of these gadgets, and is making a small fortune in this new business.

Oh, it took several years of hard work, some borrowed money, some real salesmanship, and a lot of criticism from his family, before Dick James finally decided to quit his 5,000-dollar a year job, and go after a patent on this new toy. But he had the guts to do it—so now we have "Slinky" for the kids.

How did we get where we are today? Take the case of the window cleaner in my house. I got talking to him the other day, and he told me that after he got started in this business on a small scale, he got his brother-in-law interested in it, and they hired some help. Now his sons are old enough to work at the job in his firm. He contracts for complete janitorial service for several of the large banks and office buildings in this city. Now he owns several panel trucks. Last winter, he spent a month in Florida! That's his privilege in America—the land of opportunity! Let me tell you this—don't ever scoff and sneer at any honest job in this country of ours. There's dignity and satisfaction and success in any real job if you will look for them.

How did we get where we are? Check the facts. The truth is that in 150 years we have come along further than most of the rest of the world in 600 years. With only 6 per cent of the world's area, and one-sixteenth of its population, we have practically one-half of the electric power, telephones and radios on the earth. We have 60 per cent of the world's steel production and the same percentage of the life insurance policies.

We didn't get all this by passing laws to give us "something for nothing." No, sir! We got where we are by the same individual initiative that the inventor of "Slinky" had and that our window cleaner had. That's what makes America tick.

Check the facts. Locate yourself today—you will find you aren't far from the goal-line. Don't forget how you got down there.

Let's keep America on the beam.

The second example comes from a talk by H. R. Blackwell with the descriptive title, "Four Score and Seven Years. . . ." The speaker achieves immediate interest by direct quotations of the amusing answers to a questionnaire; this is followed by observing the appropriateness of the subject and a more detailed analysis of the questionnaire; the point is then revealed by six specific references to the "Gettysburg Address"; the proof is offered in a contrast between the lobbies that exist and the true one that should exist; and the conclusion is established by the novelty of presenting the actual address.

This speech delivers a serious message of high purpose and at the same time preserves interest. It is a mistaken notion that serious things must be solemn and dull. No matter how serious your message, you will gain listeners' attention if you prepare that message in a form that is easily understood. Note the interest-getting device of breaking up the statistical report by first quoting the bizarre, then stating the point, and finally striking with the serious fact of our ignorance. If your talk is in a serious vein, pay special attention to these factors as a model.

### "FOUR SCORE AND SEVEN YEARS. . . ."

#### By H. R. Blackwell

"How should I know the Gettysburg Address? I'm a stranger here myself—just got in from Chicago."

"It was a talk given by George Washington at the end of the war."

"Lincoln gave it to free the slaves."

"It was a political talk."

"It was a debate with Douglas."

"Sure—it was made at the end of the Civil War, somewhere around 1822."

This year it will be just four score and seven years since the weary and ailing President made the "few appropriate remarks" asked of him at Gettysburg.

The date was November 19, 1863. It was to have been October 23; but Edward Everett required the extra weeks to polish the two-hour oration that preceded Lincoln's immortal two minutes. The President, invited as an afterthought, had but a fraction of a crowded two weeks to get ready.

The people, they say, were disappointed.

It is possible that Lincoln, today, might be disappointed in the people. For the words that have been engraved in gold and marble are something less than indelible in their hearts.

If ten cities recently surveyed rightly represent the nation, more than seven million adults have never even heard of the Gettysburg Address.

Sixteen per cent of those who have heard of it cannot identify the speaker. Fifty-four per cent are wrong about the occasion. Guesses about the exact date cover 185 years.

Opinions of what the talk was about range from the well-informed to many like those mentioned at the beginning of this talk.

Thirty-six per cent can repeat the first line, but only fifteen per cent even pretend to know most of the address.

One thing that does not suffer from age is Truth, and Lincoln's message has as much meaning today as it had eighty-seven years ago.

We still live in a "nation conceived in Liberty, and dedicated to the proposition that all men are created equal."

It is more than ever questionable whether "any nation, conceived, and so dedicated, can long endure."

Never before have governments "of the people, by the people, for the people" perished so rapidly from the earth.

And never, many believe, has it been so vital that "this nation under God, shall have a new birth of freedom."

It is not likely that our freedom, bought at such a price in death and suffering, can be lightly wrested from us.

But it may dribble away, drop by unnoticed drop, while we are busy rolling our own small logs.

Two hundred fifty-six organizations support lobbies in Washington today. There are lobbies for the Farmer, for Lower Taxes, for World Federalization, for the Townsend Plan, for Displaced Persons, for Railroads, for Waterways, for Real Estate. . . .

But a study of the list does not show any lobby for the United States of America.

There ought to be one—the greatest pressure group in history with every one of our 102,000,000 adult Americans as members, each pledged to put the country's good ahead of personal profit or group gain, each refusing to have his thinking done for him and delivered like the morning mail.

For there can be no real public opinion without private thinking, and there can be no national strength based on "What's in it for me?"

If this country is to have a "new birth of freedom," it will not commence with committees and councils, nor will it develop by resolution or proclamation.

It will start quietly across the land in the hearts of men and women, and it will grow into a national conviction that what others have been willing to die for may be worth some effort to preserve.

It will begin with some very small thing, as small perhaps as the 277 words of the Gettysburg Address.

Suppose—to celebrate its eighty-seventh birthday—all of us memorized it again. Most of us knew it once.

And while we were memorizing it, suppose we took time to think about its meaning, about the character of the man who gave it, about the hope it holds against the fearful background of its giving.

It might help free us from lazy cynicism, from spiritual shiftlessness, from our dangerous habit of leaving everything to a non-existent "them." It might even lead to the "new birth of freedom" that Lincoln prayed for.

It is with that hope that the Gettysburg Address is repeated:

Four score and seven years ago our fathers brought forth, upon this continent, a new nation, conceived in Liberty, and dedicated to the proposition that all men are created equal.

Now we are engaged in a great civil war, testing whether that nation, or any nation, so conceived, and so dedicated, can long endure. We are met here on a great battle-field of that war. We have come to dedicate a portion of it as a final resting place for those who here gave their lives that that nation might live. It is altogether fitting and proper that we should do this.

But in a larger sense we cannot dedicate—we cannot consecrate—we cannot hallow this ground. The brave men, living and dead, who struggled here, have consecrated it far above our poor power to add or detract. The world will little note, nor long remember, what we say here, but can never forget what they did here. It is for us, the living, rather to be dedicated here to the unfinished work which they have thus far so nobly advanced.

It is rather for us to be here dedicated to the great task remaining before us—that from these honored dead we take increased devotion to that cause for which they here gave the last full measure of devotion—that we here highly resolve that these dead shall not have died in vain; that this nation, under God, shall have a new birth of freedom; and that this government of the people, by the people, for the people, shall not perish from the earth.

The third example, "How to Sell an Idea," has been given by the author to conventions and sales meetings over a hundred times. It is included because it is an example of a speech built solely on the use of specific instances and evidence, and because it reiterates the basic theory of persuasion. It captures interest by opening with an anecdote which promises the audience a great secret; the point is stated in terms of a formula and immediately restated in popular language; eight instances are then given which illustrate the point. A further restatement of the point follows, and four more instances are given. The climax of the speech is reached through a detailed exposition of the use of the formula during the recent war. Note that specific evidence of actual leaflets is used to secure conviction. The conclusion restates the formula in terms of authority by quoting Aristotle, and ends with a final plea to use the formula in the exciting game of life.

### How to Sell an Idea

#### By David Guy Powers

Professor Ormond Drake, Assistant Dean of the College of Liberal Arts, New York University, once startled a convention of professors of public speaking with this challenge: If all the books on the art of moving human beings to action were condensed to a brief statement, what would that statement be?

The discussion lasted for two hours, and was followed by a special session of fifteen leading university and college professors. They met far into the night. Probably there never was such a distinguished group attacking this problem. They had read almost every book ever written on the subject in any language, and collectively had spent more than two hundred years teaching it in the classrooms of our country.

This is the statement they agreed held the secret: "What the mind attends to, it considers; what it does not attend to, it dismisses. What the mind attends to continually, it believes. And, what the mind believes, it eventually does!"

Let's reduce those generalities to simple procedures. Get a man thinking about your idea. Even if he rejects it, keep him thinking about it. Gradually he will become accustomed to it. Now if you persist long enough, he will believe it. And here is the pay-off; once he believes it, he will act upon it.

Professor Harry Overstreet stresses the same truth in his interesting book *Influencing Human Behavior*. "What we attend to controls our behavior," he says. "What we can get others to attend to controls their behavior. In these two sentences we have the key to the influencing of human behavior."

The psychological basis of all human action is that no one can resist continual stimulation. "As a man thinketh in his heart, so he is." Therefore, if you would persuade anyone, keep him thinking about your idea. His thoughts control his actions as his breathing controls his life.

"Repetition is reputation!" said Arthur Brisbane. Even the rankest myths assume the dignity of historic truth when repeated endlessly. The gullible swallow an oft-told tale as gospel, and the skeptical swallow it because they cannot disprove it. All those in between believe it because it is pleasanter to share a common ignorance than to be wise alone.

"Never delude yourself that because you have told your story once, that that is all that is necessary," says Bruce Barton, President of Batten, Barton, Durstine & Osborn. "Selling an idea is a day-by-day, hour-by-hour business."

George Bernard Shaw gave himself as an example of this principle of repetition when he said almost fifty years ago, "For ten years past, with an unprecedented pertinacity and obstination, I have been dinning into the public head that I am an extraordinarily witty, brilliant, and clever man. That is now part of the public opinion of England, and no power on earth will ever change it. I may dodder and dote; I may potboil and platitudinize; I may become the butt and chopping block of all the bright, original spirits of the rising generation; but my reputation shall not suffer; it is built up fast and solid, like Shakespeare's, on an impregnable basis of dogmatic reiteration."

And on his ninetieth birthday every paper in the land called him "an extraordinarily witty, brilliant, and clever man."

The DuPont Company has had its oval symbol repeated over a billion and a half times to impress it on the mind of the public, according to Mr. William Hart, head of the advertising department.

No less a personage than John Dewey, America's most distinguished philosopher, wrote to me from Hubbards, Nova Scotia, that "I am inclined to believe such influence as I have exercised in teaching and writing is more due to mass material and repetitive effect than anything else."

Napoleon Bonaparte sensed the power of repeating a theme. Calling an artist one day, he mentioned that he was small in stature, and felt that he must strike a pose that would show him to advantage. After rejecting all the poses that added girth they finally hit upon the hand-in-waistcoat-front-and-back attitude. Napoleon practiced this on every possible occasion. He became so identified with it that any child today falls into the pose when describing Napoleon.

For more than twelve years the minds of the German people were guided by Paul Joseph Goebbels, Nazi Minister of National Enlightenment and Propaganda. How did he do it? On January 29, 1942, the satanic "Little Doktor" wrote in his personal diary: "Propaganda must always be essentially simple and repetitious. In the long run only he will achieve basic results in influencing public opinion who is able to reduce problems to the simplest terms, and who has the courage to keep forever repeating them in this simplified form—despite the objections of the intellectuals."

Repetition is like pounding a nail on the head—the more you pound it the more secure it becomes. And when it begins to loosen you pound it again.

So if you would sell an idea, repeat it, repeat it, and when you get tired repeating it—repeat it again.

Now repetition need not be direct. The most skillful persuasion is indirect. Set the situation and let the person persuade himself.

Man is such a persuasive animal that he cannot resist himself. Spend your time setting the scene, arranging the details, and creating the mood for your idea. Let the eye, the ear, the touch, the smell and the situation preach to him. These items give him pictured gratifications. He is making up his mind to do what he wants—and that is exactly what you want him to do.

Take the example of Macy's in New York. They have a technique called the "unadvertised special." You have to come into the store to find out what it is. As you enter, you are handed a bill which lists the twenty or more items on sale that day. These bargains are sold below list price. Take one and you'll find that one item is on the third floor, one on the sixth, and another in the basement. It takes about sixty-seven minutes to visit the counters involved.

What is Macy buying? Why the time of the woman who came in for a bargain. She is giving her attention to the objects on display as she goes from counter to counter. She sees things she needs; she visualizes the "good" the possession of these objects will bring her. They will make her life happier, help her to do her housework more easily. She will be the envy of the neighbors if she has the variety of merchandise displayed. She senses gratifications. And by the indirection of the implanted motives, she is being persuaded to buy. No one is saying a word to her; she is persuading herself.

Is it effective? Macy's sells $160,000,000 worth of goods in a year. And the secret again is: Create the conditions of persuasion and the person will proceed to act.

When Dr. John W. Studebaker, now U.S. Commissioner of Education, conducted a survey of the Philippine Islands in 1929 he came back with one of the simplest but most far-reaching recommendations on record. He said, "Put a Sears, Roebuck catalogue in every home in the Philippines. That will raise the cultural level of the islands." Why? Because no man desires that which he does not know. No man can dream of things which are totally outside his experience. He may change, he may modify, he may even create new patterns with combinations of things. But if there is nothing in his experience, he produces nothing. However, give his imagination an image to start with, and he will outstrip you with new patterns and wild desires. In the hands of the Filipinos, we were placing the whole wealth of our creative life. We were showing them an easier way of life, a more effective pattern of living, by simply subjecting them to a visual bath of luxuries. It wasn't necessary to sell them, we had but to direct their minds. They would do the rest. And the record shows that they did.

Nancy Astor suggested the same treatment of the Russians. "The way to make Russia a part of the world," she said, "would be to put a five-and-ten-cent store in every town over there."

Another effective device is the contest scheme. You know the one. It asks you to win a thousand dollars by writing twenty-five words pointing out the wonder of soap. This technique holds a great lesson for idea sellers. Think of what the advertisers are getting for their money. They are having people focus their minds on a product for an hour or more. Not only that, the manufacturer is having people sit down and think of the glory of his product while they write. Their defense is down. They are so persuasive they convince themselves unwittingly.

Get your subject thinking in terms of your idea, and his heart and mind are your allies. Arrange a contest, make a game, offer a challenge, give a gift, or create a fashion, and you have succeeded.

The most amazing example of idea selling was carried on by Hitler and

Mussolini. All the symbols and trappings were used, and what seemed nauseous repetition to us turned the heads of half the nations of the world. In the war, German psychological machines were turned on our troops. And they were effective.

I had the opportunity to study the leaflets the Germans spent planes, pilots, and precious gas to shower on our troops. They represented the best thinking of the collective German psychological mind as it conceived what would move Americans to surrender.

As you read these, note the use of the formula: the appeals to life, to loved ones, to physical safety, to honor, and to pride. And then note the theme of each one. Millions of leaflets, a variety of appeals, but one message. One theme expressed endlessly. And what is it? A strange theme clumsily expressed? No, indeed! It is a simple expression directed to the deepest drive in man's nature—self-preservation. And it is a saying that you and I have used since childhood.

Every leaflet ended with this thought:

> DEAD MEN TELL NO TALES
> PRISONERS OF WAR DO!

Capture the attention in any way you will, but always direct it to your idea.

Picture a war-weary soldier finding this leaflet:

### A Letter from Home

My one and only,

Another day and still no news from you.

For weeks I've hardly slept a wink knowing that you are facing such danger in the midst of battle—it drives me almost out of my mind.

In September you wrote you would be home for Christmas. I knew such a thing was too good to be true. Everyone knows that this war is not over by a long shot. And now this terrible winter!

During the long and lonely nights my thoughts often turn to what I would do if suddenly the news should arrive that you have been "killed in action." The thought of this dreaded telegram which so many mothers and young wives have already received haunts me night and day.

My darling! My darling! I couldn't stand it; without you life means nothing. When you are "Out There"—so far away—I beg you with all my heart to remember our vows when we promised to belong to each other always. It doesn't matter to me if you're not a hero, just so long as you come home safely. There must be a way out! Don't forget our dreams about our little "heaven on earth." Remember our old favorite "My fate is in your hands. . . ."

I love you—I love you—I love you—

Eternally yours,

Joan

Thousands and thousands XXX

How cleverly the germ of futility is inserted at various points: "war is not over," "this terrible winter," "killed in action," "Out There," "come home safely," "a way out." The judgment being repeated is simply: Get out of danger safely, give up. And this judgment is wrapped up in a theme that has been current in our land for generations: Dead men tell no tales. They were talking to our boys in our language.

Another appeal was a soldier's children, his hostages to fortune, an appeal no man can resist. Talk to a man in terms of his children, and you talk in terms of his heart. Moreover, these appeals were combined with pictures of children. One was a picture of a little girl saying her night prayers:

". . . and please take good care of Daddy."

The dead never return

The P.O.W.'s do.

Another little girl asks a reception nurse:

"I want an appointment to see my daddy."

"Yes, darling, but. . . ."

The dead never return

The P.O.W.'s do.

A cartoon drawing of a choo-choo train and child's art efforts had this message:

Dear Daddy,

I love you, Daddy, and I want you very much. I'd like you to come home when you can. Tell the choo-choo man to hurry the train for I want you.

Bob

Dead men tell no tales

P.O.W.'s do.

A typical American boy of four years held out a Congressional Medal and with tearful eyes explained:

"My daddy was a soldier too."

Dead men tell no tales

P.O.W.'s do.

Actual pictures of American troops surrendering were used to capture attention. Then came the approach to pride and honor, followed always by the theme.

> These pals of yours had plenty of guts. It needs more courage "to pack up" when you might get killed, and your death is of no use to anyone.
> Your pals were sportsmen. They knew when the game was up. We, recognizing their sportsmanship just as we do the Geneva Convention, treat them according to the rules and respect their soldierly honour.
> Dead men tell no tales but P.O.W.'s do!

Note the excellent use of repetition in capturing a mood of despair in this one.

> Every speculation has failed. . . .
> Every promise broken. . . .
> Every hope shattered. . . .
> There's no rhyme or reason. . . .
> No end in sight. . . .
> After Germany—Japan. . . .
> If you don't fall today—then tomorrow. . . .
> Put a stop to it . . . in one way or another.

DEAD MEN TELL NO TALES
. . . But P.O.W.'s do!

The attention-catcher of the question form, and the use of repetition . . . American . . . and the theme made this one a favorite.

> Where?
>   Which?
>    Who?
>     Why?
>      When?
> Where is the stiffest fighting going on?
>          On the AMERICAN Sector.
> Which part of the front has made the most progress?
>          The AMERICAN Sector.
> Who has had the greatest losses?
>          The AMERICANS.
> Why are the British letting you do all the fighting?
> When will you come to your senses and let those who started the war fight it out?
>          Dead Men Tell No Tales. . . . P.O.W.'s do.

What is the story of all these leaflets? Only the common experience of men of all ages:

"What the mind attends to, it considers; what it does not attend to, it dismisses. What the mind attends to continually, it believes. And, what the mind believes, it eventually does!

A new theory? Not at all. One that was realized by antiquity, and expressed so well by Aristotle that it has been a theme song echoing through the ages. The greatest Grecian mind, Aristotle, put it this way: "If you would persuade men, implant motives that will lead them to freely follow your desires."

So if you would sell an idea, get the other person thinking about your idea. Make him alive to it. Put it in his mind, again and again, and again.

Can you do it? It is the most challenging contest known to man. It is the game of life.

### PROJECTS

In the speech you are about to prepare, use the simple formula constructed many years ago by Professor Richard C. Borden in his excellent book *Public Speaking as Listeners Like It*. For the action speech this formula is extremely useful. It consists of four simple steps:

1. Ho hum!
2. Why bring that up?
3. For instance!
4. So what?

Professor Borden was trying to help speakers organize their thinking in terms of audience interest. In the first step, the audience is thinking of matters which concern only themselves, so the speaker must direct their attention to his point. If he fails to capture their attention he is likely to fail throughout his talk. For example, a student of mine, talking about preparation of defenses in atomic warfare, began, "The time to bury yourself is now!" This gained immediate attention for his point that underground factories should be built now. Search out the novel aspect of your point and make the audience wake up. There are five easy ways this can be done: (1) show the audience how to get something they want; (2) arouse their curiosity or suspense; (3) state an arresting fact; (4) present a demonstration; and (5) begin with an illustration or anecdote.

Any number of ways may be used to get immediate interest in beginning your talk. For example, one student tossed a small object into the air as he explained that this was the most precious jewel in the world. After he had created sufficient suspense, he revealed that this was a human tooth. It was an effective opening to his talk on care of the teeth. Another student held up a pair of safety glasses commonly worn by factory workers, and indicated the square inch of steel that was embedded in the right eye glass. He asked the audience to imagine what would have happened had that worker failed to wear his protective goggles that day. Then he proceeded to give his talk on plant safety devices. A third student simply asked the class to close their eyes. As they did so she announced:

". . . A mantle of darkness has fallen over your eyes forever. Never again will you be able to distinguish between light and shadow. The faces of your loved ones you will never see again. You may leave this room safely and make your way to the street. There you will be powerless, groping. Everything about you may mean injury or death. You are completely at the mercy of others. You are at the mercy of the smallest prankish child. What would you give to have your sight back? . . . Now open your eyes. You can see again. *That's what a Seeing Eye dog means to a blind person. . . .*"

The principle is obvious: Capture the attention of your listeners by directly contacting as many of their senses as possible.

The second step, *Why bring that up?*, furnishes the reason the audience should continue to pay attention. The opening captures attention, but the reason sustains attention. Tell the audience why this subject is important to them, and make your point in an interesting way. Make it challenging, make it specific, make it useful, or make it novel. But be certain that you join your point with supporting reasons. Do not elaborate with proof of your reasons but use them as a bridge between your audience and your topic.

Dean Rose of Missouri State College, at Cape Girardeau, applied this technique when he determined to landscape the campus. Instead of plastering KEEP OFF THE GRASS, he painted small signs which read, GIVE US YOUNG BLADES A CHANCE, and SEEDS AT WORK. Instead of having the ash cans say REFUSE, he made them give a reason, a pictured gratification, and each gently suggested THE CAMPUS BEAUTIFUL. These instances were successful because the reason for the action was given.

In addition, you must make certain that the statement of your point is clear and obvious. The *Encyclopaedia Britannica* reports that "Nine readers out of ten take a lucid statement for a true one." And the United States Army insists that "An order that can be misunderstood will be." President Woodrow Wilson left a revealing anecdote of how his father taught him to acquire simplicity and directness in making his meaning clear. "My father was a man of great intellectual energy," said the scholarly President. "My best training came from him. He was intolerant of vagueness, and from the time I began to write until his death in 1903, when he was eighty-one years old, I carried everything I wrote to him. He would make me read it aloud which was always painful to me. Every now and then he would stop me. 'What do you mean by that?' I would tell him, and of course in doing so would express myself more simply than I had on paper. 'Why didn't you say so?' he would go on. 'Don't shoot at your meaning with birdshot and hit the whole countryside; shoot with a rifle at the thing you have to say.'"

The third step, *For instance!*, is the most persuasive part of your talk. One good example is worth a thousand words. The reason is that examples present images to the senses which attract and hold the attention of the mind. A good example is nature's pathway to the mind. But you must follow nature and be specific, vivid, sensuous, and, above all, graphic. For example, here is a short extract from a speech by Marcus Duffield on the overlapping functions in bureaus of the Federal Government:

"Overlapping functions in government bureaus are not necessary—but just plain foolish! Take highways. An ordinary public highway is built by the Bureau of Public Roads of the Department of Agriculture. If it runs through a National Park, the National Park Service of the Department of Interior builds it. If it is in Alaska, the Engineering Corps of the War Department builds it.

"Take foxes. If a man shoots a fox in Alaska, he must settle with the Department of Agriculture. But if he traps the fox, he must settle with the Department of Commerce.

"If you think two-department care of Alaskan foxes is just an accident— then take bears! The Secretary of the Interior protects grizzly bears. The Secretary of Agriculture protects brown bears. If a brown Kodiak bear has twins, one brown and one black, they are under the auspices of two different federal departments."

The fourth step, *So what?*, suggests that the speaker ask for action. To state all your facts and expect the audience to make up their minds is asking too much. You must request some specific action. And the action requested must be within the power of the audience. If you ask for the impossible, you get nothing. So set your final plea in a verb, such as "join," "contribute," "write," "telegraph," "buy," "enlist," "investigate," "convict."

Two examples of such conclusions taken from widely different fields are of value. The first is from Burke's opening speech against Warren Hastings which concludes with this solemn catalogue of impeachment:

"Therefore, it is with confidence that, ordered by the Commons, I impeach Warren Hastings, Esquire, of high crimes and misdemeanors.

"I impeach him in the name of the Commons of Great Britain in the Parliament assembled, whose parliamentary trust he has betrayed.

"I impeach him in the name of all the Commons of Great Britain, whose national character he has dishonored.

"I impeach him in the name of the people of India, whose laws, rights and liberties he has subverted; whose properties he has destroyed; whose country he has laid waste and desolate.

"I impeach him in the name and by virtue of those eternal laws of justice which he has violated.

"I impeach him in the name of human nature itself, which he has cruelly outraged, injured and oppressed, in both sexes, in every age, rank, situation, and condition of life."

The second example is from a speech by William G. Power, executive of the Chevrolet Division, General Motors, appearing before the National Institute of Real Estate Brokers. After a stirring speech on selling real estate, he concludes:

"How are we going to be better than average? How are we going to face success in a competitive market? I'll tell you how. You are going to do better than the average in your viewpoint, in your attitude toward your job, toward your organization, toward your city; you are going to work with your local committee, with your state; you are going to work with your National Association. You are going to send ideas as well as receive ideas. You are going to read bulletins. You are going to apply yourselves. You are going to start selling again. You are going to start promoting.

"Remember, two-thirds of promotion is motion!

"Motion, action, activity! Men on the march! Real estate men on the march! Real estate men out selling! You are going to be real brokers, Realtor-brokers, not Realtor-speculators. You are going to watch legislation. You are going to work with the Legislative Committee and you are going to do everything in your power to make your organization bigger and stronger, knowing that you can be no bigger nor stronger than your organization.

"*Two-thirds of promotion is motion!* Promote yourselves, promote your organization, promote your city. To do this you must have a fighting faith in yourself, a fighting faith in your profession, and a fighting faith in your organization.

"*Two-thirds of promotion is motion.* Motion, action, activity! Men on the march. I challenge you to go into 1948 with the determination to meet tomorrow's competition. Make that your battle cry, *Action, Action, Action.*"

In asking for action, be certain that you tie it up with the self-interest of the audience. Picture gratifications to your audience. Old Dr. Samuel

Johnson was once auctioning off the contents of the old Anchor Brewery in London. As he stood on the auctioneer's platform he didn't orate much about what the product intrinsically was—about physical fixtures, complete equipment, location, or capacity. Knowing human nature, the good Doctor boomed out: "We are not here to sell boilers and vats, but the potentiality of growing rich beyond the dreams of avarice." So when you write your conclusion, remember you are not merely writing an ending to your talk, you are asking for a definite action which will benefit your listeners.

### Projects

*Assignment 1*

Select some cause or drive that is being promoted in your community. It may be either the Community Chest, the Red Cross, the Cancer Drive, the Orphanage Fund, the School Appeal, or any current charity drive. Fashion a two- or three-minute speech in which you make the audience want to give. This is a real challenge. It will not be enough to make the audience aware of the need; you must make them contribute. To make this assignment real, each speaker will place a fixed sum in the general fund as he gives his speech. After all the speeches have been heard, the class will decide which cause is to receive the jackpot. Use all the appeals to emotion, all the specific instances, and all the pictured gratifications at your command to make your cause win.

*Assignment 2*

This is a Hobby Lobby assignment. There is something in which you are interested as a hobby. Something that you spend time on because you like it. Whatever that thing is it will furnish the material for an interesting speech. It is something that you have earned the right to talk about. Why not make that hobby the subject of your talk? More than likely the audience will respond enthusiastically, and the experience of success will benefit you.

*Prepare a three- to four-minute talk encouraging the class to become interested in your hobby.*

Picture for your audience the gratifications they will experience if they adopt your hobby. This usually calls for a demonstration. One student, for example, had the hobby of training homing pigeons. During his talk he held a pigeon in his hand, attached a message to it, and released the bird from the window saying, "He'll be home when I get there." Another student had the hobby of making fudge. After describing the process, she took out a box of homemade fudge and let the class sample her efforts.

Woodcraft, sketching, shell collecting, stamp collecting, or any item of human interest can be made into a good talk.

## Assignment 3

This assignment will help you to think on your feet. Select one of the following comments about life and give a two- to three-minute talk on its message.

1. You may elaborate upon its meaning.
2. You may refute it.
3. You may support it with specific examples from your own experience.
4. You may apply it to modern life and times.
5. You may maintain it is a half-truth.
6. You may relate the effect such a belief had in the life of another person.
7. You may use it as a point of departure for a related truth.
8. You may plead for its acceptance by the audience.
9. You may demonstrate it for more effective understanding.

In any or all of these nine ways you can formulate your thoughts. Use each of the nine ways to examine your thinking about the proposition and you will find that you are quickly arranging your knowledge for use. This is an excellent mental streamliner. If you practice it when reading you will start to sharpen your thinking powers.

1. Whatsoever things are true, whatsoever things are honest,
   Whatsoever things are just, whatsoever things are pure, whatsoever things are lovely,
   Whatsoever things are of good report; if there be any virtue, and if there be any praise, think on these things.

   —Philippians 4:8

2. Let your light so shine before men, that they may see your good works, and glorify your Father who is in heaven.

   —Matthew 5:16

3. A joyful mind maketh age flourishing: a sorrowful spirit drieth up the bones.

   —Proverbs

4. The man whose acquisitions stick is the man who is always achieving and advancing whilst his neighbors, spending most of their time in relearning what they once knew, but have forgotten, simply hold their own.

   —WILLIAM JAMES

5. The common error in regard to speaking is the assumption that all is necessary is to have "something to say." Utterly false! Unless that

"something to say" is said in accordance with the laws of the human mind which govern conviction, it might as well be spoken to the winds.

—PHILLIPS

6. One picture is worth ten thousand words.

—CHINESE PROVERB

7. But dost thou love life? Then do not squander time, for that's the stuff life is made of, as Poor Richard says.

—BENJAMIN FRANKLIN

8. And all men kill the thing they love,
    By all let this be heard,
Some do it with a bitter look,
    Some with a flattering word,
The coward does it with a kiss,
    The brave man with a sword!

—OSCAR WILDE

9. We are such stuff as dreams are made on, and our little life is rounded with a sleep.

—SHAKESPEARE

10. A man's praise has very musical and charming accents in another's mouth, but it is very flat and untunable in his own.

—ANONYMOUS

11. Ah Love! Could you and I with Him conspire
To grasp this sorry Scheme of Things entire,
    Would not we shatter it to bits—and then
Re-mould it nearer to the Heart's Desire!

—FITZGERALD

12. Everything comes if a man will only wait.

—DISRAELI

13. There is no new thing under the sun.

—Ecclesiastes

14. For the good are always merry,
    Save by an evil chance,
And the merry love the fiddle
    And the merry love to dance.

—YEATS

15. Freedom is obedience to self-formulated rules.

—ARISTOTLE

16. It is the silence of the god we fear, not his wrath;
Silence is the unbearable repartee.

—MEREDITH

17. I do not believe in a fate that falls on men however they act, but I do believe in a fate that falls on them unless they act.

—CHESTERTON

18. To manage men, one ought to have a sharp mind in a velvet sheath.

—GEORGE ELIOT

19. Men must be taught as if you taught them not,
And things unknown propos'd as things forgot.

—POPE

20. A man's personal defects will commonly have with the rest of the world, precisely that importance which they have to himself. If he makes light of them, so will other men.

—EMERSON

21. Give every man thy ear, but few thy voice.

—SHAKESPEARE

22. God Himself dare not appear to a hungry man except in the form of bread.

—GANDHI

23. Men are failures not because they are *stupid*, but because they are not sufficiently *impassioned*.

—STRUTHERS BURT

24. The art of understanding people is the art of assuming that they are better than perhaps even they themselves think. Most of us are fascinated by a generous portrait of ourselves and try at least for a while to live up to it.

—JOHN ERSKINE

25. The successful shepherd thinks like his sheep.

—ANONYMOUS

26. It is an old and true maxim "that a drop of honey catches more flies than a gallon of gall." So with men, if you would win a man to your cause, first convince him that you are his sincere friend. Therein is a drop of honey that catches his heart; which, say what you will, is the great high road to his reason.

—LINCOLN

*Assignment 4*

The one-point speech is a perfect example of the technique of Aesop. Take any one of his fables and you will see that he follows this simple presentation of a single point in a telling way. For example:

A lark once had a nest of young birds in a cornfield, and one morning as she went out to seek food for them she told the little larks to listen very carefully to anything they might hear the farmer say, and to tell her when she came back.

On her return they said that the farmer had been there with his son, and had arranged to ask his neighbors to come upon the next day and help him to reap the corn.

"Then," said the old bird, "there is no danger yet."

Next day the young larks told their mother that the farmer had been there again, and had told his son to ask his cousins to come and help to reap the corn. The old lark still said that there was no danger yet.

On the third day the young birds told their mother how the farmer had said that next morning he would reap the corn himself.

"Then," answered the mother lark, "it is time that we went somewhere else. The farmer's neighbors and friends were not very likely to come and help him; but if he is going to reap the corn himself we must move our home to another field."

*If you want a thing done, do it yourself!*

Select a proverb, or some truth that you have discovered by experience, and create a fable about it. This is not as difficult as it appears at first. In fact, it's fun. Present your fable to the class and ask them to find the point.

*Sample Persuasive Outline*

Speaker _____ Class _____ Date _____

  I. Topic.
 II. Purpose of speech: Indicate specific aim.
III. Attention getter.
IV. Point.
 V. Examples.
VI. Conclusion.

*Questions for Critical Discussion of Performance*

 1. Did the opening immediately capture interest? Why?
 2. Was the speaker enthusiastic?
 3. Was the purpose of the speech clear?
 4. Was the speaker's point obvious throughout?
 5. Did the speaker use the most effective appeal?
 6. Were his examples definite and specific?
 7. Were the speaker's demonstrations attractive?
 8. Was the conclusion logical and appealing?
 9. Were you persuaded by the talk?
10. How could the speaker improve this talk?

*Developing Semantic Skill*

Add to your word cards the following:

I. Words used in the speech text:

| Word | Pronunciation | Meaning |
|------|---------------|---------|
| 1. concept | | |
| 2. description | | |
| 3. exposition | | |
| 4. intellect | | |

II. Words commonly mispronounced:
   1. naïve
   2. neither
   3. New Orleans

III. Words from your own experience.

## Chapter 19

# DELIBERATIVE SITUATIONS

As a vessel is known by the sound, whether it be cracked or not,
so men are proved by their speeches whether they be wise or foolish.
—DEMOSTHENES

Deliberative situations have the common aim of making decisions or
plans. The decisions may deal with the nature of past acts or the
nature of future acts. In a trial, the court is trying to decide whether
the person is innocent or guilty of a past act so that it may pass judgment here and now. Evidence is brought to light to determine what
decision ought to be justly made. The court does not seek to carry
out its judgment, but merely to decide what is just in each case. The
sentence is a plan of retribution offered by the court, but not carried
out by the court. A special branch of government is maintained to
carry out the court's decisions. Similarly, in business the managers
meet regularly to decide what has been good or bad in their previous
sales and administrative tactics. In such conferences the goal is to
pass judgment on the past acts, to investigate and reflect on their
value. In both the above types of situation the immediate outcome
is not action but decision. The court decides the guilt or innocence,
and the business conference decides either to maintain the *status quo*
or to revise the system.

When a situation deals with the nature of future acts, the purpose
remains the same. A decision is still sought, but it is a more difficult
decision. To decide the nature of past acts simply requires a full understanding of them; such an understanding of future acts is not
possible. Hence, the participants must deal not solely in facts but
must consider possibilities and probabilities. In deciding the nature
of a past act, facts are sought; in future acts the most probable good
is sought. That the latter is no easy task may be realized from the
attempts of the present administration to formulate plans for defense. Congress is continually engaged in the task of planning laws

241

to meet emergencies that may arise in the future. Business firms are engaged year in and year out in planning sales campaigns and other future courses of action. Congress and business alike perform these functions in the communicative activity called "conference." They get their respective groups together for the purpose of decision.

The purpose of decision determines the character of the situation. The participants deliberate, take counsel, and weigh the evidence offered. The appeal is intellectual rather than emotional, seeking to convince rather than to persuade. The method of the speaker is simple and direct, and he endeavors to make known all the available facts and likely probabilities. The goal is not action, but reflection; not to do, but to decide. Such situations are "deliberative situations," and their general purpose decision or conviction.

Conviction proceeds from furnishing ample reasons to the mind. To convince is essentially to make conscious of a truth. It differs from persuasion in that the appeal is to the intellect rather than to the emotions. Hence, to convince requires the elements of clarity, orderliness, evidence, arguments, and straight thinking.

### Clarity and Orderliness

You must impress the audience with the accuracy of your thinking and the clarity of your perception. You can achieve this by stating each point in simple, precise language. Order deals first with the continuity of thought and second with the presentation of thought. As a check on the continuity of thought the form of outline called a "brief" is best. A brief gives the main thoughts in complete sentences and states the proof for each argument. The thought and the arguments supporting it are joined by causal connectives, such as "because," "for," and "since." The orderly presentation of thought centers on the simplicity and directness of language, manner, and matter. Present your facts and arguments in their simplest form and avoid complications introduced by asides or digressions.

Your technique in gaining conviction consists of (1) making the group see your position clearly, (2) making them believe the correctness of your position, and (3) making them accept the proof you offer in support of your position. You do this by stating your proposition, determining the issue, and supporting your issue with cogent arguments and valid evidence. Let us consider each of these vital elements of conviction.

## Proposition

What you assert or deny about your topic is your proposition. A simple proposition has one subject and one predicate. A composite proposition has one subject and two or three predicates. For example, "The United States should join a union of the English-speaking nations" is a simple proposition predicating that the subject, "United States," should follow a single action. However, "That the United States should join a union of the English-speaking nations, and make a stand for world democracy" is a composite proposition indicating two proposed actions for a single subject.

The simplicity of your proposition is an aid in conviction. An involved proposition leads to misunderstanding and wastes persuasive effort. Besides being simple, the proposition should be interesting, and expressed in vital language, which will make it concrete, novel, and well adapted to the audience. It is sometimes useful to make the proposition challenging. Remember that a trite expression of the proposition leaves the audience disinterested and apathetic. Search your proposition for some novel aspect; use that aspect creatively, and the problem of immediate interest will be solved.

## Issue

In every proposition there are some elements that all sides will agree to without argument. In any controversy these common points must be made clear to save time. The discovery of these common points helps determine the points at issue. Hence, it is important to determine in exactly what sense the speaker agrees and disagrees with his opponents.

There are three main types of issues: fact, definition, and justification. Issues of *fact* deal directly with the meaning of the proposition. They deny the existence of the facts asserted in the proposition—for example, "Jones is guilty of murder" being faced with "Jones is not guilty of murder." Here the fact itself is challenged, making an issue of fact. An issue of *definition* does not deny that the act took place, but denies that the act was as specified. For instance, "Jones killed the man, but he did so accidentally; hence, it was not murder." Finally, the issue may resolve around *justification* of the act. For example, "Jones murdered this man, but he did it in self-defense and was justified." Distinction of the nature of the issue clarifies the point at issue and aids in arriving at an understanding.

## Arguments

Once the issue has been determined clearly the speaker seeks to marshal his proof. This proof generally consists of a series of subordinate propositions which, if proved true, will establish the main proposition. This process is the one friends engage in continually when arguing. One says, "Well, you'll agree to this—and you'll agree to this—therefore, you have to agree to *this*." Or one may say, "You'll admit this is true—and you'll admit this is true—now, if all these are true isn't it reasonable that *this* is true?" Such techniques use the two basic forms of reasoning: deduction and induction. The first instance is the use of a syllogism: a *deductive argument* in which the reasoning proceeds from two true propositions logically connected to a third proposition necessarily true. The second instance is the use of *induction*, an argument in which a general conclusion is sought from many particulars. It is expressed in reasonable terms by offering a few select instances rather than all conceivable ones as evidence. Hence, it is not scientifically certain, but reasonably sure. However, it is in this realm of probability that men must act most frequently, for it is not possible to know absolutely all the possibilities in any case.

In seeking conviction, the cogency of the arguments will carry the greatest weight. It must not be supposed, however, that the forces of emotional appeal play no part in conviction. Indeed, in the absence of absolute certainty, the participants fall back on the character and impression of the speaker. Still, the pale light of ordered thought does eventually succeed, and truth is never wholly lost.

In all deliberative situations the determination of truth remains as the goal. Hence, your task is to ascertain truth first, but, in addition, as a speaker you must achieve the means of communicating truth. This requires an ordered sequence of thought and usually a climactic arrangement of thought. After you have decided upon the reasoning which best supports your solution, arrange your sequence of thought in its most forceful style. You achieve this by selecting the most potent arguments and introducing them in their most telling order.

## Evidence

Evidence is the means of ascertaining the truth of an alleged fact. It can be classified, depending upon how it is offered, as personal, original, or hearsay; or, according to its effect on the proposition under discussion, as direct or circumstantial. The quality of the evidence can be indicated further by reference to it as expert or ordinary.

Evidence is *personal* when it is presented by an individual and concerns his mental and physical possessions. It is distinguished from *real evidence* in which the thing offered as proof is itself presented. If a man wanted to establish that an automobile was defectively made, he might offer the personal evidence of his trouble with it, and even bring in mechanics to prove that his statements were true. These would both be personal. If, however, he produced parts of the car in court in order to demonstrate their effects, that would be real evidence. A less confusing name than real evidence is *tangible evidence*.

Evidence is *original* when the one who offers it arrived at it first-hand; it is *hearsay* when the knowledge came to the testifier from another person. As you readily realize from a study of semantics, there are numerous factors in hearsay evidence which tend to weaken its value as proof. Indeed, the court will not accept hearsay evidence. Yet, to a speaker, it is a potent force for conviction and persuasion because an audience is usually ready to accept the speaker as a truthful man and to rely on his hearsay evidence.

Evidence is *direct* when it deals directly with the issue, and *indirect* when it deals with facts not essential to the issue, but bearing upon it. Hence, direct evidence, if it be true, immediately establishes the fact to be proved by it; while indirect evidence establishes immediately collateral facts from which the main fact may be inferred. Indirect evidence is often referred to as *circumstantial* evidence. Circumstantial evidence presents objects which give mute testimony that a fact is true or false. Etymologically, the word means "standing around." The position of the inanimate objects surrounding an act usually forms the basis for circumstantial or indirect evidence.

When evidence is given orally it is called *testimony*. Testimony can be of two kinds: *expert* and *ordinary*. This distinction deals with the quality of the evidence offered. The courts draw a sharp line between these two types of evidence by stating that the expert may offer opinion in his testimony, but the ordinary witness can offer only facts. Hence, what the witness actually saw would be valid evidence, but not what he thought about the thing he saw. The expert, however, because of his skill, learning, and authority in his field, is permitted to offer an opinion relative to the worth of the material evidence offered. An authority on wood could offer an opinion that the wood in question came from the same kind of a tree and from a particular lumberyard. An ordinary witness would not be allowed to offer such evidence. All he could say would be whether or not the piece of wood looked like the one he saw at such and such a place.

*Summary*

From (1) the statement of the proposition to (2) the determination of the issue to (3) the proof of the issue by argument to (4) the submission of the evidence is the route followed in a clear speech. The introduction prepares the audience for the issue; the conclusion reminds them that the case has been established. Steps 3 and 4 together constitute the proof of the proposition and must not be supposed to occur separately. In support of each chain in your argument it may be necessary to offer evidence. The clear determination of the issue will aid you in deciding just how much evidence need be offered and on what points it is necessary. In gathering your material, follow this process as a check on your preparation. Finally, when all material is collected, strive for the most effective arrangement of your material. Align it to the audience, the occasion, and whatever other factors in the situation will assist in transmitting it to the audience.

### EXAMPLE

James A. Farley presents a compact, logical, and vital speech on the meaning of democracy. The speech is characterized by cogency of thought and simplicity of language. The speaker's style is simple and suitable for the exposition of a fundamental belief. Forcefulness in thought is achieved by the nature of the subject. He feels that if the audience understands the message behind his words they will believe. Hence, he uses the common means of clarification: definition, concrete instance, parts, authority, summary, and iteration.

The speaker exhibits the unique skill of making the philosophic real. Clear exposition of logical concepts is coupled with an astute use of the figurative. Difficult notions are made simple by placing them in common coinage. The abstract notions of personal liberty and religious freedom become vivid when related to the daily practice of democracy. The speaker ennobles his theme by a complete disparagement of its opponents. His speech may be called a "meeting of minds," for he addresses men in a contemplative mood and confines his thoughts to that mood. This crystallizes the purpose of a meeting of Christians and Jews and hence establishes a bond readily accepted. The speech was recorded in the *Congressional Record* by unanimous consent on March 31, 1941.

## NATIONAL CONFERENCE OF CHRISTIANS AND JEWS

### ADDRESS

by

HON. JAMES A. FARLEY

AT BOSTON CHAMBER OF COMMERCE, MAR. 27, 1941

Never in our history has a conference like this had greater significance. The National Conference of Christians and Jews, proclaiming as its purpose adherence to the principle of religious liberty and the promotion of that liberty, has a special meaning at this time, when democracy is being attacked all over the world. America, to a greater extent than ever before in history, is called upon to defend democracy in terms of clear thinking and vital action. It is seeking once more to prove democracy to be that form of government which has done most for the individual and most for humanity.

I shall not attempt to define the concept of democracy in exact terms. I merely wish to call attention to one or two of its aspects which are fundamental to the purposes for which we are gathered here.

If democracy means anything, it means the equality of men. That does not mean equality in all those capacities of mind and body which in the nature of things can never be equal. They cannot be equal for the simple reason that human beings are not identical. It does not apply to moral equality, for there will be some who are more kind, more charitable, and who live their lives more completely in obedience to the moral law. When the Declaration of Independence speaks of the "self-evident truth" that "all men are created equal and endowed by their Creator with certain inalienable rights" it speaks of equality in a vastly more fundamental sense. It means that no human being shall be so poor or so unfortunate or so incompetent, even so unworthy, that he is not deserving of recognition as an individual. Beyond that it means that, as an individual, he has certain rights that no one is justified in destroying or denying him. It means that so far as possible he deserves equality of opportunity—an equal chance—as an individual. It is the glory of this country that it has fought to maintain the principle that every man and woman deserves a share in the benefits of our society.

When we consider this principle of equality as the basis of our democratic faith, we must recognize two other major points. The first is that, when we proclaim that equality, we are granting the truth of a fundamental religious teaching. The belief in the political equality of men springs from the belief in the essential equality of men before the common Father. This idea of equality is part and parcel of the belief in the existence of a human soul in every individual person. More, it is part and parcel of the religious assertion that the soul is an immortal soul.

Unless it is, why should human personality be sacred? Unless it is, what inalienable rights could the individual possess? Unless it is, why do individuals give of their goods, their efforts and their lives for the sake of principle? If the individual soul is a thing that vanishes like a spark falling in the water, then it is hard to see how men can be so indifferent to their personal comfort and interest as to make any sacrifice at all for principle. Democracy, therefore, fundamentally recognizes the necessity of religion and of the teachings of religion as a guaranty of its own vitality and its own perseverance in a world of danger. The equality to which we pay reverence when we dedicate ourselves to the principle of democracy, is the equality of the human soul. To paraphrase a great American thinker, it is because the human being has moral powers, because he carries a law in his own breast and was made to govern himself, that we cannot endure to see him become another person's slave or tool. It is because we see in him the Divine image, that we demand for him means of self-development, spheres for free action, and that we call society not to fetter but to aid his growth.

The second aspect of democracy is the principle of tolerance. It is the principle of respect by the individual and for the individual. It is the principle of the many living together in a common life, maintaining peace with each other, upholding justice in their relations and, above all, actively working together to protect those who need protection in the exercise of their legitimate rights.

It is interesting that tolerance became established only slowly, only in spite of the many forces that denied the possibility of tolerance. Take the word toleration—which, I need not remind you, has a slightly different definition than tolerance. Toleration, as a national principle, came after centuries of conflict. It came after nations stood exhausted, broken up into factions and clashing armies. It was not until blood had drenched the soil of Europe that people began to recognize the essential fact that two or more religions could exist in the same nation at the same time. This principle of toleration is another name for the principle of religious liberty. It is not only the mark of a great aspiration but the mark of a very definite legal concept.

Briefly, religious liberty manifests itself in three ways.

First, it gives to the individual the right to choose his own creed, his own church, his own form of religion, so far as the exercise of that right does not impair the fundamental rights of others.

Second, it grants autonomy to a religion as an institution. It gives a religious institution the right to the pursuit of its own purposes, so far as these purposes conform with those expressed laws of the land which are designed to protect one religion as against the other. Basically, as this principle operates in America, it means that religious institutions are free to gather new members and to grow, to own property, to carry on their legitimate religious services and ceremonies, and to speak freely in the forum of public opinion.

The third characteristic of religious liberty is a recognition by the Nation of the essential equality of the different religions. That means that a small religious institution with 50 members stands within the great principle of freedom with the same rights and privileges as the largest religious institution.

It is interesting that as the nations of the world slowly came to the principle of religious freedom over past generations, the nations have differed in their ways of maintaining what they have called religious freedom. In many nations, some of them on the continent of Europe, the state actively sought to regulate religions in order, it claimed, to maintain equal status among religions. The state exercised a definite supervision over religious institutions, and in some cases made grave mistakes and committed serious injustices in exercising this supervision.

America, however, has worked on a different principle. It seeks to maintain religious freedom by the entire separation of the church and state. We are proud, here in America, that without the active interference of the state, religions have grown, have cooperated, have recognized one another's rights, and have achieved a vital and commanding place in the great community of America.

But these formal, legal, technical aspects of toleration exist because basically the principle of tolerance is a principle that is cherished in every community that dares to call itself a civilized community. Tolerance is an expression of one of the most profoundly important qualities of a civilized human being—the capacity for self-restraint. I want to stress the word "civilized" in this connection. I want to say as strongly as I can here that the absence of tolerance is characteristic of the barbarian. I know you will understand to what I refer, for I know that all Americans feel this deeply. Tolerance is that admirable thing in a human being that makes him restrain his own power in order that others may enjoy the exercise of theirs. It is the principle that permits him to grant to his fellow man the right to be heard, that recognizes the virtue in the man on the other side of the street or in the other street or in the other town. It is the principle that prevails so magnificently in every manly sport—the thing we call sportsmanship—which, despite keen competition, restrains those who participate from a ruthless and unfair exercise of temporary advantage. It is the principle to which, in these serious days, we must rededicate ourselves.

Now that the great struggle for the existence of democracy in so many parts of the world is reaching a critical stage, the ideals of this conference assume a new—a unique—importance. They are essential to the defense of our Nation. They are also essential to the playing of our proper part in world affairs. The reason they are important to our national defense is that they are an outward sign of the principle of true unity. Only a nation that is thus united can effectively survive. Of course, there is another kind of unity in the world. That is the hard, enforced, cruel unity of dictatorship. It is a false—an artificial—unity. That is why it can be only a temporary and passing manifestation. No unity enforced in a nation by arms and power has ever survived. Such a unity is the unity of the jailer and the hangman. It is the unity of the prison and the grave. Human beings will not long submit to so vicious a denial of the simple dictation of humanity.

The unity that endures is the kind of unity we have in America. It is the unity of free people recognizing that only as others are free can they be free, recognizing that only as others are permitted to speak can they be permitted to speak, recognizing that only as others have rights can they maintain their own rights. That is the unity that quickens the heart and lifts the head of an American when he sees the flag. It is the unity of free men and free religions in a free nation.

I need not remind you that those nations that maintain unity by persecution would seek and are seeking to destroy our kind of unity by dividing us among ourselves. You and I know too well how they proceed. Intolerance is the poison they use. By pamphlets, by speeches, by whispering campaigns they try to set group against group, religious believer against religious believer, neighbor against neighbor. Lying stories of the most revolting kind—from simple slander against one or two persons to elaborate fabrications involving whole groups—are spread among the gullible. These are efforts to divide us, to destroy our unity, to sap our strength, to throw us off our course, to render us ineffective; and these efforts are rewarded whenever an American says or does an intolerant thing. Whenever we make a distinction between men because of their religion or race, whenever we impute to a whole religious or social or economic group the sins or failings or the political beliefs of some of the members, whenever we spread slanderous whispers about a religion or those who believe in it—whenever we do these things, we are helping those who wish to shatter our American unity. Intolerance is the deadliest enemy of true unity. It is the destroyer of democracy.

As I have lived and grown older in this world, I have learned not only the ethical value of tolerance but its practical necessity. Whenever, in dealing with another man, we have to stop to think of that man as a Catholic or a Jew or a Protestant and shape our methods of dealing with him in accordance with a conception of something in him peculiar to his own religion, we fail in the practical purposes for which we all deal with each other. We cannot think straight and we cannot think effectively and we cannot get results when we have to stop and gear ourselves to supposed religious differences. Effective dealing with neighbors and friends and political and business associates means dealing with them as human beings and Americans, subject to the same fundamental desires and purposes. I have found that tolerance is not only a good moral principle; it is the only sound, practical means of successful living.

But much as we love our liberty and much as we extol the virtues we have learned over the generations in America, we must always be aware that there is such a thing as tolerance in our dealing with the world. Let us be proud, but not conceited. Let us avoid the self-deception practiced by the Pharisee who stood in the temple and thanked God that he was not as other men. Let us rather approach our national problems and responsibilities with the quiet assurance that our light will shine in the darkness around us because of what we are rather than because of what we say we are.

In the task before us, we must prevail in the spirit of our institutions. In combating intolerance in others we must not become intolerant ourselves. If we do, those against whom we struggle will have achieved the ultimate victory over us. They will have made us become as they are.

They will have transformed us into the evil thing we set out to oppose. Let us, in fighting for tolerance, observe among our own people, among our own religions, the finest, greatest, most enduring unity—the unity of free men and free religions.

BRIEF

*Introduction*

    I. This Conference has greater significance than ever before.
        A. It proclaims the principle of religious liberty.
        B. It proves that democracy is the best form of government.

*Narration*

    I. Democracy means the spiritual equality of men; for
        A. Men are not equal in body and mind; for
            1. Capacities differ by nature;
            2. Men are not identical.
        B. Men are not morally equal; for
            1. Some are more kind and charitable;
            2. Some live more obediently to the moral law.
        C. The Declaration of Independence speaks of spiritual equality; for
            1. Man deserves recognition as an individual;
            2. Man's rights cannot be destroyed or denied;
            3. Man deserves equality of opportunity;
            4. Man deserves a share in the benefits of society.

*Discussion*

    I. The principle of equality is the basis of our democratic faith; for
        A. Political equality arises from spiritual equality; for
            1. Equality attests the existence of a human soul in each;
            2. Equality attests that that soul is immortal; for
                 *a.* Unless it is immortal human personality is not sacred;
                 *b.* Man possesses no inalienable rights;
                 *c.* Sacrifice for principle is absurd.
            3. Equality of human souls is the basis of democracy; for
                 *a.* Man was made with the power to govern himself;
                 *b.* It is intolerable to see him a slave or tool;
                 *c.* Man is the image of the Divine;
                 *d.* Society must aid his growth and development.
        B. The principle of tolerance means respect for individuality; for
            1. It means living a common life peacefully;
            2. It means upholding justice in all relations;
            3. It means assurance of legitimate rights for all.

II. Toleration or religious liberty has been painfully achieved; for
- A. Toleration evolved after centuries of conflict; for
  1. It came only after blood drenched the soil of Europe.
- B. Toleration manifests itself in religious freedom; for
  1. It grants the right to choose one's own creed;
  2. It grants autonomy to religion as an institution;
  3. It grants recognition to the essential nature of different religions.
- C. Nations have differed in maintaining religious liberty; for
  1. Many attempted to supervise religious institutions;
  2. One (America) has striven for separation of church and state.

III. The practice of tolerance has enabled America to achieve true unity; for
- A. Tolerance is a capacity for self-restraint; for
  1. Its absence is characteristic of the barbarian;
  2. It grants to fellow men the right to be heard;
  3. It is the basis of sportsmanship and fair dealing.
- B. Conferences are the outward signs of unity; for
  1. They reveal the workings of the principle of unity;
  2. They reveal unity freely given, not forced and false.
- C. America has the kind of unity that endures; for
  1. It knows that only as others have rights have free men rights;
  2. It is a union of free men and free religions in a free nation.

*Final Plea*

I. America must safeguard its unity through tolerance; for
- A. Intolerance is the weapon of the enemy; for
  1. Intolerance is a poison used to divide us and sap our strength;
  2. Placing race against race, or religion against religion, aids the enemy.
- B. Tolerance is a practical necessity; for
  1. Prejudice deceives men in human relationships;
  2. Tolerance is the only sound means of successful living.
- C. Tolerance must characterize our dealings with the world; for
  1. We must avoid the self-deception of the Pharisee;
  2. We must not become intolerant while combating intolerance;
  3. We must fight for tolerance with the unity of free men and free religions.

## ANALYSIS

The purpose of friendliness is won by Farley in the most traditional way: by his sincerity, and the identity of purpose between himself and the audience. The introduction is calm, suggesting the philosophic strain that the proof will take. Mutual belief in religious liberty unites the group, and the speaker becomes spokesman for their common cause. The obvious good in the speaker's cause and the apparent evil in the opposition further endears the speaker to the listeners. The speaker wins the *attention* of the audience by alluding to the significance of the occasion and the subject. The occasion is shown as a unique sign of spiritual unity. A National Conference of Christians and Jews proclaims a common belief in religious liberty and demands the deliberate attention of all thinking men. The audience is *informed* by a direct statement of the proposition. The speaker humbly narrows down his treatment by referring it to the purpose of the meeting: fostering tolerance and religious liberty.

### Division of the Proof

The speaker states his proposition forthrightly at the beginning of his speech: "Democracy means the equality of men." He establishes this view by a philosophic exposition in his *narration,* by three main arguments in the *discussion,* and by a stirring *final plea.* In the *narration,* he seeks to clarify the nature of equality. Once this is treated he divides his proof into three main parts: (1) the basic spiritual structure in our democracy, (2) the dependence of democracy upon religious freedom, and (3) true unity inspired by tolerance. To these he adds his *final plea* to safeguard unity through the practice of tolerance.

### Narration

The speaker's narration explains the background necessary to complete understanding of the proposition. To talk about "equality" is vague and often misleading, and since the proposition depends on a clear understanding of this abused term, an exposition is necessary. Farley phrases this information simply, speaking of democracy as the *spiritual* equality of men, and develops the idea by definition, *explaining what a thing is.* He talks of spiritual equality and clarifies it by explaining what it does not mean. By this contrast he gives balance to the exposition of its exact meaning. As brief proof is in order, he is not content merely to state the exact meaning. He quotes authority, *citation of an unimpeachable source,* to substantiate his interpretation. Further, he uses iteration, *insistence upon a single thought,* by stating the principal parts of spiritual equality. This permits him to define his most important idea four times and repeat the truth of each of its chief characteristics. Hence, in the narration, he has established the exact sense in which "equality" is to be taken, and has prepared the audience for a discussion or proof of his proposition.

## Discussion

The speaker's first main argument, "The principle of equality is the basis of our democratic faith," is supported by two propositions:

A. Political equality arises from spiritual equality.
B. The principle of tolerance means respect for individuality.

Proposition A is developed by causes, *that which occasions or effects a result. Because* there is a common Father, *because* man possesses an individual soul, *because* that soul is immortal, there is equality among men. This is followed by a *reductio ad absurdum, a form of refutation pursuing a principle or point to its logical conclusion to show its absurd consequences.* If these things are not true, how incongruous is human action? Logically, this structure is a hypothetical syllogism, *a form of deductive reasoning in which the major premise is conditional, that is, composed of a supposition and a conclusion.* The syllogism is composed of a supposition, "if man's soul is not immortal," and a conclusion, "man's dignity, rights, and sacrifices are absurd." The speaker proceeds to deny the conclusion by an appeal to reason. He pictures the futility of existence if the conclusion be true. He reduces the conclusion to absurdity as being contrary to human experience. Man's actions are imponderable if he be no more than "a thing that vanishes like a spark falling in the water." By thus refuting the conclusion, the speaker also repudiates the supposition. Hence, man must be more than an accidental thing. Argument B is developed by an exposition of the meaning of tolerance by citing the effects of its existence.

The second main argument, "Toleration or religious liberty has been painfully achieved," is supported by three propositions:

A. Toleration evolved after centuries of conflict.
B. Toleration manifests itself in religious freedom.
C. Nations have differed in maintaining religious liberty.

Proposition *A* is developed by historical definition; proposition *B* is developed by effects; and proposition *C* is developed by contrast and serves as a transition to the third major argument. Two excellent examples of definition are used: first, the definition of evolution in setting the discovery of religious liberty as a concept, and, second, the definition by species which delineates the characteristics of that concept. Both forms of definition are useful in securing understanding. By enumeration, the speaker gains various opportunities to stress his point of view. Hence, he sets his forms of support in three simple judgments: the rights of the individual, the rights of religion as an institution, and the rights of differing religions. He expounds these three rights by reference to their limitations in regard to the fundamental rights of others. This is definition in its literal sense.

The third main argument, "The practice of tolerance has enabled America to achieve true unity," is supported by three propositions:

A. Tolerance is a capacity for self-restraint.
B. Conferences are the outward signs of unity.
C. America has the kind of unity that endures.

The exposition in proposition *A* is achieved through cause and effect. The speaker asserts the basic cause of tolerance and after a short contrast continues to elucidate the effects tolerance has in the audience's lives. In addition, he deftly inserts a clear definition, "Tolerance is that admirable thing in a human being that makes him restrain his own power in order that others may enjoy the exercise of theirs." Proposition *B* is developed by contrast, *i.e.*, the unity that typifies the conference of free men of different faiths versus the enforced artificial unity of dictatorship. Proposition *C* is developed by parts, *a technique of exposition in which the speaker enumerates the specific elements which constitute the whole.* Added to this is a keen use of reiteration in the phrase, "it is the unity of," coupled with the climactic "it is the unity of *free* men and *free* religions in a *free* nation."

*Final Plea*

The final plea, "America must safeguard its unity through tolerance," is supported by three propositions, namely:

A. Intolerance is the weapon of the enemy.
B. Tolerance is a practical necessity.
C. Tolerance must characterize our dealings with the world.

Proposition *A* is established with a communication, *a method of contact which invites the audience to deliberate with the speaker,* and an enumeration of the techniques used to spread intolerance. This is followed by a form of repetition known as "correction," *a method of supplying a better expression for the one just uttered,* as "to render us ineffective." He concludes his proof by the use of iteration, *insisting upon the same thought in a variety of forms,* with five specific instances, each beginning with the word "whenever."

Proposition *B* is an ethical appeal of personality. The speaker attests from his own experience the truth of his proposition. This is effective because the speaker's reputation is the most forceful ethical persuasive known. He reveals that tolerance is a practical as well as a moral necessity, and by showing the effects of intolerance in a hypothetical instance concludes with a climactic structure: "I have found that tolerance is not only a good moral principle; it is the only sound, practical means of successful living."

Proposition *C* concludes the talk with a direct appeal. It is supported by a résumé of the situation and an exhortation for genuine tolerance. Tolerance is insisted upon three times with a common exhortative phrase, "let us. . . ." This is followed by an obverse iteration, *stressing the thought through its opposite,* and a final balanced contrast extolling the virtue of true tolerance.

## Projects

*Assignment 1*

Assume that you have been elected a representative to the Congress of the United States. You represent your community. Select a proposal that would benefit your constituents and present it forcefully to the House of Representatives. Show how your proposed legislation is necessary, worth while, and beneficial to the country.

*Assignment 2*

Reread the speech of Bruce Barton, "Which Knew Not Joseph." Using that talk as a model, construct a three-point program advocating more effective selling, or more interesting radio programs, or more lively college spirit, or more sensible health practices, or more valuable examinations, or more ennobling religious experiences. Be certain that you use as many specific instances as possible. Give evidence and authority for your statements, and be certain that your arrangement is clear and orderly.

*Assignment 3*

Prepare a five-minute speech in defense of some virtue or habit that has been neglected in modern living. For example, meditation, selflessness, spirituality, asceticism, charity, mortification, or penance. Make special use of definition in all its forms. Cite instances which establish the valuable effects of practicing the virtue you advocate. Use contrast to develop the difference between the use and abuse of that virtue, and also the contrast between modern and olden times.

*Assignment 4*

Urge the acceptance of some belief that you hold. Present a clear definition of its essential parts and offer evidence to establish its value. Note the skilled use of definition in Farley's speech and use his technique as a guide. Most speeches whose purpose is conviction must make frequent use of all means of exposition. That means the use of balanced structures, the constant use of articles, prepositions and other words of relation, the insistence upon the same thought in a variety of guises, a use of transitions which give a comprehensive statement of what has preceded and a brief announcement of what is to come, and a brief résumé of important arguments. You cannot repeat too often, but your repetition must have variety and interest. A wealth of specific instances engenders belief.

*Sample Deliberative Outline*

Speaker _____ Class _____ Date _____

   I. Topic.
  II. Purpose of speech.
 III. Audience analysis: Consider the thinking patterns. Consult Situations Analysis Chart, Chap. 2.
 IV. Introduction: Establish friendliness; arouse interest; and state the proposition.

V. Body: Include statement of proposition, main divisions, supporting propositions, reasoning, and evidence.

A. Statement of proposition.

_____

1. Supporting proposition.

_____

   *a.* _____

   *b.* _____

   *c.* _____

2. Supporting proposition.

_____

   *a.* _____

   *b.* _____

   *c.* _____

3. Supporting proposition.

_____

   *a.* _____

   *b.* _____

   *c.* _____

VI. Conclusion: Restate proposition as proved.

*Questions for Critical Discussion of Performance*

1. Was the speaker's proposition clearly and graphically stated?
2. Did the speaker define his terms accurately?
3. Were the issues apparent?
4. Did the speaker support his position convincingly?
5. Was a full use made of evidence?
6. Was the speaker's organization easily followed?
7. Was the language clear and forceful?
8. Was the speech difficult to follow?
9. Were you conscious of any illogical props?
10. How could this speech be improved?

*Developing Semantic Skill*

Add to your word cards the following:

I. Words used in the speech text:

| *Word* | *Pronunciation* | *Meaning* |
|--------|-----------------|-----------|
| 1. evidence | | |
| 2. probability | | |
| 3. reflection | | |
| 4. *status quo* | | |

II. Words commonly mispronounced:
   1. manger
   2. mischievous
   3. municipal
III. Words from your own experience.

# PART VI. CONFERENCE SPEAKING

The ability to conduct public discussions and private conferences is a unique characteristic of the educated person. You cannot effectively participate in democratic living if you are unable to participate in group action and group decisions. Not to know the forms of democratic procedure robs you of the rights democracy confers upon you. For what you do not exercise you lose. To tell you that you have freedom of speech when you are unable to speak is to delude you. You must be able to use your rights or you do not possess them. This is precisely the challenge of the next three chapters and projects. You are to acquire skill in the exercise of rights which men have freely given their lives to preserve for you. Study these forms with intense fervor for they will determine your inheritance of the full benefits of democratic living.

A stirring event in American history occurred when all Americans joined in a war pledge of national unity. In a historic conference the leaders of American labor pledged their personal sacrifices in a "No-strike" agreement. This was achieved at the conference pictured above. The participants were John L. Lewis, United Mine Workers chief; Joseph Curran, president of the Maritime Union; Philip Murray, CIO president; R. J. Thomas, president of the United Auto Workers; Emil Rieve, president of the Textile Workers Union; and William Green, AFL president.

This is a reminder that American unity begins where all wars end—*at the conference table*. Skill in conference techniques not only ensures your freedom, but protects the right of all minorities to be heard. If you would preserve democracy, learn to effectively present your ideas in the conference situation. Learn its special requirements and prepare for leadership.

*Chapter 20*

# GROUP DISCUSSION

> The only way in which a human being can make some approach to knowing the whole of a subject is by knowing what can be said about it by persons of every variety of opinion. . . .
>
> —JOHN STUART MILL

Discussion is essentially a method for solving problems by the process of group thinking. It is therefore a cooperative activity in which certain basic steps must be followed by the entire group. It is not a one-many relationship such as we have seen in public speaking, but a technique for shared thinking. Its aim is consequently different from persuasion, for discussion seeks to extend the thought process among the minds of the entire group. This requires that the problem-solving pattern of thinking be maintained, but that many minds converge on each step in the thought process so that many shades of meaning and viewpoints will be brought to bear on the problem. The basic assumption is that many minds tend to bring more clarity and understanding to the solution of problems.

Living is a complex problem, and many situations cannot be resolved in terms of black and white. There are many fine shades of differences between these two extremes. Participation in group discussion emphasizes this complexity of human affairs. It helps the participants to realize the numerous possibilities in the situation. The final group decision growing out of the cooperative thinking of all members is a better answer to the problem for the group because it is more likely to take all aspects of the problem into consideration.

Dr. George Gallup, director of the American Institute of Public Opinion, cited an example of this means of reasoning in trying to establish the value of his famous "Gallup Polls."

A professor of physics drew a line on the blackboard and asked the members of his class to guess the length of the line which was actually five feet. Some members of the class guessed seven feet, some eight, some

263

four, some only three. But the curious thing was that the average of all their guesses proved to be exactly correct—five feet. Individual judgments may be wrong, but the sum total of all judgments is usually surprisingly right.

In like manner, if a man of perfect height existed, tall men would be sure to feel he was too small, while small men would swear that he was too tall. The average of all opinions—that he was neither small nor tall—would be very near the truth.

In addition to the value of more likely solutions to problems, discussion carries an extra power. It is the best-known technique for gaining the acceptance of the solutions finally determined. When people have been part of the making of a policy they more readily cooperate in carrying out that policy. For example, when I interviewed Mr. Arthur Hays Sulzberger, publisher of the *New York Times*, the question arose as to the amazing sense of loyalty that all members of the paper felt. Mr. Sulzberger explained it in these words:

The control that the publisher of this paper exercises over its policies is anything but arbitrary. It lies primarily in picking his associates and working with them in harmony—talking things out and, on many occasions, being willing to give *way* rather than to give *orders*.

I do not wish to appear naïve or sentimental in this matter, I merely assure you, out of twenty-seven years' experience, that you could not have a newspaper as good as this one if what I have said were not so.

J. Edgar Hoover, who built the only secret service ever to outrival Scotland Yard, declared the discussion technique with his staff was the secret of its amazing effectiveness. "There is only one procedure [discussion] in practice in the FBI, which to my mind stands out in the development of our organization. I have always taken pride in the fact that the FBI is a 'we' organization."

Group discussion, therefore, has a twofold purpose for you. It will teach you the technique of solving problems with others and it will increase your skill in winning the cooperation of those with whom you must work and live. Since you are a special creature living in a group, you must be prepared for the give-and-take of group life. The highest purpose of group achievement is attained when all the members can cooperate for a common end. This is at times difficult because individuals differ in their opinions, tastes, training, and temperament. Yet, to continue to exist, the group must arrive at some decisions that are acceptable to the majority. Discussion is the art which facilitates this cooperative interchange of ideas. It is the democratic way of life in action.

The complexity of the current American scene, and the difficulty of obtaining accurate data, uncolored by prejudice, make it necessary to study the group-discussion method. Group discussion is the American way. It gives the minority the right to express its opinions and helps the group arrive at common understandings through intelligent sharing of opinions. It furnishes a means of acquiring opinions based on facts given by experts. There is a need for leaders who are experts in handling the group and who are public-spirited enough to use their leadership to promote free discussion.

## Varieties of Discussion Forms

The most likely form of discussion for the college student is the *lecture discussion.* This is a special presentation by an authority, followed by questions and comments from members of the audience. This is the form most frequently used by the town halls throughout the country. It is most suitable for situations in which the audience desires knowledge about a special subject.

The second most likely type of discussion is the *informal,* or *round table,* discussion group. This is made up of an entire group who have agreed to find out more about a particular problem and are trying either to solve it or acquire a deeper understanding of it. In college you will encounter many of these situations. Members of the class will equip themselves with information about a social or political problem and freely discuss the values involved.

The third form of discussion is the *conference.* This is sometimes referred to as the *action-taking discussion* because it seeks to make a decision and act on that decision. Business conferences are usually of this type. A problem arises that requires action, and a conference is held to determine the most appropriate course to follow. In this form of discussion more time is spent in the stage of determining the best possible solution, and frequently a vote is taken to determine the most effective solution offered during the discussion.

*Panel* discussion is the fourth popular form. Any number of interested persons are selected for the panel to discuss their views freely before the audience. There need be no basic disagreement among the panel members; they are selected because each one has a special interest or special information about the topic. This is an excellent method to get a broad view of an intricate subject. If it is carefully planned, each panel member may represent one of the issues involved. For example, if the subject is American foreign policy, each one may select some area of our participation in international relations. Following the presentation by the panel, the audience questions the panel members.

A variation of the panel has been called the *symposium*. In a symposium, three or more persons with different views on a particular subject provide the presentation, and the audience takes part in the discussion. This form is valuable when the subject under discussion cannot be answered in a "yes" or "no" decision but is capable of several alternatives.

### The Problem-solving Formula

To arrive at a solution to a problem on the basis of shared thinking demands a logical pattern of acting. That pattern is merely a reflection of the pattern used by individuals in solving personal problems. If you would solve a problem in your own life, you would first have to determine specifically what that problem was. You would have to find the trouble. Once you had determined what was bothering you, you would set about exploring the causes of your trouble—how you got that way. Only then would you ask yourself what you should do. And after you had examined all the possibilities, you would select the best solution. That is precisely the same formula used to solve problems in group discussion.

This formula has been described in a variety of ways. A factual analysis suggests:

1. Find the facts.
2. Focus the facts.
3. Filter the facts.
4. Face the facts.
5. Follow the facts.

Another formulation from the problem-solution angle suggests:

1. Locate and define the problem.
2. Analyze and explore the problem.
3. Review and examine the possible solutions.
4. Choose the best solution.
5. Enact the best solution.

It must not be supposed that this is an infallible method for solving problems. No such method has been devised. The formula is actually a mode of thinking which provides for rational rather than emotional solutions. It safeguards the group from erratic solutions. Moreover, it assists the group in arriving at a solution rather than merely rambling about a problem. Note briefly the nature of each of these five steps:

## Finding the problem

Unless the members of the group understand the exact nature of the problem, discussion will be confusing. The leader must state the problem clearly and give sufficient background material to enable all members to understand its import. If there are strange terms involved, these should be defined. The facts demonstrating that this question is a real problem must be furnished. Moreover, the problem must have some basis in the experience of the group discussing it. For example, if the discussion is about the rising divorce rate in America, the leader must bring the seriousness of the situation to the attention of the group. He must give a brief history of the increase, opinions of experts, comparisons between our country and the world at large, and pertinent facts that relate to this group. He must crystallize the problem, incite the group's interest in it, and show its significance for them.

## Analyzing and exploring the problem

In informal discussion it is wise to simplify the process of analyzing a problem. This can be done by asking the question "What are the causes of this problem?" For it is most frequently within the causes that the true solution lies. If the group can direct their minds to a thorough scrutiny of the factors that produced the difficulty, it is more than likely that they will think deeply about the problem. Moreover, such causal thinking is the most productive activity that logic can prescribe. To consider causes is to consider the very basis of problem creation. Problem solving deals with apparent effects and seeks to determine the causes which produced these effects. The discussion, therefore, must spend much time examining critically the probable causes of the present dilemma.

In the question of divorce, it is unlikely that the exact cause can be readily ascertained. Yet if the group applies its many-minded force to the causes of divorce, a number of revealing factors become apparent. The group would consider our moral standards, our sanction of divorce, our uneven state laws, our emancipation of women, our freedom of movement, our lack of sex education, our concept of romance, our motion-picture mores, and many other causes that have operated within the experience of the audience. Such concentration prepares the group for the task of finding more intelligent solutions.

### Reviewing and examining the possible solutions

After the causes have been explored, the group is ready to examine possible solutions. This is a broadening phase of the discussion technique. It teaches every participant to be more tolerant of the opinions of others, for each individual can more readily understand solutions that come after their causes have been examined. While each may not agree with the solution, he or she can see the other person's point of view. That alone is a true sign of maturity. But, there is a more enriching value to this whole process. Ideas can be exchanged and become the property of all members of the group. For example, if I have a dollar and you have a dollar, and I give you my dollar, you have two and I have none. No increase of wealth has taken place. If you give me your dollar, the same is true. But, if I give you an idea, you have a new idea and I also have it. And we can mutually enrich each other if we share our ideas. So it is that all possible solutions to a problem are of some value. They enrich every member with a new concept of life and a deeper understanding of human beings.

In examining the solutions offered by the group, certain basic standards may be applied. First, do the proposed solutions really meet the needs of the problem? In other words, is the cure worse than the disease? Second, are the proposed solutions practicable? Or do they merely settle the problem theoretically? Third, are the solutions desirable? Sometimes it is better to live with the disease than to operate. And many problems are best solved if no active program is attempted. The magic of time cures all. These three norms can assist in assessing values to the solutions offered by the group.

### Choosing the best solution

The group will be able to solve its problem if it can first see the problem clearly; understand the points of agreement and disagreement; study the advantages and disadvantages for the various possible solutions to the difficulty; and, in the light of knowledge thrown on all aspects of the situation, finally decide what would be best for the group. If the decision is arrived at with the cooperation of all members, then the action undertaken as a result of the decision will probably receive the support of the majority of the members.

The easiest way to determine the best solution for the group is to take a vote. This, however, may not be the best solution. It may only be the best solution the group can achieve in this situation and at the moment. Added to that it may be the solution that is only best when action must be taken. In other words, a vote on the best solution is valuable when the purpose of your discussion is action, as in a conference, and when the discussion is used as a technique to gain cooperation. Otherwise, it can settle very little of the problem.

There is a more logical method of determining the best possible solution. A good solution usually has the following characteristics: *It is a clear solution without ambiguity.* It states what it means and only what it means. *It is consistent with known facts.* It does not contradict the experiences common to the group. *It makes the fewest assumptions.* That is, it is closer to reality and possesses more probability than the other solutions. It is more intimately related to the causes discovered in the discussion. *It is consistent within itself.* Solutions that do not hang together provide grave doubts. A good solution usually has a core of truth which applies to all the ramifications of the problem. A solution that applies only to one angle of the question should be reexamined very closely. Finally, *it is more intellectual than emotional.* Emotion is a persuasive factor which may be seductive. A solution that appears too attractive should be reexamined. It is likely to contain elements of wishful thinking.

## Implementing the best solution

One of the frequent complaints about discussions and conferences is that they come to nothing. There is much talk and little action. Such complaints are in part true. Discussions of policy have the purpose of exposing a problem and do not seek to attain more than understanding. Conferences, on the other hand, have the specific goal of achieving the benefits of group thinking plus the decision to act. In conferences, therefore, the leader must spend considerable time on step four—choosing the best solution—and see that some definite action is determined. He must see that measures are established which will implement the solution achieved. Step five—implementing the best solution—requires considerable discussion when the purpose of the meeting is action.

Draw the following distinction when planning your discussion: Does this problem require that action be taken? Or: Will this discussion achieve its goal if people understand the nature of the problem more thoroughly? These two questions should provide the answer for the need of implementation.

## The Leader

The most crucial position for a participant is that of the leader. He must see that the discussion gets somewhere. He must be skilled in the technique of guiding the other members and must prevent monopoly of the discussion by any member, rambling wanderings by the group, or the raising of irrelevant issues. He must at all times know just where the discussion is, where it has come from, and to what it is tending. His skill in drawing out timid members and adroitly preventing loquacious ones from holding forth too long will determine the success of the discussion.

The skill of the leader may be compared to the skill of the telephone operator. The function of the operator is to connect two parties who have something to say; the function of the discussion leader is to do the same thing. He must sense when the participants have something to say and see that they readily communicate their sentiments. For him to enter the discussion is as bad taste as to have the operator enter the conversation. The leader's finesse is a social skill embodying the graciousness of the host and the wisdom of the social scientist.

Discussion is a problem-solving activity, and the basic function of the leader is to assist the group in arriving at an acceptable solution to the problem at hand. He must see that the discussion is molded toward some definable end. His task is like that of top management. He must lay out the larger strategy which will guide the participants toward an end all desire. He must see that the forest is not missed because of the trees. This is simply to say that he must guide the participants through the logical steps of solving a problem. His concern is that they first *clarify* the problem, then *explore* the causes which produced the problem, then *direct* their minds to its solution, and finally *determine with them* which solution is most expedient. To follow this pattern skillfully demands that the leader exercise a certain aloofness. He is not a participant in a specific sense, but in a general sense. He is concerned with a formula or technique rather than with specified items. In short, he is a general directing an operation.

During one of the battles of the Civil War, General Grant provided an excellent example of this directional skill. While one of the fiercest battles was raging, he rolled up under a tree to catch a few hours' sleep. Three hours later he was awakened by an excited line officer who told him that the right flank was in full retreat, the left flank sagging, and the center in danger of being cut off. Grant thought for a moment, dismissed the officer, and went back to sleep. He had planned the engagement so thoroughly that he knew the report was wild rumor. General Grant thought in terms of over-all strategy, and that is precisely what the discussion leader must do.

The ideal discussion leader conforms to Benjamin Franklin's formula for a diplomat: "Sleepless tact, unmovable calmness, and a patience that no folly, no provocation, no blunders can shake." He must be always conscious that he is dealing with people who are sensitive about their thoughts and more sensitive about their prejudices. He must learn to distinguish between the opinion and the maker of the opinion. In other words, the leader must never comment upon the person but only upon the opinion offered. As the Church admonishes, "He must hate the sin, but love the sinner." Such humaneness is as difficult to attain as to shoot a bird in flight, but it is the essential substance of leadership.

The following ten rules are recommended as guides to the discussion leader:

1. Prepare an outline of the probable issues to be discussed.
2. Open the discussion with an impartial description of the problem.
3. Confine your remarks to statements of fact.
4. Realize that your role is to *direct* the discussion and not to solve the problem for the group.
5. See that everyone participates.
6. Keep your own point of view a top secret; you are interested in getting the group to solve the problem.
7. Make frequent but brief summaries.
8. Move the group from statement of problem to causes, to solutions, and to evaluation of solutions.
9. Ask the group for examples, reasons, and cases continually.
10. Give a final summary of the essential points discussed.

How can the discussion leader do all these things and not take over the situation? He must ask questions instead of answering them. This is the most difficult task of the leader. To keep in the discussion and yet remain out of it. Professors Henry Lee Ewbank and J. Jeffery Auer, in their excellent book, *Discussion and Debate,* offer the following suggestions on how to handle a number of situations that often confront the discussion leader: [1]

1. To call attention to a point that has not been considered:
"Has anyone been thinking about this phase of the problem?"
2. To question the strength of an argument:
"What reasons do we have for accepting this argument?"
3. To get back to causes:
"Why do you suppose Mr. X takes this position?"
4. To question the source of information or argument:
"Who gathered these statistics that you spoke of?"
"Who is Mr. X whose opinion has been quoted?"
5. To suggest that the discussion is wandering from the point:
"Can someone tell me what bearing this has on our problem?"
6. To suggest that no new information is being added:
"Can anyone add anything to the information already given on this point?"
7. To call attention to the difficulty or complexity of the problem:
"Aren't we beginning to understand why our legislators haven't solved this problem?"
8. To register steps of agreement (or disagreement):
"Am I correct in assuming that we all agree (or disagree) on this point?"
9. To suggest that the group is not ready to take action:
"I wonder if we should not think the matter over and take action at our next meeting?"
10. To suggest that nothing can be gained by further delay:
"After all, is there any information that we do not have before us?"
11. To suggest that personalities be avoided:
"I wonder what bearing this has on the question before us?"
12. To suggest that some are talking too much:
"Are there those who have not spoken who have ideas they would like to present?"
13. To suggest the value of compromise:
"Do you suppose the best course of action lies somewhere between these two points of view?"

[1] Auer, J. J., and Henry L. Ewbank, *Discussion and Debate,* p. 524. New York: Appleton-Century-Crofts, Inc., 1941.

14. To suggest that the group may be prejudiced:
"Is our personal interest in this question causing us to overlook the interests of other groups?"

## PROJECTS

*Assignment 1*

Your first assignment is a discussion of policy: How can America achieve a free and responsible press? For your preliminary reading *The Canons of Journalism* is given below, and an additional list of other interesting sources is suggested. This is to be an informal discussion, so recall the simple formula:

1. What is the problem?
2. What are the causes of the problem?
3. What are all the possible solutions?
4. What is the best possible solution?

As you prepare for your part in the discussion, try to secure specific instances which support your point of view. If you can state your opinion in the form of point-reason-example-point, your ideas will have more chance of being realized for their full value in the group thinking.

As you make your point, strive for clarity; as you give your reasons, strive for cogency; as you give your example, strive for specificity; and as you restate your point, strive for forcefulness. This process enables you to present your thought in four different forms of repetition. You state it simply, you give its logical basis, you illustrate it, and you restate it as a suggestion for acceptance. If your thought is worth expressing, it is worth expressing effectively. So spend that extra time in preparing and you will enjoy and profit from the discussion.

### THE CANONS OF JOURNALISM [2]

The primary function of newspapers is to communicate to the human race what its members do, feel and think. Journalism, therefore, demands of its practitioners the widest range of intelligence, of knowledge and of experience, as well as natural and trained powers of observation and reasoning. To its opportunities as a chronicle are indissolubly linked its obligations as teacher and interpreter.

To the end of finding some means of codifying sound practice and just aspirations of American journalism, these canons are set forth:

[2] Ethical rules adopted by the American Society of Newspaper Editors on April 28, 1923, and since endorsed by many state associations and other groups of journalists.

1. Responsibility. The right of a newspaper to attract and hold readers is restricted by nothing but considerations of public welfare. The use a newspaper makes of the share of public attention it gains serves to determine its sense of responsibility which it shares with every member of its staff. A journalist who uses his power for any selfish or otherwise unworthy purpose is faithless to a high trust.

2. Freedom of the Press. Freedom of the press is to be guarded as a vital right of mankind. It is the unquestionable right by law, including the wisdom of any restrictive statute. To its privileges under the freedom of American institutions are inseparably joined its responsibilities for an intelligent fidelity to the Constitution of the United States.

3. Independence. Freedom from all obligations except that of fidelity to the public interest is vital.

A. Promotion of any private interest contrary to the general welfare, for whatever reason, is not compatible with honest journalism. So-called news communications from private sources should not be published without public notice of their source or else substantiation of the claims to value as news, both in form and substance.

B. Partisanship in editorial comment which knowingly departs from the truth does violence to the best spirit of American Journalism; in the news columns it is subversive of a fundamental principle of the profession.

4. Sincerity, Truthfulness, Accuracy. Good faith with the reader is the foundation of all journalism worthy of the name.

A. By every consideration of good faith, a newspaper is constrained to be truthful. It is not to be excused for lack of thoroughness, or accuracy within its control, or failure to obtain command of these essential qualities.

B. Headlines should be fully warranted by the contents of the articles which they surmount.

5. Impartiality. Sound practice makes clear distinction between news reports and expressions of opinion. News reports should be free from opinion or bias of any kind. This rule does not apply to so-called special articles unmistakably devoted to advocacy or characterized by a signature authorizing the writer's own conclusions and interpretations.

6. Fair Play. A newspaper should not publish unofficial charges affecting reputation or moral character, without opportunity given to the accused to be heard; right practice demands the giving of such opportunity in all cases of serious accusation outside judicial proceedings.

A. A newspaper should not invade rights of private feelings without sure warrant of public right as distinguished from public curiosity.

B. It is the privilege, as it is the duty, of a newspaper to make prompt and complete correction of its own serious mistakes of fact or opinion, whatever their origin.

7. Decency. A newspaper cannot escape conviction of insincerity if, while professing high moral purpose, it supplies incentives to base conduct, such as are to be found in details of crime and vice, publication of which is not demonstrably for the general good. Lacking authority to enforce its canons, the journalism here represented can but express the hope that deliberate pandering to vicious instincts will encounter effective public disapproval or yield to the influence of a preponderant professional condemnation.

## ADDITIONAL SOURCES

BEMAN, LAMAR, *Censorship of Speech and the Press.* The Handbook Series. Series 3, V. 5, 1930.

———, *Selected Articles on Censorship of the Theater and Moving Pictures.* The Handbook Series. Series 3, V. 6, 1931.

Commission on Freedom of the Press, *A Free and Responsible Press.* A general report on mass communication: newspapers, radio, motion pictures, magazines, and books. Chicago: University of Chicago Press, 1947.

———, *Government and Mass Communications,* 2 vols., by ZECHARIAH CHAFFEE, JR. Chicago: University of Chicago Press, 1947.

HOCKING, W., *Freedom of the Press.* Chicago: University of Chicago Press, 1947.

JOHNSEN, JULIA, *Freedom of Speech.* Reference Shelf. Vol. 10, No. 8. New York: The H. W. Wilson Company, 1936.

SUMMERS, R., comp., *Federal Information Controls in Peace Time.* Reference Shelf. Vol. 20, No. 6. New York: The H. W. Wilson Company, 1949. "Is the American Press Really Free?" *Representative American Speeches,* pp. 159–176, 1946–47.

UN Conference on Freedom of Information, Geneva, Switzerland, Mar. 23 to Apr. 21, 1948. Report of U.S. delegates with related documents. International Organization and Conference Series. Series III, SI.70/3:5.

U.S. Advisory Commission on Information, semiannual report to Congress, March, 1949. International Information and Cultural Series. SI.67:5.

## Assignment 2

You made one of the major decisions of your life when you decided to come to college. Not only that, but if you are to gain the maximum advantages of a college education, you must have some definite goals in mind. You must know why you are here and where you are going. In order to help you achieve clear objectives, this assignment is included.

Interpret it personally and prepare to share your thinking with the class. Your preparatory reading will help clarify your thinking. Select three books or magazine articles and do some fundamental thinking about your future. Remember, you are investing four years of your life in this adventure. Its advantages should be known to you, and they should incite you to greater efforts.

The topic for discussion is: "What are the advantages of a college education?"

Do not confine yourself to reading in your preparation. Confer with your friends and your parents. Ask your friends in business and the professions what they got out of college and be prepared to enliven the discussion with specific instances. An outline is furnished to help you complete your preparation.

### Self-review Sheet for Group Discussion Project

Name _____ Class _____ Date _____

You have been rated by your listeners on many characteristics. It is useful to know what others think of you. However, "The knowledge of self is the beginning of wisdom." Rate yourself on your ability to participate effectively in a speech situation involving technique of discussion.

Use this scale: 4, generally; 3, at times; 2, rarely; 1, never.

|  | 1 | 2 | 3 | 4 |
|---|---|---|---|---|
| Ability to see issues involved............................ |  |  |  |  |
| Courtesy toward other speakers.......................... |  |  |  |  |
| Cooperation (neither talking too much nor too little)........ |  |  |  |  |
| Accuracy and scope of information....................... |  |  |  |  |
| Willingness to see good in others' viewpoints.............. |  |  |  |  |
| Ability to sense implications in situation.................. |  |  |  |  |
| Use of appropriate words............................... |  |  |  |  |
| Ability to express thought succinctly..................... |  |  |  |  |
| Knowledge of rules.................................... |  |  |  |  |
| Willingness to surrender own plan to group desire........... |  |  |  |  |

The above is a candid-camera shot of you as a participant in a discussion. Plan a program of self-development for your weakest abilities.

*Sample Outline for Group Discussion*

Name _____ Class _____ Date _____

Topic: "What are the advantages of a college education?"
Be prepared to discuss this topic under these issues:
I. Educational advantages.
   A.
   B.
   C.
II. Social advantages.
   A.
   B.
   C.
III. Economic advantages.
   A.
   B.
   C.

List three references you have consulted. Give the following information for each:
Title
Author
Date
Pages

*Developing Semantic Skill*

Add to your word cards the following:

I. Words used in the speech text:

| *Word* | *Pronunciation* | *Meaning* |
| --- | --- | --- |
| 1. opinion | | |
| 2. potential | | |
| 3. premise | | |
| 4. syllogism | | |

II. Words commonly mispronounced:
   1. pathos
   2. poignant
   3. program
III. Words from your own experience.

## References

Auer, J. J., and Henry L. Ewbank, *Handbook for Discussion Leaders*. New York: Harper & Brothers, 1947.

Baird, A. Craig, *Discussion: Principles and Types*. New York: McGraw-Hill Book Company, Inc., 1943.

Bowman, LeRoy C., *How to Lead Discussion*. New York: The Woman's Press, 1934.

Elliott, Harrison S., *The Process of Group Thinking*. New York: Association Press, 1932.

Fansler, Thomas, *Discussion Methods for Adult Groups*. New York: American Association for Adult Education, 1934.

Judson, Lyman S., and Ellen Judson, *Modern Group Discussion*. New York: The H. W. Wilson Company, 1937.

McBurney, James H., and Kenneth G. Hance, *Discussion in Human Affairs*. New York: Harper & Brothers, 1950.

Sheffield, Alfred D., *Creative Discussion*, 3d ed., rev. and enl. New York: Association Press, 1936.

Simpson, Ray H., *A Study of Those Who Influence and Those Who Are Influenced by Discussion*. New York: Teachers College, Columbia University, 1938.

Studebaker, John W., *The American Way*. New York: McGraw-Hill Book Company, Inc., 1935.

Walser, Frank, *The Art of Conference*, rev. ed. New York: Harper & Brothers, 1948.

Wiese, Mildred, Lyman Bryson, and W. C. Hallenbeck, *Let's Talk It Over*. Chicago: University of Chicago Press, 1936.

## Chapter 21

# PARLIAMENTARY PROCEDURE

Which is better in a dispute? For each side to a dispute to get something it wants, or for one side to get all and the other side to get nothing? The savage answer is, "It's better for me to get mine." The civilized man answers, "It's better to give and take, to live and let live."

—T. V. Smith

This chapter reveals the procedures useful in the normal process of club business. It seeks to make this procedure distinct from more complicated forms and portrays the conduct of meetings under normal conditions. Ordinarily, *simplicity* of procedure is the aim, but when issues become vital and feelings mount, *order* becomes the aim, and strict procedure is essential. Hence, simple and efficient methods are first indicated, and gradually the more complicated forms are introduced. Finally, the treatment is from the Chairman's point of view. He is the focal personage, the entrusted leader chosen by the majority.

No other body of laws has been subjected to the same battery of experience as parliamentary laws. Their continued existence is due to the recurring patterns of action demonstrated by men seeking group action. They are as simple and efficient in practice as they are logical in principle. They bequeath the entire experience of almost two hundred years of democratic development. To learn them is to share that heritage and ensure its permanence, in other words, to express faith in democratic procedure. To paraphrase Emerson: "Parliamentary procedures are happy ways of doing things—each originally a stroke of genius, but crystallized by repetition into a custom."

The preservation of democracy consists in the preservation of the techniques of arriving at decisions in a democratic manner. The habit of thinking democratically is developed by the exercise of free

279

speech and assembly. Four fundamental rules must be observed diligently to accomplish this:

1. The right of the minority must be protected.
2. The considered rule of the majority must prevail.
3. Respect for the dignity of all members must be assured.
4. A logical order of business must be provided.

"Order" makes for efficiency. Most meetings are intrusions upon the time of busy people. Meetings must, therefore, proceed steadily. Disorder causes delays, confuses participants, and makes for inefficiency. No organization can afford to let its meetings degenerate into the wranglings which result from lack of order. Parliamentary procedure means order. It means that the business of the meeting can proceed justly, fairly, and judiciously according to rules to which all have agreed. Learn these simple rules. Follow them carefully and watch your organization grow in efficiency as the meetings come to order.

## THE CHAIR PRESIDES

It is the privilege of the president of a society to preside at its meetings. A *meeting* is an assembly of the members of a society for any length of time during which they do not separate except for a short recess. However, at the first meeting of a new society, a meeting can only be called to order by the Chair, after he has determined that a majority of the members, *i.e.*, a *quorum*, is present. The Chair inquires of the secretary if a quorum is present. If the answer is "yes," he announces:

*Chair:* "The meeting will please come to order." If silence is not forthcoming, he may add, "Order, please!" and then wait with dignity. When no quorum can be had, the Chair suggests the only legitimate motion:

*Chair:* "As there is no quorum, a motion to adjourn is in order." In cases of extreme urgency, the Chair may conduct the meeting without a quorum. The society, however, is not bound by the business contracted unless it ratifies the action at the next legal meeting. Should a meeting start with a quorum and lose it, no vote can be taken, but discussion may be conducted. A note or order cannot be rescinded when it has resulted in any action which the group cannot undo without injury or breaking faith.

## Order of Business

The procedure by which the chairman advances from one matter to another is called the "order of business." Establishing such an order assures the progress of the meeting. The group can readjust the order at any time by a two-thirds vote, but the usual procedure is as follows:

1. Minutes of previous meeting.
2. Reports of officers, boards, and standing committees.
3. Reports of special committees.
4. Announcements.
5. Unfinished business.
6. New business.
7. Adjournment.

This procedure guarantees that the business of the day will be transacted in light of

1. Actions taken at the last meeting (minutes).
2. Actions of elected officers (reports).
3. Knowledge gained by special study (reports).
4. Actions still pending (unfinished business).
5. Information recently received (announcements).

It furnishes a check on business already contracted and protects the group from considering new problems while vital old ones remain unsettled. The Chairman must assume that the group desires strict observance of the order of business unless the group specifically indicates otherwise.

## Minutes

The official record of the business of a group is called the "minutes." In the customary order of business the minutes are read at the opening of each meeting. This serves to establish continuity in the group's affairs and offers a check on the accurate recording of the group's actions. Still, should important business be pressing, the minutes can be dispensed with by a majority vote. Such a motion is undebatable, and the minutes come up for approval at the next regular meeting. Certain organizations have found it advantageous to read the minutes at the close of each meeting while the day's actions are fresh in mind.

The minutes contain the essential business of the group. Correct minutes report:

1. Name of the group.
2. Kind of meeting, *i.e.*, regular or special.
3. Place, date, and time of meeting.
4. Name of presiding officer.
5. Approval of the minutes of previous meeting.
6. Motions introduced, their final disposition, and their proposers.
7. Time of adjournment.

Hence they contain all the decisions arrived at by the group, all motions and their proposers, the exact vote on each motion, the substance of all reports (usually given in writing to the secretary), and an indication of the approval of the previous minutes.

Minutes are introduced and sanctioned in this manner:

"Will the secretary please read the minutes?"

After the reading of the minutes:

"The minutes stand approved as read."

If corrections are suggested, the Chairman instructs the secretary to make them. Any objection, however, to the corrections necessitates a vote. In such cases the Chairman states the correction in the form of a motion and immediately takes a vote:

"Shall the proposed correction (states the correction) be made? Those in favor say 'aye,' those opposed, 'nay.'"

After a majority vote:

"The 'ayes' have it, and the correction will be made," or, "The motion has failed, and minutes stand as read."

The above process is reenacted if other corrections arise. Finally the Chairman inquires:

"Are there any further corrections to the minutes?"

If none arises, the Chairman proceeds:

"There being no further corrections, the minutes stand approved as corrected."

Minutes may be corrected at any time. If previously approved, a two-thirds vote is required. This protects the record from unwarranted changes by a temporary majority. Should notice of the intended corrections be posted previously, however, a majority vote can effect the change.

## Reports

After the acceptance of the minutes, the Chair proceeds to "reports." Reports give formal accounts of the official actions of the officers and return to the group the conclusions of appointed committees. There are two types of reports, each distinguished by its function and membership: official reports and special reports.

Official reports are the legitimate means by which officers of a society announce their actions taken in behalf of the group. The principle of distinction between reports resides in the fact of whether or not the group must accept the report. The actions of the president, a governing board, or a committee empowered to act do not need the specific approval of the group to make the actions final. Such officials hold office for a specific term, and their legitimate actions in office are binding on the group. The group controls its officials by new elections and, in extreme cases, by impeachment. These officers are the executive branch of the society, and their official reports constitute their actions to date.

The Chairman uses the following forms:

"The President wishes to report that. . . ."

or

"The Chair wishes to report the following communications received from the board of. . . ."

or

"The Chair wishes to report the following action taken by the committee on. . . ."

Such reports are received and accepted by the group unless objections arise. Objections may take the form of protests and impeachments. Such actions are unusual and take the form of motions especially designed as resolutions and appeals.

Since it is difficult to complete business with a large group, committees are usually appointed, and their decisions are reported to the organization. Committees are composed of members interested in a question and willing to spend time in reaching a solution or agreement. The communication of their deliberations is called a "special report." A committee appointed to study a matter and report back to the group is simply advisory. The group may or may not act upon the advice reported by the committee. If no recommendations are made, the report need not be accepted, and a motion to accept the report is unnecessary. The Chair simply instructs the secretary to record that "the report is received with thanks." Frequently the lack of specific recommendations is due to poor reporting, and it is wise for the Chair to inquire:

"Are there any specific recommendations?"

If recommendations are made, it is up to the group either to accept or reject them in the form of main motions. In such a case the Chair announces:

"You have heard the report of the committee. What is your pleasure?"

## Announcements

Items of interest to the group and items for the good and welfare of the society are introduced as "announcements." After the Chair has made public any communications of interest, he inquires:

"Are there any announcements to be made at this time?"

Informal discussion and questions about the announcements are in order at this point.

## Unfinished business

In order to insure progress, a society must settle old matters before proceeding to new ones. A question being considered by the group and interrupted by the adjournment of a meeting has first call on the deliberations at the next meeting. As a new meeting is a continuation of the previous meeting, the unsettled question is given preference. Such questions are in order under the item of "unfinished business."

Should more pressing business arise, the old question may be put off by a motion to postpone. When the Chair feels this action is expedient, he announces:

"In order to proceed to the more urgent matter of (state new business), a motion to postpone (state old business) is in order."

If the motion is made, seconded, and receives a majority vote, the Chair advances to "new business." Should there be no old business, the Chair announces:

"There being no unfinished business, new business is in order."

### New business

Following the final disposition of old questions, new business is in order. New business means any proposals not previously considered by the group. It is the actual business of the current meeting and concerns the regular work of the club. Correspondence and other communications to the club are introduced by the Chair as new business. Any action taken by the group is accomplished through the regular routine of motions.

### Adjournment

When the business of the meeting is accomplished, the Chair states, "If there is no further business at this time, the meeting stands adjourned." Any member may introduce a motion to adjourn at any time during the meeting. Since the motion to adjourn is always in order, and is undebatable, the Chair immediately calls for a vote: "As many as are in favor of adjourning say 'aye.' Those opposed, say 'nay.' The meeting stands adjourned," or, "The motion being lost we will continue discussion."

### A Main Motion

When a member of the group proposes that some action be taken by the group he makes a "motion." A motion is a proposal of action. To be considered by the group, at least two members must desire the proposed action. The second member "seconds" the motion. There are two main types of proposals for action: simple proposals and dual proposals. A simple proposal has one subject and advocates one action. For example, "that the X club (the subject) donate $1,000 to the X Charity (action)" is a simple proposal. It calls for specific action by the group.

A dual proposal moves that the same perform two actions. For example, "that X club (the subject) donate $1,000 to United Charity and $500 to the Elks Charity." It is obvious that this is a more complicated motion than the above. Certain members may wish to give to the United Charity but not to the Elks. In general, they may wish to vote "yes" on the first action proposed, and to vote "no" on the second action. If only one choice is allowed, they must vote "no" on both proposals in order to defeat the objectionable one. *The wise chairman anticipates difficulties and avoids them.* When the chairman perceives that a proposal will lead to difficulty, it is his privilege to advise the member to rephrase or simplify the proposal. This should be done tactfully by explaining the probable difficulty the proposal would involve.

### Procedure for main motion

Simplest form without any complications:

*Member* rises, addresses Chair, "Mr. Chairman," and waits for recognition.

*Chair* recognizes member, *i.e.*, gives him the floor by a nod or by stating his name, "Mr. Brown."

*Member* makes the *motion:* "I move that this organization send the sum of $1,000 to the United Charities Fund." Second member without waiting to be recognized says, "I second the motion." He may remain seated if the group is small. In a large group it is customary for him to stand and, without waiting to be recognized, say, "Mr. Chairman, I second the motion."

*Chair* rises and *states the question:* "It has been moved and seconded that this organization send the sum of $1,000 to the United Charities Fund. Is there any discussion?" He waits for members to discuss the question. When the members have discussed the question fully, he *puts the question* by saying: "Are you ready for the question?" The *members* indicate their readiness to have the question put by responding "Question." The Chair then puts the question, "It has been moved and seconded that this organization send the sum of $1,000 to the United Charities Fund. All those in favor say 'aye.' Those opposed say 'nay.'" The Chair *announces the vote:* "The 'ayes' have it, and the motion is carried," or "The 'no's' have it, and the motion is defeated." The Chair states the business next in order.

The above procedure is the simplest possible. The motion was in order and the Chairman could permit it to come before the assembly for consideration. There was no other motion on the floor at the time, and the motion did not conflict with the constitution or the by-laws of the organization nor with national or state laws. It did not bring up a question which had been previously considered in the meeting since it would not be feasible to consider the same question twice.

In summary, there are eight steps in the presentation and disposition of a main motion without amendments:

1. A member rises and addresses the Chair.
2. The member is recognized by the Chair.
3. The member states his proposal.
4. Another member seconds the proposal.
5. The question is stated by the Chair.
6. Discussion is conducted.
7. The Chair puts the question to a vote.
8. The Chair announces the result.

The main motion is the starting point for all the activities of the group. In small groups a great deal of informal discussion may be allowed, but in order to get business accomplished a motion must be made, duly seconded, and stated by the Chair. It is then before the group for discussion and consequent action. It is the Chairman's duty to sense the precise moment when informal discussion should cease and a formal motion be made. He does this by stating: "If specific action is desired in this matter, the floor is open for a motion."

*Amendments*

When the proposal made as a main motion needs to be modified or changed in some way, a motion to amend is in order. There are four ways that this can be done:

1. To amend by inserting.
2. To amend by adding (that is, place at the end).
3. To amend by striking out and inserting.
4. To amend by substituting a paragraph.

The form for making this motion is: "I move to amend the main motion by (inserting, adding, striking out and inserting, or substituting)." After the amendment has been discussed, the Chair states: "As many as are in favor of the amendment to (states change) say 'aye'; those opposed say 'nay.' The 'ayes' have it, the amendment is adopted, and the question is on the resolution, which is, 'Resolved, That, etc.'" The Chairman reads the resolution as amended.

A motion may be amended, and, in turn, the amendment may be amended. But the amendment of the amendment cannot be amended. In other words, for the sake of clarity, amendments can only go to the second degree. For example, the proposal is offered: "Resolved, That this organization send the sum of $1,000 to the United Charities." A motion is made to amend the main motion by striking out $1,000 and inserting $500. An amendment of the amendment is offered which proposes that $500 be stricken out and $250 be inserted. This is in order, but no amendments can be offered relative to the $250 at this time. The following graphic presentation makes the point clear.

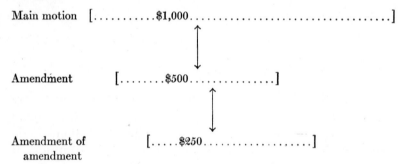

The question of the $250 cannot be further amended as that would constitute a third degree of amendment. The order of discussion would now proceed upward from the amendment of the amendment, to the amendment, and up to the main motion. The Chairman would conduct discussions on these issues: One, does the group desire that $250 become the amendment? If that carries, then two, shall the $250 become part of the main motion? On the other hand, should the change to $250 fail to amend the amendment, then the second question would be whether the $500 should become part of the main motion; three, the amended main motion is then open to discussion and other amendments using the same process.

Simplicity is the keynote of skilled use of amendments. The Chairman should try at all times to keep the group discussing the issue before the assembly. Using the illustration one step further, the issues to be discussed are as follows:

Main motion  [.........$1,000...................]    *Issue to be discussed:*
                                                     Shall the main motion
                       ↑                             read $500 or remain
                       |                             as is?
                       ↓
Amendment    [.........$500.........]

During the discussion on the above issue, a motion is duly made
and seconded to strike out $500 and insert $250.

Amendment    [.........$500.........]               *Issue to be discussed:*
                                                    Shall the amendment
                     ↑                              read $250 or remain
                     |                              as is?
                     ↓
Amendment of    [.........$250.........]
  amendment

The experienced Chairman usually guides the group through
these amendments by using set forms when putting the question to
a vote. This eliminates considerable confusion, for a group cannot
act as efficiently as an individual, and a skilled leader assists them
in crystallizing their desires. Here are the forms to be used.

1. When putting the question on the amendment of the amendment, the Chairman says:

"It has been moved and seconded that the amendment be
amended by striking out $500 and inserting $250. All those in favor
of the amendment reading $250 say 'aye'; those opposed, 'nay.'"

2. When putting the question on the amendment, the Chairman
says:

"It has been moved and seconded to amend the main motion by
striking out $1,000 and inserting $500. All those in favor of the main
motion reading $500 say 'aye'; those opposed, 'nay.'"

These forms may appear lengthy but they assure the group of
what they are voting upon. Moreover, the Chairman is subtly in-
structing the group in proper procedure as he explains each step.

In conclusion, it is well to point out that while there cannot be
amendments to the third degree, there is no limit to the number of
amendments that can be offered. In other words, after the amendment of the amendment on the $250 was decided, another amend-
ment of the amendment was in order. And after the amendment on
the $500 was settled, amendments to other parts of the proposal

were in order. Amendments are the techniques used to modify the proposal so that it suits the desires of the group. The one restriction on amendments is that they be "germane," *i.e.*, relevant to, or closely associated with, the main proposal. The difficulty arises that an amendment may be "hostile" to the main proposal and still be germane. An excellent example of each of these is given by Henry M. Robert in his *Rules of Order*.[1]

A resolution of censure may be amended by striking out the word "censure" and inserting the word "thanks," for both relate to opinion of certain conduct; refusing to censure is not the same as expressing thanks.

It is obvious that the amendment is "hostile" to the main motion but it is still "germane." An example of germaneness is:

A resolution to purchase some books could not be amended by striking out the words relating to books and inserting words relating to a building. Suppose a resolution pending directing the treasurer to purchase a desk for the secretary, and an amendment is offered to add the words, "and to pay the expenses of the delegates to the State Convention"; such an amendment is not germane to the resolution, as paying the expenses of the delegates is in no way related to purchasing a desk for the secretary, and is therefore out of order. But if an amendment were offered to insert the word "desk," it would be in order, because both are articles to enable the secretary to perform his duties.[2]

The question of germaneness calls for the exercise of good judgment on the part of the Chairman. The temperate judgment is always the wiser, but every judgment or ruling should be accompanied by an explanation from the Chairman.

## Order of precedence of motions

Precedence refers to the regulation governing the motion which determines whether it has the right to be debated before another motion. The motion of higher rank has first right to the attention of the assembly. Thus the motion to amend has precedence over a main motion, because the amendment must be settled before the main motion can be voted upon. Otherwise the members could not

[1] Robert, Henry M., *Rules of Order*. New York: Scott, Foresman & Company, 1921, p. 144.

[2] *Ibid.*, p. 144.

vote upon the main motion as they would not know whether it had been changed or not. The order of rank has been long established through custom, but its basis is in the fundamental principle of orderly procedure. First things must come first or there is chaos.

All the details governing special cases will be given in the Chart of Parliamentary Procedure. The usual motions rank as follows, the lowest being at the bottom and the highest at the top of the list.

1. Fix the time at which to adjourn.
2. Adjourn.
3. Take a recess.
4. Raise a question of privilege.
5. Call for the orders of the day.
6. Lay on the table.
7. Previous question (requires a two-thirds vote).
8. Limit or extend limits of debate (requires a two-thirds vote).

(*All the above motions are undebatable.* The following are debatable:)

9. Postpone to a certain time.
10. Commit or refer.
11. Amend.
12. Postpone indefinitely.
13. A main motion.

### EXPLANATION FOR THE CHART ON PARLIAMENTARY PROCEDURE

Sometimes students find difficulty in getting their club started because the majority of members have had little experience with parliamentary procedure. They do not understand the simple principles upon which it is based and do not know how to word the motions. The chart has been devised by work with a group of such students and is intended to fulfill their needs. Hence the minimum of time may be spent on theory and the maximum of time on practice. The student who contributes by making a good motion can realize the function of the procedure more vividly than the student who has studied the rules from a book. This chart enables the student to get the necessary information readily and assures intelligent participation by all.

| What is the motion? | When is it in order? | What is its function? | Must it be sec-onded? | Amend-able? | Debat-able? |
|---|---|---|---|---|---|
| I. *Principal* | When no other business is before house | Put new subject for consideration before house | | | |
| 1. Main | As above | As above | Y | Y | Y |
| 2. Rescind (Repeal) | When for some reason (*e.g.*, too late) it is impossible to reconsider | To render void a rule or order | Y | Y | Y |
| II. *Privileged* | Take precedence over all others. Yield only to privilege of higher rank | Concern rights and privileges of members—urgent—important | | | |
| 1. To fix time and place for adjournment | In order at any time—wiser to provide for this during early part of meeting | To fix time, place for reassembly | Y | Y | N |
| 2. To adjourn | Cannot be made before vote is completed, but is in order before announcement of result | To close meeting | Y | N | N |
| 3. To take a recess | In order as 2 is; yields only to 1 and 2 | Interrupt session for a limited time | Y | N | N |

| Limit debate to pending motion? | Recon- sidered? | Subs. motions? | Vote? | Notes: What is customary wording of motion? What special rules govern it? |
|---|---|---|---|---|
| | | | | Member rises, addresses Chair, "Mr. President," or, "Mr. Chairman—Mr. Brown." Chair recognizes member. Member states motion, *e.g.*, "I move that. . . ." Another member seconds motion. The member may withdraw or amend motion before it has been stated by Chair. However, no motion can be acted upon by assembly until it has been stated by the Chair. It is courteous to ask consent of one who seconds it, but the member may withdraw it without asking for this (before it has been stated by Chair). |
| Y | Y | Y | M | Main motion should be in writing, stated simply in as few words as possible. Member must write out each motion or the Chair must do so unless (as in most organizations) the secretary does this. The Chairman states the motion: "It has been moved and seconded that. . . . Are there any remarks?" Once the motion has been so stated it becomes the property of the group and cannot be then withdrawn except by general consent or by a motion to withdraw. |
| Y | Y | Y | M | Constitutions generally require a $\frac{2}{3}$ vote for repeal of a rule and may demand previous notice and publishing of proposed change to be read and studied by the members. When these conditions are not determined by such ruling, then the motion is treated as a main motion. |
| . . . . . . . . . | Y | Y | M | Any question may be made a privileged question if group decrees it—customary ones are enumerated. Member rises, interrupts business. "I rise to a question of privilege." Chairman directs him to state question. Decides whether or not it is in order. |
| . . . . . . . . . | N | N | M | This cannot be debated if moved when another question is before house. It may be used to arrange for a special meeting. It is necessary for the life of an organization which has not fixed its regular time and place for reassembly. |
| . . . . . . . . . | Not neces- sary to rec. Y | Y | M | "I move that the meeting be adjourned." In a society that meets regularly, this motion closing meeting causes the business to come up before next meeting as unfinished business. However, if adjournment brings a session to a close, then the unfinished business cannot come up unless introduced by new propositions or motions. "I move that the organization now take a recess (for twenty minutes, until one o'clock or subject to the call of the Chair)." This merely interrupts the meeting for a time. Usually, the members confer with each other during the recess. This motion is amendable only in regard to the length of the recess. |

[*Continued on next page.*]

| What is the motion? | When is it in order? | What is its function? | Must it be sec- onded? | Amend- able? | Debat- able? |
|---|---|---|---|---|---|
| 4. Question of privilege | Takes precedence over all others ex- cept 1, 2, 3 | To secure rights and privileges to group and to members | Y | Y | Y |
| 5. Orders of day | Takes precedence over all others ex- cept 1, 2, 3, 4 | Put proper business before meeting in place of other business being discussed | N | N | N |
| III. *Subsidiary* | Have precedence over main ques- tion and over each other in rank. Yield to privilege and incidental motions | To amend or dis- pose of other mo- tions | | | |
| 1. Considera- tion | Immediately after main motion has been stated | Questions the con- sideration of main motion | N | N | N |
| 2. Lay on table | Takes precedence over all subsidi- ary except 2 above. Yields to privilege and in- cidental motions | Postpone action— allows group to proceed to more urgent matters | Y | N | N |
| 3. Order previ- ous question | May be applied to any debatable question | Suppress debate— secure a vote on the question | Y | N | N |
| 4. Postpone to a certain time | Takes precedence over 5, 6, 7. Yields to privileged and incidental | Defer action | Y | Y | Y |

**PARLIAMENTARY PROCEDURE** (*Continued*)

| Limit debate to pending motion? | Recon- sidered? | Subs. motions? | Vote? | Notes: What is customary wording of motion? What special rules govern it? |
|---|---|---|---|---|
| Y | Y | Y | M | "I rise to a question of privilege." The speaker may interrupt even when another speaker has the floor. Any disturbance to the group, *e.g.*, noise, presence of nonmembers, quarrels between members, etc., justifies a question of privilege. An individual may use this to secure his rights. |
| ......... | N | N | M | "I call for the orders of the day." Organization must have regular orders or they cannot be called for. If this motion is defeated, then group discusses business before meeting and the call for order of day can be presented again. Orders must be called for in definite order and disposed of in order before group can get to important business it wants to consider. |
| | | | | The rank of subsidiary motions varies in groups according to customary practice of groups. |
| ......... | N | N | M | "I raise question of consideration," or, "I object to consideration of the question." Chairman then puts question of consideration to vote. "Shall this question be considered?" This question must be raised at once, immediately after main motion has been stated and before debate has started. It is not often raised, but is useful to save time. |
| ......... | N | N | M | "I move that the question be laid on the table." It is not proper to specify time at which question is to be taken from table. |
| ......... | Rec. is super- fluous N | N | ⅔ | "I call for the previous question." Chairman then says, "Shall the main question be now put?" When this motion has been put to vote, if result is affirmative, then it is carried out by first putting to vote amendments and then the main motion. Previous questions may be limited to discussion of amendment only, and in such case affect just the amendment to which they apply. This still allows debate on the main motion. |
| Y | Y | Y | M | "I move that question be postponed until the twentieth of March." This allows time for further study. |

[*Continued on next page.*]

| What is the motion? | When is it in order? | What is its function? | Must it be sec-onded? | Amend-able? | Debat-able? |
|---|---|---|---|---|---|
| 5. Refer to a committee | Takes precedence over 6, 7. Yields to substitute, priv-ileged, incidental | Further study | Y | Y | Y |
| 6. Amend | Takes precedence only over a main motion. Yields to all others | Modify the motion under considera-tion | Y | Y | N.B. |
| 7. Postpone in-definitely | Takes precedence over nothing else but main motion | Really kills action on motion | Y | N | Y |
| IV. *Incidental* | Have no fixed order of rank. Yield to privilege, take precedence over subsidiary | Arise out of other motions inciden-tal to debate | | | |
| 1. Order | Take precedence over question that gives rise to it | To secure proper enforcement of order | N | N | N |
| 2. Appeal from decision of Chair | Immediately after the decision is made. Take pre-cedence over all except privilege | Appeal for group decision on some action of the Chair | . . . . . . . | N | Y |
| 3. Reading of papers | In order when neces-sary | To request reading of document for information | Y | N | N |
| 4. Withdrawal of motion | | To remove motion | N | N | N |
| 5. Suspend rules | In order pending question to which it relates. Yields to privileged mo-tions | In order to secure some urgent ac-tion which is for-bidden by rules | Y | N | N |
| 6. Make special order | When a suspension of rules would be in order | To fix a certain time for consid-eration of motion | Y | N | N |

PARLIAMENTARY PROCEDURE (*Continued*)

| Limit debate to pending motion? | Recon- sidered? | Subs. motions? | Vote? | Notes: What is customary wording of motion? What special rules govern it? |
|---|---|---|---|---|
| Y | Y | N.B. N | M Y | "I move that the question be referred to a committee," or, "I move that this question be referred to a committee of ten to be appointed by the Chair." It cannot be reconsidered once the committee has begun its study. The committee can be discharged by a motion to that purpose (⅔ on vote). |
| | Y | Y | M | "I move to amend motion by (1) striking out, (2) inserting, (3) dividing question, (4) substituting." Motion is undebatable when motion to which it is applied is undebatable. Cannot amend to third degree. Amendment must be genuine. No limit to number of amendments that can be voted upon in turn. |
| N | N | Y N | M | "I move that the question be postponed indefinitely." Some manuals permit reconsideration; others say this cannot be reconsidered. The motion really prevents action on the motion. The use of it in many organizations is questioned. It opens main question to debate and enables opponents of motion to sound out the group on the motion. |
| | | | | Since these questions arise out of debate on other questions, they are decided before the question to which they are incidental. Therefore, they have no fixed rank, for their rank varies with the question out of which they arise. |
| ......... | N | N | M | May interrupt the speaker. "I rise to a question of order." The Chair should enforce rules. When a member observes a breach of order, he may insist upon correction of irregularities in procedure. |
| ......... | Y | Y | M | "I appeal from decision of the Chair." Chairman puts question, "Shall the decision of the Chair stand?" These appeals should not be used lightly. They should only be made in cases of gross error or unfairness. |
| ......... | Y | N | M | This is usually allowed if member desires information. If other member objects, it must be put to vote. |
| ......... | N.B. | N | M | Once motion has been made, seconded, and stated by Chair, it becomes property of group and cannot be withdrawn except by general consent or vote. N.B. An affirmative vote on this cannot be reconsidered. |
| ......... | N | N | Unan. consent ⅔ | "I move that the rules which would prevent (specify desired action) be suspended." It is not permissible to make a blanket motion suspending rules; motion must be specific. |
| ......... | N | N | M | "I move that motion be a question of special order on May 1—etc." A special order takes precedence over all general orders. If it is not reached at specified time, it has no special privilege. |

[*Continued on next page.*]

| What is the motion? | When is it in order? | What is its function? | Must it be seconded? | Amendable? | Debatable? |
|---|---|---|---|---|---|
| 7. Determine mode of procedure | Incidental to question out of which it arises | To limit debate or to determine way of voting | Y | Y | N |
| 8. Divide question | When main motion is before house | To separate question into distinct parts | . . . . . . | Y | N |
| 9. Nominating | In order when Chair calls for nomination | To name member for some office | ? Y | N | Y |

## PROJECTS

*Assignment 1*

You need training in the use of parliamentary procedure. A fairly adequate knowledge of the intricacies of the procedure can be learned if the class is turned into a club. You can practice the techniques as you study them and thus understand the purpose and function of each procedure. This knowledge is valuable as most organizations carry on their business with at least a modified form of this procedure.

The first lesson should be devoted to a discussion of the purpose and function of parliamentary procedure. Once the student understands the difference between the informal procedure suitable to the meanings of small groups, and the formal procedure necessary for the meetings of large groups, he can approach the study of the formal procedure with the proper attitude. This first discussion should reveal the danger of sacrificing the purpose of a meeting to the formalities of procedure and allowing time to be wasted in splitting hairs over minor points. Such disputes are relatively insignificant when considered in the light of the major business of the meeting. The danger of a superficial knowledge of the rules cannot be overemphasized. Therefore, this first class period should stress the fact that all the rules have been devised to facilitate the business of the meeting, that they must never be used as ends in themselves, that the procedure of groups differs according to the type of organization, and that such differences are usually set forth in the bylaws of the group. Of course, even this procedure cannot prevent unscrupulous, aggressive members from

PARLIAMENTARY PROCEDURE (*Continued*)

| Limit debate to pending motion? | Recon- sidered? | Subs. motions? | Vote? | Notes: What is customary wording of motion? What special rules govern it? |
|---|---|---|---|---|
| . . . . . . . . . | Y | N | ⅔ M | These do not establish a rule for they apply only to the motion in question. Include special motions for limiting debate, determining mode of procedure, manner of rating, etc. Cannot be made to apply to some action covered by a rule. |
| . . . . . . . . . | N | Y | M | This must separate the question into distinct propositions. The motion must specify how the division is to be made. It is useful for members who would accept a distinct part of question, but not whole question. |
| Y | N | Y | M | "I nominate Mr. Brown for president," etc. |

foisting their viewpoints upon the group and using the technicalities of the procedure to hinder rather than to facilitate the purpose of the meeting. However, given a group of members eager to accomplish business with the least amount of friction, the knowledge of the rules will be of inestimable value.

For the second class meeting, the members of the class should read the Introduction in *The New Cushing's Manual of Parliamentary Law and Practice,* revised by Charles Gaines, which explains the fundamental principles on which procedure is based, the nature and origin of the rules and the need for revision of parliamentary procedure. Also read the explanation of the organization of a permanent society as described in Robert's revised *Rules of Order,* which gives directions for the first meeting, the second meeting, and the regular meetings of such organizations. You will then be ready to organize into a permanent society at the second meeting of the class. From then on, the club functions as such, and all the regular business is conducted in a realistic manner; the members elect officers, work out a constitution, select the name of the club, etc. The idea works most successfully if the members decide that the purpose of the club will be the study of parliamentary procedure as an aid to intelligent participation in all the outside organizations to which they belong.

*Assignment 2*

Test your knowledge of parliamentary procedure by answering the following questions:

1. What is parliamentary procedure? What is its function? Is a knowledge of parliamentary procedure a necessary part of the citizen's equipment for life in a social group? What is the fundamental principle upon which parliamentary procedure is based? Illustrate your answer by specific references either to experiences with parliamentary procedure in class or in other groups.

2. What is a motion? Explain the following terms as used to describe motions: "takes precedence," "rank," "disposed of," "yield to," "in order," "out of order," "amenable to," "applied to." Illustrate your answer by references to specific motions.

3. What is a principal motion? How many kinds are there? When are they in order? What specific regulations apply to them? Give examples of kinds of principal motions.

4. What is a privileged motion? What are its functions? How many kinds are there? Name each kind.

5. Demonstrate, define, and illustrate each type of privileged motion.

6. What is a subsidiary motion? Classify this motion as a class; name each of the various kinds of subsidiary motions.

7. Explain fully, with specific illustrations, each kind of subsidiary motion.

8. What is an incidental motion? Classify these motions as a class.

9. Explain fully, with specific illustrations, each type of incidental motion.

10. Describe the way you would go about organizing a permanent club. Describe the preliminary steps you would take and the essential procedure to be followed in the first few meetings. Use a specific illustration to lend definiteness to your discussion.

### References

Chafee, E., *Parliamentary Law*. New York: The Thomas Y. Crowell Company, 1930.

Cushing, Luther S., *The New Cushing's Manual of Parliamentary Law and Practice*, rev. by Charles Kelsey Gaines. New York: Thompson Brown Co., 1928.

Deschler, Lewis, *Rules of the House of Representatives*. (Also contains Thomas Jefferson's famous *Jefferson's Manual*.) Washington, D.C.: United States Government Printing Office, 1941.

Hall, Alta B., and Alice F. Sturgis, *A Textbook on Parliamentary Law*. New York: The Macmillan Company, 1930.

Leigh, Robert D., *Modern Rules of Parliamentary Procedure*. New York: W. W. Norton & Company, 1937.

ROBERT, HENRY M., *Parliamentary Law.* New York: D. Appleton-Century Company, 1923.

———, *Rules of Order,* rev. ed. Chicago: Scott, Foresman & Company, 1921.

———, *Parliamentary Practice.* New York: D. Appleton-Century Company, 1921.

*Senate Manual of the United States Senate.* Washington, D.C.: United States Government Printing Office, 1933. (For sale by the Superintendent of Documents, Washington, D.C.)

STURGIS, ALICE F., *Standard Code of Parliamentary Procedure.* New York: McGraw-Hill Book Company, Inc., 1950.

## Chapter 22

## DEBATE

When a thing ceases to be a subject of controversy, it ceases to be a subject of interest.

—WILLIAM HAZLITT

Debate is an exercise in controversy. It is an argument on the merits of a stated proposition affirmed by one side called the "affirmative," and denied by the other side called the "negative." There are usually two teams of three members each. After a definition of terms has been established, the teams prepare their briefs in light of the issues involved. The first speaker presents the case for the affirmative and indicates the issues to be defended by his two colleagues. The negative prepares in like manner. A rebuttal speaker is chosen for each side, and after the formal speeches have been presented, the rebuttal speakers present their refutations.

Since debating skill is only acquired by practice, an outline for two different types of debating is provided in this chapter. For a description and analysis of a proposition, an issue, arguments, and evidence, see Chap. 19.

In your review of Chap. 19, be certain that you understand how the proposition is narrowed by the issue to the exact sense in which the positive and negative sides disagree. In addition, review carefully the types of evidence and the norms that are given for testing the validity of such evidence. Spend some time in studying the manner in which James A. Farley supports each of his minor propositions with cogent arguments. This is most evident in the excellent brief for the speech. Note how the brief is constructed in complete sentences, and how each point is an integral unit of reasoning. Use this speech as a model in constructing your debate brief.

## Preparation of the Debate

The preparation of the debate is a group task. Each member of the team must do his share in preliminary study and research. The first step is the selection and wording of the proposition. Once the negative and the affirmative sides have been chosen, each team begins its preparation. The terms should be defined and the origin and history of the subject should be studied. Each member can now begin the organization of his materials for the issue which he is to defend. The study and research for debate, like that for the public talk, give value to the material presented. The debater must find interesting, pertinent support for his issue. He must take adequate notes and be prepared to contribute to the preparation of the brief, which is the next joint task for the members of each team. Each member must also prepare his speech for delivery. Preliminary preparation for the rebuttal must be made, but the speakers must be ready to adapt this part of their material to the needs of the occasion. The debater must prepare as diligently as the public speaker and he must also be ready to adapt his material so as to meet the arguments presented by his opponent.

## Cross-examination Debate

Interest is often added to debating when the cross-examination debate is used. This is a more difficult form of debating and requires more thorough preparation than the formal style. The procedure is as follows: The first speaker of the affirmative presents his formal speech, and immediately he is cross-examined by the first speaker for the negative. After seven minutes of examination, the questioner is allowed four minutes to summate for the audience what admissions he has secured by the cross-examination. He is restricted to what he has actually gained by admissions, and can introduce no new evidence or arguments. Following this, the second member of the negative presents the negative case, and is then cross-questioned by the second member for the affirmative. The cross-questioning technique is quite difficult and requires skill in pertinent use of language.

A questioner's outline has been worked out as a means of preparation for this type of debate. The questioner can best prepare by summarizing the points at issue between the two teams and isolating the admissions that must be procured to break down the opposition's case. Such admissions should be a logical chain destroying the opposition. If the admissions are inadequate proof, the case is lost before the questioning begins. Take special care to narrow the issues to the exact points of difference. Once the admissions are clearly set, the problem of skillful and purposeful questioning needs attention. By setting pointed questions aligned to the admissions desired, you direct the witness to make admissions. Your preparation outline should have a set of salient questions cautiously worded. Other questions will undoubtedly be needed, but the skilled questioner works these around to his well thought-out questions at the proper moment. Once an admission has been gained, proceed to your next point. Your summation will provide time to remind the audience of the admissions gained.

### The Art of Questioning

Questioning is an art. Being an art, its acquisition requires assiduous practice and a complete command of the media employed. That medium is not the static pigment, brush, clay, or mallet, but the intangible combination of thought, feeling, and expression. It is the medium that changes even in the very framing of the product. The command of such variable material demands skill. No one attempts to play the violin without a long period of practice and study, but the more difficult art of questioning is readily assumed to be the common property of mankind.

The question form differs basically from the statement in purpose and in use. A question must be answered, a statement may go unchallenged; a question must be interpreted, a statement merely accepted; a question must be orientated in light of the individual's experience, a statement may occasion no reaction. Such differences provide the real field of battle for wit and thought. Questions reach truth more quickly than any other technique known. To the degree that a question ascertains truth, it is a valid means of research and a boon to men in search of truth. It is more than that; it is a means of guiding serious men to better understandings, more communal enterprises, and better human relationships.

The most frequent source of misunderstanding in questioning proceeds from irrelevance. All questions which do not bear a causal relation to the proposition suffer some degree of irrelevance. For instance, in the simple question "Does A owe B $100?" a vast number of complications that are irrelevant may be introduced. The lawyer asks: "Is it not a fact that A owes everyone in town?" Here the counsel objects on the ground of irrelevance. The objection is sustained despite the fact that A does owe everyone in town—a seeming unfairness, but actual justice, because: *There is no logical connection between this case and the other instances of A's debts.* This is summed up in the legal axiom "Bad men may have good lawsuits." The point at issue is not what kind of a life A has led, but what is the just decision in this case.

When Governor Dewey was district attorney of New York, he received instructions from Judge Pecora in the art of proper questioning. The following interesting exchange took place in New York on August 17, 1938. It illustrates the difference between a leading question and a direct inquiry.

Testimony of Weinberg [1]

*George Weinberg of 286 Fort Washington Avenue, a confederate of the late Arthur (Dutch Schultz) Flegenheimer in the operation of the numbers racket in New York, who pleaded guilty to the indictment and appeared as a witness for the State, testified as follows:*
Direct examination by Mr. Dewey:
Q.—Mr. Weinberg, you are the George Weinberg who is named in the indictment which is now on trial? A.—Yes, sir.
The Court—Keep your voice up, Weinberg.
Q.—I think you are going to have to talk about five times that loud. Do you think you can? A.—I can.
Q.—You pleaded guilty to this indictment, have you not? A.—I did.
Q.—All thirteen counts? A.—I did.
Q.—I want to ask you at this time only about one conversation. In the Spring of 1932 did you receive a message from Dutch Schultz to come to a meeting? A.—I did.
Mr. Stryker—One moment, please. Watch me and don't answer till the Court rules. I object to it.
Mr. Dewey—May I suggest that counsel—
Mr. Stryker—As incompetent, irrelevant and immaterial.
Mr. Dewey—Just a moment. I ask the Court to direct counsel to address the Court and not the witness.

[1] *New York Times*, Aug. 18, 1938.

*The Court*—That direction will be given now to both counsel in the case for not only present purposes but the future conduct of the trial. Mr. Witness, whenever a question is put to you by the District Attorney in the course of this examination, and you see this gentleman, Mr. Stryker, who is the attorney for the defendant, getting up on his feet, that is an indication that Mr. Stryker proposes to interpose an objection to the question. When you see Mr. Stryker doing that, withhold your answer until Mr. Stryker has stated his objection and the Court has ruled upon it. Do you understand that?

*The Witness*—I do.

*Mr. Stryker*—Now, for the purposes of my motion, will you first strike out the answer, so that we can then dispose of it, because it was given before I had a chance to object.

*The Court*—Strike it out.

*Mr. Stryker*—I object to the question on the ground that it is incompetent, irrelevant, immaterial, hear-say, conversation with a deceased person, in no way germane to any issue in this case, and not in furtherance of any allegation in the indictment, and also on the further ground that the question is leading and puts into the witness's mouth the answer.

*Mr. Dewey*—Dutch Schultz is a named co-conspirator in this indictment.

*Mr. Stryker*—Yes, I know that, although dead.

*The Court*—Read the question. I want to see if it is leading.

(Question read.)

*The Court*—Objection overruled.

*Mr. Stryker*—I except.

*The Court*—Keep your voice up now.

*Q.*—I am referring to the meeting at which the defendant Hines was present.

*Mr. Stryker*—One moment. I object to that.

*The Court*—Strike that out.

*Mr. Stryker*—On the ground—

*The Court*—The jury is instructed to disregard that.

*Mr. Stryker*—That it is a mere statement.

*The Court*—Do not make any statements. Ask questions of the witness.

*Mr. Stryker*—And furthermore on the ground that the question is improper and a mere statement of the District Attorney. I ask for the withdrawal of a juror and a mistrial on the ground of the improper statement.

*The Court*—No; the motion is denied.

*Mr. Stryker*—Exception.

*The Court*—The jury is instructed to disregard the statement made by the District Attorney. Eliminate it entirely from your minds, gentlemen.

*Q.*—Did you go to a lot of meetings? *A.*—I did.

*Q.*—All right. Now I am trying somehow to identify a particular meeting.

*Mr. Stryker*—I object to that, too, the form of the question. "I am trying somehow to suggest a particular meeting." Let him ask a plain, straight question.

*Mr. Dewey*—I suggest that counsel defer his characterizations for his summations and refrain till then.

*Q.*—I am referring to a meeting—trying to identify it—which occurred on Ninety-eighth Street.

*Mr. Stryker*—I object to that. It is a pure leading question, improper in form.

*The Court*—Let the witness give the testimony, Mr. Dewey.

*Mr. Dewey*—Your Honor, I would be delighted if someone would suggest to me how I can isolate one from a dozen meetings, if I cannot say which one I mean or who was present, in a question.

*The Court*—I will try to do it for you.

By the Court:

*Q.*—Mr. Weinberg, do you remember any occasion when you received a message from a man that you knew as Dutch Schultz to go to any meeting sometime in or about the month of March, 1932? *A.*—I do.

*Q.*—Did you go to any such meeting? *A.*—I did.

*Q.*—Where was the meeting? *A.*—At 16 East Ninety-eighth Street.

*Mr. Dewey*—May I suggest, Your Honor, that you permit me to examine the witness?

*The Court*—Just let me ask one more question.

*Q.*—Who was present at that meeting? *A.*—Dutch Schultz.

*Mr. Stryker*—I cannot hear him.

*Q.*—A little louder. *A.*—Dutch Schultz, Jimmy Hines, my brother, Bo Weinberg, and Lulu Rosenkranz.

*The Court*—Now go ahead from that point.

## Hypothetical questions

A hypothetical question has its use in introducing the testimony of an expert. A hypothetical question is phrased this way:

*Q.*—Assuming a man is thirty-two years old, weighs 130 pounds, and is 6 feet tall, would the facts, Doctor, that he lifted a 50-pound package, and thereafter spat blood, indicate a tubercular condition?

Such a question is proper for an expert because it allows him to give his opinion objectively, that is, in regard to a set of facts and with no relation to any person.

*Linguistic questions*

The linguistic questions receive most publicity because of their humorous character. From the current "Is so-and-so sober today?" to the ancient "Have you stopped beating your wife?" humorists have used the question form of linguistic misinterpretations. However, attempts at humor in questioning are very dangerous, and are often turned back on the instigator. When an Italian contractor was sued for completing a poorly constructed wall, the cross-examiner was attempting to show that the contractor's employees, Italian masons, were inferior workmen.

Q.—Was Domenico a good mason?
A.—Oh, yes, verra fine mason.
Q.—And Giuseppi, was he a good mason?
A.—Even better.
Q.—How about Giovanni?
A.—Best of the three.
Q.—(*Slurringly*) I suppose, then, that you claim all masons are good masons?
A.—No—no—justa lika lawyers—soma good—soma rotten.

Questions that tend to cast disregard on the answerer frequently have the opposite effect. Aristotle quotes Gorgias as saying that we must ruin our opponent's earnestness with our jocularity, and his jocularity with our earnestness. In the above, the disparaging question of the lawyer was overthrown by the sincerity of the workman.

In the serious business of seminars and examinations, more subtle difficulties arise. To get behind the symbols used in the question and ascertain the exact meaning involved is a difficult matter. Consider the variety of meaning almost all words have, the skill or lack of skill in the questioner, and the possible interpretations by the questioned. Great care and precision should be used in framing your questions. Such care should not lead to a too cautious question, as:

I am not sure this question can be answered, but a realization that it exists makes it important enough to bring to mind; that is, if you feel that it should be brought to mind, and I'm quite conscious some don't feel that way, but at any rate I should like to know what you think, in light of your own experience, about the, etc.—

Such ruminations belong to silent speech. A question is not graced by a preface, nor is a statement transformed into a question through a rising inflection. Do not distinguish yourself out of existence.

The ambiguous question is one which calls for great tolerance on both sides. It is so easy to slip into personal bickering when what is obvious to you is not obvious to someone else. Usually, it seems the answerer is avoiding the question. Yet it may be that the terms of the question are not clear in light of the other person's background. This difficulty is not new. Aristotle in his *Rhetoric* warns: "In replying you should meet ambiguous questions by a reasonable definition of terms, and not answer curtly." The curt answer carries a barrier that a hundred questions cannot remove. The matter of distinguishing, as practiced by the schoolmen, is not without merit in such cases. Words grow and assume new meanings with age. Frequently the connotative meaning overtakes the denotative meaning, and a lack of common references results. The word "awful," for instance, once meant awe-inspiring. Consider the difference in meaning today between an awe-inspiring class and an awful class.

Distinction may be applied to the motives behind a question. Some questions can only be answered in light of the reason which prompted the person to act. In the following example, Aristotle shows the use of distinction at its best:

So, too, the Lacedaemonian, when he was being examined for his conduct as ephor, was asked whether he thought that his fellow ephors had been justly put to death. "Yes," he said. "Well," said the other, "did you not act in concert with them?" "Yes," was his reply. "Well, then," asked his opponent, "would not you too be justly put to death?" "Not at all," said he; "they acted so because they were bribed; I acted, not for money, but from conviction."

Distinctions should not be made too hastily or too quickly or they will be missed. Reason with the other person until the point at issue evolves clearly, and then distinguish. Most linguistic difficulties in questions can be sifted until a common meaning is achieved; only at that moment should questions be answered. No one can satisfactorily answer a question that he does not understand.

## Opinion and fact questions

A question should seek some definite piece of information, whether it be an opinion or a fact. The more specific and exact the question is, the more readily it can do its work. To invoke again the analogy of questioning in court, note the specific nature of the following questions:

Q.—Did you see a spot on the coat?
A.—Yes.
Q.—What was the color of the spot?
A.—Dark brown.
Q.—Was it blood?

That question was ruled out by the Court as calling for an opinion of the witness. The ordinary witness can only testify to what he has observed by means of his own senses. Only an expert must testify as to the nature of the spot! The precaution taken in legal instances is necessary in debating; fact questions must be distinguished from opinion. Fact-seeking questions should not be phrased "Do you think?" "In your opinion," etc. Matters of fact are true and independent of opinion.

The question put by an expert in a field differs from the question of the average inquirer. When the man whose knowledge is limited asks a question, he reveals a wealth of ignorance that tries the patience of the authority. It is not sufficiently remembered that a degree of knowledge is needed before a good question can be asked. Insistent questioning without basic knowledge leads to grave misunderstanding.

The law furnishes another instance of this in a case of the great English barrister, Sir James Scarlett. Sir James was questioning a well-known actor and musician, Tom Cooke, who was subpoenaed as an expert witness in a musical-piracy case.

Q.—(*Rather flippantly*) Sir, you say that the two melodies are the same but different. Now, what do you mean by that?
A.—I said the notes in the two copies are alike, but with a different accent, the one being in a common time and the other in six-eight time; and consequently the position of the accent of the notes was different.
Q.—What is a musical accent?
A.—My terms are nine guineas a quarter, sir. (*A laugh*)
Q.—Never mind your terms here; I ask you what is a musical accent? Can you see it?
A.—No, Sir James.
Q.—Can you feel it?
A.—A musician can. (*Great laughter*)
Q.—(*Very angry*) Now pray, sir, don't beat about the bush, but explain to his Lordship, and the jury, who are expected to know nothing about music, the meaning of what you call accent.

A.—Accent in music is a certain stress laid upon a particular note in the same manner as you would lay stress upon a given word for the purpose of being better understood. Thus, if I were to say, "You are an ass," the accent would rest on "ass"; but if I were to say, "You are an ass," it rests on "you," Sir James.

The skilled questioner tries to determine the answer before he asks the question. William Lyon Phelps once recounted his difficulties in making out examinations. To the question "Can you name the four greatest writers of English prose?" he received the answer "I can." And when he tried "What eventually happened to Maud?" he got the reply "Eventually she died." He had to accept both answers as correct.

In summary, when you are using the questioning technique, remember that questions possess three major frailties. Such frailties arise from logical, linguistic, or prejudicial bases. The logical frailties involve a lack of relationship, the linguistic a lack of meaning, and the prejudicial a lack of understanding. Such considerations are serious enough to give rise in the law to a strict code for questioning. The lawyer's objection of "irrelevant, immaterial, and incompetent" mirrors the norm to be observed in all questioning. The pertinency, the importance, and the source of a question are as essential in answering as the surrounding colors are to a chameleon.

Study the following rules and apply them in your cross-examination debate.

*Rules for Questioning*

1. Know all you can about the proposition being discussed before questioning the speaker.
2. Be sincere in seeking information.
3. Don't inquisition the speaker.
4. Be brief, *i.e.*, formulate the question before asking it.
5. Don't be unduly minute, this leads to verbalism.
6. Rid your question of emotional bias.
7. Ask questions; don't accuse, harass, browbeat, or upset the speaker. Achieve an attitude of fair play, not trickery.
8. Have a purpose to your question, *i.e.*, gaining information, clarifying an issue, seeking explanation of reasoning involved, or reviewing evidence brought forth.
9. Ask specific questions.
10. Avoid sophistry—questions designed to demonstrate your own skill.

*Assignment 1*

One of the most difficult things to learn is the discipline of finding the facts. All of us are prone to engage in rationalizations—especially when the facts are not readily accessible. Debate is the discipline which teaches us to base our arguments on facts.

There is a club in New York called the Black and White Club. In order to keep the club together, its chairman, Mr. John Cashman, invented this fact-finding assignment:

> To put an end to this futile bickering, I instituted what we now call Black and White Sessions. If the debate involves a matter within the realm of proven fact (as all our debates now do), all speakers must come to the meeting armed with facts—in black and white. Instead of throwing a controversial subject into the teeth of the Society and tearing it apart on the spot, the members of the Society vote pro and con, and then are divided into groups according to their vote. The groups then are given a week to collect their data, make notes, study the subject and its ramifications, and when they meet they bring with them the information they have collected.
>
> For the first time since the Society was formed, the chairman was invested with a real, working authority that was absolute, and the weapon with which he calmed the irascible and kept the rebellious in order was the power voted him to accept or reject proof of an argument submitted by an individual or group. The line drawn between the admissible and inadmissible in proof is clear: the work of newspaper or columnists, radio commentators, or other writers and speakers in whose work bias or prejudice could play a part is absolutely inadmissible, as are unsigned newspaper clips in which the news is slanted either to Right or Left. Quotes from public officeholders submitted as proof are not admissible. Admissible are excerpts from any work of chronological or historical value proven in authenticity. This covers newspaper clips of past events, the encyclopedias, transcripts of radio broadcasts in which the facts have already been proved, or any other work or works which tend to deal only with facts.
>
> Thus was eliminated the great bugaboo which haunts any order-loving chairman—hearsay.

*Organize a fact-finding session for the next class meeting. Each student will bring a sample of definite proof. Select one of your favorite points of view and try to establish it beyond reasonable doubt.*

*Assignment 2*

In class discussion select several interesting questions of controversy and plan a series of debates. These questions can be drawn from the current items of business before the House of Representatives or the United States Senate. Taking a current issue increases interest and also provides a ready source of information in newspapers and magazines.

*Sample Debate Outline, I*

Speaker _____ Class _____

Side _____ Date _____

A. Statement of proposition.
B. Issues involved.
    1. First speaker.
    2. Second speaker.
    3. Third speaker.
C. Main speech: Introduction, definition, analysis, exposition.

*Sample Debate Outline, II*

Speaker _____ Class _____

Side _____ Date _____

A. Order of arguments: Kinds and distinctions.
    1.
    2.
    3.
B. Refutation.
    1.
    2.
C. Conclusion.

*Sample Questioner's Outline, Cross-examination Debate*

Speaker _____ Class _____

This is an additional outline. The regular debate outline should also be filled out completely.

A. Opponents' probable issues.
    1.
    2.
    3.

*B.* Admissions to be gained.
  1.
  2.
  3.
  4.
  5.
  6.
*C.* Purposeful questions: To be used in cross-examination.
  1.
  2.
  3.
  4.
  5.
  6.
  7.
  8.
  9.
  10.
*D.* Probable questions: To be asked of you.
  1.
  2.
  3.
  4.
  5.

*Sample Critical Debate Chart*

Student Critic _____ Date _____

Debate _____

## Mark

1. poor     2. fair     3. adequate     4. good     5. excellent

| Speech skill | Affirmative speaker | | | Negative speaker | | |
|---|---|---|---|---|---|---|
| | 3 | 2 | 1 | 3 | 2 | 1 |

### Debate

| | | | | | | |
|---|---|---|---|---|---|---|
| Analysis of proposition | | | | | | |
| Presentation of issues | | | | | | |
| Division of proposition | | | | | | |
| Pertinence of arguments | | | | | | |
| Arrangement of arguments | | | | | | |
| Validity of evidence | | | | | | |
| Summation | | | | | | |

### Rebuttal

| | | | | | | |
|---|---|---|---|---|---|---|
| Extemporaneous expression | | | | | | |
| Wit | | | | | | |
| Attack on significant issues | | | | | | |

## REFERENCES

BAIRD, A. CRAIG, *Argumentation, Discussion, and Debate.* New York: McGraw-Hill Book Company, Inc., 1949.

CROCKER, LIONEL, *Argumentation and Debate,* Chaps. I and II. New York: American Book Company, 1944.

EWBANK, H. L., and J. J. AUER, *Discussion and Debate,* Chaps. I–III. New York: Appleton-Century-Crofts, Inc., 1941.

FOSTER, W. T., *Argumentation and Debating,* rev. ed., Chap. I. Boston: Houghton Mifflin Company, 1932.

NICHOLS, E. R., and J. H. BACCUS, *Modern Debating.* New York: W. W. Norton & Company, 1936.

O'NEILL, J. M., and J. H. McBURNEY, *The Working Principles of Argument.* New York: The Macmillan Company, 1931.

———, C. LAYCOCK, and R. L. SCALES, *Argumentation and Debate.* New York: The Macmillan Company, 1917.

# PART VII. SPEECH ARTS

Speech is the most universal art. Its use proclaims a man to be either a mere copyist or one endowed with the sublimest gifts. Since all men speak, it is not the miracle of speaking which attracts attention but that significant feature of art called "form." Form is the organization of perceptual material into intelligible patterns. Form in speech deals with the complete act, the coordinated, significant sound pattern. This conceptual form gains effectiveness as art in direct proportion to the adequacy of expression involved. Naturally, all speakers cannot be great artists, but all can achieve a certain dexterity and a degree of form.

Your final speech activities center about the mutual enjoyment of aesthetic experiences. Under this heading are all situations whose aim is the appreciation of sublime thought beautifully expressed. In such situations the participants gather together to enjoy each other's company and to experience some lofty sentiment or ideal. Beauty and goodness hold sway. The participants desire the cadence of poetry, the action of drama, and the beautiful expression of language. Such activities have been called the "impressive arts" for the appeal is to the imagination. The necessary actions of the world are forgotten, and its beauty and magnificence are realized. Such situations reveal man and nature in moments of exquisite perfection.

Laurence Olivier is the leading actor of our time. He combines superb vocal skill with an unusual sense of dramatic values. He has shown dexterity in virtually all the dramatic forms. Whether it be a popular play or a Shakespearean performance the audience finds him revealing new depths of character through flawless interpretations. He illustrates the finest combination of the social, semantic, vocal, and phonetic skills coupled with the artistry indicative of a rich personality. His motion pictures of Shakespearean plays have brought a new dimension to the screen.

## Chapter 23

# ORAL INTERPRETATION OF LITERATURE

He ceas'd; but left so pleasing on the ear
His voice, that list'ning still they seemed to hear.
—HOMER, *Odyssey*

The mind and spirit of man grow by what they feed on. If you wish to gain power in expression, you must read the works of the great authors who are masters of the art of selecting words. There is no more ennobling experience than contact with great literature. Reading the best that has been thought and expressed in all ages by the truly significant thinkers of each age is of inestimable value.

Many critics maintain that all art is conceived in terms of music before actual expression in any media. Perhaps we may more certainly say that all art is originally conceived in terms of sound. At any rate, no poet conceives of his works in terms of written symbols. He merely tries to preserve them in written symbols for those who cannot share the present vocal rendition. But you as an interpreter, and consequently sharer and re-creator with the poet, must capture not the barren symbols, but the true aesthetic experience that forced the poet to write.

Consider the overwhelming desire to communicate his "vision of the good" that forced the poet to discipline himself to expression in a conventional form; to capture and frame his dream in a sonnet, epic, ballad, lyric, or ode. This was more difficult for the poet than it is for us as his audience. His was the genius, yours the company of genius. Yet, if you come to him as an understanding companion in thought, it is not impossible that you may leave him as his master embarked on a purer dream, a more Dantesque vision.

This chapter is an attempt to acquaint you with the real meaning of poetry, to introduce you to the intimate companionship of men of superb gifts. Begin the study of poetry with this attitude, and it will form a source of enjoyment throughout your life. Never be satisfied with your initial reading of a poem. Read it aloud many times. Each time you will find new meaning and freshness in the lines. Each reading will gain in power.

*Questions in Analyzing a Poem for an Understanding of the Art Process*

1. What is the general conception or significance of a poem or of some other writing?
2. What is the first impression you received?
3. What in this first impression is most interesting, striking, or unusual?
4. What is most pleasing? Least pleasing? Why?
5. What was the artist's idea which made him write this poem or piece of writing? What did he want to share? Was this worth while?
6. How did he use the mechanism of literature to achieve this effect?
7. Did his feeling come to you more acutely because of characterization, arrangement of detail, emphasis, or rhythm?
8. Do subject matter and rhythm seem to coordinate?
9. How would you develop this theme?
10. Do the rhythm, arrangement, imagery, and expression appeal to you more or less than the thought expressed?
11. Do all the last comprise a unity of the whole?
12. What rhythm is used? Is the rhythm broad and easily discernible, or is it a diffused atmospheric blending creating an esoteric mood?
13. Is the theme preserved?
14. Is this theme borne out in onomatopoetic language, in smooth, flowing, delicate, rough, jagged words, or sound patterns?
15. Are the themes unified and supplementary?
16. Is there a hierarchy of themes? One central theme with supplementary themes?
17. Are all these themes unified in a significant pattern?
18. Is the poem realistic, dramatic, romantic, or naturalistic?
19. What significance has the above on its development? Are there lights and shadows which enhance the idea or emotion of the poet?
20. What are the shadings within the poem? Does the language suggest dullness, bleakness, darkness, vividness, clearness, dinginess, quietness, gorgeousness, monotony, confusion, or boresomeness?
21. Are ideas juxtaposed for effect?
22. How does the language reveal hues and tints in emotional reaction?
23. What is the result of general pattern: monotonous, confused, unified, concrete, totality of theme?
24. What provisions does this poem furnish for individuality of interpretation? What expressive real arts could be implied in enriching the poem?

25. How does the poet rise to the highest point in interest and emotion in his poem? Where is the highest point? How attained? By what means? What is the hierarchy of points of emphasis? How is it attained?

26. What is the predominate emotion? What color best describes this? How would you conceive of this poem in a painting?

27. Is there a transition in the poem? How would you achieve that transition through voice?

28. Are treatment of theme and type of poem consonant?

29. Are there parts to the poem which stand apart, or do all harmoniously blend? Is one cumulative effect produced?

### Questions in Analyzing a Poem for Oral Interpretation

1. Who is speaking in the poem? What kind of a person: old, young, sophisticated, naïve? What is the person's mood? What kind of a life has he led? Why is he speaking?

2. To whom is the person speaking? What relationship exists between the two?

3. What is the situation?

These questions may sound simple, but they give the cue to interpretation. Edna St. Vincent Millay's "Departure" may be given widely different interpretations according to the decisions the interpreters make concerning the age of the girl and what has happened to make her speak. Many readers completely miss the tragedy in Eugene Field's "Little Boy Blue." Your interpretation of "My Last Duchess" will differ according to your idea of the Duke's character. Is he a man who cannot stand the indiscriminate likings of his wife, or is he a cruel, haughty, and overbearing aristocrat without cause? Are his feelings natural, or are they artificial? Did she die of a broken heart, or was she put to death? Would you like the Duke as a friend? Why? Unless you the interpreter think through the above questions and others of a similar nature, you will not have an adequate impression of the poem. Without this impression you cannot reveal its beauty to others.

The first series of questions sought to make you conscious of the art process that is the basis of all poetry and of all art. The process in drama, architecture, sculpture, or painting is the same, the incidental of media alone differs. Apply these questions to other art forms. The second set of questions attempts to give you a view of the individuality of a poem as such. It seeks to make you cognizant of the particulars of a poem and its distinguishing features as a form of art. It further seeks to help you to realize the thoughts and emotions expressed in terms of people and actions. This should lead to a visualization of the important details and a keen insight into the accentuation and subordination of details. Here the form of technique and the thoughts and emotions of persons become one. The following set of questions helps you to translate your impressions into adequate expression.

### Questions in Selecting the Techniques of Expression

1. Have you ever known anyone similar to the person speaking in the poem? How did this person talk? Can you make your voice sound appropriate? What is the difference between a young voice and an old voice? How does the voice portray mood? What is the characteristic tempo of this person? What pitch would he be likely to use? Would his voice have much flexibility?

2. Have you ever witnessed a scene between two people similar to the one you are about to portray? Many ways are used to display the same emotion. Which one would be the most effective in this situation? Experiment with the various ways and select the one which you feel is most effective.

3. If there is no similar experience in your life, try to recall something that is akin to it. For instance, if you have never lost a hundred dollars it would be hard for you to interpret the emotions of a man who had. Yet this could be done quite adequately if you recalled the loss of some money and its consequent discomfiture and multiplied that to an extreme degree. By this process of fuller feeling, you acquire fuller living. Make poetry and its interpretation aid you in attaining a fuller sensitivity to life.

### PROJECTS

#### Assignment

Select a poem and read it aloud at home. Be prepared to read the poem to the class. If it is short, memorize the poem. If it is long, memorize certain lines which are particularly meaningful to you.

#### Suggested Selections for Practice

| Author | Poem |
|---|---|
| Arnold, Matthew | The Study of Poetry |
| Belloc, Hilaire | Tarantella |
| Brooke, Rupert | The Great Lover |
| Broun, Heywood | My Sort of God |

| *Author* | *Poem* |
|---|---|
| Browning, Elizabeth B. | A Musical Instrument |
| Browning, Robert | An Incident in a French Camp, The Last Ride Together |
| Carroll, Lewis | The Walrus and the Carpenter |
| Daly, T. A. | Mia Carlotta |
| De la Mare, Walter | Old Susan, Silver |
| Eliot, T. S. | The Hollow Men |
| Frost, Robert | The Pasture, Mending Wall, Birches, Stopping by Woods on a Snowy Evening, The Death of the Hired Man |
| Housman, A. E. | When I Was One-and-Twenty |
| Kipling, Rudyard | Gunga Din |
| Knibbs, Henry H. | Roll a Rock Down |
| Lindsay, Vachel | General Booth Enters into Heaven, The Congo, Abraham Lincoln Walks at Midnight |
| Lowell, Amy | Sea Shell, Patterns, Lilacs |
| Masefield, John | A Consecration, Sea-Fever |
| Millay, Edna St. Vincent | Renascence, Ballad of the Harp Weaver, The Buck in the Snow |
| Noyes, Alfred | The Barrel Organ, The Admiral's Ghost, Forty Singing Seamen |
| Poe, Edgar Allan | The Bells, Annabel Lee |
| Robinson, Edwin A. | Richard Cory, Miniver Cheevy |
| Ruskin, John | Traffic |
| Sandburg, Carl | Cool Tombs, Grass, Chicago, Gone |
| Sarett, Lew | Four Little Foxes, Wind in the Pines, The World Has a Way with Eyes |
| Schauffler, Robert H. | Scum o' the Earth |
| Seeger, Alan | I Have a Rendezvous with Death |
| Shakespeare, William | Sonnets |
| Sill, Edward R. | The Fool's Prayer |
| Teasdale, Sara | Barter |
| Wylie, Elinor | Golden Bough |

*Suggested Anthologies*

| Author | Title | Publisher |
|---|---|---|
| Campbell, O. J., and J. F. A. Pyre | *Great English Poets* | Crofts |
| Clarke, G. H. | *A Treasury of War Poetry* | Houghton Mifflin |
| Colum, Padraic | *Anthology of Irish Verse* | Boni and Liveright |
| Drinkwater, John | *An Anthology of English Verse* | Collins |
| Hoffenstein, Samuel | *Poems in Praise of Practically Nothing* | Garden City Pub. Co. |
| Kronenberger, Louis | *An Anthology of Light Verse* | The Modern Lib. |
| Le Gallienne, Richard | *The Le Gallienne Book of English and American Poetry* | Garden City Pub. Co. |
| Lieberman, Elias | *Poems for Enjoyment* | Harper |
| Monro, Harold | *Twentieth-century Poetry* | Chatto & Windus |
| Monroe, Harriet, and Henderson | *The New Poetry* | Macmillan |
| Quiller-Couch, A. T. | *The Oxford Book of English Verse* | Oxford |
| Quiller-Couch, A. T. | *The Oxford Book of Victorian Verse* | Oxford |
| Robinson, E. A. | *Collected Poems* | Macmillan |
| Robinson and Thurston | *Poetry Arranged for the Speaking Choir* | Expression Co. |
| Sandburg, Carl | *Chicago Poems* | Holt |
| Stedman, E. C. | *An American Anthology* | Houghton Mifflin |
| Teasdale, Sara | *Flame and Shadow* | Macmillan |
| Untermeyer, L. | *Modern American Poetry* | Harcourt, Brace |
| Untermeyer, L. | *Modern British Poetry* | Harcourt, Brace |
| White, N. I., and W. C. Jackson | *An Anthology of Verse by American Negroes* | Trinity College Duke University Press |
| Whitman, Walt | *Leaves of Grass* | Macmillan |
| Wilkinson, Marguerite | *New Voices: An Introduction to Contemporary Poetry* | Macmillan |

*Sample Outline for Oral Interpretation*

Student _____ Class _____ Date _____

To read a poem effectively, you must (1) understand the poem fully and (2) express the thought and emotion vividly for your audience.

### ANALYSIS OF POEM

Thought:
1. The theme of poem is _____
2. The poet's purpose in writing poem was _____

3. The words which must be defined for the audience are _____

_____

Emotion:
1. The mood of poem is _____
2. The poem is (lyric, dramatic, epic, etc.) in style _____
3. The element which should receive major emphasis is _____

_____

### INTERPRETATION OF POEM

Read the poem aloud several times, preferably to someone who can criticize your reading. If you find your expression of thought and emotion is inadequate, try experimenting with the different techniques described in the first chapters of this book, *e.g.*, mark the words or lines which should receive major emphasis because of thought or emotion. Subordinate other thoughts to these and make them prominent by using the means of emphasis outlined. Beware of artificiality. You must be sincere in your reading, for an audience can readily detect affectation. It is often possible to increase the effectiveness of your reading by prefacing it with a short introductory talk in which you set the mood for your poem and explain any strange terms the poet may have used. Write out a short paragraph which you could use in introducing your poem to the audience. It will clarify your own thinking in regard to the poem.

*Developing Semantic Skill*

Add to your word cards the following:

I. Words used in the speech text:

| *Word* | *Pronunciation* | *Meaning* |
|--------|-----------------|-----------|
| 1. Dantesque | | |
| 2. esoteric | | |
| 3. hierarchy | | |
| 4. media | | |

II. Words commonly mispronounced:
 1. saline
 2. sinecure
 3. suite

III. Words from your own experience.

## Chapter 24

# DRAMATIC READING

Then read from the treasured volume
The poem of thy choice,
And lend to the rhyme of the poet
The beauty of thy voice.
—LONGFELLOW

If you have never had the opportunity of taking part in a dramatic production, you have missed an exhilarating experience. Working with other members of the cast for a successful production provides invaluable contacts with people. These contacts alone would make the experience worth while. In addition, the creative art involved in portraying a character on the stage includes many skills useful in life. The body control and poise required for satisfactory stage presence will prove an asset in business and social life. Moreover, getting completely out of one's self and becoming an entirely different person is a good experience for everyone. Dramatic activity offers increasing mental and emotional stimulation. Shakespearean actors all agree that they find something vital and fresh in each interpretation they study. For this reason the dramatic readings suggested for you are taken from the best in literature. This assures you that the time and energy put forth in perfecting the reading will not be wasted.

Your first problem is to find a reading which will merit your study. The dramatic reading should be one which will continue to hold your interest. Freshness of approach comes from your own enthusiasm about the material. So make your selection one which encourages you to spend your time wisely. Once you have selected the reading, study it carefully. Think about it. Analyze the selection from all angles. Have a clear concept of the selection as a whole before you begin to work on the individual parts. Remember, you must practice the selection aloud many times before you can expect to achieve a convincing interpretation. Practice with verve, keeping always in mind that your purpose is to lift your audience into the realm of imagination. Bring new life to the character through your interpretation.

Let us take a scene from *Macbeth* to illustrate the way dramatic readings should be prepared. In Act V, Scene 1, the doctor and the gentlewoman await the appearance of Lady Macbeth. Terrified by these sleep-walking scenes, the gentlewoman has asked the doctor to wait with her. As you read the scene through, you realize the artistry with which Shakespeare created the mood. The doctor asks the gentlewoman what she has overheard Lady Macbeth say during these scenes. The gentlewoman refuses to tell him despite the fact that he is the doctor and, as he reminds her, " 'tis most meet" that she should tell him. The full significance of the scene is immediately apparent, for the woman still refuses to tell what she has heard. Your first reading of the scene gives you pertinent leads which help in making your interpretation vivid. It is good to write out even a brief summary of the scene after you have read it as a starting point for your study.

The meaning of the scene might be expressed as follows: Alone at the castle, Lady Macbeth feels remorse for the crimes her evil prompting has led Macbeth to commit. In her sleep she relives all the moments of horror. The scene reveals the disintegration of a powerful personality. Once you have this concept clearly in mind, you can begin to work on the meaning of the individual lines. The doctor notices that she keeps rubbing her hands, and the gentlewoman explains that this is an accustomed action continued for periods of time. Therefore, when Lady Macbeth says, "Yet here's a spot," you know she refers to the bloodstains she received when she took the daggers from the terrified Macbeth to put them near the grooms. The line must be read slowly to bring out the full significance of the horror she now experiences in being unable to remove the stains of blood. You know the importance of this phobia, for Lady Macbeth keeps referring to it throughout the scene.

Notice the variety of emotions expressed from line to line. "Yet here's a spot" is said slowly to show her terror. The very next line, "Out, damned spot! out, I say!" is read rapidly with great force for it expresses her accustomed way of dealing with problems. She is one who commands rather than entreats. The next line, "One: two:

why, then 'tis time to do't" can be whispered as Lady Macbeth counts off the hours warning Macbeth to get ready to commit the murder. A quickening of the tempo in the second half of the line and a rise in pitch may indicate the tense excitement. The next line is one of biting sarcasm as she goads Macbeth on to the deed: "Fie, my lord, fie! a soldier, and afeard?" The tone could be harsh for the first part of the line to indicate her brusqueness. The sarcasm can be brought out by using circumflex inflection on "soldier" and "afeard." She taunts her husband and drives him on when he would weaken.

Thoughts of the great power they will have once Macbeth becomes king give strength and assurance to the following statement: "What need we fear who knows it, when none can call our power to account?" Let your voice express confidence, security in being the absolute rulers. This emotion is then strongly contrasted with the very next statement, "Yet who would have thought the old man to have had so much blood in him." Again the horror of the murder returns, and we see a crushed and terrified woman. In imagination, she feels her hands to be stained with blood and even stronger than his. "Here's the smell of the blood still; all the perfumes of Arabia will not sweeten this little hand." You must practice to bring out the full tragedy of this line, for a woman has so forgotten her essential femininity as to drive her husband on to the murder and, when he weakened, to carry out the plans by attempting to make it seem as though the grooms had committed the murder.

As you study the reading, each line takes on meaning. By reading the line aloud and practicing until you can bring out its full import, you gradually build an interpretation which is tremendously effective.

## PROJECTS

*Assignment*

Select a scene from one of Shakespeare's plays, or one of the following excerpts, and prepare it for reading in class. The reading must not exceed five minutes. Memorize the selection.

### REMORSE

Filled with horror at the murders which she and her husband have instigated, Lady Macbeth reveals her true feelings in her anguished murmurings during this sleep-walking scene.

Scene 1. Dunsinane. A Room in the Castle. *Enter a Doctor of Physic, and a waiting Gentlewoman.*

DOCT.: I have two nights watch'd with you, but can perceive no truth in your report. When was it she last walk'd?

GENT.: Since his Majesty went into the field, I have seen her rise from her bed, throw her night-gown upon her, unlock her closet, take forth paper, fold it, write upon it, read it, afterwards seal it, and again return to bed; yet all this while in a most fast sleep.

DOCT.: A great perturbation in nature, to receive at once the benefit of sleep and do the effects of watching! In this slumb'ry agitation, besides her walking, and other actual performances, what, at any time, have you heard her say?

GENT.: That, sir, which I will not report after her.

DOCT.: You may to me: and 'tis most meet you should.

GENT.: Neither to you, nor to any one; having no witness to confirm my speech.

*Enter Lady Macbeth, with a Taper.*

Lo, you, here she comes! This is her very guise; and, upon my life, fast asleep. Observe her; stand close.

DOCT.: How came she by that light?

GENT.: Why, it stood by her. She has light by her continually: 'tis her command.

DOCT.: You see her eyes are open.

GENT.: Ay, but their sense is shut.

DOCT.: What does she now? Look how she rubs her hands.

GENT: It is an accustom'd action with her, to seem thus washing her hands; I have known her continue in this a quarter of an hour.

LADY M.: Yet here's a spot.

DOCT.: Hark, she speaks. I will set down what comes from her, to satisfy my remembrance the more strongly.

LADY M.: Out, damned spot! out, I say!—One: two: why, then 'tis time to do't.—Hell is murky!—Fie, my lord, fie! a soldier, and afeard?—Yet who would have thought the old man to have had so much blood in him?

DOCT.: Do you mark that?

LADY M.: The thane of Fife had a wife; where is she now?—What, will these hands ne'er be clean?—No more o' that, my lord, no more o' that; you mar all with this starting.

DOCT.: Go to, go to; you have known what you should not.

GENT.: She has spoke what she should not, I am sure of that: Heaven knows what she has known.

LADY M.: Here's the smell of the blood still; all the perfumes of Arabia will not sweeten this little hand. Oh, oh, oh!

DOCT.: What a sigh is there! The heart is sorely charg'd.

GENT.: I would not have such a heart in my bosom for the dignity of the whole body.

DOCT.: Well, well, well—

GENT.: Pray God it be, sir.

DOCT.: This disease is beyond my practice; yet I have known those which have walk'd in their sleep who have died holily in their beds.

LADY M.: Wash your hands, put on your night-gown; look not so pale. —I tell you yet again, Banquo's buried; he cannot come out on's grave.

DOCT.: Even so?

LADY M.: To bed, to bed! there's knocking at the gate. Come, come, come, come, give me your hand. What's done cannot be undone.— To bed, to bed, to bed. (*Exit Lady Macbeth.*)

DOCT.: Will she go now to bed?

GENT.: Directly.

DOCT.: Foul whisp'rings are abroad; unnatural deeds
Do breed unnatural troubles; infected minds
To their deaf pillows will discharge their secrets.
More needs she the divine than the physician.
God, God, forgive us all! Look after her;
Remove from her the means of all annoyance,
And still keep eyes upon her. So, good-night.
My mind she has mated, and amazed my sight.
I think but dare not speak.

GENT.: Good-night, good doctor. (*Exeunt.*)

### FREE WILL

A theme often expressed by Shakespeare—man's free will—is here depicted in graphic terms. As you prepare this selection, note the cumulative effect of the philosophizing. From the general reflections about the world, he comes down to his own case, with ever-increasing feeling. Try to distinguish between the general reflections and the personal feeling.

This is the excellent foppery of the world, that, when we are sick in fortune—often the surfeit of our own behaviour—we make fuilty of our disasters the sun, the moon, and the stars: as if we were villains by necessity; fools by heavenly compulsion; knaves, thieves, and teachers, by spherical predominance; drunkards, liars, and adulterers, by an enforced obedience of planetary influence; and all that we are evil in by a divine thrusting on: an admirable evasion of man, to lay his goatish disposition to the charge of a star! My father compounded with my mother under the dragon's tail; and my nativity was under Ursa major; so that it follows, I am rough and lecherous. Fut! I should have been that I am had the maidenliest star in the firmament twinkled on my bastardizing.

—SHAKESPEARE

### GLOUCESTER'S SOLILOQUY

John Barrymore did a memorable recording of this speech on the Victor Record 6827-B. It is probably in your college library. This soliloquy is a challenge requiring every type of vocal variety you possess. Note the use of irony and contrast; the wrath and abandon of the soul-searching cry of Richard against his fate.

Ay, Edward will use women honourably.
Would he were wasted, marrow, bones, and all,
That from his loins no hopeful branch may spring,
To cross me from the golden time I look for!
And, yet, between my soul's desire and me—
The lustful Edward's title buried—
Is Clarence, Henry, and his son young Edward,
And all the unlook'd for issue of their bodies
To take their rooms, ere I can place myself: . . .
Well, say there is no kingdom then for Richard;
What other pleasure can the world afford?
I'll make my heaven in a lady's lap,
And deck my body in gay ornaments,
And witch sweet ladies with my words and looks.
O miserable thought! and more unlikely
Than to accomplish twenty golden crowns!
Why, love forswore me in my mother's womb;
And, for I should not deal in her soft laws,
She did corrupt frail nature with some bribe,
To shrink mine arm up like a wither'd shrub;
To make an envious mountain on my back,
Where sits deformity to mock my body;
To shape my legs of an unequal size;
To disproportion me in every part,
Like to a chaos, or an unlick'd bear-whelp
That carries no impression like the dam.

And am I then a man to be belov'd?
O monstrous fault, to harbour such a thought!
Then, since this earth affords no joy to me
But to command, to check, to o'erbear such
As are of better person than myself,
I'll make my heaven to dream upon the crown
And, whiles I live, t'account this world but hell,
Until my mis-shap'd trunk that bears this head,
Be round impaled with a glorious crown. . . .
And from that torment I will free myself
Or hew my way out with a bloody axe.
Why, I can smile, and murder whiles I smile,
And cry "Content" to that which grieves my heart,
And wet my cheeks with artificial tears,
And frame my face to all occasions. . . .
Can I do this, and cannot get a crown?
Tut, were it farther off, I'll pluck it down.
—*Henry the Sixth*, Part III, Act III, Scene 2

### THE DIALOGUE OF ORLANDO AND ROSALIND

This is an excellent dialogue for the nuances of expression required.
The insinuations should be subtle but telling.

ORLANDO: What were his marks?
ROSALIND: A lean cheek, which you have not; a blue eye and sunken,
which you have not; an unquestionable spirit, which you have not;
a beard neglected, which you have not; but I pardon you for that,
for simply your having in beard is a younger brother's revenue. Then
your hose should be ungarter'd, your bonnet unbanded, your sleeves
unbutton'd, your shoe unti'd, and everything about you demonstrating a careless desolation. But you are no such man; you are rather
point-device in your accoutrements, as loving yourself than seeming
the lover of any other.
ORLANDO: Fair youth, I would I could make thee believe I love.
ROSALIND: Me believe it! you may as soon make her that you love believe it. . . . But, in good sooth, are you he that hangs the verses
on the trees, wherein Rosalind is so admired?
ORLANDO: I swear to thee, youth, by the white hand of Rosalind, I am that
he, that unfortunate he.
ROSALIND: But are you so much in love as your rhymes speak?
ORLANDO: Neither rhyme nor reason can express how much.

ROSALIND: Love is merely a madness, and, I tell you, deserves as well a dark house and a whip as madmen do; and the reason why they are not so punish'd and cured is, that the lunacy is so ordinary that the whippers are in love too. Yet I profess curing it by counsel.

ORLANDO: Did you ever cure any so?

ROSALIND: Yes, one; and in this manner. He was to imagine me his love, his mistress, and I set him every day to woo me; at which time would I, being but a moonish youth, grieve, be effeminate, changeable, longing and liking, proud, fantastical, apish, shallow, inconstant, full of tears, full of smiles; for every passion something and for no passion truly any thing. . . . And thus I cur'd him; and this way will take upon me to wash your liver as clean as a sound sheep's heart, that there shall not be one spot of love in't.

ORLANDO: I would not be cured, youth.

ROSALIND: I would cure you, if you would but call me Rosalind and come every day to my cote and woo me.

ORLANDO: Now, by the faith of my love, I will. Tell me where it is.

ROSALIND: Go with me to it and I'll show it you; and by the way you shall tell me where in the forest you live. Will you go?

ORLANDO: With all my heart, good youth.

ROSALIND: Nay, you must call me Rosalind. . . .

—*As You Like It*, Act III, Scene 2

### YOUTH OR AGE?

One of the most celebrated exchanges in parliamentary debate took place when Sir Robert Walpole attacked Mr. Pitt in a perfect example of the argument from *ad hominem*. Select a partner and reenact this famous debate.

### "Sir Robert Walpole against Mr. Pitt"

I was unwilling to interrupt the course of this debate while it was carried on, with calmness and decency, by men who do not suffer the ardor of opposition to cloud their reason or transport them to such expressions as the dignity of this assembly does not admit. I have hitherto deferred answering the gentleman who declaimed against the bill with such fluency of rhetoric and such vehemence of gesture,—who charged the advocates for the expedients now proposed with having no regard to any interests but their own, and with making laws only to consume paper, and threatened them with the defection of their adherents, and the loss of their influence, upon this new discovery of their folly and ignorance. Nor do I now answer him for any other purpose than to remind him how little the clamors of rage and the petulancy of invective contribute to the end for which this assembly is called together; how little the discovery of truth is promoted, and the security of the nation established by pompous diction and theatrical emotion. Formidable sounds and furious declamation, confident assertions and lofty periods may affect the young and inexperienced; and, perhaps, the gentleman may have contracted his habits of oratory by conversing more with those of his own age than with such as have more opportunities of acquiring knowledge, and more successful methods of communicating their sentiments. If the heat of his temper would permit him to attend to those whose age and long acquaintance with business give them an indisputable right to deference and superiority, he would learn, in time, to reason rather than declaim, and to prefer justness of argument, and an accurate knowledge of facts, to sounding epithets and splendid superlatives, which may disturb the imagination for a moment, but leave no lasting impression on the mind. He will learn that to accuse and prove are very different; and that reproaches, unsupported by evidence, affect only the character of him that utters them. Excursions of fancy, and flights of oratory, are, indeed, pardonable in young men, but in no other; and it would surely contribute more, even to the purpose for which some gentlemen appear to speak (that of depreciating the conduct of the administration), to prove the inconveniences and injustices of this bill, than barely to assert them, with whatever magnificence of language, or appearance of zeal, honesty, or compassion.

### "Reply of Mr. Pitt"

The atrocious crime of being a young man, which, with such spirit and decency, the honorable gentleman has charged upon me, I shall neither attempt to palliate nor deny; but content myself with hoping that I may be one of those whose follies cease with their youth, and not of that number who are ignorant in spite of experience.

Whether youth can be imputed to a man as a reproach, I will not assume the province of determining; but, surely, age may become justly contemptible if the opportunities which it brings have passed away without improvement, and vice appears to prevail when the passions have subsided.

The wretch who, after having seen the consequences of a thousand errors, continues still to blunder, and whose age has only added obstinance to stupidity, is surely the object either of abhorrence or contempt, and deserves not that his gray hairs should secure him from insult. Much more is he to be abhorred, who, as he has advanced in age, has receded from virtue, and becomes more wicked with less temptation:—who prostitutes himself for money which he cannot enjoy, and spends the remains of his life in the ruin of his country.

But youth is not my only crime. I am accused of acting a theatrical part. A theatrical part may either imply some peculiarity of gesture, or a dissimulation of my real sentiments, and an adoption of the opinions and language of another man.

In the first sense the charge is too trifling to be confuted, and deserves only to be mentioned that it may be despised. I am at liberty—like every other man—to use my own language: and though, perhaps, I may have some ambition to please this gentleman, I shall not lay myself under any restraint, nor very solicitously copy his diction or his mien, however matured by age or modeled by experience. But if any man shall, by charging me with theatrical behavior, imply that I utter any sentiments but my own, I shall treat him as a calumniator and a villain: nor shall any protection shelter him from the treatment he deserves. I shall, on such an occasion, without scruple, trample upon all those forms with which wealth and dignity intrench themselves; nor shall anything but age restrain my resentment:—age, which always brings one privilege—that of being insolent and supercilious without punishment.

But, with regard to those whom I have offended, I am of opinion that if I had acted a borrowed part I should have avoided their censure. The heat that offended them was the ardor of conviction, and that zeal for the service of my country which neither hope, nor fear, shall influence me to suppress. I will not sit unconcerned while my liberty is invaded, nor look in silence upon public robbery. I will exert my endeavors, at whatever hazard, to repel the aggressor and drag the thief to justice,—whoever may protect him in his villainies and whoever may partake of his plunder.

### SPARTACUS TO THE GLADIATORS AT CAPUA

This is a stirring and emotional speech requiring the abandon of true emotional delivery. Try to capture the depth of feeling that inspired Spartacus. Let your voice ring out with fulsome volume.

Ye call me chief; and ye do well to call him chief who, for twelve long years, has met upon the arena every shape of man or beast the broad empire of Rome could furnish, and who never yet lowered his arm. If there be one among you who can say, that ever, in public fight or private brawl, my actions did belie my tongue, let him stand forth, and say it. If there be three in all your company dare face me on the bloody sands, let them come on. And yet I was not always thus—a hired butcher, a savage chief of still more savage men!

My ancestors came from old Sparta, and settled among the vine-clad rocks and citron groves of Cyrasella. My early life ran quiet as the brooks by which I sported; and when, at noon, I gathered the sheep beneath the shade, and played upon the shepherd's flute, there was a friend, the son of a neighbor, to join me in the pastime. We led our flocks to the same pasture, and partook together our rustic meal.

One evening, after the sheep were folded, and we were all seated beneath the myrtle which shaded our cottage, my grandsire, an old man, was telling of Marathon and Leuctra; and how, in ancient times, a little band of Spartans, in a defile of the mountains, had withstood a whole army. I did not then know what war was; but my cheeks burned, I knew not why, and I clasped the knees of that venerable man, until my mother, parting the hair from off my forehead, kissed my throbbing temples, and bade me to go to rest and think no more of those old tales and savage wars. That very night, the Romans landed on our coast. I saw the breast that had nourished me trampled by the hoof of the war-horse; the bleeding body of my father flung amid the blazing rafters of our dwelling!

To-day I killed a man in the arena; and, when I broke his helmet-clasps, behold! He was my friend. He knew me, smiled faintly, gasped, and died—the same sweet smile upon his lips that I had marked, when, in adventurous boyhood, we scaled the lofty cliff to pluck the first ripe grapes, and bear them home in childish triumph! I told the pretor that the dead man had been my friend, generous and brave; and I begged that I might bear away the body, to burn it on a funeral pile, and mourn over its ashes. Ay! upon my knees, amid the dust and blood of the arena, I begged that poor boon, while all the assembled maids and matrons, and the holy virgins they call Vestals, and the rabble, shouted in derision, deeming it rare sport, forsooth, to see Rome's fiercest gladiator turn pale and tremble at sight of that piece of bleeding clay! And the pretor drew back as if I were pollution, and sternly said—"Let the carrion rot; there are no noble men but Romans!" And so, fellow-gladiators, must you, and so must I, die like dogs.

O Rome! Rome! thou hast been a tender nurse to me. Ay! thou hast given to that poor, gentle, timid shepherd-lad who never knew a harsher tone than a flute-note, muscles of iron and a heart of flint; taught him to drive the sword through plaited mail and links of rugged brass, and warm it in the marrow of his foe:—to gaze into the glaring eye-balls of the fierce Numidian lion, even as a boy upon a laughing girl! And he shall pay thee back, until the yellow Tiber is red as frothing wine, and in its deepest ooze thy life-blood lies curdled!

Ye stand here now like giants, as ye are! The strength of brass is in your toughened sinews; but to-morrow some Roman Adonis, breathing sweet perfume from his curly locks, shall with his lily fingers pat your red brawn, and bet his sesterces upon your blood. Hark! hear ye yon lion roaring in his den? 'Tis three days since he tasted flesh; but to-morrow he shall break his fast upon yours—and a dainty meal for him ye will be!

If you are beasts, then stand here like fat oxen, waiting for the butcher's knife! If ye are men,—follow me! Strike down yon guard, gain the mountain passes, and there do bloody work, as did your sires at old Thermopylæ! Is Sparta dead? Is the old Grecian spirit frozen in your veins, that you do crouch and cower like a belabored hound beneath his master's lash? O comrades! warriors! Thracians!—if we must fight, let us fight for ourselves! If we must slaughter, let us slaughter our oppressors! If we must die, let it be under the clear sky, by the bright waters, in noble, honorable battle!

—E. KELLOGG

### NO, I THANK YOU

No more exquisite description of individuality has been written than Rostand's speech of personal independence. Re-create its vigor and note especially the reiteration of the phrase "No, I thank you." [1]

CYRANO: And what should a man do? Seek some grandee, take him for patron, and like the obscure creeper clasping a tree-trunk, and licking the bark of that which props it up, attain to height by craft instead of strength? No, I thank you. Dedicate, as they all do, poems to financiers? Wear motley in the humble hope of seeing the lips of a minister distend for once in a smile not ominous of ill? No, I thank you. Eat every day a toad? Be threadbare at the belly with groveling? Have his skin dirty soonest at the knees? Practice feats of dorsal elasticity? No, I thank you. With one hand stroke the goat while with the other he waters the cabbage? Make gifts of senna that counter-gifts of rhubarb may accrue, and indefatigably swing his censer in some beard? No, I thank you. Push himself from lap to lap, become a little great man in a great little circle, propel his ship with madrigals for oars and in his sails the sighs of the elderly ladies? No, I thank you. Get the good editor Sercy to print his verses at proper expense? No,

[1] From *Cyrano de Bergerac*, by Edmond Rostand. Copyright 1898, 1926. Reprinted by permission of Doubleday & Company, Inc., publishers.

I thank you. Contrive to be nominated Pope in conclaves held by imbeciles in wineshops? No, I thank you. Work to construct a name upon the basis of a sonnet, instead of constructing other sonnets? No, I thank you. Discover talent in tyros, and in them alone? Stand in terror of what gazettes may please to say, and say to himself "At whatever cost, may I figure in the Paris Mercury!" No, I thank you. Calculate, cringe, peak, prefer making a call to a poem,—petition, solicit, apply? No, I thank you! No, I thank you! No, I thank you! But . . . sing, dream, laugh, loaf, be single, be free, have eyes that look squarely, a voice with a ring; wear, if he chooses, his hat hind-side afore; for a yes, for a no, fight a duel or turn a ditty! . . . Work, without concern of fortune or of glory, to accomplish the heart's-desired journey to the moon! Put forth nothing that has not its spring in the very heart, yet, modest, say to himself, "Old man, be satisfied with blossoms, fruits, yea, leaves alone, so they be gathered in your garden and not another man's!" Then, if it happens that to some small extent he triumph, be obliged to render of the glory, to Caesar, not one jot, but honestly appropriate it all. In short, scorning to be the parasite, the creeper, if even failing to be the oak, rise, not perchance to a great height, . . . but rise alone!

### FROM A CHRISTMAS CAROL

"A merry Christmas, uncle! God save you!" cried a cheerful voice. It was the voice of Scrooge's nephew, who came upon him so quickly that this was the first intimation he had of his approach.

"Bah!" said Scrooge. "Humbug!"

He had so heated himself with rapid walking in the fog and frost, this nephew of Scrooge's, that he was all in a glow; his face was ruddy and handsome; his eyes sparkled, and his breath smoked again.

"Christmas, a humbug, uncle!" said Scrooge's nephew. "You don't mean that, I am sure."

"I do," said Scrooge. "Merry Christmas! What right have you to be merry? What reason have you to be merry? You're poor enough."

"Come, then," returned the nephew gaily. "What right have you to be dismal? What reason have you to be morose? You're rich enough."

Scrooge, having no better answer ready on the spur of the moment, said "Bah!" again, and followed it up with "Humbug!"

"Don't be cross, uncle!" said the nephew.

"What else can I be," returned the uncle, "when I live in such a world of fools as this? Merry Christmas! What's Christmas time to you but a time for paying bills without money; a time for finding yourself a year older, and not an hour richer: a time for balancing your books and having every item in 'em through a round dozen of months presented dead against you? If I could work my will," said Scrooge indignantly, "every idiot who goes about with Merry Christmas on his lips, should be boiled in his own pudding, and buried with a stake of holly through his heart. He should."

"Uncle!" pleaded his nephew.

"Nephew," returned his uncle sternly, "keep Christmas in your own way, and let me keep it in mine."

"Keep it," repeated Scrooge's nephew. "But you don't keep it."

"Let me leave it alone, then," said Scrooge. "Much good may it do you. Much good has it ever done you!"

—Charles Dickens

*Additional Selections from Shakespeare*

## Richard the Second

1. Act I, Scene 1

Duke of Norfolk: Then, Bolingbroke, as low as to thy heart,
   Through the false passage of thy throat, thou liest. . . .

2. Act II, Scene 1

John of Gaunt: Methinks I am a prophet new inspir'd
   And thus expiring do foretell of him: . . .

3. Act III, Scene 2

King Richard: Needs must I like it well; I weep for joy
   To stand up on my kingdom once again. . . .

4. Act III, Scene 2

King Richard: No matter where; of comfort no man speak: . . .

5. Act IV, Scene 1

King Richard: Ay, no; no, ay; for I must nothing be;
   Therefore no no, for I resign to thee. . . .

## Hamlet

1. Act I, Scene 2

Hamlet: O, that this too too solid flesh would melt,
   Thaw, and resolve itself into a dew! . . .

2. Act II, Scene 2

Hamlet: Now I am alone.
   O, what a rogue and peasant slave am I! . . .

3. Act I, Scene 3

Polonius: Yet here, Laertes! aboard, aboard, for shame! . . .

4. Act III, Scene 1

Hamlet: Speak the speech, I pray you,— . . .

## Macbeth

1. Act I, Scene 7

MACBETH: If it were done when 'tis done, then 'twere well
　　It were done quickly. If the assassination . . .

2. Act II, Scene 1

MACBETH: Is this a dagger which I see before me,
　　The handle toward my hand? Come, let me clutch thee. . . .

3. Act V, Scene 1

LADY MACBETH, DOCTOR, GENTLEWOMAN:
　　Out, damned spot! out, I say!—One: two: why, . . .

4. Act V, Scene 5

MACBETH, SEYTON, MESSENGER:
　　Hang out our banners on the outward walls; . . .

*Sample Outline for Dramatic Reading*

Student ——————————————— Class ————— Date ————

Since you cannot give to others what you do not possess, you must understand a scene thoroughly before you can interpret it for an audience. The items listed below should assist you in your careful study of the scene.

ANALYZING SELECTION

Thought analysis:

1. Dominant theme of play is ————————————————
2. Scene is important because ————————————————
3. The situation in scene is ————————————————
4. The characters are ————————————————
5. The tempo of scene is ————————————————
6. The climax occurs ————————————————

Emotional analysis:

1. The character I am portraying has the following traits: ————
(physical) ————— (mental) ————— (emotional) ————
2. His dominant emotion in this scene is ————————————
3. He reveals this emotion by ————————————————

Vocal analysis:

1. This character would have the following pitch level: ————
2. The emotional impact is captured by using these vocal elements:

————————————————————————————

3. The appropriate force, volume, and tempo are ————————

*Developing Semantic Skill*

Add to your word cards the following:

I. Words used in the speech text:

| Word | Pronunciation | Meaning |
|------|---------------|---------|
| 1. character | | |
| 2. climax | | |
| 3. drama | | |
| 4. pantomime | | |

II. Words commonly mispronounced:
1. tomato
2. thwart
3. tremor

III. Words from your own experience.

*Chapter 25*

# CONVERSATION

The best of life is conversation.
—EMERSON

This inscription placed over an open fire typifies the joy of fellowship. Old friends gathered together to share their lives. Such is conversation at its best. There is a free give-and-take of ideas and feelings. The talk changes from one topic to another in free-and-easy exchange. The cares of ordinary existence seem far away, and the members of the group relax and enjoy each other's company. You have probably at some time or another had such an experience. Such moments make you feel life is well worth living.

The full pleasure of conversation is only experienced on rare occasions. The great majority of conversations never get going. They lack zest. A number of factors destroy ordinary conversations. Sometimes the place hinders conversation. For example, if you have ever tried to talk in a crowded subway train, or in a room that was noisy, you can appreciate the importance of the setting for conversation. A good host sets the stage for the kind of evening he wants his guests to enjoy. A large room will tend to keep the conversation formal; a small room with an open fireplace will make the guests feel informal. The importance of atuning the conversation to the setting is emphasized by William Lyon Phelps in his essay "Human Nature." He tells the story of the man who overtook him on the way to a football game, and as they were walking along with the gay excited crowds, his companion inquired about the condition of contemporary American poetry. The purpose of this chapter is to keep you from being just such a bore.

The presence of bores in the group contributes to the failure of conversation. A bore is a person who insists upon talking when someone else wants to talk. Approach the conversation from the point of view of the listener, and take your cues from the interest of your listeners. The greatest profit can come from conversation when you concentrate on drawing the other person out, leading him to talk about his interests, or telling him about the things he is most likely to be interested in hearing. There is an old saying, "He who looks for trouble, finds it." Deliberately looking for pleasure from conversation is the surest way to find pleasure. So develop your skill as a conversationalist by study of the things in others which annoy you; analyze the types of bores you meet and try *not* to be like them.

### Bores

The worst bore is the one who wearies you with endless details. He omits nothing, whether it has anything to do with the story or not. In the middle of one story, he launches into another, and before he's halfway through that, has thought of a third equally boring sidetrack. He never gets you to the station. If he is your boss, you have to listen to his ramblings or escape him. He can teach you a lesson, however, in your own conversation. Avoid telling meaningless details! Select, build your story, get to the point as quickly as possible, and *stop*. Be brief.

### The "that-reminds-me" bore

The "detail" type of bore is very closely related to the bore who jumps from one topic to another in a bewildering jumble of utterly unrelated ideas. The discussion on baseball reminds him of his cousin who was at a baseball game the day he was run over; and speaking of accidents, did you hear about the terrible accident on the subway; it's really wonderful the way they build subways so far underground nowadays, and so on, ad infinitum. He leaves no room for comment or interruption, and his leap from one topic to another leaves you dizzy.

### The one-track bore

He has an opposite in the bore who gets on one topic and stays there. He may be interested in the topic for any number of reasons. Sometimes he's a reformer who is ready to swing into action on any and all occasions. At other times, he's just a person with a one-track mind. Or he may be a man with a hobby who assumes everyone is as interested as he is, and goes on from there. It is very easy to become this kind of a bore. A person who has been perfectly normal before his trip to Europe suddenly becomes very adept in turning every topic to travel. Everyone who meets him spends the evening taking the trip—minus the pleasure of it. If you've had any unusual experience in which others might be interested, you may use it judiciously to add to your conversational powers; if you overdo it, you lose all the advantage of the experience as material for conversation. There is no more boring experience than conversing with someone interested in only one topic. The antidote is to develop a wide variety of interests.

Certain irritating personality traits make people boring in conversation. The person who is sure he is right on any and all decisions is a typical bore. He plows into the person who has ventured an opinion and sets him right on the matter. He presents quite a problem for the host or hostess, and timid guests are his meat. One or two blasts from him and they are effectively silenced for the evening. At times aggressive guests come to grips with him, and awkward situations arise which ruin the gaiety of an evening.

## The namby-pamby bore

The person who has no opinion is equally boring. He ruins all discussions by trying to agree with everyone. It is no fun to discuss matters with him for he vacillates from one position to another. In this matter, as in many others, it is wise to seek the pleasant mean. One of the advantages of conversation is that, in conversing with others, you become acquainted with many ways of solving problems, and your own thinking is refined in this process. By closing your mind to the opinions of others you shut off rich sources of growth, and by failing to form an opinion for yourself, you make yourself the prey of every wave of opinion which passes over you. The story of the man with the donkey who tried to take everyone's advice is ample warning against the second condition.

## The tactless bore

No list of bores would be complete without reference to the tactless person who makes everyone squirm. The old rule that the topics to be avoided in conversation are "money, religion, nationality, politics, and unpleasant topics such as sickness and death" is still a good one. Don't open up a conversation with such statements as "All Republicans are idiots" unless you are absolutely sure there are no

Republicans present, and, even then, it is better not to get into the habit of making such tactless statements. Sooner or later you will make the statement without thinking of who is present, and the results are likely to be unpleasant.

Tact is an art which can be developed. It is easy to be tactless, for tactlessness comes from lack of consideration for the rights and feelings of others. A particularly irritating form of tactlessness is that of asking personal questions. A very good rule to follow is never to ask a personal question. Get out of the habit of asking your friend what he paid for his suits, or how much rent he pays, or what his father did, or where he made his money, or any question which touches upon his private affairs. The greatest trial of family life is the lack of privacy accorded each member by the others. So the joy of friendship is marred by questions the person would rather not be asked. Be especially careful what you say to a friend when you meet him with another friend. The horror of meeting the old home-town crony with all the stories centering around the theme "I knew him when" can hardly be overestimated. Some people actually consider it funny to ask a friend whom they meet with a business associate how he's making out since he was fired from the last position. Such atrocities are inexcusable.

### The "I-knew-you-when" bore

When you meet a friend, and he introduces you to the person he is with, you should avoid all references to personal matters. Keep the conversation general. Talk about current figures in the news or any other safe topic. You cannot possibly know how much the stranger knows about your friend. A remark made at this time which would be perfectly permissible at another time might embarrass your friend. He may have dressed very carefully to create an impression upon this person. Your remark, "All dressed up, aren't you?" may defeat his purpose. Since you can't possibly know just how much the person knows about your friend, avoid all personal remarks.

### The "I" bore

The tactless person can spoil everyone's pleasure very quickly, but he has a close rival in the person who is conceited. The tendency to use every topic as a means of showing how clever you are should be watched. A very useful trick is to fine yourself a dime every time you find yourself beginning a story with "I." Change it, and lead the other fellow into telling you about himself. He will think you are an unusually intelligent person for listening attentively to his words of wisdom. However, it is not good to be too self-effacing. The timid souls and the "Weary Willies" who are always finding the world against them, have a deadening effect on the spirits of even the most skillful conversationalists. Good taste should keep you from going to this extreme.

## The punster

The people who make a practice of punning, asking trick questions, and giving flippant answers to serious questions are in a class by themselves. If you permit yourself to use more than one pun during the course of a conversation, you are well on the way to becoming a public nuisance. The strain of trying to live up to the "brilliant sallies" of an habitual punster is irritating in the extreme. You should avoid all such mannerisms.

## How to Acquire Conversational Skill

The list of bores points out dangers to be avoided in the art of conversation. There is a stimulation to good conversation which will repay you for any efforts you may make to become skillful as a conversationalist. Look upon conversation as the source of broad, enriching experiences. Be enthusiastic in your study of it. Your attitude toward conversation can change your life. If you once experience the thrill of directing conversation from dullness to brilliance, you will have started on a most enriching hobby.

Conversation is a speech situation, and the principles which apply to the acquisition of good speech apply to the art of becoming a good conversationalist. All other things being equal, the more intrinsically interesting the person, the better the conversationalist. The exception to this rule is the person who has had thrilling experiences but whose telling of them is uninteresting. You cannot hope to be a good conversationalist unless you have something interesting to talk about. If your life is rather humdrum, you can still be a good conversationalist by using listening techniques to acquire a fund of information.

A famous hostess was once asked the secret of her success. She explained that on the afternoon before her dinner parties, she read up on the topics in which her guests were interested so that she would be able to ask intelligent questions to draw out her guests. Remember, it is a basic human desire to feel important. So read widely that you may be able to ask intelligent questions of the people you meet. Every person has had some unique experiences, and you can learn something from his experiences if you can get him to talk about them.

There are two parts to the process by which you can become a good conversationalist. One part of the process concerns you; the other is concerned with your power to get the other fellow talking. First, *you must have something to say.* College should give you the interest in a wide variety of topics which are the subject materials for conversation: art, music, drama, political science, psychology, literature, science. Practice in conversation should give you the ability to use these materials effectively. This chapter should motivate you to eliminate any personal mannerisms which might make you boring in conversation.

The second part of the process is equally important: *you must make a study of dealing successfully with all kinds of people.* Don't excuse your failures. Some students who have merely been exposed to the college influence feel a tremendous sense of their own importance. When they meet strangers and fail in conversation, they attribute the failure to their superiority. If you cannot converse with all types of people, you are closing avenues of growth to yourself. Learn to talk with everyone you meet—even the bores. They can be handled if you study the proper techniques. A conceited person can be handled easily by deferring to his opinion. Let him know you think he is clever. Never argue with a pompous person. Become conveniently deaf or change the subject when someone asks you a personal question. You are under no obligation to answer such a question. Most bores are interesting if you learn how to handle them. Further, let no human failing irritate you. Decide that such quirks make people more interesting and you will be surprised at the change in the effect of your conversation.

Read the accounts of the conversations of famous people. They contain good hints as to how to develop skill in repartee. The special articles on this topic which appear in *Reader's Digest* are excellent. Keep a notebook of good stories, interesting anecdotes, and clever witticisms, to be read over in your spare moments. You can become a good conversationalist if you put your mind to it. It is worth the effort because conversation is the source of the richest, most stimulating social experiences in life.

## PROJECTS

*Assignment*

Read one good article on conversation. Come prepared to participate in a class discussion on conversation. Have some suggestions as to suitable topics for conversation and ways of developing conversational skills.

## REFERENCES

CLAPP, JOHN M., and EDWIN A. KANE, *How to Talk*, Chap. 4, "Conversation."

DE QUINCEY, THOMAS, *The Art of Conversation.*

HARRINGTON, WALTER, and M. G. FULTON, *Talking Well.*

HELESTINE, OLIVE, *Conversation.*

WRIGHT, MILTON, *The Art of Conversation and How to Apply Its Technique.*

*Chapter 26*     •

# RADIO AND TELEVISION SPEAKING

Radio and television speaking are the result of the ever-increasing desire of modern man to extend the use of personal contact and communication. They present immense opportunities for the skillful speaker and actor, but only if you acquire the additional skills that these new media require. Essentially, of course, the act of speaking remains the same, and the factors studied in this course form the basis of all types of speaking. But radio and television make additional demands that fashion the situation into a new style. For example, the skill of forcefully holding a vast throng must be replaced by a new concept of enticing one to seven people in the quiet of their homes to listen to your message. The audience is still vast, but the approach must be reconditioned because you are now talking to millions in separate intimate groups.

Another amazing difference is the competition in speaking that the new speaker encounters. In a public talk, you have the audience within your sight. But in radio and television, all you can see is a mike or a camera. Moreover, you must capture the audience in the first few seconds or you have lost them to another program. You cannot wait to warm up to your subject nor can you expect the audience to cease what they are doing and listen unless you have captured their attention. Bruce Barton, chairman of the board of B.B.D. & O., compares the radio audience to the passing throng on the boardwalk at Atlantic City. "They are as a stream of humanity passing by. You have one shot at them and in that shot you must stop them and then talk with them. If you miss, it matters little what you have to give them. They are gone; and your message is lost."

The final basic difference is the absence of audience reaction. As a sensitive speaker you depend a great deal upon the encouragement of your audience. Their laughter, their applause, and their murmured approval are the very core of good audience contact. Such reactions help you pace the speech and give you a sense of pausing and climactic effect. But radio and television are quiet, reactionless media. True, there are announcers, engineers, and camera technicians. But they are busy men, silently intent upon performing a totally different function from an audience. If you expect even the slightest reaction from them, you will be sadly mistaken. Indeed, if you look for their reactions, you will be more easily disconcerted. You and you alone must proceed with an imagined audience and sense their reactions to your performance.

## Types of Radio and Television Speaking

The variety of speeches, conferences, dramatic productions, and fellowship situations are almost endless. Never before in history has the spoken word held such sway in the affairs of people. From morning until night every home in the country is furnished a full fare of speaking performances. For example, there are the informative talks such as the movie gossip, the book talks, the inspirational talks, the commentaries, the sportscasts; for fellowship situations you find the quiz program, the variety show, and the interview; for persuasion you will need but be reminded of the almost endless commercials; and for deliberative speeches, the political talks and religious sermons are freely afforded for your edification; for conference speaking there are debates, town halls, and people's platforms; while the drama can be said to have truly come into its own with the advent of the serial, radio drama, television theater, and endless dramatic variation.

## Radio and Television Scripts

The most obvious difference between speaking and broadcasting is that, in the latter, what you are going to say must be written down. It is not enough to have an outline. *You must prepare a script.* This has become standard practice to protect the station from legal entanglements and to protect the audience from unprepared rambling. The only exception to this is the spontaneous interview such as Mary Margaret McBride and Nancy Craig carry on; but even these are set up with meticulous prearrangements. So resolve to learn the subtle technique of writing a good script.

The radio or television script has seven fundamental requirements.

1. *The opening should be an attention getter.* Radio audiences shop around on their dials. They patiently listen to the end of a program, but they are most attentive the next thirty seconds of the new program. That is the deadline of interest. The new program has thirty seconds to convince the listener to stay with it. In those thirty seconds you must promise the audience something worth while. Note how John B. Kennedy did just that in his opening on a book program:

This is John B. Kennedy and I have a tremendous piece of news for the whole family! Men and women by the thousands are overwhelming the author of a remarkable new book in a mass outpouring of thanks such as I have seldom witnessed in my long years of covering the news. An incredibly beautiful and exciting retelling of the Life of Christ by one of our greatest living authors has just been published and is sweeping the country like a tidal wave. It's called *The Greatest Story Ever Told* by Fulton Oursler. . . .[1]

Sydney Walton used the same technique in opening an inspirational program:

What are you getting out of life? Are you making the most of your opportunities? Listen to a few minutes which may change your whole life. Dr. ——— has already helped thousands find the key to true happiness. Perhaps he can help you.

In television, the same interest opener is necessary. Note this Dollar Mystery Club opener:

DOUBLEDAY & CO.
11–11:15 P.M.

WARREN HULL
MONDAY APRIL 24

STATION: CBS

| *AUDIO* | *VIDEO* |
|---|---|
| MINOR:<br>If *you* murdered somebody, keep away from this camera! It has already convicted 50 guilty people! | CUE OF CAMERA, NEWSPAPER GRAFLEX TYPE ON TABLE (SAME TABLE AS USUAL BOOKS) |

[1] Scripts are used with the permission of Huber Hoge & Sons, New York City.

*AUDIO*  *VIDEO*

THEME:

PULL BACK TO
TAKE IN BOOKS ON
TABLE

SUPER: DOUBLE-
DAY & CO.

FLIP TO: "THE
WARREN HULL
SHOW"

CUE HULL TO PICK
UP CAMERA THEN
PULL BACK
JOIN HULL—

CUE HIM

HULL: (*Smiling*)
Yes, friends, if you are guilty of murder stay away from
this camera! It's used by two of the most famous de-
tectives in mystery fiction—Flash Casey and Kent Mur-
dock, newspaper photographers extraordinary! A little
hard on the outside, perhaps, but for the right people,
their hearts are as big as ostrich eggs. They're the
smartest, fastest thinking newspaper men that ever dug
up a story—thanks to their gifted author, George Har-   CARTOON OF COX
mon Cox, who has held us spellbound with his active
gripping detective stories, year after year. And now I'd
like you to meet Casey's creator in person—George   SHOW COX STAND-
Harmon Cox!   ING NEXT TO 30 OR
SO BOOKS PILED UP
HIGH

Any of the established ways of gaining attention may fashion an
effective opening. You may start with a pertinent question and
sprinkle others throughout, for questions keep interest alive and vary
the pace of your style. Or you may touch people on common points
of human interest. Make them say, "Yes, that is just like me." Or you
can quiz them about some failing they sense deeply; for example,
"Do you make these mistakes in English?" Above all, be certain that
you have emotional appeal in your opening. Promise the listening
audience some pictured gratification. Describe in vivid image-bearing terms what good will come to the listener if he continues to
listen. Finally, do not be afraid to be dramatic. Use humanized facts
in dramatic situations and keep your portrayals alive with word pictures and emotional appeals.

2. *The script should be timed.* Time is of the essence in radio and television. Your talk must begin and end upon a given signal. So the simplest thing to do is to determine at what rate you speak most easily and tailor your speech to that rate. You will find that the average speaker broadcasts at between 140 and 160 words per minute. This may be shortened for heavy emotional material, or lengthened to 180 for quick, light, and amusing chatter. After you have determined with a stop watch just how much copy you can read in one minute, your timing problem is solved. *Put only that much copy on each page of your script.* You are then certain of at least eleven checks during a fifteen-minute broadcast. The other three and a half minutes will be used by the announcer and the commercial. Above all, don't try to get too much in one broadcast. It is far more important to repeat one idea five times than to give five ideas in one broadcast. The audience simply cannot absorb ideas that quickly. Moreover, if you have too much in your script, you may well have to cut the ending and thus lose the most important part of the performance.

In addition to your *one-page-one-minute* script, place one or two possible cuts near the end of the broadcast. Simply enclose a number of lines in a bracket. These are to be left out if time does not permit their inclusion. The vast benefit of this is that you do not have to cut at a minute's notice, and the deleted material does not impair the logic of your talk. It also removes the fear and nervousness that come when the broadcast is about to go off the air and you have not finished. Most speakers also provide an extra minute of copy on a separate piece of paper to be inserted if the reading has been accelerated. The announcer will signal you whether or not to use the insert. With these two safety measures, the timing should gradually become a routine process.

3. *The script should be marked for delivery.* A variety of script forms has been evolved. All have the common purpose of making the reading sound conversational and natural. Reading from any page tends to formalize your message. As you know, this style loses the attention and interest of the listeners. Just what form is best for you is a matter of personal taste, and a little experience will reveal the most effective type script. The following are the usual devices:

*a.* Caps and dots for pauses.

MUSICALLY SPEAKING, THE PROGRAM TODAY IS ON THE POPULAR SIDE. SOME OF IT'S ROMANTIC . . . SOME LIGHT AND BREEZY . . . AND SOME OF IT NOSTALGIC. . . .

*b.* Parentheses for subordination.

Then, of course . . . you'll hear a chapter from the Passing Parade. (But let's get right into it) My first number is Moya's "Song of Songs."

*c.* Underlining keywords for emphasis.

"These are not small, illustration-size pictures, but range in size up to 11 x 14 inches. They can be framed . . . or hung on any wall / in any room in your home / ."

*d.* Bars for pauses.

"*Start* a system of your own *today* // As you grow with your system / you will get more out of it // As you *develop* it / *your* mind will establish a *mental habit* // Make your beginning humble / and *increase* the complication of your system as you use it // . . . *Remember* / the function of charts is to give an *over-all view* // to see relationship // and to *sense* proportions."

*e.* Triple spacing for ease in reading.

"My wife and I looked *all over* the South for a place to live // and *one morning* in June we drove into this paradise / Roanoke // Virginia."

An example of a professionally marked script gives an insight to the care that top announcers use in preparing a commercial for broadcast:

And for lovers of good books and fine art / here's an unusual opportunity! // If you join the Family Reading Club immediately, / you will receive as a FREE gift for joining . . . 20 . . . yes . . . 20 of the world's greatest works of art! // Yes, / this astonishing collection of art masterpieces is yours FREE / as a new member of the FAMILY READING CLUB . . . the book club that brings you the very highest type of bestseller entertainment at huge savings! // As the club's new way of advertising, / new members get FREE / 20 magnificent full-color reproductions of the greatest art the world has ever seen. // They were originally made available through the cooperation of the Metropolitan Museum of Art, / The Louvre, / The Whitney Museum, / and famous private collections; / but now / in this special drive to win new members, / THE FAMILY

READING CLUB will ship all 20 of them to new members absolutely FREE! // . . .

4. *The script should be rehearsed for readability.* When the script is ready, it should be read several times for difficult phrases and awkward constructions. Such lush phrases as "the inexorable processes of democracy" have a way of never coming over the broadcast just that way. Sentences with an overabundance of sibilant sounds are most difficult in rendition. Possible tongue twisters are unrecognizable until spoken. For example, try "She stood at the door awelcoming him in," or "I don't think this could be Poughkeepsie." Both of these are credited with breaking up otherwise good scenes.

Many commentators refuse to write scripts and use a stenographer to take down their extemporaneous remarks in order to acquire a conversational manner in their delivery. This is a wise method of procedure. It affords a real opportunity to capture the pattern of your normal speech. But even the most carefully prepared script will sometimes meet with difficulty in reading. Bill Stern, the famous commentator, once recalled some of these blurts in this way:

Radio is a business where mistakes are costly, sometimes funny. Announcers don't always mean what they say. . . . Bob Elson is one of America's top sport announcers yet Bob let fly with, "It's printed in clear tripe easy to read." Don Wilson likes to forget the time he stated, "Now, ladies, I will climb up the fire escape with one hand and talk with the other." It was André Baruch who on the "American Album of Familiar Music" stated, "When you have a headache, ask for it by its full name." Or the time David Ross on CBS introduced Tito Guizar and his guitar by saying, "And now we present Tito Guitar and his guizar." Or maybe you like the one Harriet Hilliard pulled last season on the Red Skelton show, "This is the bed George Slepington washed in."

A final word must be said about sentences. Keep your sentences short. It is difficult for the listener to follow a number of distinctions drawn out in modifying phrases and clauses. The listening span is short, and long sentences confuse the hearer. Break up your sentences and use repetition. The wise commentator strives more for analogies, comparisons, and homely similes than for extended argument or reasoning. An illustration drawn in specific pictures is ten times more effective than the most logical argument. So use short, descriptive sentences. They will be easier to read, and easier listening for the audience.

5. *The script should have emotional appeal.* Specific and definite pictures touch the hearts of the listeners. In your script, strive to have an emotional touch. You can do this by crystallizing the feelings of the moment. All good speakers develop a sense of knowing how to say what the audience wishes it had the ability to say. In other words, the closer you can come to expressing the heart's desire of the audience, the nearer you are to true eloquence. This need not be arched in flowery language, it but needs to be direct as an arrow aimed at the heart. Two of the finest examples of this simplicity of emotional appeal are worthy of study and restudy. The first was the speech of Winston Churchill which inspired an all but beaten nation to start a march to victory; and the second is a talk at the funeral of one of the great men of our time, Knute Rockne.

Notice in the Churchill speech the power of the ever-forward surge of emotional appeal:

I have nothing to offer but blood, toil, tears, and sweat.

We have before us an ordeal of the most grievous kind. We have before us many, many long months of struggle and of suffering. You ask, What is our policy? I will say: It is to wage war, by sea, land and air, with all our might and with all the strength that God can give us: to wage war against a monstrous tyranny, never surpassed in the dark, lamentable catalogue of human crime. That is our policy. You ask, What is our aim? I can answer in one word: Victory—victory at all costs, victory in spite of all terror, victory however long and hard the road may be; for without victory there is no survival. Let that be realized; no survival for the British Empire; no survival for all that the British Empire has stood for; forward towards its goal. But I take up my task with buoyancy and hope. I feel sure that our cause will not be suffered to fail among men. At this time I feel entitled to claim the aid of all, and I say, "Come, then, let us go forward together with our united strength."

In the following example, notice how President Charles O'Donnell of the University of Notre Dame gave a memorable radio address at the burial of Knute Rockne by relating the tragic feeling of the nation when a beloved football coach passed away in a plane crash at the height of his career.

In this holy week of Christ's Passion and death there has occurred a tragic event which accounts for our presence here today. Knute Rockne is dead. And who was he? Ask the president of the United States who dispatched a personal message of tribute to his memory and comfort to his bereaved. Ask the king of Norway who sends a special delegation as his personal representatives to this solemn service. Ask the several state legislatures now sitting that have passed resolutions of sympathy and condolence. Ask the university senates, the civic bodies and societies without number; ask the bishops, the clergy, the religious orders, that have sent assurances of sympathy and prayers; ask the thousands of newspapermen whose labor of love in his memory has stirred a reading public of 125,000,000 Americans; ask men and women from every walk of life; ask the children, the boys of America; ask any and all of these who was this man whose death has struck the nation with dismay and has everywhere bowed heads in grief.

Was he perhaps a martyr who had died for some great cause, a patriot who laid down his life for his country, a statesman, a soldier, an admiral of the fleet, some heaven-born artist, an inventor, a captain of industry or finance? No, he was Knute Rockne, director of athletics and football coach of Notre Dame. He was a man of the people, a husband and father, a citizen of South Bend, Indiana. Yet had he been any of these personages that have been mentioned the tribute of admiration and affection which he has received could not be more universal or more sincere.

6. *The television script should be easy to memorize.* Sometimes we forget that the Shakespearean actors memorized their long scripts with comparative ease. As you have used the voice exercises in this book, you have probably had the same easy experience. The secret is that speeches that have a simple rhythm are easily memorized. And a simple rhythm is one that is near to your natural expression under the stress of emotion. In other words, those expressions that come nearest to the way you would naturally react are the most easily memorized.

In television broadcasts, memorization is as necessary as it is on the stage. It is true that many commentators surreptitiously sneak a glance at notes, but the true performer gives a lifelike rendition of the script. Television has added to the script the need of memorization. In this sense it has freed the performer from the power that pictureless radio had. You are no longer tied to a script, but you no longer have the absence of personal factors that so forcefully communicate. You must use all the facial expressions and gestures that enhance your message with meaning and emotion. Every part of the body communicates a particular aspect of your story. Hence, all these factors must be coordinated into a whole which presents your talk.

You must realize that there is no short cut to memory. Your memory is a remarkable faculty yet it is the most neglected sense you have. And it is the most easily developed sense you possess. In fact, simple steps can make any memorization of a script a pleasant task:

1. Read the script through several times for continuity.
2. Read each paragraph, noting the theme sentence.
3. Study each paragraph and then close the script and repeat it aloud. Try not to refer to the script until you have gotten through the paragraph.
4. Review the whole script twice more for final overview.

Finally, keep in mind that clarity in the writing of your script makes for easy memorization and easy listening. You can test the clarity of your speech by asking two questions: (1) "Have I cut out all the superfluous matter?" and (2) "Have I used the simplest language I know?" Make these two questions a habit and you will streamline your broadcast style. You will find yourself substituting image-bearing words for technical terms, relating the unknown in terms of the known, and reiterating your points in a variety of ways that create interest. Remember, it is generalities that are most difficult to memorize and that are most easily forgotten by the listeners and viewers. Avoid them.

7. *The script should be tied together logically.* A loose and rambling script soon loses the audience. You have the responsibility to make your talk proceed from one point to another with the least friction. You can do that by using words that help the listener form connections. As you well realize, part of the tediousness of travel is in making connections. Everyone worries about making trains. In like manner, part of the difficulty of reasoning is in putting thoughts together. If the speaker doesn't arrange his thoughts, the listener must do so, for the human mind requires order. It assimilates ideas in units and is confused by disorder. You can assist your hearer by tying your talk together. Make frequent use of summaries, and note the constant use of these connectives in good speaking:

Remember. . . .
Consequently. . . .
As you can see. . . .

Gradually. . . .
Since. . . .
As I have shown. . . .
In due time. . . .
Despite. . . .
After all. . . .
In view of. . . .
As you know. . . .
As we see it. . . .
There is no doubt. . . .
As a result. . . .
Soon. . . .
Now. . . .
Instead. . . .

A logical talk must have an ending which recapitulates what has gone before. Most starting speakers forget this vital fact. Your conclusion is often the only thought that the audience remembers. That is why most programs end with a commercial. No matter how forcefully you have made your point, the audience expects you to pull the talk together for them. If you neglect to do so they go away with a confused impression of your message. So tie up the talk in a neat package that can be easily carried home.

## Summary

Jot down these seven fundamental requirements of good scripts and keep them before you as you prepare your radio or television script:

1. The opening should be an attention getter.
2. The script should be timed.
3. The script should be marked for delivery.
4. The script should be rehearsed for readability.
5. The script should have emotional appeal.
6. The television script should be easy to memorize.
7. The script should be tied together logically.

### Projects

Plan a radio jamboree. Professional scripts of a variety of actual broadcasts are included for your study and use. You may use them as models and construct your own radio jamboree, or you can practice with these materials which cover several types of radio and television speaking situations. Five different types of professional scripts are included for your study and imitation: the special feature, the interview, the sportscast, the commercial, and the artist commentator. A variety of others are at your disposal at the flick of a dial on your radio and television set. This assignment can be an exciting and profitable adventure. For example, should you decide to have a program of your own, open it with a news commentary. Have in it the opening headline summary, the straight news, a human-interest story, a flash, the weather report, and for dramatic effect, a "sixty-second round the world roundup." Use the special talents of the class and have a gay radio parade.

### A SPECIAL FEATURE

Elizabeth Donahue has given us a notable example of the human-appeal special spot broadcast. Notice the personal elements so skillfully mingled with the forward movement of the event. This is an exquisite piece of atmosphere building.

WASHINGTON—MADAME CHIANG KAI-SHEK MET AMERICAN REPORTERS EN MASSE FOR THE FIRST TIME TODAY AND ADMITTED THAT THE ENCOUNTER FRIGHTENED HER MORE THAN HER VISITS TO CHINA'S FIGHTING FRONTS. NEWSMEN AND WOMEN PILED HELTER-SKELTER INTO THE PRESIDENT'S OFFICE FOR THE CONFERENCE. THE TINY WIFE OF THE CHINESE GENERALISSIMO WAS SEATED BETWEEN MR. AND MRS. ROOSEVELT. SHE NERVOUSLY FINGERED A SQUARE GOLD COMPACT, WRAPPED IN A HANDKERCHIEF.

MADAME CHIANG APPARENTLY WAS UNFAMILIAR WITH THE TRICKS OF AN AMERICAN SWIVEL CHAIR, WHICH TWICE ALL BUT SPILLED HER BACKWARDS. FOLLOWING A BRIEF TALK, SHE AGREED TO ANSWER QUESTIONS. THE PRESIDENT BARRED NEWSMEN FROM ASKING "CATCHY" ONES.

IN REPLYING TO EACH QUESTION, SHE ROSE TO HER FEET. SHE WAS IMMEDIATELY TRANSFORMED FROM AN ALMOST CHILDLIKE FIGURE TO A NATIONAL LEADER VOICING IN CLEAR, DETERMINED TONES CHINA'S NEEDS FOR PLANES AND FUEL.

WITH HER EYES FIXED ON THE GREAT SEAL OF THE UNITED STATES CARVED ON THE CEILING OF THE EXECUTIVE OFFICE, MADAME CHIANG SPOKE FOR HER COUNTRY WITH AN EMPHASIS THAT SOMETIMES AMOUNTED TO ANGER AGAINST THE SUFFERING OF HER PEOPLE.

MADAME CHIANG LOOKED MORE AMERICANIZED THAN WHEN SHE ADDRESSED THE CONGRESS YESTERDAY. TODAY SHE WORE THE NOW-FAMILIAR

ANKLE-LENGTH CHINESE GOWN. BUT INSTEAD OF JADE ORNAMENTS SHE
WORE TINY GOLD BEADS IN HER EARS. ON HER ENGAGEMENT FINGER WAS
A TRIPLE CIRCLE OF DIAMONDS AND SAPPHIRES. SHE WORE THE SILVER
WINGS OF THE CHINESE AIR FORCE OF WHICH SHE IS HONORARY COM-
MANDER.

SHE WAS FLANKED BY THE PRESIDENT AND MRS. ROOSEVELT, BOTH TALL
AND TOWERING ABOVE HER. OCCASIONALLY SHE GLANCED AT THEM FOR A
NOD OF ENCOURAGEMENT AS SHE TACKLED HER UNFAMILIAR ROLE. THE
PRESIDENT FREQUENTLY NODDED SILENTLY IN APPROVAL OF HER WORDS.

MADAME CHIANG PROVED A PAST-MASTER OF THE AMERICAN IDIOM IN
SPEECH. SHE NEVER HESITATED IN CATCHING THE MEANING OF THE BRISK
QUESTIONS. ALTHOUGH SHE SAID EMPHATICALLY THAT HER VISIT WAS A
PERSONAL ONE, SHE TOOK EVERY OPPORTUNITY TO DRIVE HOME HER
COUNTRY'S NEEDS FOR MORE AND MORE FIGHTING EQUIPMENT.

THE NOTED WOMAN CARRIED OUT HER ROLE AS A GUEST-WITH-OUT-
STRETCHED-HAND WITH TACT AND CHARM, BUT THERE WAS NO MISTAK-
ING THE SERIOUSNESS OF HER MISSION NOR THE BURNING SINCERITY OF
HER HOPES.

### AN INTERVIEW

An excellent example of an interview with meaning and significance
occurred when John B. Kennedy interviewed the famous editor of the
*Reader's Digest*, Fulton Oursler. Note the dignified introduction and the
skilled lead-in questions coupled with necessary background material.

KENNEDY: Dean Inge, called the Gloomy Dean of St. Paul's Cathedral in
London because he insisted on telling the British the plain, unpleasant truth—as a matter of fact the retired Dean Inge is not gloomy,
but a charming and witty gentleman—but the Dean is reported to
have been in an unusually cheerful mood: he had probably presided
at the obsequies of an eminent politician, but he stretched out his
arms to writhing Europe and inquired, "Is Christianity to be a failure?" Well, the answer to that is that Christianity probably will not
be a failure if the world ever tries it in international affairs. Librarians
the world over outside the Iron Curtain report intense interest in
spiritual and religious reading—not seeking escape, but seeking
strength. And the sensational success of Fulton Oursler's book, *The
Greatest Story Ever Told,* bears them out. Now we shall hear from
the man responsible for *The Greatest Story Ever Told,* distinguished
author and playwright, senior Editor of the *Reader's Digest* . . .
Fulton Oursler. First, Mr. Oursler, the obvious question—how did

you come to be inspired to write this book *The Greatest Story Ever Told?*

OURSLER: It was on my second visit to the Holy Land. I had been there once before and wrote a book about it. . . .

KENNEDY: I remember that one; it was called a *Skeptic in the Holy Land.*

OURSLER: That's correct. I went to the Holy Land a skeptic, but as Mrs. Oursler will testify, I became a pilgrim. I was then frankly agnostic, and had been for years. When we toured Galilee, Samaria, Judea and Transjordania—visiting the holy places, quite literally following in the footsteps of Christ and His Disciples, I felt stirred; but unconvinced. As I've said: I was a skeptic.

KENNEDY: But skepticism is quite often the stepping-stone to faith.

OURSLER: That was so in my case. My intense curiosity regarding the Christian story returned to me, and I returned to the Holy Land.

KENNEDY: Was it just curiosity that impelled you? After all, Mr. Oursler, you've been a success all your life since you were in your twenties when your play, *The Spider,* was a smash hit on Broadway. Success and piety don't often mix.

OURSLER: Don't get me wrong. I wasn't pious. I doubt if I am now, although I am a convinced and confirmed believer. But the mystic impact of the Holy Land stamped on my soul not only the religious enormousness, but the historical validity of *The Greatest Story Ever Told*, the story of the Greatest Life Ever Lived—that of Jesus Christ. Rabbi Solomon Freehof of Pittsburgh first planted the seed in my mind that brought fruit in *The Greatest Story Ever Told*—when he lamented to me once that Bible-reading had been largely abandoned in this country. I investigated and found that this was scandalously true. Ordinary folk I'd meet everywhere and anywhere could quote the latest Hollywood wisecrack but they didn't know what was meant by "Thirty Pieces of Silver"—or by "E'er the cock crows twice, thou shalt betray me thrice." They know the Ten Commandments by hearsay and the Book of the Prophets not at all. I decided to do something about it as far as the New Testament was concerned. So I studied the Gospels of Matthew, Mark, Luke and John . . . on their home grounds, in the Holy Land—and wrote the story.

KENNEDY: And in writing *The Greatest Story Ever Told* you seem to have pleased not only Christians, but also Jews, as I see the distinguished Otto Frankfurter says, "My fellow Jews will value *The Greatest Story Ever Told* for its historic interpretation of a most illustrious member of our race, Jesus of Nazareth." You know, Mr. Oursler, I can personally testify to the astonishing pace, movement and suspense there is in *The Greatest Story Ever Told.* I remember only too well when

I was editing Colliers how difficult it was to get manuscripts on great religious themes simply because the writers somehow always seemed to get completely involved in complicated theological dissertations. But by some magic you seem to have recaptured in simple moving words the ancient setting in which the 12 disciples and the Master moved . . . the very atmosphere of the Holy Land. Every once in a while I caught myself feeling as if I were actually witnessing the great moments of this, the greatest life ever lived . . . walking with, and listening to John the Baptist, Simon called Peter, John, Matthew, Judas . . . the money lenders . . . the people. You have done a perfectly marvelous job! Now, Mr. Oursler, have you any message for our listeners?

Oursler: May I say that many of you listening to me now, may be, as I was for so many years, so wrapped up in daily problems, that you give practically no time to your religion. You may have even grown skeptical as I did. But if you'll only *make* the time to give religion . . . the great religious truths of all creeds a chance to help you in your daily life, whether you are Catholic, Protestant, Jew, Moslem, or Buddhist, you will find days and nights of inner peace unfolding before you. And today with tragic undertones rumbling behind the headlines, we can well take to heart the words of Voltaire. When asked by Benjamin Franklin to bless his 17-year-old grandson, he stretched his hand over the boy's head and said, "My child, God and Liberty. . . . Remember those two words!" Here in this great land we are becoming more and more aware of the meaning of Liberty every time we look at the paper and contemplate the happenings abroad. . . . And as for things of the spirit, I'd like to tell every one of you . . . whatever your faith . . . whatever you do . . . where ever you live, there's wonderful help, comfort, inspiration and hope in the deeds and words of Jesus of Nazareth!

### A SPORTSCAST

Year after year, the superb sportscasts of Bill Stern have brought games, fights, and races into American homes. This fiery and exciting presentation is typical of his skill. You may wish to bring it up to date by describing a current sports event.

The ball goes over to the Army and that is the third time today that Notre Dame has failed to score . . . when they were within scoring distance. Troxel comes back in at fullback and Roberts comes back in at quarterback for Army. . . . At the end of the first quarter,

Navy leads Pennsylvania 7 to 0; the Pennsylvania team that defeated the Army last week 19 to 0 and the same Navy team that Notre Dame defeated last Saturday 9 to 0 are playing today in Franklin Field, Philadelphia and Navy leads 7 to 0. . . . All right . . . the Army team has Roberts, Maiser, Troxel and Hill in the backfield. It's a single wingback over the left with Hill leading. Hill takes a pass at center, breaks into the clear, smashes down to the end of the 33 yard line before he is stopped by Louis Rimkiss. . . . A gain in that play of 8 yards . . . 8 yards, second down; one; that was Hill No. 17, the right halfback of the Army, smashing down to the 34 yard line of the Army before he was finally stopped. . . . The ball 15 yards in from the east side of the field. . . . He was tackled by Clayton Miller, the right halfback of Notre Dame. . . . Out of the huddle comes the Army team, . . . single wingback off to the right, Maiser in the fullback position. The ball goes to Henry Maiser who gives it to Callaher; . . . Callaher is running wide; he is up there and knocked out of bounds. That was the end of round play . . . the end of round play with Callaher carrying the ball loses yardage for the Army. They lose four yards on the play, back to the 30 yard line. . . . The tackler was Joseph Lamonte. . . . So it's third down, about 3½ Army's ball, 15 yards in from the west side of the field, the score nothing to nothing in the second period. . . . This is the Blue Network presentation of the game of the day from Yankee Stadium New York City. . . .

### COMMERCIALS

The thing that sustains American broadcasting and television is sponsorship. The sponsor demands three minutes out of every fifteen that comes on the air. This means that twelve minutes of every hour of sponsored programs are concerned with persuasion. And the programs that stay on the air are those that influence the listening and viewing audiences to buy. This situation has made a fine art of the short persuasive talk known as the "commercial."

The following two book-club program commercials show the wide gamut that such commercials can cover. The first is a home-building cultural appeal for the Family Reading Club, and the second is a popular, fast-paced mystery-club offer, as portrayed by the Mystery Guild.

### 1. *The Family Reading Club*

And for lovers of good books and fine art, here's an unusual opportunity! If you join the Family Reading Club immediately, you will receive as a FREE gift for joining . . . 20 . . . yes, 20 of the world's greatest works of art! Yes, this astonishing collection of art masterpieces is yours FREE as a new member of the FAMILY READING CLUB . . . the book club that brings you the very highest type of best seller entertainment at huge savings! As the club's new way of advertising, new members get FREE, 20 magnificent full color reproductions of the greatest art the world has ever seen. They were originally made available through the cooperation of the Metropolitan Museum of Art, The Louvre, The Whitney Museum and famous private collections, but now in this special drive to win new members, the FAMILY READING CLUB will ship all 20 of them to new members absolutely FREE!

These are not small, illustration-size pictures, but range in size up to 11 x 14 inches. They can be framed or hung on any wall in any room in your home . . . on a large living room wall, in the children's room . . . in those awkward, hard to decorate corners that often give so much trouble. Yes, friends, if you join the FAMILY READING CLUB today . . . we will ship you in one package "The Strange Child" by Titian, a Degas Dancer, a magnificent Rembrandt Self-Portrait, "The Last Supper" by Da Vinci, Botticelli's "Madonna," "The Card Players" by Cézanne. . . . A Goya, a Renoir. Yes, 20 glorious art masterpieces for your home ranging from Picasso's "Harlequin" to the "Flower Vendor" by Diego Rivera. Think of it! The originals as they hang in museums or private collections are priced from $15,000 to $100,000—but all 20 reproduced in glorious full color are yours FREE if you join the FAMILY READING CLUB. When the postman brings your art masterpieces to you plus the Club's first selection the three dollar smash hit, *Shannon's Way*, pay nothing for your priceless art collection, your free gift for joining! Deposit only $1.89, plus a small postal and handling charge for the tender love story that skyrocketed to the top of the best-seller list, *Shannon's Way*. Examine your paintings and your book free for a week. If not delighted, return for your money back. Or, keep them, and continue to get the best of the best sellers for your whole family at savings up to 50%. And you need accept only four books a year. Rush a card or a letter with your name and address to FAMILY READING CLUB, Box ——— Garden City, New York. (*Repeat.*)

## 2. *The Mystery Guild*

Mystery fans! How would you like to get $12 worth of smash-hit mysteries in handsome library editions for only $1. And how would you like to *continue* to get the cream of the newest $2.50 to $3 mysteries in beautiful bindings for only $1 each? Yes, friends, that's what you get if you join the famous Dollar Mystery Guild today. You get five top-flight mysteries by your favorite authors worth $12 for only $1. You'll also continue to get the newest $2.50 to $3 mysteries for only $1 each. Now there's no catch to this: You *need* only agree to accept just 4 mystery stories a year for only $1 each. That's your only obligation. If you agree to accept only 4 mysteries a year at only $1 apiece, here's how membership in the DOLLAR MYSTERY GUILD gets you 3 times more for your money. Listen! While non-members paid $2.50 for the latest Michael Shayne thriller, *A Taste for Violence,* Mystery Guild members didn't pay $2.50. They got a handsome library edition for only $1. While non-members paid $2.50 for Rex Stout's baffling spine-chiller, *Trouble in Triplicate,* Mystery Guild members didn't pay $2.50. They got it for only $1. And while non-members paid $2.75 for Ngaio Marsh's high-tension thriller, *A Wreath for Rivera,* Mystery Guild members didn't pay $2.75 or anywhere near it. They got it for only $1! How can the Dollar Mystery Guild do it? Mass production. Over 100,000 handsome library editions printed at one time. Members save up to 75% on each handsome mystery novel! And if you join today, here's what you get FREE for joining. First, you get free for joining, Ellery Queen's latest $2.50 thriller. . . . *Cat of Many Tails,* complete, unabridged . . . and yours FREE. Second, you get Agatha Christie's $2.50 puzzler, *The Crooked House* . . . complete, unabridged and yours FREE. Third, you get the new Mr. & Mrs. North mystery . . . *The Dishonest Murderer,* complete, unabridged and yours FREE. And, as your fourth FREE book for joining you get Perry Mason's *Case of the Cautious Coquette,* by Erle Stanley Gardner . . . complete, unabridged and yours FREE. Send no money. Pay postman nothing for your four free books. Pay only $1 plus a small postal and handling charge for your first club selection . . . Rex Stout's *Second Confession!* $12 worth of mysteries for only $1. Keep them for a week. If not delighted, return for money back. Or keep your five books and continue to get the best new mysteries at savings up to 75%. Remember, you can choose as few as four mysteries a year at only $1 each, and still remain a member. You may not hear this offer again, so act today. Rush a card or letter with your name and address to Mystery Guild, ⸻. That's Mystery Guild, ⸻

### THE ARTIST COMMENTATOR

More and more the audience is desiring that the artist do his own commentary. This brings him closer to the audience as a person. John Charles Thomas is one of the best at this type of commentary. In your jamboree you may wish to form a program from the talent in the class. Use this as a model.

ANNCR: To you, America, Westinghouse presents John Nesbitt, Victor Young and the Orchestra, Ken Darby and the Westinghouse Chorus and—John Charles Thomas!

*Music: Orchestra and chorus swell and down to (sings)* "Home on the Range" . . . *First two lines . . . Music out.* . . .

THOMAS: Good afternoon, dear friends, this is John Charles Thomas. Welcome to the Westinghouse Program. Musically speaking, the program today is on the popular side . . . for the most part. Some of it's romantic . . . some light and breezy . . . and some of it nostalgic. Then, of course . . . you'll hear a chapter from John Nesbitt's Passing Parade. (But let's get right into it.) My first number is Moya's "Song of Songs."

*Music:* "Song of Songs" .................................*Thomas.*

THOMAS: The beautiful music in the picture "For Whom the Bell Tolls" was composed and conducted by our own Victor Young. Vic has done a great job and—we're all very proud of him. And we're exceptionally happy he's playing the overture and love theme from the score today, since it's Vic's birthday.

*Music: Overture from* "For Whom the Bell Tolls" ..........*Orchestra.*

THOMAS: Some years back it was a pretty sure bet that when you walked into a parlor, you'd find on the piano a copy of "Indian Love Lyrics"; one of the great songs from this collection is "The Kashmiri Love Song," and here it is.

*Music:* "Kashmiri Love Song" ............................*Thomas.*

THOMAS: The barbershop quartette addicts among you are in for a chuckle when I announce the title of the number Ken Darby and the chorus have dug up for today—because they really went back to dig up this one! It's "Mr. Jefferson Lord" . . . (remember the gentlemen who played "That Barbershop Chord"?) well, here it is—with "A Tavern in the Town" for company.

*Music:* "Tavern in the Town" and "Mr. Jefferson Lord" .........*Chorus.*

THOMAS: This is John Charles Thomas.

And now, as every Sunday, we come to story-telling time, with another tale from our eloquent Westinghouse Storyteller, John Nesbitt.

Today, John once again looks seaward to bring us a little-known true story that eventually gave birth to something you and I are mighty thankful for today. What it is . . . is for John to tell you. Go ahead, John Nesbitt.

(*The story of the first Coast Guard unit formed in England, told by Nesbitt.*)

THOMAS: Thank you, John Nesbitt.

Victor Young has selected a lively little tune for the orchestra to play now, composed by that English jack-of-all-trades, Noel Coward, the name of it is "Dance, Little Lady." All right, Vic, dance the little lady on.

*Music:* "Dance Little Lady" . . . . . . . . . . . . . . . . . . . . . . . . . . . . .*Orchestra.*

THOMAS: And now. For a finale, the chorus and I will sing "Let Me Be Born Again."

"Let Me Be Born Again" . . . . . . . . . . . . . . . . . . . . . . . . . . . . .*Ensemble.*

Well, it's good-bye time again. But we're looking forward to being with you again next Sunday afternoon at this same hour . . . and that goes for all of you from all of us . . . John Nesbitt, Victor Young, Ken Darby and myself . . . and

THOMAS: The entire Westinghouse organization. Until next Sunday, then, dear friends . . . this is John Charles Thomas saying . . . good-bye . . . to you all.

### REFERENCES

ABBOT, WALDO, *Handbook of Broadcasting*, 2d ed., New York: McGraw-Hill Book Company, Inc., 1950.

CHESTER, GIRAUD, and GARNET R. GARRISON, *Radio and Television.* New York: Appleton-Century-Crofts, Inc., 1950.

DUNLAP, ORRIN E., *Talking on the Radio.* New York: Greenberg Publisher, Inc., 1936.

GOULD, SAMUEL B., and SIDNEY A. DIAMOND, *Training the Local Announcer.* New York: Longmans, Green & Company, Inc., 1950.

HENNEKE, BEN G., *The Radio Announcer's Handbook.* New York: Rinehart & Company, Inc., 1948.

HOFFMAN, WILLIAM G., and RALPH L. ROGERS, *Effective Radio Speaking.* New York: McGraw-Hill Book Company, Inc., 1944.

HUTCHINSON, THOMAS H., *Here Is Television.* New York: Hastings House Publishers, Inc., 1946.

KEITH, ALICE, *How to Speak and Write for Radio.* New York: Harper & Brothers, 1944.

McGILL, EARL, *Radio Directing.* New York: McGraw-Hill Book Company, Inc., 1940.

Sposa, Louis, *Television Primer of Production and Direction*. New York: McGraw-Hill Book Company, Inc., 1947.

Weaver, Luther, *The Technique of Radio Writing*. New York: Prentice-Hall, Inc., 1948.

Wylie, Max, *Radio and Television Writing*. New York: Rinehart & Company, Inc., 1950.

# VISUAL-AIDS BIBLIOGRAPHY

The instructor should note the fact that many of the films listed here were not produced specifically for the college level. Most of these listed as produced by Coronet, for instance, were intended primarily for high-school instruction and are set in high-school situations. The material included, however, is in itself pertinent, but the instructor is advised to preview wherever possible to determine for himself the grade-level suitability.

Films may be obtained from the producer or primary distributor listed with each title. A Directory of Sources is appended at the end of the bibliography. It will be more convenient in most cases to order films from local distributors, or your state university film library, if they happen to be available from those sources.

All films are black and white, sound, 16 mm, unless otherwise indicated. They were specially selected for inclusion in this bibliography by Prof. Beatrice Jacoby, Ph.D., Chairman of the Committee on Classroom Films, Speech Association of America, and Prof. Robert Sonkin, of the City College of New York.

### Social Skill

*How to Develop Interest* (Cor, 10 min b/w or color). Developing interest is not only a teacher's job but also the responsibility of individual class members. This film demonstrates how this responsibility can be met.

*How to Observe* (Cor, 10 min b/w or color). Students are shown that observation can be developed as a skill and can be improved through applied and guided practice.

*How to Think* (Cor, 12 min b/w or color). Suggested procedures for clear and careful thinking toward problem solving.

*Speech: Function of Gestures* (YAF, 11 min). Explains the function of gestures in public speaking and discusses the use of the right gesture at the right time.

### Semantic Skill

*Build Your Vocabulary* (Cor, 10 min b/w or color). Mr. Willis finds himself at a loss for words at a public meeting, takes a cue from his son, Pete, and embarks upon a campaign of vocabulary improvement.

*Do Words Ever Fool You?* (Cor, 10 min b/w or color). Illustrates the danger of being tricked by the use of words in our everyday life—in newspapers, advertisements, politics, and propaganda.

*Propaganda Techniques* (Cor, 10 min b/w or color). The methods of recognizing and evaluating propaganda, urging the student to adopt a judicious critical attitude.

*What Makes Words?* (Cor, 10 min b/w or color). Indicates the important ways our language grows, through "borrowing," invention, and meaning change.

## VOCAL SKILL

*Fundamentals of Acoustics* (EBF, 11 min). Explains the phenomenon of hearing and the modification of sound between the source and the hearer.

*How the Ear Functions* (KB, 11 min). Outlines the structure and function of the human ear and explains the nature of sound waves.

*Physiology of Speech* (Univ of Mich, 30 min).

*Speech: Using Your Voice* (YAF, 11 min). Points out that most speech faults are due to carelessness and demonstrates how one may correct such faults.

*Your Voice* (EBF, 10 min). Describes the four phases of voice production—respiration, phonation, resonance, and articulation.

## PHONETIC SKILL

*American Spoken Here* (TFC, 10 min). A dramatized history of several slang expressions, showing how they originated and came to be included in the American idiom.

*Improve Your Pronunciation* (Cor, 10 min b/w or color). Walter realizes his own shortcomings while practicing a speech to be delivered at a class banquet. He formulates a program for pronunciation improvement, which the film explains in detail.

*Movements of the Tongue in Speech* (IFB, 14 min color). Movements of the tongue and lips are shown during the speech of a male patient whose right cheek was removed by surgical operation.

*We Discover the Dictionary* (Cor, 10 min b/w or color). A class learns how to use the dictionary to answer questions accurately about the meaning, spelling, and pronunciation of words.

## PUBLIC SPEAKING

*Describing an Incident* (Cor, 10 min b/w or color). Shows an incident poorly described and the same incident interestingly, completely, and colorfully described.

*Fundamentals of Public Speaking* (Cor, 10 min b/w or color). Importance of public speaking in a real life situation is stressed, followed by the steps in achieving an effective speech.

*How to Make a Sales Presentation Stay Presented* (Modern, 30 min). Charts in dramatic form the course of a successful sale, and analyzes the steps which make it successful.

*How to Vote* (TFC, 10 min). A satirical presentation of a political meeting with exaggerated emphasis on the buncombe present in some political speeches.

*Jefferson Davis Declares Secession* (TFC, 6 min). An excerpt from a theatrical film, embodying the speech of Jefferson Davis at the outbreak of the Civil War.

*Speech: Platform Posture and Appearance* (YAF, 11 min). The importance of good appearance and proper posture to the success of the public speaker.

*Speech: Stage Fright and What to Do about It* (YAF, 11 min). Analyzes the cause of stage fright and shows the inexperienced speaker what he can do to overcome it.

*Watch That Quotation* (Cor, 10 min b/w or color). The importance of quoting accurately, and of having authority behind statements. How to quote in speech and writing.

## CONFERENCE SPEAKING

*Discussion in Democracy* (Cor, 10 min b/w or color). A typical group of students learn the importance and the techniques of discussion.

*How Not to Conduct a Meeting* (GM, 10 min). Colonel Stoopnagle burlesques the common errors and omissions so frequently encountered in a poorly planned meeting.

*How to Judge Authorities* (Cor, 10 min b/w or color). Demonstrates intelligent evaluation of statements of "authorities."

*How to Judge Facts* (Cor, 10 min b/w or color). Like Jim, who writes a "sensational" story for his school newspaper, students will learn from this film to guard against platitudes, false analogies, assumptions, and double meanings.

*Learning from Classroom Discussion* (Cor, 10 min b/w or color). The value and necessity of worthwhile class discussion is explained, and some of the ingredients of good discussion are outlined.

*Parliamentary Procedure in Action* (Cor, 13 min b/w or color). In a session of a well-run high-school club we see the proper procedures and parliamentary forms correctly used.

## SPEECH ARTS

*Air Waves—Radio Broadcasting* (UWF, 10 min).

*Henry Wadsworth Longfellow* (EBF, 20 min). Describes his early love for poetry and his full life as teacher, scholar, and poet. Includes selections from his poems.

*Julius Caesar* (BIS, 19 min). The forum scene is played by a large company of English actors, with Leo Genn delivering Mark Antony's funeral oration.

*Let's Read Poetry* (Bailey, 10 min). Pointers on how to read poetry, with a participation effect at the end in which the audience is led in the reading of a poem by the narrator.

*Macbeth* (BIS, 16 min). The murder scene and the sleepwalking scene are presented by a cast of English players headed by Wilfred Lawson and Cathleen Nesbitt.

*Master Will Shakespeare* (TFC, 11 min). A fictionized story of the life of Shakespeare, including scenes from *Romeo and Juliet*.

*Nature Speaks* (TFC, 10 min). A photographic study of natural mountain, lake, and sea scenery, accompanied by poetry read by David Ross.

*On the Air* (Westinghouse, 28 min). The story of radio broadcasting, from its beginning in a garage workshop of Dr. Conrad to our complex networks of today.

*Othello* (Eastin, 44 min). In this condensed version of *Othello* a talented English cast enacts the principal scenes from the play.

*Radio and Television* (Mahnke, 11 min). An analysis of the radio industry from the vocational guidance standpoint, with the many jobs involved treated in detail.

*Romeo and Juliet* (TFC, 39 min). A classroom edition of the Metro-Goldwyn-Mayer feature production.

*Television* (RCA, 10 min). A brief description of how television works, with a demonstration of the broadcast of two programs.

*Ways to Better Conversation* (Cor, 10 min b/w or color). Points out what constitutes good conversation and how skill in conversation can be improved.

### DIRECTORY OF SOURCES

Bailey—Bailey Films Inc., 2044 N. Berendo St., Hollywood 27, Calif.

BIS—British Information Services, 30 Rockefeller Plaza, New York 20.

Cor—Coronet Instructional Films, 65 E. South Water St., Chicago 1.

Eastin—Eastin Pictures Co., Box 598, Davenport, Iowa.

EBF—Encyclopaedia Britannica Films, 1150 Wilmette Ave., Wilmette, Ill.

GM—General Motors Corporation, Department of Public Relations, Film Distribution Section, General Motors Building, Detroit.

IFB—International Film Bureau, 6 N. Michigan Ave., Chicago 2.

KB—Knowledge Builders, 625 Madison Ave., New York 22.

Mahnke—Carl F. Mahnke Productions, 215 E. 3 St., Des Moines 9.

Modern—Modern Talking Picture Service, 45 Rockefeller Plaza, New York.

RCA—Radio Corporation of America, Rockefeller Center, New York.

TFC—Teaching Films Custodians, 25 W. 43 St., New York 18.

Univ of Mich—University of Michigan, Ann Arbor, Mich.

UWF—United World Films, 1445 Park Ave., New York.

Westinghouse—Westinghouse Electric Corporation, 306 Fourth Ave., Box 1017, Pittsburgh 30.

YAF—Young America Films, 18 E. 41 St., New York 17.

# INDEX